Lecture Notes in Computer Science 11027

More information about this series at http://www.springer.com/series/7408

Abhinav Bhatele · David Boehme ·
Joshua A. Levine · Allen D. Malony ·
Martin Schulz (Eds.)

Programming and Performance Visualization Tools

International Workshops, ESPT 2017 and VPA 2017
Denver, CO, USA, November 12 and 17, 2017
and ESPT 2018 and VPA 2018
Dallas, TX, USA, November 16 and 11, 2018
Revised Selected Papers

Springer

Editors
Abhinav Bhatele
Lawrence Livermore National Laboratory
Livermore, CA, USA

David Boehme
Lawrence Livermore National Laboratory
Livermore, CA, USA

Joshua A. Levine
The University of Arizona
Tucson, AZ, USA

Allen D. Malony
University of Oregon
Eugene, OR, USA

Martin Schulz
Technical University of Munich
Munich, Germany

ISSN 0302-9743 ISSN 1611-3349 (electronic)
Lecture Notes in Computer Science
ISBN 978-3-030-17871-0 ISBN 978-3-030-17872-7 (eBook)
https://doi.org/10.1007/978-3-030-17872-7

LNCS Sublibrary: SL2 – Programming and Software Engineering

This Springer imprint is published by the registered company Springer Nature Switzerland AG
The registered company address is: Gewerbestrasse 11, 6330 Cham, Switzerland

Preface

This volume contains the proceedings of two instances each of two workshops, held in conjuction with the International Conference on High Performance Computing, Networking, Storage and Analysis (SC). The workshops are – Workshop on Extreme-Scale Programming Tools (ESPT) and International Workshop on Visual Performance Analysis (VPA).

ESPT 2017

The 6th Workshop on Extreme-Scale Programming Tools (ESPT) was held in conjunction with the International Conference on High Performance Computing, Networking, Storage and Analysis (SC) in Denver, Colorado, USA, on Sunday, November 12, 2017. The workshop focused on how the path to exascale computing challenges HPC application developers in their quest to achieve the maximum potential that the machines have to offer. Factors such as limited power budgets, clock frequency variability, heterogeneous load imbalance, hierarchical memories, and shrinking I/O bandwidths make it increasingly difficult to create high performance applications. Tools for debugging, performance measurement and analysis, and tuning are needed to overcome the architectural, system, and programming complexities envisioned in exascale environments. At the same time, research and development progress for HPC tools faces equally difficult challenges from exascale factors. Increased emphasis on autotuning, dynamic monitoring and adaptation, heterogeneous analysis, and so on require new methodologies, techniques, and engagement with application teams.

The ESPT 2017 workshop served as a forum for HPC application developers, system designers, and tools researchers to discuss the requirements for exascale-enabled tools and the roadblocks that need to be addressed. It was the sixth instantiation of successful SC conference workshops organized by the Virtual Institute – High Productivity Supercomputing (VI-HPS), an international initiative of HPC researchers and developers focused on parallel programming and performance tools for large-scale systems. The workshop topics of interest included:

- Programming tools (e.g., performance analysis, tuning, debuggers, IDEs)
- Methodologies for performance engineering
- Tool technologies for extreme-scale challenges (e.g., scalability, resilience, power)
- Tool infrastructures and environments
- Evolving/future application requirements for programming tools and technologies
- Application developer experiences with programming and performance tools

More information can be found at: http://www.vi-hps.org/symposia/espt/espt-sc17.html.

ESPT 2017 was a full-day workshop consisting of a keynote address in the morning followed by research paper presentations and an open debate in the afternoon. All submitted research papers underwent a rigorous review process. A total of 13 papers were submitted, with three to four reviews provided for each paper. The ESPT organizers made final decisions on paper selection. A total of eight papers were accepted and each paper was allotted 30 minutes for presentation. This volume contains seven of the eight accepted papers from the ESPT 2017 proceedings.

Organizing Committee

William Jalby (Chair)	Université de Versailles St-Quentin-en-Yvelines, France
Allen D. Malony (Vice-chair)	University of Oregon, Eugene, USA
Martin Schulz	Technische Universität München, Germany
Judit Gimenez	Barcelona Supercomputing Center, Spain

Program Committee

Jean-Baptiste Besnard	ParaTools, SAS, France
Michael Gerndt	Universität München, Germany
Kevin Huck	University of Oregon, Eugene, USA
Andreas Knüpfer	Technische Universität Dresden, Germany
Heike McCraw	University of Tennessee, Knoxville, USA
Barton P. Miller	University of Wisconsin, Madison, USA
Pablo Oliveira	Université de Versailles St-Quentin-en-Yvelines, France
Sameer Shende	University of Oregon, Eugene, USA
Jan Treibig	Friedrich-Alexander-Universität Erlangen-Nürnberg, Germany
Felix Wolf	Technische Universität Darmstadt, Germany
Brian Wylie	Jülich Supercomputing Centre, Germany

Special thanks: Marc-Andre Hermanns, Jülich Supercomputing Centre, Germany

ESPT 2018

The 2018 Workshop on Extreme-Scale Programming Tools (ESPT) was held in conjunction with the International Conference on High Performance Computing, Networking, Storage and Analysis (SC) in Dallas, Texas, USA, on Friday, November 16, 2018. It was the seventh instantiation of successful SC conference workshops organized by the Virtual Institute – High Productivity Supercomputing (VI-HPS), an international initiative of HPC researchers and developers focused on parallel programming and performance tools for large-scale systems.

The path to extreme computing keeps broadening: Large-scale systems toward exascale and beyond, growing many-core systems with deep memory hierarchies and massively parallel accelerators are just a few of the platforms we can expect. This trend will challenge HPC application developers in their quest to achieve the maximum potential that their systems have to offer, both on and across nodes. Factors such as limited power budgets, heterogeneity, hierarchical memories, shrinking I/O bandwidths, and performance variability will make it increasingly difficult to create productive applications on future platforms. To address these challenges, we need tools for debugging, performance measurement and analysis, and tuning to overcome the architectural, system, and programming complexities expected in these environments. At the same time, research and development progress for HPC tools faces equally difficult challenges from exascale factors. Increased emphasis on autotuning, dynamic monitoring and adaptation, heterogeneous analysis, and so on require new methodologies, techniques, and engagement with application teams.

Like its predecessors, the ESPT 2018 workshop served as a forum for HPC application developers, system designers, and tools researchers to discuss the requirements for exascale-enabled tools and the roadblocks that need to be addressed. The workshop topics of interest included:

- Programming tools (e.g., performance analysis, tuning, debuggers, IDEs)
- Methodologies for performance engineering
- Tool technologies for extreme-scale challenges (e.g., scalability, resilience, power)
- Tool support for accelerated architectures and large-scale multi-cores
- Tool infrastructures and environments
- Evolving/future application requirements for programming tools and technologies
- Application developer experiences with programming and performance tools

More information can be found at: http://www.vi-hps.org/symposia/espt/espt-sc18.html.

ESPT 2018 was a half-day workshop consisting of two keynote addresses and a session of research paper presentations. All submitted research papers underwent a rigorous review process. A total of five papers were submitted, with three to five reviews provided for each paper. The ESPT organizers made final decisions on paper selection. A total of four papers were accepted and each paper was allotted 30 minutes for presentation. This volume contains the ESPT 2018 proceedings.

Organizing Committee

Martin Schulz	Technische Universität München, Germany
David Boehme	Lawrence Livermore National Laboratory, USA
Marc-André Hermanns	Jülich Supercomputing Centre, Germany
Felix Wolf	Technische Universität Darmstadt, Germany

Program Committee

Dorian C. Arnold	Emory University, USA
Jean-Baptiste Besnard	ParaTools, France
Karl Fürlinger	Ludwig Maximilian University of Munich, Germany
Michael Gerndt	Technical University of Munich, Germany
Judit Gimenez	Barcelona Supercomputing Center, Spain
Marc-André Hermanns	Forschungszentrum Jülich, Germany
Kevin Huck	University of Oregon, USA
William Jalby	Université de Versailles St-Quentin-en-Yvelines, France
Andreas Knüpfer	Technical University of Dresden,Germany
John Linford	ARM, USA
Allen D. Malony	University of Oregon, USA
John Mellor-Crummey	Rice University, USA
Bart Miller	University of Wisconsin Madison, USA
Heidi Poxon	Cray Inc., USA
Nathan Tallent	Pacific Northwestern National Laboratory, USA
Christian Terboven	RWTH Aachen University, Germany
Josef Weidendorfer	Leibniz Supercomputing Centre, Germany
Gerhard Wellein	University of Erlangen-Nürnberg, Germany
Felix Wolf	Technical University of Darmstadt, Germany
Brian J. N. Wylie	Forschungszentrum Jülich, Germany

VPA 2017

The Fourth International Workshop on Visual Performance Analysis (VPA 17) was held in conjunction with the International Conference on High Performance Computing, Networking, Storage and Analysis (SC 17) in Denver, Colorado, USA, on Friday, November 17, 2017 and in cooperation with TCHPC: The IEEE Computer Society Technical Consortium on High Performance Computing.

Over the past decades an incredible amount of resources has been devoted to building ever more powerful supercomputers. However, exploiting the full capabilities of these machines is becoming exponentially more difficult with each new generation of hardware. To help understand and optimize the behavior of massively parallel simulations, the performance analysis community has created a wide range of tools and APIs to collect performance data, such as flop counts, network traffic, or cache behavior at the largest scale. However, this success has created a new challenge, as the resulting data are far too large and too complex to be analyzed in a straightforward manner. Therefore, new automatic analysis and visualization approaches must be developed to allow application developers to intuitively understand the multiple, interdependent effects that their algorithmic choices have on the final performance.

This workshop brought together researchers from the fields of performance analysis and visualization to discuss new approaches of applying visualization and visual analytics techniques to large-scale applications. The workshop topics of interest included:

- Scalable displays of performance data
- Data models to enable scalable visualization
- Graph representation of unstructured performance data
- Presentation of high-dimensional data
- Visual correlations between multiple data source
- Human–computer interfaces for exploring performance data
- Multiscale representations of performance data for visual exploration

More information can be found here: https://vpa17.github.io.

VPA 17 was a half-day workshop consisting of a keynote address by Dr. Lucy Nowell of the U.S. Department of Energy titled "Visual Performance Analysis for Extremely Heterogeneous Systems" as well as a panel discussion on "Challenges and the Future of HPC Performance Visualization." Research paper presentations were mixed into these two sessions. All submitted research papers underwent a rigorous review process. A total of six papers were submitted, with five reviews provided for each paper. The VPA workshop chairs made final decisions on paper selection. A total of three papers were accepted and each paper was allotted 25 minutes for presentation. This volume contains two of three accepted papers from the VPA 2017 proceedings.

Workshop Chairs

Fabian Beck	University of Duisburg-Essen, Germany
Abhinav Bhatele	Lawrence Livermore National Laboratory, USA
Judit Gimenez	Barcelona Supercomputing Center, Spain
Joshua A. Levine	University of Arizona, USA

Steering Committee

Peer-Timo Bremer	Lawrence Livermore National Laboratory, USA
Bernd Mohr	Jülich Supercomputing Center, Germany
Valerio Pascucci	University of Utah, USA
Martin Schulz	Lawrence Livermore National Laboratory, USA

Program Committee

Harsh Bhatia	Lawrence Livermore National Laboratory, USA
Holger Brunst	TU Dresden, Germany
Alexandru Calotoiu	Technical University Darmstadt, Germany
Todd Gamblin	Lawrence Livermore National Laboratory, USA
Marc-Andre Hermanns	Jülich Supercomputing Center, Germany
Kevin Huck	University of Oregon, USA
Katherine Isaacs	University of Arizona, USA
Yarden Livnat	University of Utah, USA
Naoya Maruyama	Lawrence Livermore National Laboratory, USA

Bernd Mohr	Jülich Supercomputing Center, Germany
Ananya Muddukrishna	KTH Royal Institute of Technology, Sweden
Matthias Mueller	RWTH Aachen University, Germany
Valerio Pascucci	University of Utah, USA
Paul Rosen	University of South Florida, USA
Carlos Scheidegger	University of Arizona, USA
Chad Steed	Oak Ridge National Laboratory, USA

VPA 2018

The Fifth International Workshop on Visual Performance Analysis (VPA 2018) was held in conjunction with the International Conference on High Performance Computing, Networking, Storage and Analysis (SC 2018) in Dallas, Texas, USA, on Sunday, November 11, 2018.

Over the past decades an incredible amount of resources has been devoted to building ever more powerful supercomputers. However, exploiting the full capabilities of these machines is becoming exponentially more difficult with each new generation of hardware. To help understand and optimize the behavior of massively parallel simulations, the performance analysis community has created a wide range of tools and APIs to collect performance data, such as flop counts, network traffic, or cache behavior at the largest scale. However, this success has created a new challenge, as the resulting data are far too large and too complex to be analyzed in a straightforward manner. Therefore, new automatic analysis and visualization approaches must be developed to allow application developers to intuitively understand the multiple, interdependent effects that their algorithmic choices have on the final performance.

This workshop brought together researchers from the fields of performance analysis and visualization to discuss new approaches of applying visualization and visual analytics techniques to large-scale applications. The workshop topics of interest included:

- Scalable displays of performance data
- Case studies demonstrating the use of performance visualization in practice
- Data models to enable scalable visualization
- Graph representation of unstructured performance data
- Presentation of high-dimensional data
- Visual correlations between multiple data source
- Human–computer interfaces for exploring performance data
- Multi-scale representations of performance data for visual exploration

More information can be found here: https://vpa18.github.io.

VPA 18 was a half-day workshop consisting of a keynote address by Dr. Allen Malony of the University of Oregon, USA titled "Not Your Mama's Angry Fruit Salad: Ruminations on 30 Years of Performance Visualization and Visual Performance Analysis" and research paper presentations. All submitted research papers underwent a rigorous review process. A total of five papers were submitted, with three to five reviews provided for each paper. The VPA workshop chairs made final decisions on paper selection. A total of four papers were accepted and each paper was allotted 25 minutes for presentation. This volume contains the VPA 2018 proceedings.

Workshop Chairs

Abhinav Bhatele	Lawrence Livermore National Laboratory, USA
Katherine Isaacs	University of Arizona, USA
Kevin Huck	University of Oregon, USA

Steering Committee

Peer-Timo Bremer	Lawrence Livermore National Laboratory, USA
Bernd Mohr	Jülich Supercomputing Center, Germany
Valerio Pascucci	University of Utah, USA
Martin Schulz	Lawrence Livermore National Laboratory, USA

Program Committee

Harsh Bhatia	Lawrence Livermore National Laboratory, USA
Holger Brunst	TU Dresden, Germany
Alexandru Calotoiu	Technical University Darmstadt, Germany
Todd Gamblin	Lawrence Livermore National Laboratory, USA
Judit Gimenez	Barcelona Supercomputing Center, Spain
Marc-Andre Hermanns	Jülich Supercomputing Center, Germany
Aaditya Landge	Twitter, Inc., USA
Joshua A. Levine	University of Arizona, USA
Yarden Livnat	University of Utah, USA
Naoya Maruyama	Lawrence Livermore National Laboratory, USA
Matthias Mueller	RWTH Aachen University, Germany
Paul Rosen	University of South Florida, USA

Contents

ESPT 2017

Enhancing PAPI with Low-Overhead `rdpmc` Reads

Yan Liu and Vincent M. Weaver(✉)

University of Maine, Orono, ME 04469, USA
{yan.liu,vincent.weaver}@maine.edu

Abstract. The PAPI performance library is a widely used tool for gathering self-monitored performance data from running applications. A key aspect of self-monitoring is the ability to read hardware performance counters with minimum possible overhead. If read overhead becomes too large then the act of measurement will start to interfere with the gathered results, adversely affecting the performance analysis.

On Linux systems PAPI uses the perf_event subsystem to access the counter values via the `read()` system call. On x86 systems the special `rdpmc` instruction allows userspace measurement of counters without the overhead of entering the operating system kernel. We modify PAPI to use `rdpmc` rather than `read()` and find it typically improves the latency by at least a factor of three (and often a factor of six or more) on most modern systems. The improvement is even better on machines using a KPTI enabled kernel to avoid the Meltdown vulnerability. We analyze the effectiveness and limitations of the `rdpmc` interface and have gotten the rdpmc interface enabled by default in PAPI.

1 Introduction

PAPI [16] is a portable, cross-platform library for accessing hardware performance counters. These counters are found on most modern CPUs and are widely used when evaluating system and program performance. Various tools are available that can read the values of these performance counters (such as perf [7], LIKWID [23] and VTUNE [27]). While all of these tools can measure overall aggregate counts and perform statistical sampling, PAPI is one of the few that allows easy *self-monitoring*.

Self-monitoring is the ability to read the values of the counters from within the running program, allowing fine-grain "caliper" measurements solely around the code of interest. Other tools can provide overall counts for an entire program run, or gather samples periodically that can be used to extrapolate statistically where a program spends most of its time. However a self-monitoring tool like PAPI is required to get exact fine-grained measurements for a single function, or to measure the impact of just a few lines of program code.

Self-monitoring is a powerful methodology, but care must be taken to keep overhead low. To use PAPI the code of interest must be instrumented, which

A. Bhatele et al. (Eds.): ESPT/VPA 2017/2018, LNCS 11027, pp. 3–20, 2019.
https://doi.org/10.1007/978-3-030-17872-7_1

involves adding extra code to the program. If the extra code needed to read the counter values becomes too long or intrusive then the resulting measurements will start to be affected. Mytkowicz et al. [17] found that instrumentation which increased instruction count by just 2.5% interfered with properly correlating performance results. Mytkowicz et al. [18] also showed that simply adding an additional PAPI counter could be enough to cause noticeable perturbations. Low overhead is critical for accurate performance measurements.

Instrumenting a program with PAPI is a multi-step process. First, setup code is added to the beginning of the program that initializes PAPI and sets up an "event set" with the chosen performance events of interest. These setup routines can end up calling a large amount of library code, but since this is run only once during program initialization it has minimal impact on a long-running process. Next, caliper code is added around the region of interest. It is critical that that code has minimal overhead. The routines involved are `PAPI_start()` which starts the measurements, `PAPI_read()` which reads the counters, and `PAPI_stop()` which stops the measurements. The `PAPI_start()` and `PAPI_stop()` calls can be put away from the critical code section to avoid overhead by using two reads (before and after) and calculating the difference. This leaves `PAPI_read()` as the most important routine requiring low-overhead.

In an ideal system a hardware counter read would simply be an assembly language instruction loading from the special CPU counter register, followed by a store of the value to memory for later analysis. On actual systems there is additional overhead caused by the operating system, as well as indirection and housekeeping overhead inside the measurement library. The PAPI library is a cross-platform abstraction layer and so the read call involves additional instructions, memory accesses, and branches. In addition, reading counters on Linux traditionally involves using the `read()` system call which involves a relatively slow entry to the Linux kernel. This is essentially a software interrupt which brings the CPU to a halt, changes to privileged mode, branches to internal kernel code that does some housekeeping, reads the value from the CPU, ensures all buffers are valid, writes the results out to userspace, and then finally switches back to the original running program. All of this overhead can take hundreds to thousands of cycles, much higher than the tens of cycles needed for a raw counter read [24].

Much of this overhead can be avoided if we bypass the `read()` system call and read the counters directly from userspace, without involving the operating system at all. On x86 systems there is a special `rdpmc` instruction which allows exactly this. Setting up and using this instruction can be complex and it was not available in the initial perf_event release. Once the Linux kernel added support, PAPI's perf_event still lacked `rdpmc` support and used the `read()` interface. We extend PAPI to use the lower-overhead `rdpmc` interface and run a number of tests to evaluate the change in performance. We run on a wide variety of x86 machines and find a typical speedup of around six times when using the new interface. The work revealed four bugs in the low-level Linux interface, but we have gotten these fixed upstream. Due to our work, PAPI uses `rdpmc` by default as of the 5.6 release of the library.

2 Background

The concept of performance counters is straightforward: they are hardware counters that increment when certain architectural events happen on a processor. Gathering these results in a fast, efficient fashion involves complex interactions between the hardware, operating system, libraries, and applications.

2.1 Performance Counter Hardware

Hardware performance counters are configured by setting values in a series of special low-level CPU registers. On x86 machines these are called Model Specific Registers (MSRs) which are described in the vendor documentation [2,9].

Recent x86 processors tend to have between four to seven counters per CPU, as can be seen in Table 1. This number can be affected by the existence of hardware multithreading. These counters are used to measure per-core architectural events such as cache behavior, branch predictor behavior, cycle and instruction counts, etc. Recent CPUs often have additional events, such as "uncore" and RAPL power measurement; these are measured by a different interface and cannot be accessed via the `rdpmc` interface we describe here.

To start measurement the desired events (from a list of potentially hundreds) are programmed into the event configuration registers. A bit is set in another configuration register to start the counting. The current values can be read out of the counter registers, typically from 40 to 48 bits in size. An interrupt can be configured for when the counter overflows; this allows both statistical sampling as well as keeping track of total event counts when they overflow.

2.2 Linux perf_event Interface

Access to performance counter registers requires supervisor level permissions; because of this the operating system is usually responsible for the interface. The operating system might further restrict access for security reasons, as a clever user can monitor in detail what a system is doing based on the fine grained performance information (one prime worry is being able to reverse engineer encryption happening on other cores by monitoring cycle or cache miss counts). The standard counter interface on Linux is known as `perf_event` and the primary way of accessing it is the `perf_event_open()` system call [25]. This system call is used to configure and open a performance counter event; it is a complex call with over forty interacting parameters. The system call returns a file descriptor which can be used to control and access the event. Values can be read with the `read()` system call, and memory can be set up with `mmap()` that allows both sampling to a circular buffer as well as gathering additional information about the event. Various `ioctl()` calls are used to start and stop the events. Advanced features, such as event scheduling, event multiplexing, and save/restore on context switch, are all provided by the interface.

2.3 PAPI Library

The PAPI performance library [16] is a cross-platform library designed to allow access to performance counters on a wide variety of machines. On current Linux machines PAPI uses the perf_event interface. Before perf_event became standard (in 2009 with the Linux 2.6.31 release) PAPI used the perfmon2 [6] and perfctr [21] interfaces (which required custom patching of your Linux kernel). perfctr in particular has extremely fast counter reads due to using the `rdpmc` call, something perf_event initially lacked.

2.4 Linux `rdpmc` Support

The merging of perf_event into Linux was not without controversy. Due to the complaints from the PAPI developers about the high overhead of the `read()` system call, a userspace interface to allow fast `rdpmc` reads was eventually added with the Linux 3.4 release in 2012. An interface-breaking bug was found and fixed in the 3.11 release in 2013 [4] involving overlapping fields in a union which had unintentionally disabled some of the functionality. This was fixed, but this makes fully supporting both old and new kernels in a backwards compatible way tricky.

2.5 PAPI `rdpmc` Code

The `rdpmc` instruction itself only takes a short amount of time to run, on the order of a few tens of cycles [24]. Enabling userspace `rdpmc` support on x86 is simply a matter of the kernel setting a bit in the special `CR4` system register. After that, one might think access would be as simple as inserting `rdpmc` instructions into your code. However the complications of modern multi-tasking operating systems lead to a more complicated interface. Because there might be multiple users of perf_event, we cannot simply set counters to be free-running and use an assembly-language call to `rdpmc` to access them (this was a typical way to use `rdpmc` before perf_event was merged into Linux).

The recommended code for using `rdpmc` with perf_event is complicated, as seen in the example code found in Fig. 1. This boilerplate code more than doubles the overhead of a read, on the order of a few hundred cycles. Despite this overhead, this code all runs in userspace, so it is still much faster than using the default `read()` interface which must go through the kernel.

The reason for the extra code is that PAPI needs to be sure that the event configuration has not been changed by the kernel since the last time the event was read. The kernel is free to rearrange event counter mappings at any time. This might happen on a context switch, or due to multiplexing.

Multiplexing is when the kernel allows adding more events than the physical number available, providing estimated total event counts as if the hardware had that many counters. This is done by periodically stopping the counters and swapping in ones currently not running, so all events have a turn to run. The time an event has actually spent running is tracked, so by scaling this based on the total time you can estimate how many counts would have happened if

```
do {
   /* The kernel increments pc->lock any time */
   /* perf_event_update_userpage() is called  */
   /* So by checking now, and the end, we     */
   /* can see if an update happened while we  */
   /* were trying to read things, and re-try  */
   /* if something changed                    */
   /* The barrier ensures we get the most     */
   /* up-to date version of pc->lock          */

   seq=pc->lock;
   barrier();

   /* For multiplexing */
   /* time_enabled: time the event was enabled */
   enabled = pc->time_enabled;
   /* time_running: time the event was */
   /* actually running */
   running = pc->time_running;

   /* if cap_user_time is set we can use rdtsc */
   /* to calculate more exact enabled/running  */
   /* for more accurate multiplex calculations */
   if ( (pc->cap_user_time) &&
      (enabled != running)) {
      cyc = rdtsc();
      time_offset = pc->time_offset;
      time_mult = pc->time_mult;
      time_shift = pc->time_shift;

      quot = (cyc>>time_shift);
      rem = cyc & (((uint64_t)1<<time_shift)-1);
      delta = time_offset + (quot * time_mult) +
         ((rem * time_mult) >> time_shift);
   }
   enabled+=delta;

   /* Index of register to read               */
   /* 0 means stopped/not-active              */
   /* Need to subtract 1 to get rdpmc() index */
   index = pc->index;

   /* count is the value of the counter the*/
   /* last time the kernel read it.        */
   /* If we don't sign extend, we get negative */
   /* numbers which break if IOC_RESET is done */
   width = pc->pmc_width;
   count = pc->offset;
   count<<=(64-width);
   count>>=(64-width);

   /* Only read if rdpmc enabled and index    */
   /* valid, otherwise return the older count */
   if (pc->cap_usr_rdpmc && index) {

      /* Read counter value */
      pmc = rdpmc(index-1);

      /* sign extend result */
      pmc<<=(64-width);
      pmc>>=(64-width);

      /* add value into existing kernel count */
      count+=pmc;
      running+=delta;
   }

   barrier();

} while (pc->lock != seq);

if (en) *en=enabled;
if (ru) *ru=running;

return count;
```

Fig. 1. Sample code for a perf_event rdpmc read.

the event had been running the full time. Multiplex handling is a big part of the extra rdpmc measurement code, as due to multiplexing the events currently scheduled might be changed by the operating system at any time. Also, before reporting the final event counts, you need to scale any events that did not run for the full time during measurement.

The perf_event interface provides helper information that can be mapped into the program's address space with a call to `mmap()`. Each event you want to read via `rdpmc` must have an associated `mmap()` page. This potentially adds overhead issues: the `read()` interface allows grouping multiple events so they can be read with one single call. However with `rdpmc` each event needs to be read individually and with large numbers of events this could potentially hurt performance. In addition each `mmap()` page takes up a valuable TLB slot and could hurt performance if a large number of events are mapped. On architectures with large page sizes events can take up large amounts of RAM, which can be troublesome since by default the amount of mmap area that perf_event can pin into memory is limited to 516kB.

A `rdpmc` read involves the following series of events. First, the `seq` sequence field is read, followed by a memory barrier to make sure it is synchronized with the kernel. Next, check `time_running` and `time_enabled`. If they are equal then multiplexing is not happening, otherwise the result needs to be scaled appropriately. The `count` value (which needs to be sign extended) holds the value from the last time the kernel has read the counter. This needs to be accounted for, as the value in the actual counter might have been reset on context switch, CPU migration, or if an overflow happened. Finally use `rdpmc` to obtain the current counter value which is added to `count`. While all of this is happening various things could happen that would make the values inconsistent (such as a context switch). To verify this has not happened, the `seq` value should be read again to verify it matches the earlier value. If this has changed then the whole process needs to be repeated until we complete the process without a change. From our experiments we find it is rare for `seq` to change unless the system is under heavy load. A livelock could potentially happen where the sequence checking could never make progress if the kernel is busy updating the page. Code could be added to break out and fall back to a `read()` in this situation.

This code path may seem like it has a lot of overhead, but it still much faster than performing a `read()` system call (which is slow, disruptive to the CPU, and involves running an unpredictable amount of kernel code).

This code has been added to PAPI and is enabled by default in the 5.6 release of the library. Use the `--enable-perfevent-rdpmc=yes/no` configure option to explicitly enable or disable the feature when building and installing.

2.6 Linux `rdpmc` Bugs Found

Once we started testing the `rdpmc` code in PAPI, the PAPI regression tests turned up a number of bugs. After some analysis, most of these bugs were found to be in the Linux kernel implementation.

The first bug found was that various pthread tests would randomly cause general protection faults (GPF) and crash. This is due to a change made in the Linux 4.0 kernel that disabled `rdpmc` support when a process had no events running. Prior to this, when perf_event was started the `CR4` bit that enables `rdpmc` support was globally enabled, so even processes without active events could still read the counter values. This is a possible information leakage security issue, so the kernel was modified to only allow using `rdpmc` if a process was actively using an event. There was a bug in the implementation of this fix: a wrong field was checked and sometimes when multiple threads were active the reference count would get out of sync and `rdpmc` support would be disabled while events were still running, leading to a GPF. This bug was reported by us and fixed in the Linux 4.12 release.

Another related bug happened when a process created a perf_event mmap mapping, but then called the `exec()` system call without closing the mapping first. This would cause the mmap reference count to go negative and again GPFs would happen on `rdpmc` access. This bug was reported by us and fixed in the Linux 4.13 release.

Another test that failed was one that created a large number of events in a large number of threads. This was a kernel limitation: the number of `mmap()` pages is limited by the value in `sysctl kernel.perf_event_mlock_kb` to a default of 516kB. We were hitting this limit and PAPI was crashing. We modified PAPI to only use 1 mmap page per process when using `rdpmc` (except when sampling), and if mmap space runs out it will now fall back to using `read()` which is slower but should always work.

The final bug involves time accounting when attaching to another process. With perf_event it is possible for one process to monitor another by specifying a process id at event creation time (this is how tools like perf can monitor a separate process). The `enabled_time` accounting code did not handle the case where an event was disabled while the attached processor was asleep, leading to the value being reported as negative. PAPI saw the non-matching enabled and running times and assumed this was a multiplexed event and scaled the results accordingly leading to impossibly large values. This bug was reported by us and fixed in the Linux 4.13 release.

3 Related Work

Low-overhead counter access is an important area with a lot of previous research. PAPI is widely used and is often the comparison point for such studies.

3.1 Lower-Level Interface Overhead

Prior to the introduction of perf_event with the 2.6.31 Linux kernel, there were external patches to provide performance counter support to Linux. PAPI used two of these: perfctr [21] (which had `rdpmc` support) and perfmon2 [6] (which did not). Most previous PAPI comparisons predate the introduction of perf_event and use one of these interfaces. These results are out of date now, as work on the alternate interfaces stopped once perf_event was merged into the mainline Linux kernel.

We [26] previously investigated the overhead of perf_event in terms of start/stop/read overhead on various x86_64 machines. The measurements are at the raw system call level, one level lower than the PAPI interface we investigate. We found that perf_event `read()` has relatively high overhead, but that the perf_event `rdpmc` interface could be competitive with the previous perfctr and perfmon2 interfaces.

3.2 PAPI Overhead

Our work, as well as much of the previous work, primarily looks at the effect in cycle time when adding instrumentation. Instrumentation can affect other metrics, and the reduced overhead from `rdpmc` should help in these cases too.

Maxwell et al. [12] and Moore et al. [15] compare the overhead of PAPI, including read calls, on various architectures available in 2002. This predates perf_event so making direct comparisons to our work is difficult.

Lehr [10] finds that even though PAPI instrumentation causes less than a 10% slowdown in SPEC CPU 2006, the actual counter measurements (including stores and cache events) can be perturbed enough to give misleading results.

Huang et al. [8] investigate the power overhead of using PAPI. This is not directly related to our work, but any/time instruction overhead is also going to lead to a certain amount of power and energy overhead.

Babka and Tůma [3] investigate the overhead of PAPI in both cycle count and other metrics on AMD and Intel machines. Their primary concern is overhead of memory metrics. Their measured overhead is high, as it appears they were using perfmon2. Using a `rdpmc` capable interface would reduce the overhead.

Zaparanuks, Jovic and Hauswirth [28] investigate measurement overhead of both user and user+kernel counters using PAPI on top of perfmon2 and perfctr, as well as using perfmon2 and perfctr directly. It is a detailed investigation into obtaining minimum overhead on these interfaces, but predates the introduction of perf_event.

3.3 Other Performance Counter Tools

Röhl et al. [22] investigate the performance of likwid-perfctr and the LIKWID Marker API under the Linux OS on Intel IvyBridge-EP, Intel Haswell and AMD Interlagos. At the time LIKWID did not support the perf_event interface, and instead directly accesses the relevant MSRs using the Linux `/dev/msr` interface. Using `/dev/msr` still requires entry/exit from the kernel so can still have high overhead. The Marker API allows calipered measurement of code, although it is not full self-monitoring as the values measured are written straight to disk without the running application having access. They find that moving to `rdpmc` would greatly reduce overhead, but since the kernel disables `rdpmc` by default if not using perf_event, they cannot use it without patching the kernel. They compare their results to PAPI, but do not break out the read overhead separately. LIKWID does show an advantage over PAPI in their results, but this was before our addition of `rdpmc` support.

Table 1. Machines used in this study. Note that on Intel machines more counters may be available if hyperthreading is disabled.

Processor		Counters available	
Intel	Pentium II	2 general	
Intel	Pentium 4	18 general	
Intel	Core 2 P8700	2 general	3 fixed
Intel	Atom Cedarview D2550	2 general	3 fixed
Intel	IvyBridge i5-3210M	4 general	3 fixed
Intel	Haswell i7-4770	4 general	3 fixed
Intel	Haswell-EP E5-2640	4 general	3 fixed
Intel	Broadwell i7-5557U	4 general	3 fixed
Intel	Broadwell-EP E5-2620	4 general	3 fixed
Intel	Skylake i7-6700	4 general	3 fixed
AMD	fam10h Phenom II	4 general	
AMD	fam15h A10-6800B	6 general	
AMD	fam15h Opteron 6376	6 general	
AMD	fam16h A8-6410	4 general	

Demme and Sethumadhaven propose LiMiT [5], a Linux interface to provide fast, userspace access to performance counters reminiscent of the much older perfctr project. It requires patching the Linux kernel, and a note on the project's website notes that the patch is unstable and can cause system crashes. They claim LiMiT is 90× faster than PAPI and 23× faster than perf_event, although the test is not described in detail nor what kernel versions used for the test so it is a bit unclear what is being compared. The addition of `rdpmc` support to PAPI should make it compare more favorably since pure userspace accesses are being used.

AMD proposed an advanced Lightweight Profiling [1] interface providing userspace-only access to all aspects of controlling performance counters, not just reads. This could potentially speed up much more than reads, however the Linux kernel developers have refused to add support for the interface unless it was moderated by the kernel, which would defeat the entire purpose [14].

4 Experimental Setup

We test on fourteen different machines as shown in Table 1. This covers multiple generations of Intel and AMD processors from a 20 year old Pentium II machine up to and including more modern machines. Most machines are running the Linux 4.9 kernel provided with the Sid release of Debian Linux. A few of the machines are running the 3.16 kernel provided with Jessie Debian Linux. A full list of operating system, compiler, and cpu information is available for download along with our raw measurement information.

Most of our experiments are against a PAPI development git snapshot from March 2017, as at that time no full PAPI release contained `rdpmc` support. For comparison we also look at the 5.4.0, 5.4.1, 5.4.3, 5.5.0, and 5.5.1 official PAPI releases.

We measure the overhead of the core PAPI calls using the `papi_cost` utility that comes with PAPI. This runs each PAPI library call of interest one million times, measuring the latency using `PAPI_get_real_cyc()`. On x86 systems this maps to a `rdtsc` read timestamp instruction. We extend `papi_cost` to also return the median and 25th and 75th percentile values so that we could use those to make boxplots. For the more complicated results, such as the outlier analysis, we modify `papi_cost` further to log performance counter data for each iteration. In addition, we instrument the STREAM [13] and Linpack [20] benchmarks to investigate how the `PAPI_read()` overhead changes when a system is under load.

5 Results

We compare the overhead for traditional PAPI using `read()` to our modified PAPI using the `rdpmc` instruction.

Table 2 summarizes the `read()` vs `rdpmc` speedup found on the fourteen x86 machines. The results are given based on the median out of 1 million consecutive calls to read. We use the median, and not the average, as the measurement code occasionally has extremely large outliers which skew the average and standard deviation. See Sect. 5.1 for more discussion of these outliers. The speedup found is at least 2.6× in all cases, and is typically around 6× on recent Intel machines. This speedup is still large, but not quite as high on AMD machines and low end machines such as the Atom processors.

Figure 2 shows the `PAPI_read()` overhead gathered for the past few PAPI releases, as well as the current git snapshot we use for testing. This was mostly a sanity check to make sure the values have not changed greatly over time. The plots are boxplots: the black box shows the range between the 25th and 75th percentiles, the white line is the median, and the lines are showing the maximum outliers. Since the outliers are large, we zoom in on the plot and label at the top of the graph their numerical value. It can be seen that the overhead has not changed much in the recent past on the Haswell machine that we measure on.

By default the `papi_cost` benchmark measures two events. That is a typical number to measure, especially if you are interested in metrics such as Instruction per Cycle (IPC). To get a wider range of results we modify `papi_cost` to measure from one to four events. Figure 3 shows how the overhead increases on a Haswell machine. Both the `read()` and `rdpmc` results increase, but the increase is linear as expected.

Table 2. Median rdpmc speedup in **papi_cost** running the read test 1 million times.

Vendor	Machine	read() cycles	rdpmc cycles	Speedup
Intel	Pentium II	2533	384	6.6×
Intel	Pentium 4	3728	704	5.3×
Intel	Core 2	1634	199	8.2×
Intel	Atom	3906	392	10.0×
Intel	Ivybridge	885	149	5.9×
Intel	Haswell	913	142	6.4×
Intel	Haswell-EP	820	125	6.6×
Intel	Broadwell	1030	145	7.1×
Intel	Broadwell-EP	750	118	6.4×
Intel	Skylake	942	144	6.5×
AMD	fam10h Phenom II	1252	205	6.1×
AMD	fam15h A10	2457	951	2.6×
AMD	fam15h Opteron	2186	644	3.4×
AMD	fam16h A8	1632	205	8.0×

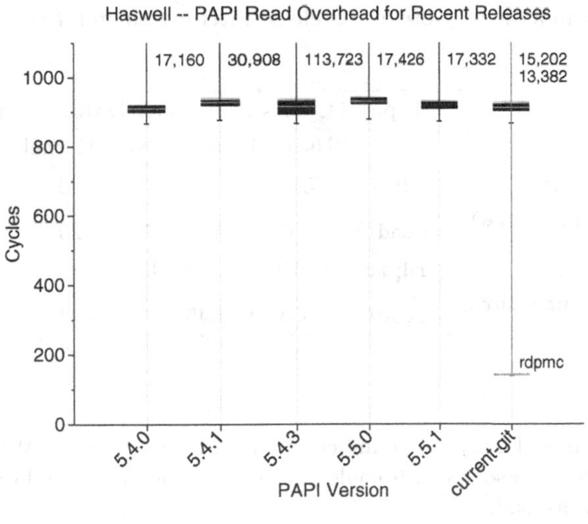

Fig. 2. Boxplot comparison of read overheads for the past few releases of PAPI.

The **read()** code uses the perf_event format group feature to read multiple events with a single system call. Despite grouping multiple events into on system call, the time still grows linearly as the internal kernel code still has to read the counters out one by one. The **rdpmc** code must read out the results one by one, with the additional overhead from the fixup code for each read. There has been an interface suggested [29] that would allow grouping multiple events into one mmap() page but this interface has not been implemented yet.

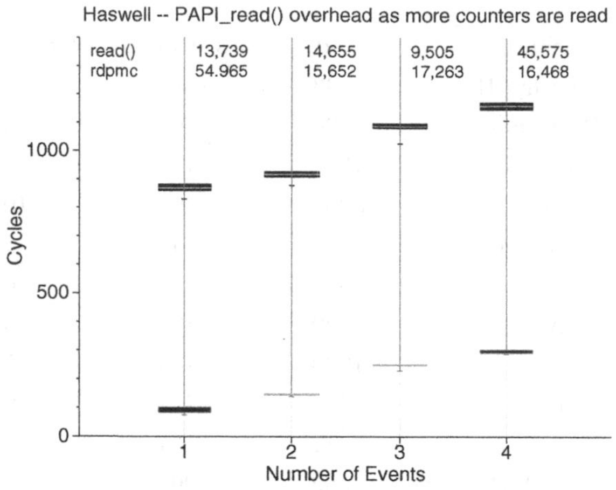

Fig. 3. Boxplot comparison of read overheads as more simultaneous events are measured.

Table 3. Results under load. Note: the cycle counter cycles aren't necessarily the same as rdtsc cycles.

Routine	Type	Cycles		L1 DMiss		DTLB Miss	
		User	Kernel	User	Kernel	User	Kernel
`HPL_pdpanel_init` (`low memory pressure`)	`rdpmc`	512	0	5	0	0	0
	`read()`	461	1,755	7	20	0	0
`HPL_pdfact` (`high memory pressure`)	`rdpmc`	4,019	0	39	0	11	0
	`read()`	4,551	13,545	43	123	16	16

Table 4. TLB misses for various number of simultaneous events. When using `rdpmc` more mmap pages are used, which could potentially increase the TLB pressure on a memory-intense workload.

Routine	Type	2 Events		3 Events		4 Events	
		User	Kernel	User	Kernel	User	Kernel
`HPL_pdpanel_init` (`low memory pressure`)	`rdpmc`	0	0	0	0	0	0
	`read()`	0	0	0	0	0	0
`HPL_pdfact` (`high memory pressure`)	`rdpmc`	11	0	14	0	16	0
	`read()`	16	16	15	17	16	18

In addition to the `papi_cost` results, which only look at overhead when doing `PAPI_read()` calls and nothing else, we also investigate overhead found in more real-world situations. We look at the architectural overhead of the `PAPI_read()` call. This is difficult, as the traditional way of gathering such measurements would be to use PAPI, but using PAPI to measure PAPI does not work well. Instead we put raw calls to `rdpmc` around the `PAPI_read()` calls under the assumption that for such short time intervals it is unlikely that the kernel will move events around.

Table 3 shows results for the overhead of `PAPI_read()` while instrumenting two different Linpack functions: `HPL_pdpanel_init()` and `HPL_pdfact()`. The former does not access memory much, and so the cycle count, L1 misses, and TLB misses are low. (Note that the cycle counts reported here are CPU cycles, which are not the same as the rdtsc bus cycles reported for other results in this paper). The `rdpmc` results show that the kernel is not entered at all, and that some of the `read()` overhead is caused by cache misses when running kernel code. The `HPL_pdfact()` routine is memory intensive, so the addition of `PAPI_read()` to the code causes cache and TLB misses which generate a lot more overhead than when the same routine is added to `HPL_pdpanel_init()`. In both cases the `rdpmc` version of `PAPI_read()` has much lower overhead overall.

Table 4 investigates the same routines as more events are being measured by `PAPI_read()`. This is to see if the additional mmap pages required by the rdpmc interface cause enough TLB pressure to adversely affect the measured overhead. While the TLB misses do grow, overall they are still less than for the `read()` version of the code.

5.1 Outliers

Our overhead results mostly cluster around the median, but there are occasional outliers of over an order of magnitude. We initially suspected the `rdtsc` cycle measurements, but on newer x86 processors the cycle counter has had many improvements to make it invariant in the face of frequency scaling. PAPI follows most of the suggestions by Intel for how to obtain accurate cycle readings [19].

An example of the magnitude of the outliers can be seen in Fig. 4 which shows the overhead of the first 3000 `rdpmc` reads in a `papi_cost` run. We use the performance counter results to determine the source of the outliers. For these results we are using an AMD A10 machine as it has a richer set of events to choose from (including a hardware interrupt event and a SMI system monitoring interrupt event). We find that many of the extreme outliers (but not all of them) are caused by a hardware interrupt happening in the middle of a read.

There are also some interesting recurring patterns every 500 reads or so. Figure 5 plots a different run, this time showing L2 cache misses. We observe L2 cache misses are happening approximately every 500 iterations. The benchmark, outside of the critical measurement loop, stores the gathered values (which are 64-bit integers) to a large array for later analysis. If you write 512 8-byte values to memory, that works out to be 4096 bytes, which is the size of a page. So our

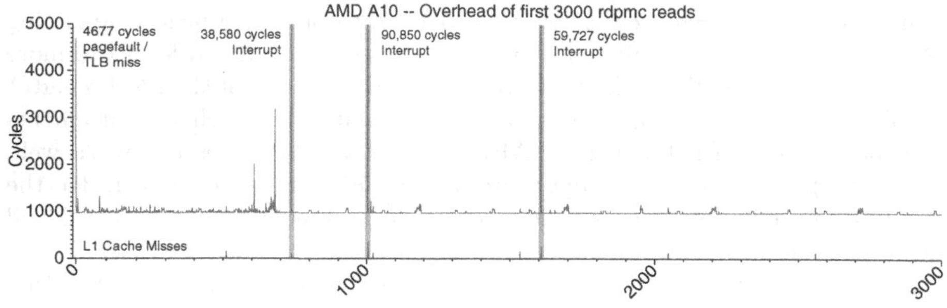

Fig. 4. Overhead seen in the first 3000 iterations of a rdpmc `papi_cost` run. The larger outliers are caused by hardware interrupts, while the initial is caused by a pagefault from the first access to the mmap() page.

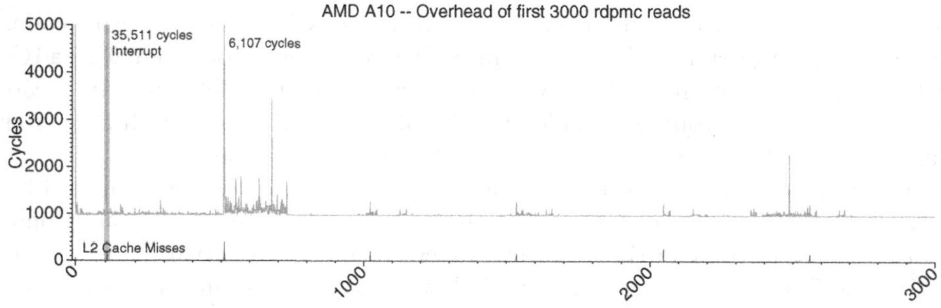

Fig. 5. Overhead seen in the first 3000 iterations of a different rdpmc `papi_cost` run. This plots L2 instead of L1 cache misses. There is a repeating pattern approximately every 500 iterations, likely caused by accesses to our results array (512 64-bit writes will fill one 4096 byte page).

measurement code is potentially causing a TLB or cache miss when crossing a page boundary which is likely the cause of that regular pattern.

The outlier immediately at the beginning on both plots is caused by a pagefault and TLB miss the first time the mmap page is accessed. We noted this previously [26], and suggested using `MAP_POPULATE` or touching the mmap page to avoid this issue. However, in Fig. 5 we tried enabling `MAP_POPULATE` and it did not help. The initialization of the event happens so far in advance of the first read that by the time it gets to our read code the page is no longer in the TLB so preloading does not help. This behavior is probably typical of what would be found in most PAPI instrumented code. This page-fault issue means that if you are using PAPI to do a single read, the first `rdpmc` overhead is large. However when using `read()` the first-access overhead is high for other reasons (including shared-library setup if you are the first user of the system call) so `rdpmc` is still better. In both cases, if more than one read is done, the initial first read overhead is mitigated.

5.2 Historical Comparison

Table 5 and Fig. 6 show a comparison of the performance interfaces historically supported by PAPI on Linux. The results are on a Core 2 machine, as the older interfaces do not support more modern CPUs as they are no longer maintained now that perf_event became standard with Linux 2.6.31. The perfctr interface has a custom `rdpmc` interface that is similar to the one used by perf_event,

Table 5. Comparison of various historical perf counter interfaces on a Core 2 machine. Core 2 is used as the older interfaces do not support more modern CPUs.

Interface	Kernel	Read results	slowdown vs perf_event `rdpmc`
`perf_event rdpmc`	3.16	199	—
`perfctr rdpmc`	2.6.32	200	1.0×
`perfmon2 read()`	2.6.30	1216	6.1×
`perf_event read()`	3.16	1587	8.0×
`perf_event KPTI read()`	4.15-rc7	3173	15.9×

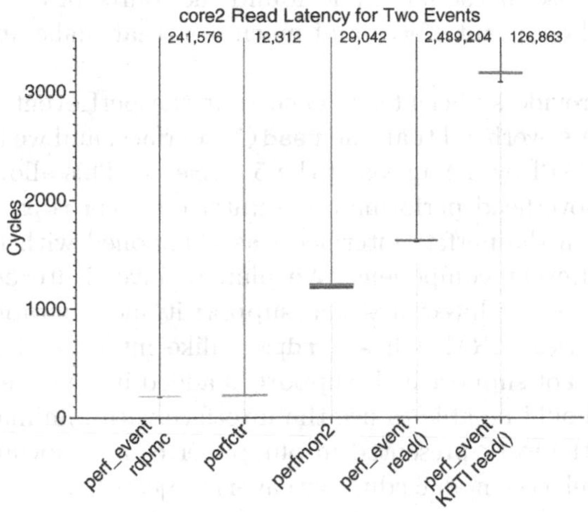

Fig. 6. Boxplot comparison of historical PAPI methods of doing reads. The few outliers are large, off the graph.

Table 6. Overhead caused by the KPTI work around for the Meltdown security vulnerability found on Intel processors.

Processor	rdpmc	KPTI = off read	KPTI = on read
Core2	199	1634 (8.2×)	3173 (15.9×)
Haswell	139	958 (6.9×)	1411 (10.2×)
Skylake	142	978 (6.9×)	1522 (10.7×)

whereas perfmon2 does not have a `rdpmc` interface. We find that the perf_event `rdpmc` interface is more or less the same speed as perfctr and much faster than perfmon2 and perf_event `read()`. It appears that after a many year absence, PAPI read overhead can finally return to the levels that were seen back when perfctr was the primary method of accessing performance counters.

One additional change to recent Linux has affected these results. The release of the Meltdown security vulnerability [11] on Intel processors has led to the Kernel Page Table Isolation (KPTI) patchset being enabled by default. This moves the kernel and user address spaces to be completely different, causing a costly TLB flush on every system call. We measure the overhead caused by this and indeed the read() overhead is much larger, as seen in Table 6.

6 Conclusion and Future Work

We have added userspace (`rdpmc`) performance counter read support to the PAPI library and found that we can reduce overhead by at least three times (and more typically around six times) on a wide variety of x86 hardware. We have validated the results, which resulted in finding and getting fixed a number of bugs in the Linux kernel. We also investigated and found the source of the large outliers in the results (found on all interfaces and machines) that make analysis of timing results difficult.

Our results provide sufficient evidence that the perf_event rdpmc interface consistently has less overhead than the `read()` interface, and we have enabled the new interface in PAPI by default as of the 5.6 release. This allows PAPI to once again obtain low-overhead performance counter data via `rdpmc`, a feature that had been lost when the perfctr interface was abandoned with the introduction of the Linux perf_event component. We plan to investigate adding userspace read support on other architectures that support it, most notably the ARM and ARM64 architectures. ARM64 has a `rdpmc` alike interface, but currently the Linux kernel does not support it. If support is added in a perf_event compatible way then PAPI should be able to use the interface with minimal changes.

Full data for the work presented in our paper can be downloaded from our website: http://web.eece.maine.edu/~vweaver/projects/papi-rdpmc/.

The reduced overhead provided by `rdpmc` should greatly help users of PAPI, especially those in the high performance computing community. Performance analysis will be greatly aided by the detailed performance results obtained with less overhead than was recently possible.

Acknowledgment. This work was supported by the National Science Foundation under Grant No. SSI-1450122.

References

1. Advanced Micro Devices: Lightweight Profiling Specification (2010)
2. AMD: AMD Family 15h Processor BIOS and Kernel Developer Guide (2011)

3. Babka, V., Tůma, P.: Effects of memory sharing on contemporary processor architectures. In: Annual Doctoral Workshop on Mathematical and Engineering Methods in Computer Science, pp. 15–22 (2007)
4. Corbet, J.: A perf ABI fix. Linux Weekly News, September 2013. https://lwn.net/Articles/567894/
5. Demme, J., Sethumadhavan, S.: Rapid identification of architectural bottlenecks via precise event counting. In: Proceedings of the 38th IEEE/ACM International Symposium on Computer Architecture, June 2011
6. Eranian, S.: Perfmon2: a flexible performance monitoring interface for Linux. In: Proceedings of the 2006 Ottawa Linux Symposium, pp. 269–288, July 2006
7. Gleixner, T., Molnar, I.: Performance counters for Linux (2009)
8. Huang, S., Lang, M., Pakin, S., Gu, S.: Measurement and characterization of Haswell power and energy consumption. In: Proceedings of the 3rd International Workshop on Energy Efficient Supercomputing, November 2015
9. Intel Corporation: Intel® 64 and IA-32 Architectures Software Developer's Manual Volume 3: System Programming Guide, June 2015
10. Lehr, J.: Counting performance: hardware performance counter and compiler instrumentation. In: Jahrestagung der Gesellschaft für Informatik. LNI, vol. P-259, pp. 2187–2198. GI, September 2016
11. Lipp, M., et al.: Meltdown. arXiv e-prints, January 2018
12. Maxwell, M., Teller, P., Salayandia, L., Moore, S.: Accuracy of performance monitoring hardware. In: Proceedings of the Los Alamos Computer Science Institute Symposium, October 2002
13. McCalpin, J.: STREAM: sustainable memory bandwidth in high performance computers (1999). http://www.cs.virginia.edu/stream/
14. Molnar, I.: Re: [RFC 0/3] basic support for LWP (2010). http://marc.info/?l=linux-kernel&m=128630554614635
15. Moore, S., Teller, P., Maxwell, M.: Efficiency and accuracy issues for sampling vs counting modes of performance monitoring hardware. In: Proceedings of the DoD High Performance Computing Modernization Program's User Group Conference, June 2002
16. Mucci, P.J., Browne, S., Deane, C., Ho, G.: PAPI: a portable interface to hardware performance counters. In: Proceedings of the Department of Defense HPCMP User Group Conference, June 1999
17. Mytkowicz, T., Diwan, A., Hauswirth, M., Sweeney, P.: Understanding measurement perturbation in trace-based data. In: Proceedings of the 21st IEEE/ACM International Parallel and Distributed Processing Symposium, March 2007
18. Mytkowicz, T., Diwan, A., Hauswirth, M., Sweeney, P.: We have it easy, but do we have it right? In: Proceedings of the 22nd IEEE/ACM International Parallel and Distributed Processing Symposium, April 2008
19. Paoloni, G.: How to Benchmark Code Execution Times on Intel IA-32 and IA-64 Instruction Set Architectures. Intel Corporation, September 2010
20. Petitet, A., Whaley, R., Dongarra, J., Cleary, A., Luszczek, P.: HPL—a portable implementation of the high-performance linpack benchmark for distributed-memory computers. Innovative Computing Laboratory, Computer Science Department, University of Tennessee, v2.2, December 2017. http://www.netlib.org/benchmark/hpl/
21. Pettersson, M.: The PERFCTR interface (1999). http://user.it.uu.se/~mikpe/linux/perfctr/2.6/

22. Röhl, T., Treibig, J., Hager, G., Wellein, G.: Overhead analysis of performance counter measurements. In: International Conference on Parallel Programming Workshops, pp. 176–185, September 2014
23. Treibig, J., Hager, G., Wellein, G.: LIKWID: a lightweight performance-oriented tool suite for x86 multicore environments. In: Proceedings of the First International Workshop on Parallel Software Tools and Tool Infrastructures, September 2010
24. Weaver, V.: [PATCH] perf_event use RDPMC rather than RDMSR when possible in kernel (2012). https://lkml.org/lkml/2012/2/20/418
25. Weaver, V.: perf_event_open manual page. In: Kerrisk, M. (ed.) Linux Programmer's Manual, December 2013
26. Weaver, V.: Self-monitoring overhead of the Linux perf_event performance counter interface. In: Proceedings of the IEEE International Symposium on Performance Analysis of Systems and Software, March 2015
27. Wolf, J.: Programming Methods for the Pentium™ III Processor's Streaming SIMD Extensions Using the VTune™ Performance Enhancement Environment. Intel Corporation (1999)
28. Zaparanuks, D., Jovic, M., Hauswirth, M.: Accuracy of performance counter measurements. In: Proceedings of the IEEE International Symposium on Performance Analysis of Systems and Software, pp. 23–32, April 2009
29. Zijlstra, P.: Re: [PATCH 1/2] perf/x86/intel: enable CPU ref_cycles for GP counter, May 2017. https://marc.info/?l=linux-kernel&m=149616517431438&w=2

Generic Library Interception for Improved Performance Measurement and Insight

Ronny Brendel[1(✉)], Bert Wesarg[2], Ronny Tschüter[2], Matthias Weber[2], Thomas Ilsche[2], and Sebastian Oeste[2]

[1] Oak Ridge National Laboratory, Oak Ridge, USA
`ronnybrendel@gmail.com`
[2] Technische Universität Dresden, Dresden, Germany
`{bert.wesarg,ronny.tschueter,matthias.weber, thomas.ilsche,sebastian.oeste}@tu-dresden.de`

Abstract. As applications grow in capability, they also grow in complexity. This complexity in turn gets pushed into modules and libraries. In addition, hardware configurations become increasingly elaborate, too. These two trends make understanding, debugging and analyzing the performance of applications more and more difficult.

To enable detailed insight into library usage of applications, we present an approach and implementation in Score-P that supports intuitive and robust creation of wrappers for arbitrary C/C++ libraries. Runtime analysis then uses these wrappers to keep track of how applications interact with libraries, how they interact with each other, and record the exact timing of their functions.

Keywords: Clang · Instrumentation · Library · LLVM · Performance analysis · Performance optimization · Software module · Tracing · Wrapper

1 Introduction

To push science and businesses further, today's software becomes increasingly powerful but also complex. Software libraries allow offloading this complexity into subunits, so that developers can focus on adding functionality by using

This manuscript has been authored by UT-Battelle, LLC, under contract DE-AC05-00OR22725 with the US Department of Energy (DOE). The US government retains and the publisher, by accepting the article for publication, acknowledges that the US government retains a nonexclusive, paid-up, irrevocable, worldwide license to publish or reproduce the published form of this manuscript, or allow others to do so, for US government purposes. DOE will provide public access to these results of federally sponsored research in accordance with the DOE Public Access Plan (http://energy.gov/downloads/doe-public-access-plan).

A. Bhatele et al. (Eds.): ESPT/VPA 2017/2018, LNCS 11027, pp. 21–37, 2019.
https://doi.org/10.1007/978-3-030-17872-7_2

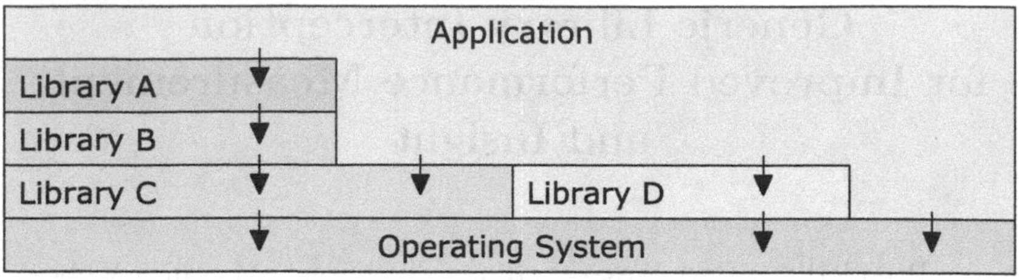

Fig. 1. Typical software stack with an application relying on four libraries.

them, rather than implementing every detail themselves. But the complexity does not disappear—It gets pushed down to lower levels. The gained development convenience is traded for an increased effort of debugging and overall reasoning about the application including its performance characteristics. Figure 1 depicts a typical application and its software dependencies.

A similar development takes place in computer architecture. The adoption of multiple cores per CPU, heterogeneous architectures, complex cache/memory hierarchies, elaborate interconnect networks, as well as deep I/O hierarchies gives rise to a multitude of potential performance problems. This increasing complexity in software and hardware makes performance analysis an integral part of the software life cycle.

Tool chains providing modern performance analysis capabilities include Linux Perf [23], NVIDIA profiling tools [26], Intel VTune Amplifier [30], Score-P [20], Arm MAP [2] and HPCToolkit [1]. These tools combine multiple data collection techniques, like sampling, call stack unwinding, tools interfaces, library wrapping, compiler instrumentation, and manual instrumentation in various ways. The goal is to gather data as detailed as needed while alleviating the disadvantages of individual techniques. For example, it is common to combine sampling and call stack unwinding with library wrapping for important libraries. Sampling gives coarse-grained stochastic timing information of the application's function call sequence, while library wrappers count and measure exact timings of library calls. Aside from counting calls and measuring time, libraries like POSIX Threads [6], and I/O libraries like HDF5 [16] and ADIOS [22] are commonly wrapped to extract semantic information (e.g. written bytes) from arguments passed to library functions.

Which wrappers are available is limited to what each performance tool supports. Even if an application developer is interested in exact function call tracking of certain libraries, there is no well supported way to achieve this in any performance analysis tool today.

To address this, we introduce *user library wrapping*, which is included in the upcoming release of the open-source performance monitor Score-P. The feature empowers application developers to easily generate library wrappers for any C/C++ library. This is significant, because:

- With just link time changes, developers can now get exact performance information on any C/C++ library they want.
- They can analyze closed-source libraries, like the Intel MKL [24].
- They can track function calls from a library to itself and between libraries.

Score-P benefits from user library wrapping for the following reasons. First, regular compiler instrumentation provides no call-backs upon library entry/exit. Second, compiler instrumentation often yields high event rates, which leads to diminished performance and large event recordings. This necessitates a filtering workflow that in turn complicates the whole measurement process. With user library wrapping, developers can forego compiler instrumentation and still capture critical performance data, and have a small low-overhead recording at the same time—no filtering needed. Third, wrappers give exact function call counts and timings as opposed to the statistical information from sampling and call stack unwinding. Additionally, it simplifies creating fixed wrappers that capture library semantics not only in Score-P, but for all tools that rely on library wrappers.

We took great care to make wrapper creation and usage as intuitive and simple as possible. Numerous checks with polished error messages ensure the wrapper works correctly or let the developer know why it might not.

This paper is divided as follows: Sect. 2 enumerates related work. Section 3 first presents basics on library wrapping. It then details the workflow for creating and using wrappers while highlighting some implementation choices, by the example of wrapping the QtWidget and QtGui modules. Section 4 demonstrates how our approach aids investigating the performance characteristics of two real-world scientific applications. The last two sections offer conclusions and indicate points of interest for future development.

2 Related Work

Wrapping C/C++ libraries is not new. SWIG [4], first released in 1996, generates wrappers for C/C++ libraries so they can be called from other languages like Python, Go and Lua. SWIG does not provide library interception for extracting, e.g., performance data. Furthermore, it is not possible to create C++ or C wrappers for C/C++ libraries. SWIG uses its own C/C++ preprocessor and parser.

Recently, Google released the C++ Language Interface Foundation (CLIF) [8] which provides similar functionality to SWIG. It uses Clang [7] to analyze the library headers, and for now only generates wrappers for Python.

Some libraries, like OpenMP 5 [13] and CUDA [10], offer a so-called *tools interface* for analysis tools to hook into. In that case, library wrapping is not needed. But for most libraries, wrappers are required to gain insight into their usage. MPI [25] provides a special *profiling interface*, which helps create wrappers by providing all functions as weak symbols so that they can be overridden. Wrapper functions call the actual MPI functions through a `P`-prefixed symbol, e.g. `PMPI_Send`.

One possible application for tools interfaces and library wrappers is to check for correct API usage. For example MUST [19] uses MPI's profiling interface to ensure correct use and to detect possible deadlocks. The wrapping code is generated manually with a simple proprietary wrapper generator.

Software performance analysis tools commonly use fixed wrappers to gain insight into the use of specific libraries. For example Arm MAP [2] is a commercial profiler specialized in analyzing multi-paradigm applications. It wraps MPI and OpenMP functions and uses the tools interface of CUDA. Various open-source performance analysis tools exist. Some of them are Extrae [14], HPCToolkit [1] and Score-P [20]. All three support a variety of parallelization schemes and hardware platforms. They differ in techniques, focus and user interface, but are similar in terms of utilizing library wrapping.

VampirTrace includes a simple implementation of user library wrapping [11]. It is based on CTool [9] (abandoned in 2004), supports only C, has several technical limitations and needs manual intervention in most cases. Score-P is VampirTrace's successor.

TAU offers user library wrapping via the `tau_wrap` and `tau_gen_wrapper` commands [28]. It uses the Edison Group's commercial C/C++ parser [12]. TAU's implementation has multiple limitations. For example, it does not support C++, cannot wrap functions with function pointers or ellipsis arguments, and compile and link flags are not customizable.

3 Methodology

Our goal is to provide a simple and robust way to record performance data on library function calls. For this, we need an opportunity to intercept them. That means whenever a library function is called, the measurement system has to be invoked.

3.1 Library Call Interception

We distinguish two wrapping methods based on when interception is set up: *link time* and *runtime*. These two methods also differ in the kind of functions that can be intercepted.

Link Time: The first approach is based on the `--wrap` option of the GNU linker[1]. For example, to wrap the function `foo`, we have to implement the corresponding wrapper function `__wrap_foo`. The original function is available via the `__real_foo` symbol. Then specifying `--wrap foo` in the link command enables wrapping `foo`, and the GNU linker resolves these symbols appropriately. This approach is limited to instances where the link step of the application can be modified, as the symbols of interest need to be specified at link time. Wrapping symbols called from shared libraries does not work, because the linker resolves these symbols at runtime.

[1] https://sourceware.org/binutils/docs-2.28/ld/Options.html.

Runtime: At the start of executing an application, the dynamic linker loads and links all dependent shared libraries. The second approach modifies the order in which the dynamic linker loads them. To wrap a function, we provide a replacement function with the same symbol name as the wrapped function. The linker, then, needs to link the wrapper before the target library. One way to achieve this is modifying the link step to put the wrapper library before the original one. Alternatively, let the environment variable `LD_PRELOAD`[2] point to the wrapper library before executing the application. The latter method has the advantage that it does not need to modify the link step. Once called, the wrapper function loads the target library via `dlopen`, searches for the address of the original symbol using `dlsym`, and then forwards the original call. With link step modification, this approach can intercept all calls that link time wrapping can, plus those that originate from shared libraries. The `LD_PRELOAD`-based version can only intercept calls to shared libraries, not to statically linked ones.

Both mechanisms require wrappers that pose as the original functions. For each call, a wrapper function notifies the performance monitor before and after forwarding the call to the original function. In the next section we present the workflow with which users create their own library wrapper.

3.2 Workflow

In this work we extend Score-P—a state-of-the-art software performance monitor. Figure 2 shows its high-level architecture.

The goal is to make calls to library functions available for performance analysis. For this, we add functionality to record timestamped *enter*- and *exit*-events for these calls.

The process of generating a library wrapper is intricate and error-prone. Thus, the highest priority in the design of user library wrapping is to make it reliable. To guide the user through these potential problems we introduce a workflow, which the following paragraphs explain. We motivate some of the implementation choices by highlighting the intricacies that necessitate them. Figure 3 depicts the steps involved.

Initialize the Working Directory. The tool `scorep-libwrap-init` initiates the bootstrapping process. For this it creates a working directory where all subsequent steps take place in. The command takes a number of arguments that concern compilation setup, linking setup, and the name of the user library wrapper. Essentially, the user specifies how to compile and link an application using the target library.

In this step, Score-P tries to locate potential shared versions of the target libraries. It lets the user know if it cannot find any to avoid confusion due to failing `dlopen`-calls later on.

---

[2] http://man7.org/linux/man-pages/man8/ld.so.8.html.

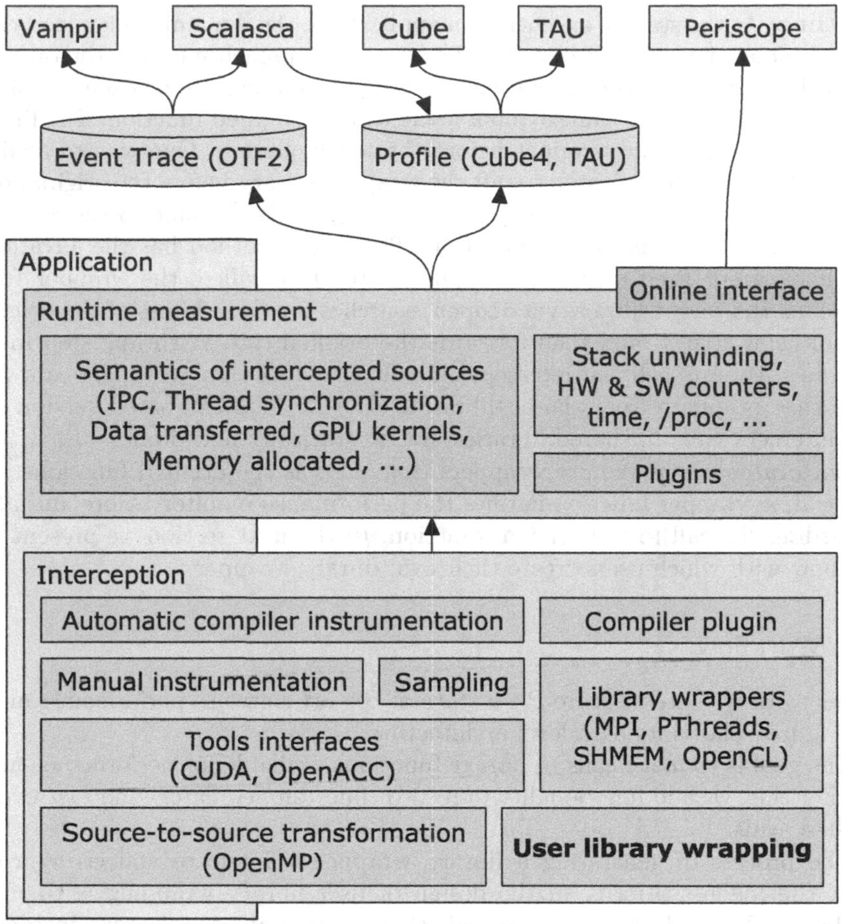

Fig. 2. Overview of the Score-P measurement system architecture. User library wrapping provides an additional interception mechanism.

`scorep-libwrap-init` creates a number of files in the new working directory:

- A detailed documentation with explanations of possible warnings and errors
- A `Makefile` that guides the user through the next steps
- Stub source-, header-, and filter-files, which subsequent paragraphs explain

At the end, the command prints out what the next steps are.

For example, the following command initializes the working directory for a library wrapper of the QtGui and QtWidget modules [27][3]:

[3] Full example: https://github.com/score-p/scorep_libwrap_examples/tree/1564c2723 11d04575f9886cd982fc611e07eb295/qt5/qtgui-and-qtwidgets.

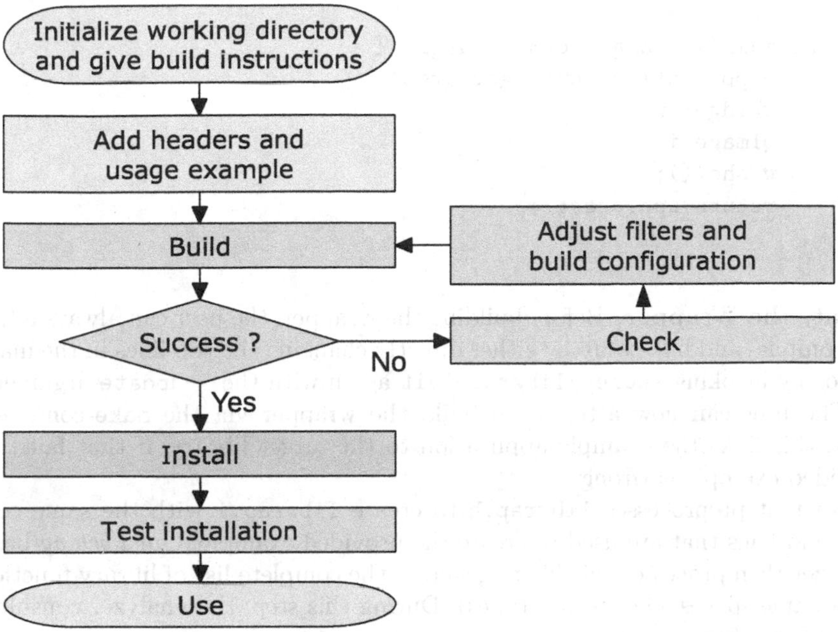

Fig. 3. High-level workflow for creating a user library wrapper.

```
$ scorep-libwrap-init -x c++                               \
   --name qtgui_and_qtwidgets                              \
   --display-name "Qt Gui & Widgets"                       \
   --cppflags "-fPIC -I${QT_INCLUDE}"                      \
   --ldflags "-fPIC"                                       \
   --libs "-lQt5Widgets -lQt5Gui -lQt5Core"
```

Add Library Headers. Next, the user adds an include-statement for each header an application usually includes from the target library to `libwrap.h`. This approach allows the user to specify a sequence of includes and preprocessor macros, which the wrapper generator can then process. Continuing the example, we add:

```
#include <QtGui/QtGui>
#include <QtWidgets/QtWidgets>
```

Create an Example Application. To be able to verify the results, the process needs a test case. For this, the user adds a small usage example to `main.c/cc`. It will be compiled, linked and executed later to test whether the target library and wrapper work. Continuing the example, we write a simple Qt application that opens a window and creates an unused image:

```
int main(int argc, char** args) {
    QApplication app(argc, args);
    QWidget w;
    QImage i;
    w.show();
    return app.exec();
}
```

Create the Wrapper. Before building the wrapper, the user can always adjust the compile- and link-setup by either directly changing the top lines in the makefile, or by invoking `scorep-libwrap-init` again with the `--update` argument.

The user can now attempt to build the wrapper via the `make`-command. First, this links the example application to the target library. If that fails, the provided example is wrong.

Next, it preprocesses `libwrap.h` to create `libwrap.i` with the same compiler and flags that are used to create the provided example. Our *libclang*-based analyzer then processes this file to generate the complete list of library functions (plus name spaces, classes and types). During this step, the analyzer consults a *filter file* for functions to ignore.

The generated list of functions is then used to create an example application, which contains a call to each of these functions. If linking this application to the target library fails, there are wrapper functions that do not have an original function in the target library. For example this happens for some class constructors and inline functions.

If `make` fails, the next step is `make check`, which the next paragraph explains. If `make` passes, it creates the wrapper. The wrapper consists of up to four different wrapper libraries. One dimension is whether the wrapper is a shared or static library. The other dimension is whether the wrapper contains the code for link time or runtime wrapping. All four versions are useful depending on the application/library/system setup. If this succeeds, the user can move on and install the wrapper.

While processing the header files, there are a number of warnings and errors that can occur. For example, the wrapper warns about functions that contain ellipsis arguments, because they cannot be forwarded in C. In case a v-version (like `vprintf` is to `printf`) exists, the `LIBWRAP_ELLIPSIS_MAPPING_SYMBOLS`-variable in the makefile lets the user create a mapping so the wrapper can forward the call to the v-version via the `va_arg` argument.

In C, having an empty argument list in a function declaration means the argument list is unknown, i.e. *variadic*. In C++, on the other hand, the same syntax means it is really empty. In C, you need to use `(void)` as argument list for this. Calling a variadic function without parameters is valid C. This means valid C can trip up library wrapping, if the library developer did not use `(void)` for an empty argument list. To work around this, the makefile provides the `LIBWRAP_VARIADIC_IS_VOID_SYMBOLS`-variable, which names functions that are to be treated as having an empty argument list.

In our example, the `make`-step warns about a number of ellipsis functions, for example in the `QMessageLogger` and `QString` classes. It exits with an error message, because there is a mismatch between functions found in the headers and the symbols in the library. To find out which functions these are, we need to run `make check` and then adjust the filter.

Verify the Wrapper. Because the function list generated by the library header analysis rarely matches the symbol table in the library, for each wrapper function, `make check` generates a source file, and tries to compile and link it with and without the target library. The result is a complete list of symbols that are missing from the target library, and a list of symbols where linking works even without the target library. The latter tries to weed out functions that are not intended to be wrapped, because they are in system libraries.[4]

Using the two generated lists, the user has to adjust the filter to remove unwrappable, and perhaps some unwanted functions. This not only ensures the soundness of the wrapper, but also makes sure the user chooses the functions deliberately. Accidentally wrapping more than intended should be avoided.

After this, the user has to repeat `make` and `make check` until `make` succeeds.

Executing this step in our example first informs us that it is doing this check for over 13,000 functions, and this may take some time. Looking at the list of these functions (in the `.wrap`-file), we notice that it wraps more than just QtGui and QtWidget's components. This is because the header analysis cannot read the users intention perfectly. It initially only includes functions that it finds in files in directories specified via the `-I`-compilation-flag.[5] Thus we refine the filter from

```
INCLUDE /usr/include/x86_64-linux-gnu/qt5/*
```

to

```
INCLUDE /usr/include/x86_64-linux-gnu/qt5/QtGui/*
INCLUDE /usr/include/x86_64-linux-gnu/qt5/QtWidgets/*
```

and repeat `make check`. This yields a list of 818 missing functions, which we add to the filter. No symbols were found that exist when not linking to Qt.

Repeating `make` still fails due to a restriction in libclang with C++. If a function uses a type that is created via `typedef` or `using` in a class, our header analysis cannot always determine the fully qualified type. This case requires user intervention. In our example we can fix this by looking up the types in Qt's documentation and adding the class scopes via text replacement to the wrapper code.[6]

---

[4] Creating a source file for each function and try compiling and linking it is a common technique among configure tools. Doing this in one compile-link-step would require parsing the output of each supported compiler and version, which is not portable across compilers and linkers.

[5] Not doing this would initially always wrap everything including functions from system headers.

[6] https://github.com/score-p/scorep_libwrap_examples/blob/1564c272311d04575f988 6cd982fc611e07eb295/qt5/qtgui-and-qtwidgets/fix-type-scopes.sh.

Install the Wrapper. Once the wrapper builds, make install installs it. If not specified otherwise, this installs the wrapper into Score-P's installation directory.

Verify the Installed Wrapper. Invoking make installcheck links the example application to the link time and runtime wrapper library in the same way the user would. This step creates two executables, and prints out how to run and check the resulting Score-P measurement.

Running the example yields a profile with over 5000 calls to 251 unique Qt functions. Figure 4 shows an excerpt. Without the wrapper, compiler instrumentation would only recognize and record the main-function. Sampling with stack unwinding yields a more detailed call graph (e.g., it includes system and desktop system functions), but misses many function calls due to the nature of sampling, and it also cannot capture exact timing and call counts.

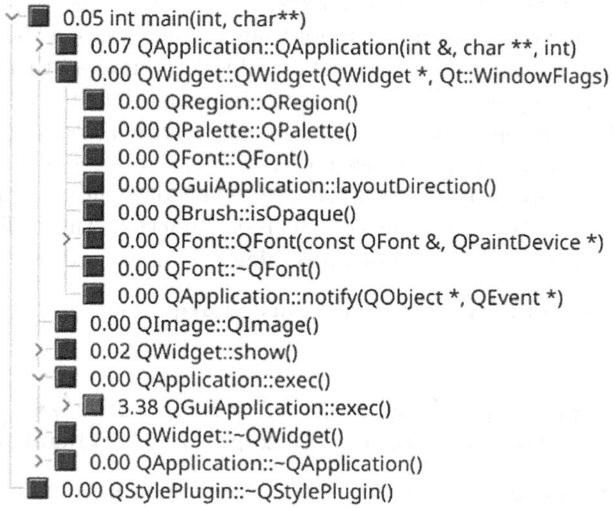

Fig. 4. Partially collapsed Cube profile of the Qt example application. It accurately resembles the source code. Numbers are seconds, inclusive execution time for collapsed entries and exclusive for expanded ones.

Use the Wrapper. If the wrapper has not been installed into Score-P's installation directory (the default), the environment variable SCOREP_LIBWRAP_PATH (PATH-like) needs to point to the wrapper's path before using it.

Score-P's new --libwrap=<wrappername>-flag then modifies the link step to activate one or more wrappers.

To use our example Qt wrapper, we link the to-be-analyzed application according to the instructions we initially gave scorep-libwrap-init and simply prefix it with scorep --libwrap=qtgui_and_qtwidgets. I.e.:

```
$ scorep --libwrap=qtgui_and_qtwidgets g++ \
    -fPIC -I${QT_INCLUDE}                  \
    application.cc                         \
    -fPIC -lQt5Widgets -lQt5Gui -lQt5Core  \
    -o application
```

Optionally, the user can specify the wrap method by prefixing the wrapper name with either `linktime:` or `runtime:`.

Auxiliary Commands. In HPC centers, we expect support staff, not only users themselves, to install wrappers of analysis-worthy libraries alongside a Score-P installation. Users can still install wrappers into their own directories. One advantage is that the staff can update the wrappers at the same time as they update Score-P or the target libraries.

The command `scorep --help`, among other information, gives a list of installed wrappers. Users can invoke `scorep-info libwrap-summary`, with an optional wrapper name, to view wrapper configurations in greater detail.

3.3 Implementation Details

Because compile-time commands, e.g., `#ifdef`, can influence the list of declared functions, we decided to employ the user's compiler to preprocess the library's headers. To generate this list of functions, we read the header using libclang. This mismatch between preprocessor and reader can sometimes lead to problems because they might not agree on the language standard to use. Specifying the standard explicitly solves this.

During development we realized that Score-P's configured compiler cannot always link libclang to the wrapper generator. The configure step would need to know the compiler with which libclang has been created. To circumvent this, contrary to other parts of Score-P, it builds the wrapper generator using Clang, if available.

The presented approach relies on wrapping facilities offered by the linker and dynamic linker. Many C++ libraries heavily rely on inlining and templates. Wrapping libraries based on symbols being present in the target library means that this technique is unable to intercept inlined function calls.

4 Case Study

The previous section proves that our approach is robust by wrapping two Qt modules. This section demonstrates how user library wrapping benefits performance analysis for two real-world scientific applications. We repeat all measurements five times, and pick the median.

4.1 GROMACS

GROMACS [29] is a popular molecular dynamics package specialized in simulating proteins, lipids and nucleic acids. To leverage the compute power of HPC systems, GROMACS relies on MPI, OpenMP, CUDA and either FFTW 3 [17] or the Intel Math Kernel Library for discrete Fourier transforms.

For our demonstration we use GROMACS' current version 2016.3, and simulate a lysozyme in water [21] using one tenth of the default number of time steps. We run the simulation on Oak Ridge National Laboratory's Titan, a Cray XK7 supercomputer. Each node has one AMD Opteron 6274 CPU with eight Bulldozer modules and one NVIDIA Tesla K20X graphics card. We choose to run on two nodes, with four processes each. Every process spawns one additional thread—a total of 16 threads. On the software side, we load the default GNU-based environment, which uses GCC 4.9.3 and FFTW 3.3.4.11.

Executing GROMACS normally takes 330 s, of which it spends 193 in the main part, the actual simulation of the protein (*Production MD*).

To instrument GROMACS with Score-P, we replace the compilers `cc` and `CC` in the CMake-command with Score-P's compiler wrappers `scorep-cc` and `scorep-CC` and prefix the command with `SCOREP_WRAPPER=off`. Building works the same as before. Score-P then, by default, enables automatic compiler instrumentation and injects the performance monitor by modifying compile and link commands. We only use this instrumented GROMACS build on the expensive Production MD part, and execute all other parts with the normal build. Executing this increases Production MD's execution time to 375 s (+94.3%). Score-P registers 3.04 billion function calls, 2.96 billion of which are user functions. The other 80 million are OpenMP loops/calls and MPI calls. `scorep-score` estimates that a trace of this execution is 76 gigabytes (GB) large.

For technical reasons Score-P requires instrumenting MPI and OpenMP events. Therefore, a reduced recording without any user functions takes 214 s (+10.9%), contains 79 million calls, and a trace of this configuration is 3.0 GB large.

Score-P's default (automatic compiler instrumentation) adds significant overhead, and should not be used in tracing mode as is. By following Score-P's filtering workflow we can reduce the overhead and trace recording size. Alternatively we can switch off compiler instrumentation to record a very small amount of information. But none of these three options record anything about FFTW.

To track calls into FFTW, we need to create a wrapper library for it following the workflow described in Sect. 3.2. One thing that confuses our process is that Cray's compiler wrapper `cc` pulls in modules, like FFTW, automatically, if the module is loaded. Thus, to compile a program using FFTW we don't need to add compile and link flags. This is not a problem, but disarms one of our checks and makes wrapper creation slightly confusing. To circumvent this we change the environment variable `PE_PKGCONFIG_PRODUCTS` to not include `PE_FFTW`. The full instructions for building the wrapper are available online[7].

[7] https://github.com/score-p/scorep_libwrap_examples/tree/1564c272311d04575f988 6cd982fc611e07eb295/fftw3.

To configure GROMACS with the FFTW wrapper, run CMake with Score-P's compiler wrappers as in the previous case. Then build it using

```
SCOREP_WRAPPER_INSTRUMENTER_FLAGS="--libwrap=fftw3" make
```

instead of just `make` to enable the wrapper. With this, Production MD takes 214 s (the same as the minimum instrumentation) and counts additional 5.9 million function calls. The corresponding trace is 3.1 GB large.

By analyzing this recording, we discover that GROMACS spends the majority of time in OpenMP loops (Fig. 5(a)). FFTW occupies only about 2.4% of the execution time. Nevertheless, for the low amount of time spent in it, there are

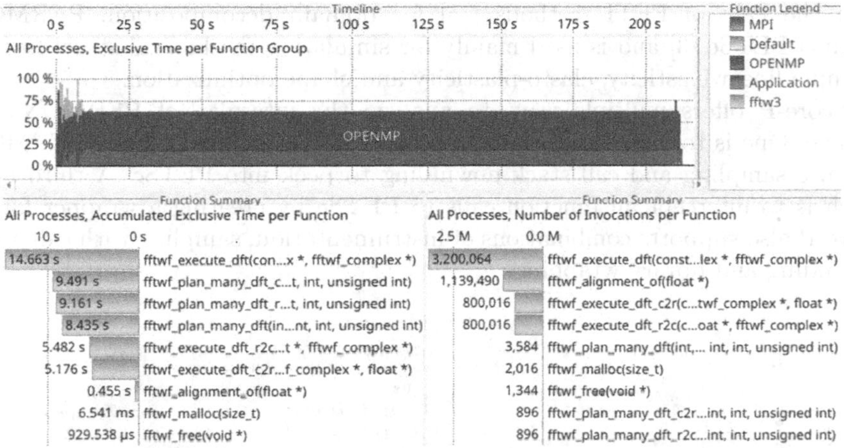

(a) Top: Overview of the whole execution. Bottom left: Accumulated (over all threads and processes) exclusive time for all FFTW functions. Bottom right: Accumulated invocation counts.

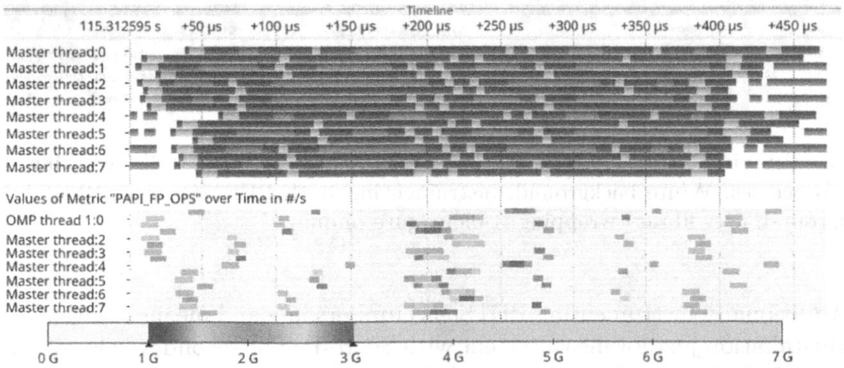

(b) Top: Currently active function active per process and thread. Orange is FFTW. Bottom: FLOPS encoded in color displayed in the same layout.

Fig. 5. Visual analysis of the trace run of GROMACS with Vampir [5] (Color figure online) a lot of calls to FFTW. This suggests that, if possible, putting more work into one iteration should be considered. Because the vast majority of calls to FFTW take below three milliseconds, a sampling-based analysis would show a distorted picture.

With this exact instrumentation of FFTW, we can now, for example, investigate how efficiently it exploits the underlying hardware by recording performance counters. Figure 5(b) shows how FFTW's use of the floating-point unit varies between calls, and is generally subpar.

4.2 PERMON

The software package PERMON [18] solves quadratic programming problems with the help of FETI methods [15] for domain decomposition. PERMON extends PETSc [3] and is used mainly for simulating mechanical structure, for example linear elasticity, elasto-plasticity and shape optimization.

Score-P offers multiple ways to analyze the interplay of PERMON and PETSc. One is to instrument both. A second way is to analyze only PERMON and use sampling and call stack unwinding to peek into PETSc. A third approach is to intercept all function calls to PETSc by creating a wrapper for it. Score-P also supports combinations of instrumentation, sampling with call stack unwinding and library wrapping.

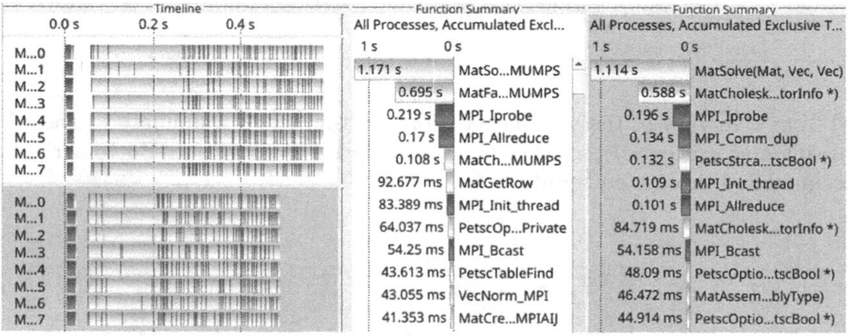

Fig. 6. Vampir Master Timeline and profile excerpt of a PERMON run using eight MPI processes. White background: instrumenting both PERMON and PETSc, blue background: user library wrapping (Color figure online)

Additionally instrumenting PETSc is cumbersome and means creating a custom installation just for measurement with Score-P. The second way is good from an ease-of-use perspective, but has drawbacks. It does not record all PETSc calls, cannot count the number of calls, and cannot record the exact timing of calls. Employing user library wrapping yields a good level of detail while alleviating the drawbacks of the other two methods.

Figure 6 shows the resulting traces from the first and third approach side-by-side. The full instrumentation creates a 112 megabyte trace, whereas the run without automatic compiler instrumentation and with library wrapping results in a 84 megabyte recording. Both recordings are similar in detail and characteristics.

5 Conclusions

In this work we present *user library wrapping*, an extension to Score-P that allows exact tracking of function calls to any C/C++ library. It enables in-depth performance analysis of applications in conjunction with their underlying libraries. Furthermore it tracks calls between libraries and offers insight into closed-source libraries like the Intel Math Kernel Library.

We offer a simple, well-crafted workflow to create and use library wrappers. This workflow guides the user through an otherwise difficult procedure, and minimizes mistakes.

Our approach differs from previous incarnations in that it supports C++, is mature, robust and well documented. It requires minimal manual work and uses modern Clang/LLVM facilities to analyze library headers.

We demonstrate its robustness for non-trivial use-cases by wrapping the QtWidgets and QtGui modules. Furthermore we show how user library wrapping enables better performance analysis for two real-world scientific applications.

6 Future Work

There are multiple interesting areas to pursue. By using compilation databases provided by CMake and GNU Autotools, we might be able to drop the requirement to specify how to build an example application in the first workflow step.

Because HPC systems install multiple versions of the same library, it would be beneficial to explicitly support versioning.

The presented approach forwards parameters from the wrapper to the target function, but does nothing with it. Extending our approach to record parameter values, for example like a performance counter, can be useful.

In order to ensure the soundness of each wrapper, the presented workflow involves a number manual checks. Technically, each wrapper needs to updated if its target library or Score-P is updated. Repeating this procedure for every update is unnecessarily burdensome. Therefore, the workflow should be extended to include automatic updating of generated wrappers.

Due to close consideration of the circumstances of header preprocessing and the symbol tables of library files, each wrapper is tied to the machine it has been created on. It should be investigated how to enable reusing the wrappers across different machines. Ultimately, a public archive of wrappers is desirable.

Score-P hinges on modifying compile and link commands to instrument an application. Some features, user library wrapping included, can be used with just link time changes. But that is not strictly necessary. By loading all of Score-P at runtime using `LD_PRELOAD`, we could skip link command line changes, and attach the performance monitor to an unmodified binary.

Because there are many runtime analysis tools relying on library wrappers, we would like to offer our wrapper creation facility to these projects. Up until now, there was no well-supported, generic way to wrap C/C++ libraries for analysis. Developers need to create wrappers, regularly update them, and keep track of new versions of the target library.

Acknowledgments. This research used resources of the Oak Ridge Leadership Computing Facility at Oak Ridge National Laboratory, which is supported by the Office of Science of the Department of Energy under Contract DE-AC05-00OR22725.

This work is supported in part by the German Research Foundation (DFG) within the CRC 912 - HAEC.

References

1. Adhianto, L., et al.: HPCToolkit: tools for performance analysis of optimized parallel programs. Concurrency Comput.: Pract. Exp. **22**(6), 685–701 (2010)
2. Arm MAP—Arm, August 2017. https://www.arm.com/products/development-tools/hpc-tools/cross-platform/forge/map
3. Balay, S., et al.: PETSc users manual revision 3.7. Technical report, Argonne National Lab. (ANL), Argonne, IL (United States) (2016)
4. Beazley, D.M., et al.: SWIG: an easy to use tool for integrating scripting languages with C and C++. In: TCL/TK Workshop (1996)
5. Brunst, H., Weber, M.: Custom hot spot analysis of HPC software with the vampir performance tool suite. In: Cheptsov, A., Brinkmann, S., Gracia, J., Resch, M., Nagel, W. (eds.) Tools for High Performance Computing, pp. 95–114. Springer, Heidelberg (2013). https://doi.org/10.1007/978-3-642-37349-7_7
6. Butenhof, D.R.: Programming with POSIX Threads. Addison-Wesley Professional, Boston (1997)
7. Clang: a C language family frontend for LLVM, August 2017. http://clang.llvm.org
8. Google/clif: Wrapper generator foundation to wrap C++ for Python and other languages using LLVM, August 2017. https://github.com/google/clif
9. CTool library, August 2017. http://ctool.sourceforge.net
10. CUDA zone—NVIDIA developer, August 2017. https://developer.nvidia.com/cuda-zone
11. Dietrich, R., Ilsche, T., Juckeland, G.: Non-intrusive performance analysis of parallel hardware accelerated applications on hybrid architectures. In: 2010 39th International Conference on Parallel Processing Workshops (ICPPW), pp. 135–143. IEEE (2010)
12. Edison design group, August 2017. http://edg.com
13. Eichenberger, A.E., et al.: OMPT: an OpenMP tools application programming interface for performance analysis. In: Rendell, A.P., Chapman, B.M., Müller, M.S. (eds.) IWOMP 2013. LNCS, vol. 8122, pp. 171–185. Springer, Heidelberg (2013). https://doi.org/10.1007/978-3-642-40698-0_13
14. Extrae—BSC tools, August 2017. https://tools.bsc.es/extrae

15. Farhat, C., Roux, F.X.: A method of finite element tearing and interconnecting and its parallel solution algorithm. Int. J. Numer. Methods Eng. **32**(6), 1205–1227 (1991)
16. Folk, M., Heber, G., Koziol, Q., Pourmal, E., Robinson, D.: An overview of the HDF5 technology suite and its applications. In: Proceedings of the EDBT/ICDT 2011 Workshop on Array Databases, pp. 36–47. ACM (2011)
17. Frigo, M., Johnson, S.G.: FFTW: an adaptive software architecture for the FFT. In: Proceedings of the 1998 IEEE International Conference on Acoustics, Speech and Signal Processing, vol. 3, pp. 1381–1384. IEEE (1998)
18. Hapla, V., Horak, D., Pospisil, L., Cermak, M., Vasatova, A., Sojka, R.: Solving contact mechanics problems with PERMON. In: Kozubek, T., Blaheta, R., Šístek, J., Rozložník, M., Čermák, M. (eds.) HPCSE 2015. LNCS, vol. 9611, pp. 101–115. Springer, Cham (2016). https://doi.org/10.1007/978-3-319-40361-8_7
19. Hilbrich, T., Schulz, M., de Supinski, B.R., Müller, M.S.: MUST: a scalable approach to runtime error detection in MPI programs. In: Müller, M., Resch, M., Schulz, A., Nagel, W. (eds.) Tools for High Performance Computing, pp. 53–66. Springer, Heidelberg (2009). https://doi.org/10.1007/978-3-642-11261-4_5
20. Knüpfer, A., et al.: Score-P: a joint performance measurement run-time infrastructure for Periscope, Scalasca, TAU, and Vampir. In: Brunst, H., Müller, M., Nagel, W., Resch, M. (eds.) Tools for High Performance Computing, pp. 79–91. Springer, Heidelberg (2012). https://doi.org/10.1007/978-3-642-31476-6_7
21. Lemkul, J.A.: Gromacs tutorial: Lysozyme in water, September 2017. http://www.bevanlab.biochem.vt.edu/Pages/Personal/justin/gmx-tutorials/lysozyme/index.html
22. Lofstead, J.F., Klasky, S., Schwan, K., Podhorszki, N., Jin, C.: Flexible IO and integration for scientific codes through the adaptable IO system (ADIOS). In: Proceedings of the 6th International Workshop on Challenges of Large Applications in Distributed Environments, pp. 15–24. ACM (2008)
23. de Melo, A.C.: Performance counters on Linux. In: Linux Plumbers Conference (2009)
24. Intel® math kernel library (intel® mkl)—intel® software, August 2017. https://software.intel.com/en-us/mkl
25. Message Passing Interface (MPI) forum, August 2017. http://mpi-forum.org
26. Profiler: CUDA toolkit documentation, August 2017. http://docs.nvidia.com/cuda/profiler-users-guide/index.html
27. Qt—cross-platform software development for embedded & desktop, August 2017. https://www.qt.io/
28. Shende, S., Malony, A.D., Spear, W., Schuchardt, K.: Characterizing I/O performance using the TAU performance system. In: PARCO, pp. 647–655 (2011)
29. Van Der Spoel, D., Lindahl, E., Hess, B., Groenhof, G., Mark, A.E., Berendsen, H.J.: GROMACS: fast, flexible, and free. J. Comput. Chem. **26**(16), 1701–1718 (2005)
30. Intel® VTune™ Amplifier, August 2017. https://software.intel.com/en-us/intel-vtune-amplifier-xe

Improved Accuracy for Automated Communication Pattern Characterization Using Communication Graphs and Aggressive Search Space Pruning

Philip C. Roth(✉)

Oak Ridge National Laboratory, Oak Ridge, TN 37831, USA
rothpc@ornl.gov

Abstract. An understanding of a parallel application's communication behavior is useful for a range of activities including debugging and optimization, job scheduling, target system selection, and system design. Because it can be challenging to understand communication behavior, especially for those who lack expertise or who are not familiar with the application, I and two colleagues recently developed an automated, search-based approach for recognizing and parameterizing application communication behavior using a library of common communication patterns. This initial approach was effective for characterizing the behavior of many workloads, but I identified some combinations of communication patterns for which the method was inefficient or would fail. In this paper, I discuss one such troublesome pattern combination and propose modifications to the recognition method to handle it. Specifically, I propose an alternative approach that uses communication graphs instead of traditional communication matrices to improve recognition accuracy for collective communication operations, and that uses a non-greedy recognition technique to avoid search space dead-ends that trap the original greedy recognition approach. My modified approach uses aggressive search space pruning and heuristics to control the potential for state explosion caused by its non-greedy pattern recognition method. I demonstrate the improved recognition accuracy and pruning efficacy of the modified approach using several synthetic and real-world communication pattern combinations.

This manuscript has been authored by UT-Battelle, LLC, under contract DE-AC05-00OR22725 with the US Department of Energy (DOE). The US government retains and the publisher, by accepting the article for publication, acknowledges that the US government retains a nonexclusive, paid-up, irrevocable, worldwide license to publish or reproduce the published form of this manuscript, or allow others to do so, for US government purposes. DOE will provide public access to these results of federally sponsored research in accordance with the DOE Public Access Plan (http://energy.gov/downloads/doe-public-access-plan). This research is sponsored by the Office of Advanced Scientific Computing Research in the U.S. Department of Energy.

A. Bhatele et al. (Eds.): ESPT/VPA 2017/2018, LNCS 11027, pp. 38–55, 2019.
https://doi.org/10.1007/978-3-030-17872-7_3

1 Introduction

An accurate and concise description of a parallel application's communication behavior can be highly useful. For the application's developers, this description supports debugging and performance optimization, and the selection of a target system whose architecture and configuration are a good fit for the application's communication demands. Job scheduling software might use such descriptions to avoid network contention among running jobs. And system designers can use such descriptions to tailor their system designs for a desired workload. With two of my colleagues, I recently proposed an automated approach for recognizing and parameterizing communication patterns in MPI-based parallel applications [12]. Starting with a communication matrix generated by a modified version of the mpiP [14] lightweight MPI profiler (such as the example shown in Fig. 1a), the approach identifies a collection of common communication patterns that best account for the data in the communication matrix. The technique uses an automated search through a "pattern space" defined by the contents of a pattern library. At each step of its search, it attempts to recognize the patterns from its library in the matrix containing the communications data that has not yet been explained (called the *residual*). If it recognizes a pattern, it removes the contribution of that pattern from the residual, and recursively applies the pattern search to the new residual. Because it may recognize more than one pattern at any step in the search, its search may branch and so it explores a *search tree* within the search space. I call each path through this tree a *search path*. When it has refined search path as far as it can, it determines which search path accounts for the most communication data in the original matrix, and outputs the collection of parameterized patterns along this path as the ones that best explain the original matrix. It outputs this collection of patterns as a concise, parameterized expression.

The original approach has several attractive characteristics. It is capable of characterizing complicated pattern combinations in many workloads. Also, its output expressions convey more information than summary statistics but require much less storage than detailed event traces. Despite its positive characteristics, the approach has several shortcomings. First, by representing the application's communication behavior as a traditional communication matrix, it fails to capture enough information to allow a pattern recognition approach to discern details about collective communication operations. Second, because the approach uses a greedy pattern recognition approach that attributes as much data as possible to a pattern that it recognizes, it can fall into "traps" in the search space that keep it from accurately recognizing the actual combination of patterns used by the application. Third, the approach is inefficient, in that it does not recognize when it is attempting to recognize a combination of patterns that is equivalent to another combination that it has already considered.

To address these problems, I modified the original approach in several ways. Instead of a traditional communication matrix, I use an *augmented communication graph* (ACG) that allows the approach to retain the information about collective operations that is missing from the matrix representation. I use a non-greedy technique for accounting for observed communication data that allows my new approach to recognize combinations of patterns that the original approach cannot recognize. And my new approach determines when it is considering a permutation of a collection of patterns that it has already considered, and prunes its search to avoid doing redundant work. Because my non-greedy recognition technique is susceptible to considering many more potential pattern parameters than the original, I added heuristics for identifying parameters that have a higher likelihood of matching the application's actual behavior.

2 Characterizing Application Communication

2.1 Augmented Communication Graphs

A traditional communication matrix represents the behavior of an N-process application run as an $N \times N$ matrix in which the (i, j)th entry expresses some characteristic of the communication from process i to process j (e.g., volume of data transferred or number of transfers). Although this representation has several good qualities (familiar to those in the HPC community, well-defined mathematical operations with memory-efficient and high performance implementations widely available), the traditional communication matrix representation is unable to capture some aspects of an application's use of collective communication operations. For example, given the communication matrix shown in Fig. 1b we cannot tell whether the program's rank 0 process used a broadcast to transfer data to all other processes, or a sequence of point-to-point operations that transferred data to each process individually. Because the amount of data transferred to each receiving process is the same in this example, we might guess that the application used a broadcast, but taking this perspective only shifts the problem: if the amount of data transferred were different for each process, we would not be able to tell if the program used a variable-length scatter operation or multiple point-to-point operations. The communication matrix visualized in Fig. 1c represents an extreme: it is impossible to determine from this matrix alone whether the program performed one all-to-all operation, multiple broadcast operations, multiple reduce operations, or many point-to-point operations. I might argue that for some uses of the resulting communication characterization, it doesn't matter which was actually used as long as the representation correctly identifies the amount of data transferred and between which processes. But in other cases, such as my case study with a plasma surface interactions model (Sect. 5), being able to discern the two is quite useful.

In my new automated communication characterization approach, I represent communications behavior using an *augmented communication graph* (ACG) instead of a traditional communication matrix. Per graph theory, a communication matrix can be interpreted as the adjacency matrix for a directed graph whose vertices represent the processes of a program run, with an edge from vertex i to vertex j indicating that process i communicated with process j during the run. However, the ACG is not simply the graph form of a traditional communication matrix. Because it is the information about collective communication

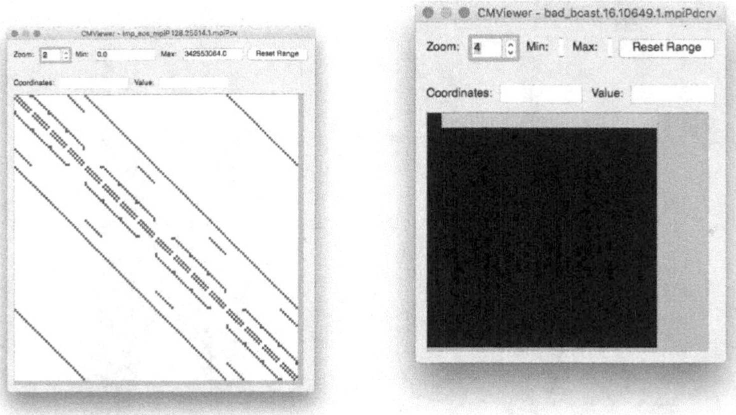

(a) Example communications graph. (b) Broadcast or multiple point-to-point?

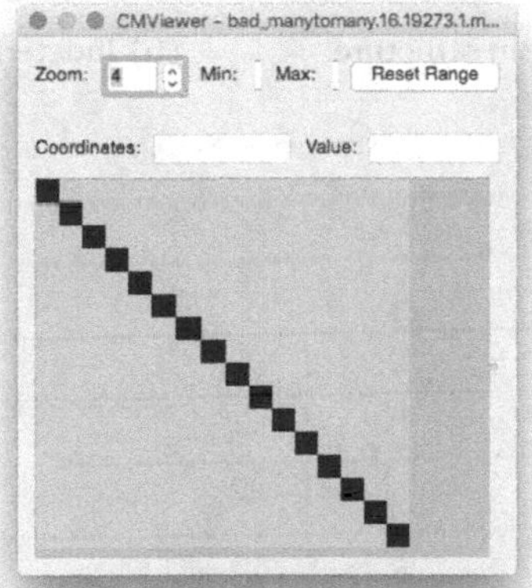

(c) Worst case.

Fig. 1. Visualizations of communication matrices with the cell at row r and column c colored according to the amount of data transferred from process r to process c. (a) Total point-to-point communication volume for 128-process run of the LAMMPS [11] molecular dynamics simulation application, EAM benchmark problem, with volume indicated by shades of blue and white indicating no data transferred; (b) and (c) "Difficult" communication matrices using rainbow color palette with black indicating no data transferred. *Using these "difficult" visualizations alone, it is impossible to discern the actual communication operation(s) used by the application.* (Color figure online)

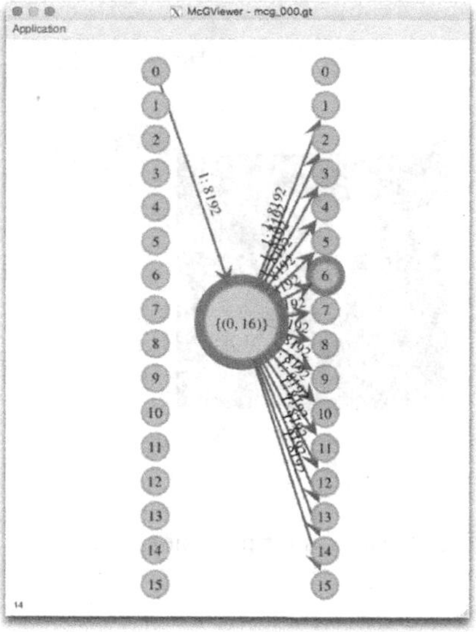

(a) Broadcast obvious from structure.

(b) Indeterminate collectives.

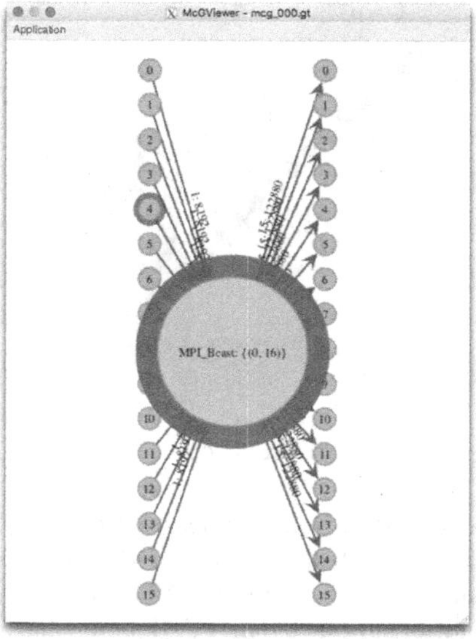

(c) Definitely multiple broadcasts.

Fig. 2. Augmented communication graphs collected from the same applications that produced the "difficult" communication matrices of Fig. 1.

operations that is lacking with the matrix representation, in an ACG I include vertices representing the MPI communicators involved in the application's collective operations. Each process vertex is labeled with its associated process' rank number within MPI_COMM_WORLD, and each communicator vertex is labeled with the set of ranks associated with the communicator's group of processes. An ACG models a collective communication operation as a data transfer from one or more process vertices into and/or out of a communicator vertex. For example, unlike the matrix shown in Fig. 1b, the ACG shown in Fig. 2a allows us to say with certainty that the application used a broadcast operation.

ACGs also differ from the graph form of a traditional communication matrix in terms of their edge labels. In an ACG, an edge between a source vertex and a sink vertex is labeled $c : v$ where c indicates a number of transfers and v indicates the amount of data transferred between the processes or communicators represented by the source and sink vertices. Although my original data capture library collected operation counts, my original characterization approach does not use that information. As described in Sect. 2.2, the operation count information is invaluable for accurate recognition of some combinations of communication patterns.

Although I seek techniques for automatically characterizing application communication behavior in this work, it is often still useful to visualize a representation of that behavior (e.g., when debugging the automated characterization tools). For clarity, instead of visualizing the ACG itself I usually visualize its corresponding *expanded ACG*. An expanded ACG splits each application process vertex into two vertices, one representing the process as a data source and the other as a data sink. By convention, I arrange the source process vertices at the left of ACG visualizations and the sink process vertices at the right. Note that I split process vertices for visualization purposes only—the implementation of my characterization approach operates on graphs that contain a single vertex for each application process.

As presented thus far, my approach allows us to discern whether the application used point-to-point or collective operations, but does not let us easily determine whether the application used *one* all-to-all collective operation or multiple one-to-all (or all-to-one) operations. A simple extension allows us to tell the difference: instead of a single vertex to represent an MPI communicator, I could add multiple vertices for a given communicator, each labeled with a specific collective operation. Figure 2c illustrates how such an extension makes it clear that the application used a sequence of broadcast operations to accomplish this pattern, as opposed to an all-to-all or sequence of reduce operations. This functionality comes at a price: it increases the storage requirements for the graph, and increases the cost of analyzing the graph and applying arithmetic operations during automated pattern recognition. The amount of increase depends on the number and type of collective operations used by the application. Still, I hypothesize that in all but the most pathological cases, the increase in storage required will be relatively small, and labeling the communicator vertices with an operation *category* (e.g., one-to-many) instead of specific operation (e.g., broadcast, scatter) might be sufficient to mitigate the cost without sacrificing too much information.

2.2 Non-greedy Volume Attribution

When the original approach recognizes a pattern, it attributes as much data volume as possible to the pattern. For example, if the original recognized a broadcast from rank 0 to all other program ranks, it finds the minimum of the entries in the 0th row of the communication matrix and uses this as the *scale* of the broadcast. When it subtracts this parameterized pattern from the residual matrix, any entries in that row that formerly held this scale value now hold 0, indicating all communication between process 0 and the corresponding rank has been accounted for.

There are pattern combinations for which this greedy technique prevents the original approach from identifying all the patterns that comprise the combination. For example, the following simple combination of patterns are not recognized correctly by the original approach:

- broadcast: {'scale': 4096, 'root': 0}
- broadcast: {'scale': 512, 'root': 3}
- reduce: {'scale': 16, 'root': 2}
- many-to-many: {'scale': 1024}

The original greedy technique first recognizes a many-to-many pattern, and attributes 1040 bytes as the scale of the pattern because that is the minimum amount associated with any of the edges involved in the pattern. But, removing a many-to-many pattern with this scale from the graph results in an invalid graph: some of the resulting edges have zero volume but non-zero counts. For this pattern combination, the broadcasts and reduce result in "extra" volume that is indistinguishable from a many-to-many pattern. Considering the broadcast or reduce pattern before the many-to-many is no better: removing one of these patterns first results either in an invalid graph or consumes too much data volume, precluding the recognition of some other pattern.

To address the problem of attributing too much data to a recognized pattern, my new approach determines when removal of a recognized pattern would result in an invalid ACG, and if so it attempts to recognize the pattern with a smaller scale. More precisely, upon recognizing a pattern P with scale S_{MAX} in a residual graph R and determining that removing $P(S_{MAX})$ from R would result in an invalid ACG, my new approach identifies one or more scales $S_i < S_{MAX}$ to consider. For each S_i, it refines its search by removing $P(S_i)$ from R, and recursively applies its search strategy to the resulting residual graph. If there are more than one such S_i, the search branches just as it would if more more than one pattern were recognized in R.

As presented so far, my approach suffers from an unfortunate problem: if $P(S_{MAX})$ can be recognized in the residual graph R, then P can be also recognized within R for *every* integer $0 < S < S_{MAX}$. Branching the search for every such S would often result in an explosion in the number of pattern space states my approach needs to consider, making the characterization problem intractable. To control the potential for state space explosion, I use a heuristic technique for identifying "interesting" scales to consider. My strategy considers *differences* between the counts and volumes associated with the ACG edges involved in a recognized pattern. In particular, I look for pairs of edges coming into or out of communicator vertices whose transfer counts differ by one. If I find such a pair, I compute the difference S_{Diff} between their counts, and add $S_{MAX} - S_{Diff}$ to the set of candidate scales. I have found this heuristic to be effective in producing useful pattern scales to consider. Indeed, with this heuristic my approach correctly identifies the troublesome four-pattern combination listed at the beginning of the section. The strategy is not a panacea, however. For some pattern combinations, it causes my recognition approach to recursively consider every scale between S_{MAX} and 0 in increments of S_{Diff}. If S_{MAX} is large and S_{Diff} is small, I might still consider a very large number of potential scales. More investigation is needed into heuristics that further limit the number of interesting scale values. Labeling ACG communicator vertices with specific collective operations might also help overcome this problem by making it easier to identify how much volume was associated with each collective operation, but I leave investigation of this alternative also to future work.

2.3 Search Space Pruning

In addition to its inability to recognize some pattern combinations, the original characterization approach is susceptible to performing a significant amount of redundant work. Consider the following collection of patterns, used in the original AChax paper to demonstrate its functionality:

- broadcast: {'scale': 4096, 'root': 0}
- broadcast: {'scale': 512, 'root': 6}
- reduce: {'scale': 16, 'root': 3}
- 2D 5pt nearest neighbor: {'dims': (8, 8), 'scale': 8192, 'periodic': [True, True]}
- 2D 5pt nearest neighbor: {'dims': (16, 4), 'scale': 1024, 'periodic': [False, False]}
- many-to-many: {'scale': 1024}
- optional "noise" (to make recognition more difficult).

Figure 2 of the original paper [12] showed the search results tree produced from applying AChax to the communication matrix representing this combination of patterns. I refer readers to the original paper for a more complete description of concepts related to search results trees, but provide a brief overview here. In a search results tree, the edges along a path from any tree node to the root node comprise a *search path* through the search space. A recognized, parameterized pattern is associated with every edge in the search path. Each node is labeled with a *residual* containing the data from the original communications data that has yet to be explained by the patterns on the search path from the node to the root node. The amount of data represented by a node's residual is a measure of the quality of the search path, with smaller amounts indicating higher quality (because the patterns along such paths account for more of the original communications data than the patterns along a path with a larger residual data volume). In the original paper's Fig. 2, many sub-trees are elided because they represent results that are redundant to those shown in detail. In fact, the original AChax approach produces a search results tree with 506 nodes, 180 of which are leaves (i.e., nodes representing the termination of a search path). Surprisingly, there are only *three* distinct residual values associated with these leaves. The vast majority of the search paths AChax examined are permutations of other paths it also examined.

To avoid doing redundant work, in my new approach I extended the search results tree so that each tree node maintains the set of parameterized patterns that were considered for search refinement from the node. When the search engine recognizes a parameterized pattern in the residual associated with a search results tree node n, it also checks the search paths from root to other tree nodes at the same depth as n to see if n's search path is a permutation of any of those other paths. If it finds a permutation, it prunes its current search path at node n because the collection of patterns along both search paths account for the same portions of the original communications data.

As a performance optimization, I also added the capability to "short-circuit" the search if it identifies a combination of patterns that completely explains the original communications data.

3 Implementation

I implemented my augmented communication characterization approach by augmenting the original Python-based AChax tool. The original tool uses the NumPy [10] and SciPy [13] Python modules for matrix arithmetic and I/O operations, and uses the widely-supported MatrixMarket exchange format [2] for persistent storage of communication matrices. My modified version, which I call AChaxG, uses the Graph-tool Python module [6] for I/O, analysis, and visualization of ACGs. In addition to its own binary file format, the Graph-tool module supports the widely-used GraphML, GML, and dot file formats, plus flexible, powerful graph visualization support for common graphics software like Cairo, GTK+, and graphviz. I used this support to develop the simple ACG viewer tool that was used to produce the ACG visualizations in this paper.

The original communications data capture library was a modified version of the mpiP lightweight profiling library [14]. This library collects data about *all* of an application's communication operations, in contrast to the stock mpiP version that uses statistical sampling to control overhead and data volume. Because the only functionality that I actually *need* from an MPI communications data capture library is the ability to interpose instrumentation at the MPI profiling interface, and because I sought to improve productivity in developing and maintaining the MPI data capture library, I developed a new communications data capture library called Grabber that is implemented in C++ using the C++ Standard Library, a small number of Boost C++ libraries [3], and Todd Gamblin's powerful and flexible MPI wrapper generator tool [4].

When a user runs an application linked with the Grabber library, the instrumentation in each application process builds a *local* communication graph that reflects only the operations in which the process participates. When the program terminates, Grabber aggregates these local graphs into a global communication graph that describes the entire application's communication behavior, and writes this global graph to a file in the Graph-tool module's native file format. For applications with multiple behavioral phases, Grabber can output a global communications graph for each phase, but the user must instrument the application code to indicate the end of each phase.

4 Evaluation

4.1 Augmented Communication Graphs

To evaluate my decision to use ACGs instead of traditional communication matrices, I consider not only that the ACGs contain more information about the program's run than a traditional communication matrix (Sect. 2.1), but also must compare how much storage they require and how costly they are to manipulate. For this comparison, I used synthetic workloads generated on the Eos Cray XC30 system deployed in the Oak Ridge Leadership Computing Facility (OLCF). As a synthetic workload, I used the same collection of patterns that I used to demonstrate the original AChax implementation as described in Sect. 2.3. Because I wanted to evaluate my approach's functionality for a range of process counts, I varied the values used for the dimension parameters of the 2D 5-point nearest neighbor patterns. In all cases, different pairs of values were used as dimensions for the two nearest neighbor patterns.

Figure 3a shows the ACG file sizes for a range of process counts from 8 to 4096, and compares those file sizes to that of traditional communication matrix files produced by the original AChax implementation for the same collection of patterns. Note that the original implementation's data capture library produces communication matrices in Matrix Market sparse format, a text-based format, and that the original communication characterization approach uses only communication volume matrices (i.e., without information about operation counts) and so that is what I report here as the communication matrix file size data. The figure includes data points for ACGs and matrices with and without "noise" (point-to-point communication between randomly-selected pairs, with number of pairs and communication volume determined by pattern parameters). Because my example workload includes a many-to-many pattern, I was not surprised that the original AChax implementation's sparse matrix representation produced the largest files, and that the file size was the same for matrices with and without noise. Figure 3b shows the file sizes for the example pattern combination excluding the many-to-many pattern. As expected, the matrix representations require much less storage for this pattern combination than the one that includes the many-to-many pattern, because there are many more zeros in the matrices that

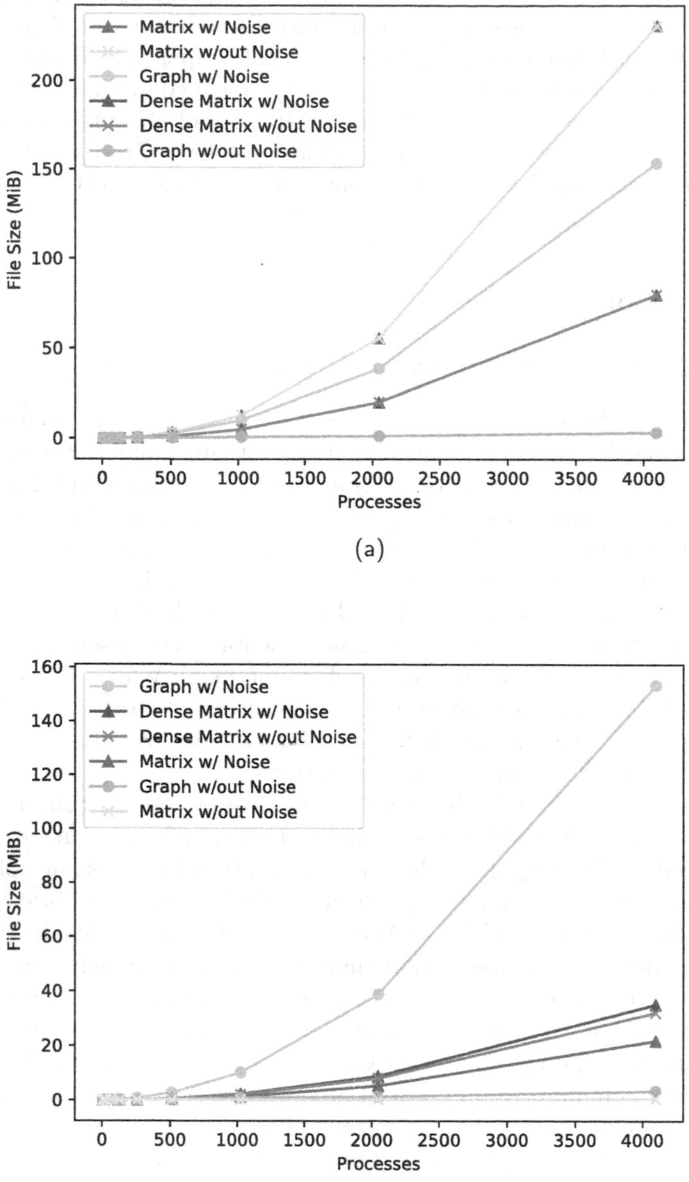

Fig. 3. Size of augmented communication graph and traditional communication matrix files for a synthetic workload that includes a many-to-many pattern (a) and excludes that pattern (b).

exclude the many-to-many pattern.[1] Interestingly, the file size for the graph representation is almost the same whether the many-to-many pattern is included or not. This is because the pattern combination includes both broadcast and reduce operations that require the same set of edges as the many-to-many pattern, and because the inclusion or exclusion of this single pattern does not change the number of characters required to represent the edge operation count labels for this example workload. Although I do not present detailed measurements due to lack of space, the time required to create the ACG files was substantially larger than that required to create matrix files.

My file size and file creation time comparisons suggest that the ACG-based approach's improved ability to discern details about collective communication operations comes at a price: the ACG is more expensive to generate, and depending on workload, may also be more expensive to store than the traditional communication matrix. I discuss a possible approach for addressing these problems in Sect. 7.

4.2 Aggressive Pruning

As noted in Sect. 2.2, my non-greedy data volume attribution method has the potential to consider substantially more scale parameter values than the original AChax approach when it recognizes a pattern. I added heuristic scale selection and aggressive pruning techniques (Sects. 2.2–2.3) to limit the negative impact of having to consider these additional search space states. To determine the impact of such pruning, I used AChaxG to characterize the synthetic workload ACGs described in Sect. 4.1 with pruning enabled and with it disabled. I also implemented a search short-circuiting feature (Sect. 2.3) as a user-configurable option, so that I could examine its impact on characterization time and results quality. As a measure of the quality of the search pruning/short-circuiting features, I compared the time required to do the characterization and the number of vertices in the resulting search results trees.

Figure 4a compares the number of vertices in the search results trees for a range of process counts under a variety of search configurations. The number of vertices in the results tree is an indicator of how much work the search engine had to do to characterize the input workload, with a lower number being better. For all configurations, the search recognized *all* of the patterns in the input workload, so the quality of the characterization results is the same for each configuration—only the amount of work needed to achieve those results varied between configurations. As shown in the figure, the configurations fall into four categories with respect to the number of nodes in their search results trees. AChaxG had to do the least work to characterize the input workload when the input workload had no noise, and it could use pruning and short-circuiting

[1] Although they contain the same number of values, the dense matrix files that exclude the many-to-many pattern are smaller than those that include it because the Matrix Market format is a text format, and it takes fewer characters to represent a zero than a non-zero value.

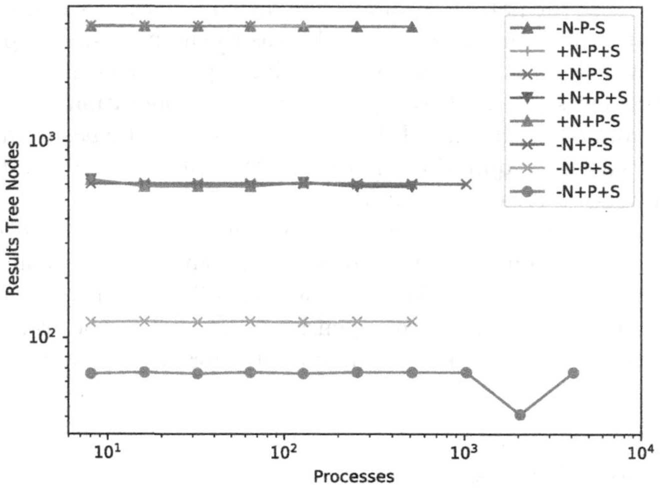

(a)

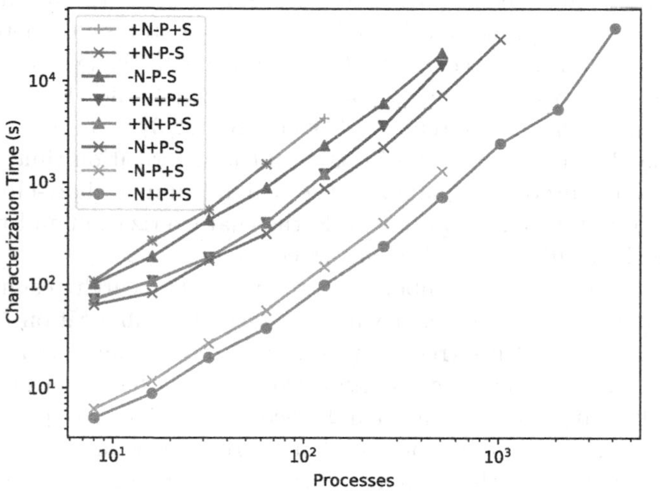

(b)

Fig. 4. Number of results tree vertices (a) and characterization time (b) for characterizing the synthetic workload combination of patterns. *Lines are labeled indicating whether the workload included noise (+/−N), whether pruning was used during characterization (+/−P), and whether short-circuiting was used (+/−S).*

(the line labeled `-N+P+S`). In this case, after producing a search results tree with approximately 66 vertices,[2] it identified a search path that completely explained the input communication data and stopped its search. Without pruning (line `-N-P+S`), AChaxG produced a search results tree with approximately 120 vertices, showing the positive impact of search pruning. When characterizing input with noise, pruning exhibited an even greater benefit (lines `+N+P*S` with approximately 612 vertices vs. lines `+N-P*S` with 3892 vertices).[3] Based on these results, I conclude that search pruning is an effective and desirable way for AChaxG to avoid doing redundant, unnecessary work when characterizing application communication patterns. Short-circuiting may also be beneficial, but only if AChaxG has a pattern library sufficient to recognize all of the input communication data. To address this limitation, it may be useful to relax this test by allowing the user to stop the search when it has accounted for a high percentage of the input data as opposed to the entire input data.

Figure 4b shows the time required for AChaxG to characterize the synthetic workload for a range of process counts and a variety of search configurations. These measurements reinforce the results from Fig. 4a in that it takes longer for AChaxG to produce a search results graph with many nodes than one with fewer nodes. These timings also support my conclusion from Sect. 4.1 that manipulations of ACGs implemented using the Python Graph-tool module become prohibitively expensive as the number of processes represented in the ACGs increase. Even with the most aggressive search pruning configuration on the most favorable input workload (i.e., noise-free), AChaxG still required nearly 1.5 h to characterize the 2048-process workload. It took over 9 h to characterize the 4096-process workload. In Sect. 7 I suggest two strategies I plan to pursue for reducing these excessive characterization times in future versions of AChaxG.

5 Case Study: Xolotl

Xolotl [8] is a plasma surface interactions model used to study the impact of a burning plasma on the surface of its container, such as within a tokamak fusion reactor. Xolotl is written in C++, uses the Portable, Extensible Toolkit for Scientific Computation (PETSc) [1] as a solver, and MPI for communication and synchronization. I ran Xolotl, instrumented with my Grabber library, on the OLCF Eos Cray XC30 system as a 32-process job for 5 time steps on a 1D input problem witih 2048 grid points. I chose this small Xolotl problem to allow for interactive visualization of the resulting ACG.

Characterizing and visualizing the ACG produced from this Xolotl run provided unexpected insights into the application's communication behavior. My tool correctly recognized and parameterized the application's Broadcast, Reduce,

---

[2] As currently implemented, the AChaxG search should be deterministic, so I am investigating why we observed a variation in the number of results tree vertices for some combinations of search control features.

[3] For inputs with noise, the short-circuiting optimization is never triggered because AChaxG does not ever completely account for the input communication data.

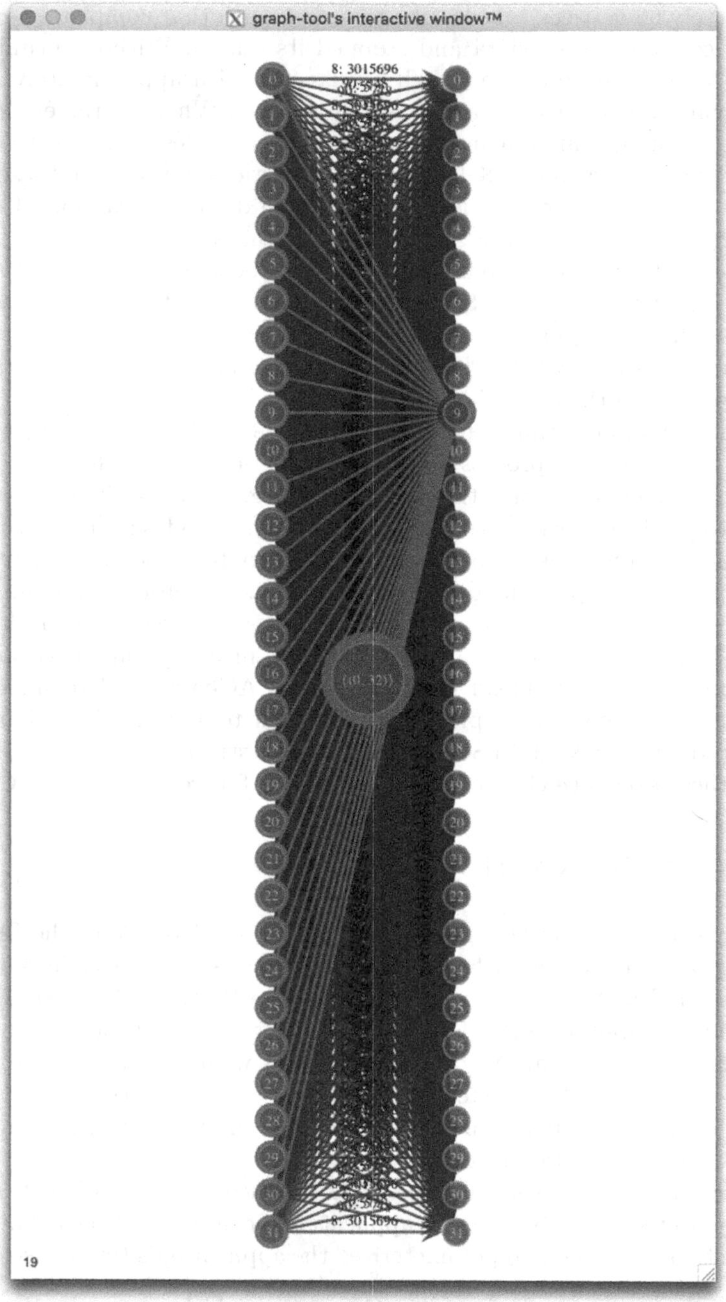

Fig. 5. Augmented Communication Graph for the Xolotl plasma surface interactions model, with the vertex corresponding to rank 9 highlighted.

and 1D nearest neighbor patterns. However, these patterns accounted for only a small fraction of the observed communication data volume. Figure 5, showing the ACG with process 9's "consumer" vertex highlighted, revealed the reason by clearly showing Xolotl having done point-to-point communication from every process to process 9. By selecting several process vertices in their sending and receiving roles, I determined that each Xolotl process *sends* point-to-point messages to every other process, and *receives* point-to-point messages from every other process. This interactive visualization demonstrated the value of the ACG for debugging and optimization: a traditional communication matrix would not have exposed that the program did both MPI collective operations *and* "do-it-yourself" point-to-point-based collective operations. Because the pattern of point-to-point operations was unexpected, I ran the program under a parallel debugger and determined that it was the PETSc library issuing these point-to-point operations to implement a scatter operation. Despite the benefit that visualizing the ACG helped us identify and understand an unexpected behavior, it also exposes a gap in my current pattern library in that it does not attempt to recognize common collective patterns implemented "do-it-yourself" using point-to-point operations outside the MPI library.

6 Related Work

This work is an evolution of the initial automated communication pattern recognition approach and its implementation in the AChax tool [12]. My current approach differs from the initial approach by using communication graphs instead of matrices, by using a non-greedy pattern recognition technique, and by using heuristics and aggressive pruning to avoid doing redundant work.

Like the original AChax work, my approach uses automated search through a space defined by a library of known communication patterns. My inspiration to use automated search comes directly from the Performance Consultant of the Paradyn performance tool [9], with additional inspiration from the Periscope performance tool [5]. My tool uses search for a different purpose than to find application performance problems in a performance problem search space, but the general concepts of searching through a space by refining one's idea of the best explanation for observed behavior, and of representing search results using an annotated tree, are firmly founded on my experience with Paradyn and knowledge of Periscope.

My communication pattern recognition approach is similar to that of Kerbyson and Barker [7] in that both use a library of known communication patterns, and both dynamically generate a representation of a communication pattern and compare it to the observed communication behavior. Their approach requires manual instrumentation of application source code, and supports only point-to-point communication operations. In contrast, my approach is designed for discerning details regarding collective communication via use of augmented communication graphs, and relies upon MPI's standardized profiling interface instead of application source code instrumentation.

7 Summary and Future Work

Determining how an application behaves can be a tedious, error-prone task, even for the most experienced performance analyst. Tools that simplify the task, such as my AChax automated communication pattern recognition tool, are beneficial to novices and experts alike. The original AChax approach can be effective at characterizing the communication patterns of some applications, but has several flaws including its ability to discern details about collective communication operations, failure to recognize some pattern collections, and susceptibility to performing redundant work. In this paper, I proposed modifications to the original approach to address these problems. This new approach uses augmented communication graphs that capture more detail about collective operations than traditional communication matrices, and a non-greedy method for attributing communication data volume to recognized patterns. Using AChaxG, I demonstrated that my approach is more accurate at recognizing communication pattern combinations than the original approach. The increased accuracy comes at a price, however: AChaxG usually considers many more potential pattern parameters than the original. To address this problem, I added heuristic and pruning methods, and demonstrated that they are effective.

Despite the impact of my pruning and short-circuiting strategies on reducing the number of possibilities that AChaxG considers, there is clearly work to do to address the problem of excessive characterization times. I plan to pursue two strategies to improve characterization times. First, because I recognize that it is the *information* in an ACG that is important for characterization accuracy, I plan to modify my AChaxG implementation to use a matrix representation of the ACG. This will require extending a traditional communication matrix with additional rows and columns that represent MPI communicators, adding metadata that indicates the mappings of MPI communicators to these "extra" rows and columns, and changing each matrix entry to include an operation count in addition to communication volume. Second, because automated search through distinct parts of the pattern space is largely independent, I plan to parallelize the search. Avoiding considering of permutations of the same pattern collection, and for short-circuiting the search when the termination criteria is met, will require some coordination among parallel threads of execution.

Acknowledgements. This research used resources of the Oak Ridge Leadership Computing Facility at the Oak Ridge National Laboratory, which is supported by the Office of Science of the U.S. Department of Energy under Contract No. DE-AC05-00OR22725.

References

1. Balay, S., et al.: PETSc users manual. Technical report ANL-95/11 - Revision 3.7, Argonne National Laboratory (2016). http://www.mcs.anl.gov/petsc
2. Boisvert, R.F., Pozo, R., Remington, K.A.: The matrix market exchange format: initial design. Technical report NISTIR 5935, National Institutes of Standards and Technology (1996)

3. Boost C++ libraries (2017). http://www.boost.org
4. Gamblin, T.: MPI wrapper generator, for writing pmpi tool libraries (2017). https://github.com/LLNL/wrap
5. Gerndt, M., Ott, M.: Automatic performance analysis with periscope. Concurr. Comput.: Pract. Exp. **22**(6), 736–748 (2010). https://doi.org/10.1002/cpe.1551
6. Graph-tool: Efficient network analysis (2017). https://graph-tool.skewed.de
7. Kerbyson, D.J., Barker, K.J.: Automatic identification of application communication patterns via templates. In: Proceedings of the 5th International Conference on Software Engineering, pp. 114–121. ISCA, September 2005
8. Maroudas, D., Blondel, S., Hu, L., Hammond, K.D., Wirth, B.D.: Helium segregation on surfaces of plasma-exposed tungsten. J. Phys.: Condens. Matter **28**(6), 064004 (2016). http://stacks.iop.org/0953-8984/28/i=6/a=064004
9. Miller, B.P., et al.: The Paradyn parallel performance measurement tool. Computer **28**(11), 37–46 (1995). https://doi.org/10.1109/2.471178
10. Numpy (2017). http://www.numpy.org
11. Plimpton, S.: Fast parallel algorithms for short-range molecular dynamics. J. Comput. Phys. **117**, 1–19 (1995)
12. Roth, P.C., Meredith, J.S., Vetter, J.S.: Automated characterization of parallel application communication patterns. In: Proceedings of the 24th International Symposium on High-Performance Parallel and Distributed Computing, HPDC 2015, Portland, Oregon, USA, pp. 73–84, August 2015. https://doi.org/10.1145/2749246.2749278
13. Scipy library (2017). https://www.scipy.org/scipylib/index.html
14. Vetter, J.S., McCracken, M.O.: Statistical scalability analysis of communication operations in distributed applications. SIGPLAN Not. **36**(7), 123–132 (2001). https://doi.org/10.1145/568014.379590

Moya—A JIT Compiler for HPC

Tarun Prabhu(✉) and William Gropp

University of Illinois, Urbana-Champaign, Urbana, IL, USA
tprabhu2@illinois.edu

Abstract. We describe Moya, an annotation-driven JIT compiler for compiled languages such as Fortran, C and C++. We show that a combination of a small number of easy-to-use annotations coupled with aggressive static analysis that enables dynamic optimization can be used to improve the performance of computationally intensive, long-running numerical applications. We obtain speedups of upto 1.5 on JIT'ed functions and overcome the overheads of the JIT compilation within 25 timesteps in a combustion-simulation application.

1 Introduction

HPC applications rely on the compiler to produce high-quality code. This can be challenging because correctly estimating the profitability of any given transformation at compile-time can be difficult. Consider the code in lines 11–19 of Fig. 1. This loop nest is a simplified approximation of the heart of the computation in a combustion simulation application, PlasComCM [7]. All the compilers that we tested, GCC, Clang and ICC, vectorized the innermost loop on line 4, yet the performance was not significantly better than the unvectorized code. This is because the innermost loop corresponds to a stencil operation and typically has a trip count of either 5 or 9. A more profitable optimization decision would be to unroll the innermost loop and vectorize the loop on line 3. There is no way that the compiler can know this without explicit directives from the programmer.

While there are several ways around this problem, none are ideal. Directives instructing the compiler to unroll the innermost loop are not portable and using them would either restrict the programmer to a single compiler or would force her to clutter the code with a different directive for every compiler that she might ever use. The other option is to manually interchange the loops on lines 12 and 13. While this transformation is easily done in this particular case, it comes at the expense of readability.

A JIT compiler, if invoked at the right time, would see all the loop bounds and would appropriately unroll and vectorize the loops. In addition, other entities in the code such as `N1` and `N2` are problem-specific parameters whose values can also be folded in, decreasing the number of loads and the size of the working set in the data cache since their values can be encoded within the instruction stream.

In this paper, we present Moya, a JIT compiler for compiled languages and discuss dynamic constant propagation, the main JIT-specific optimization that

A. Bhatele et al. (Eds.): ESPT/VPA 2017/2018, LNCS 11027, pp. 56–73, 2019.
https://doi.org/10.1007/978-3-030-17872-7_4

Moya performs. We show that a combination of a small number of easy-to-use programmer annotations, aggressive JIT-aware static analysis and dynamic optimizations can be used to improve the performance of code that has not been extensively hand-optimized. Moreover, we also demonstrate that a runtime system could be designed such that the overhead of JIT compilation does not noticeably degrade performance even when the JIT compiler is unable to uncover additional optimizations—such as when aggressively hand-optimized code is JIT'ed. We have evaluated Moya on the NAS Parallel Benchmarks [3] and PlasComCM. We show that the JIT'ed code produced by Moya often outperforms the code produced by a regular compiler.

2 Motivation

Most HPC applications operate in distinct input, compute and output phases. Typically, no input is performed during the compute phase which is characterized by high arithmetic operation density. Even in the case of applications which have multiple input-compute-output cycles, the boundary between the cycles and the phases within them is usually clear.

Consider Fig. 1 which is a highly simplified skeleton of PlasComCM. We can clearly see the input, compute and output phases on lines 21–22, 25–29 and 31 respectively.

```
1  struct State {
2    int curr, steps, N1, N2;
3    int is, ie, js, je, ks, ke, ls, le;
4    double *vals, *dF, *F;
5  };
6  #pragma moya specialize
7  void derivative(struct State &s){
8    int is = s.is;
9    // Similarly: ie, js, je, ks, ke, ls
10   //           le, N1, N2, vals, F,dF
11   for(int k = ks; k < ke; k++)
12    for(int j = js; j < je; j++)
13     for(int i = is; i < ie; i++)
14      for(int l = ls, l < le; l++) {
15       int w = ((k-1)*N2 + (j-1))*N1;
16       int t = w + i + l;
17       dF[i] += vals[l] * F[t];
18      }
19 }
20 int main(int argc, char* argv[]) {
21   struct State s;
22   setup(s);
23 #pragma moya jit
24   {
25    while(timestep(s)) {
26     bc(s);
27     derivative(s);
28     rhs(s);
29    }
30   }
31   output(s);
32 }
```

Fig. 1. PlasComCM skeleton

Many entities in these applications are "dynamic constants". Dynamic constants are those program entities whose values are constant w.r.t. some region of code. In particular, the configuration parameters are constant during the compute phase after having been initialized during the input phase. Since their values are not known to a regular compiler, they are treated as variables throughout the code. If a JIT compiler were to run after the input phase, the values of these dynamic constants could be safely folded into the JIT'ed code where, as we have already described, they can affect the compiler's choice of optimizations.

In Fig. 1, the fields `N1`, `N2`, `is`, `ie`, `js`, `je`, `ks ke` and `steps` of `state` are dynamic constants w.r.t. the compute phase of lines 25–29.

Since HPC applications are typically written in compiled languages like Fortran and C++, a JIT compiler is unlikely to improve performance by JIT'ing code indiscriminately. Ideally, only that code where there is runtime information to profitably exploit should be JIT'ed. This JIT'ed code would need to be reused to amortize the cost of the dynamic compilation. Finally, to reduce both the compilation and reuse overheads, runtime ought to be minimized.

The challenges which need to be overcome to make JIT profitable are:

1. Identify "what" parts of the program should be JIT'ed.
2. Determine "when" to JIT. This involves identifying the compute phase of the program since that is when we are likely to see the most benefit of JIT'ing.
3. Identify dynamic constants and other entities in the program which can be exploited at JIT-time.

We address these challenges using a combination of programmer annotations and compile-time static analysis which inform the dynamic optimizations. We now briefly describe each of these.

2.1 Programmer Annotations

We assume that the programmer has some idea of which parts of the program are "hot" and would benefit from JIT'ing and therefore require him to explicitly annotate "what" should be JIT'ed. Since we only support JIT'ing entire functions, the programmer must identify the functions to be JIT'ed.

We also require the programmer to annotate the code to demarcate "JIT regions". A region typically ought to encompass most or all of the compute phase of the program. This indicates "when" something should be JIT'ed since the JIT compiler is only active within a "JIT region".

2.2 Compile-Time JIT-Aware Static Analysis

At compile time, we perform one or more JIT-aware static analyses that inform the dynamic optimizations. Currently, the major JIT-time optimization we perform is dynamic constant propagation. To identify dynamic constants in each "JIT region", we perform a whole-program mutability analysis at compile-time.

2.3 Dynamic JIT-Time Optimizations

These optimizations use the results of the JIT-aware static analyses described in Sect. 2.2 and augment them with runtime information. This enables more aggressive optimizations. For instance, a JIT-time loop vectorizer can determine the disjointness (or otherwise) of arrays accesses by simply looking at the incoming pointers and loop bounds.

3 Moya

At a high-level, Moya can be thought of as consisting of three distinct parts, a preprocessor which handles the Moya annotations (Pilot), and instruments the code, a compiler that performs the JIT-aware static analyses (Aeryn) and a runtime system which carries out the actual JIT compilation (Talyn). Pilot relies on several Clang and GCC plugins to parse the annotations for C/C++ and Fortran respectively. Aeryn and Talyn are both built on top of LLVM [23].

First, Pilot processes the annotations which involves adding calls to Talyn and collecting information that is needed by the JIT-aware static analyses. At compile-time, Moya produces LLVM bitcode for each file, performs some cleanup and static analysis on this and stashes it into the object files. At link-time, the bitcode in the object files being linked are retrieved and linked together and the main JIT-aware static analyses are performed as a whole-program analysis. The results of the analysis and the bitcode for the code that will be JIT'ed are all stashed inside the executable where they are used at JIT-time by Moya's runtime system.

When a function to be JIT'ed is called, the hooks inserted during annotation processing result in control being transferred to Moya. Moya produces different variants of the function being JIT'ed and picks one if it has already been compiled. If not, the function is JIT'ed and cached for future reuse. JIT'ing only takes place within a JIT region explicitly demarcated by the programmer.

4 Programmer Annotations

We now describe the programmer annotations that enable Moya. As discussed in Sect. 2, these annotations are needed to specify "what" is to be JIT'ed and "when". Each annotation consists of a sentinel, a directive and zero or more parameterized clauses. We first present the general syntax of the annotations followed by a description of the more commonly used directives.

C/C++ : `#pragma moya <directive> <clause>*`
Fortran : `!$moya <directive> <clause>*`

JIT: The `jit` directive is used to demarcate JIT regions. The block comprising of a region must satisfy the SESE (Single Entry Single Exit) property. This ensures that the entire code within the region can be outlined into a separate function which is necessary for the static analysis. The region can then be treated as a subgraph of the callgraph of the program consisting of all the functions than can be called (directly or

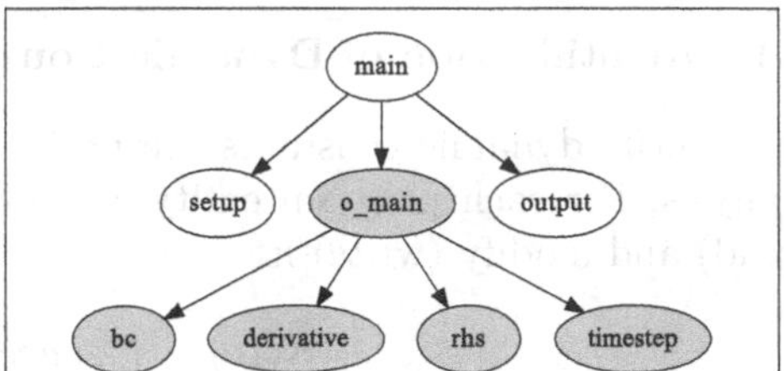

Fig. 2. Callgraph of Fig. 1. Functions reachable from the JIT region are shaded. `o_main` contains the demarcated code

indirectly) from the demarcated code region. Figure 2 shows the callgraph of the program with the region (lines 25–29 from Fig. 1) outlined into `o_main`.

Specialize: The `specialize` directive marks functions that are to be JIT'ed and is added immediately before a function definition. The `ignore` clause lists those function arguments which are to be ignored during function argument specialization while the `max` clauses limits the number of variants of the function that are JIT'ed. In Fig. 1, the `derivative` function has been tagged with this directive.

5 Compile-Time Analysis

In this section, we formalize the notions of JIT regions and dynamic constants and discuss the JIT-aware object mutability analysis that enables the JIT-time dynamic constant folding optimization.

Region: We define a region $\mathcal{R}$ to be a sequence of instructions $\mathcal{I}$ bounded by instructions i_b and i_e such that:

$$\begin{aligned} \forall i \in \mathcal{I},\ & i_b \text{ dominates } i \\ & i_e \text{ post-dominates } i \end{aligned}$$

The instructions i_b and i_e must be part of the same function. However, the scope of $\mathcal{R}$ itself includes all the functions transitively called from within $\mathcal{R}$.

Dynamic Constant: A program entity e is said to be a dynamic constant w.r.t. a region $\mathcal{R}$ iff e is immutable within $\mathcal{R}$. In other words, if e is not modified by any function which can be called transitively within $\mathcal{R}$, then e is a dynamic constant w.r.t. $\mathcal{R}$.

These definitions guarantee that if code is JIT'ed within some region $\mathcal{R}$, then all entities e_c, which are dynamic constants w.r.t. $\mathcal{R}$, can be replaced with their runtime values in the JIT'ed code. As long as this code is only called from within $\mathcal{R}$, it will remain valid, since the runtime values of e_c will not have changed. However, once control exits $\mathcal{R}$, this JIT'ed code becomes invalid.

5.1 Identification of Dynamic Constants

To identify dynamic constants, we perform a whole-program object mutability analysis. For each program entity, we obtain a set of functions f, that access (read) and modify (write) it.

$$\begin{aligned} K_r(e) &= \{f \mid accesses(f, e)\} \\ K_w(e) &= \{f \mid modifies(f, e)\} \end{aligned}$$

In addition, the analysis conservatively determines the functions that are called at each callsite. Therefore, for every region $\mathcal{R}$ in the program, we can obtain the transitive closure of all functions which may be called from within $\mathcal{R}$.

$$F(\mathcal{R}) = \{f \mid f \text{ is called from } \mathcal{R}\}$$

A program entity e is a dynamic constant w.r.t. $\mathcal{R}$ iff

$$F(\mathcal{R}) \cap K_w(e) = \emptyset \quad (1)$$

In other words, a program entity e is a dynamic constant w.r.t. some region $\mathcal{R}$, iff no function that modifies e can ever be called from within $\mathcal{R}$.

5.2 Mutability Analysis

The mutability analysis that we have implemented proceeds in a manner similar to an abstract interpretation [10] in that it conservatively "simulates" the execution of the program. In the course of this simulation, it tracks all functions that read and/or write each program entity. Since this is implemented as a whole-program analysis, we obtain, for each program entity the set of all functions that access it at any point during the execution of the program. For each region $\mathcal{R}$ demarcated in the program, we then filter out those functions which do not belong to the transitive closure of functions reachable from $\mathcal{R}$. This allows us to determine the entities that are dynamic constants using Eq. 1. Unlike prior work on mutability analysis [2], this is done entirely statically and is implemented as a link-time analysis in LLVM.

Data Structures

Store(σ): The store is used to simulate the structure and behavior of physical memory and consists of cells, each of which has a unique address. Each cell contains a set of zero or more abstract objects $\{\mathcal{C}\}$, each of which has a unique scalar or pointer type. The store also maintains mappings of functions to callsites and tracks the accessors (readers and writers) of each cell. In order to facilitate compile-time pointer arithmetic, the cell addresses are implemented as unique integers. We provide more details when discussing the handling of allocation instructions.

Abstract Objects($\mathcal{C}$): Abstract objects are used during the analysis to represent concrete objects which may exist at runtime. These include scalars whose value n is known at compile-time $\mathcal{C}_s$, scalars whose values are not known at compile-time $\mathcal{C}_r$, functions $\mathcal{C}_f$ and structs $\mathcal{C}_c$. In addition, we also have abstract objects representing valid store addresses ($\mathcal{C}_a$) that are analogous to pointers in that they "point" to a single cell in the store. An invalid store address ($\mathcal{C}_p$) is used to represent a cell address that cannot be uniquely determined at analysis-time. For instance, if we attempt to compute a compile-time unknown offset, $\mathcal{C}_s$ from a pointer $\mathcal{C}_a$, we get an invalid store address. Arrays are handled as a special case which we shall discuss when describing how indexing is performed during the analysis.

Environment(ρ)**:** The environment is a mapping from program entities to sets of abstract objects. Since we perform our analysis on LLVM-IR, each program entity in this case is an LLVM Value. An LLVM Value could be an instruction, global variable, function or constant.

Instruction Processing

We now describe how certain instructions are handled during the analysis.

Load: Load instructions correspond to reads and writes to cells in the store. The pointer operand is first looked up in the environment. This should return a set of valid store addresses $\{\mathcal{C}_a\}$. If an invalid store address is returned by the lookup, it triggers an error state and the analysis terminates. Otherwise, the cells that the store addresses point to are read, the sets of abstract objects in each of them merged and returned. A mapping is added in the environment from the load instruction to this merged set.

Store: The store instruction is the inverse of the load. The value operand of the store instruction is looked up in the environment and the set of abstract objects are merged into the cells pointed to by the valid store addresses returned by looking up the pointer operand. Once again, if an invalid store address is returned on looking up the pointer operand, it triggers an error state.

Allocation: When allocating a scalar in the store, a cell of the corresponding type is created with some integer address m. The pointer to this memory is returned as a store address object $\mathcal{C}_a(m)$. When allocating a composite type such as a struct, we recursively allocate each subtype of the struct. The cell addresses are chosen such that they correspond to the layout of successive objects in physical memory on the target system. For instance, when allocating successive 4-byte integers on X86, if the first were allocated at address m_0, the second would be allocated at address m_0+4. This allows us to easily translate the concrete pointer arithmetic that is performed in the LLVM IR to the abstract pointer arithmetic that needs to be performed on our addresses. All arrays, even those who lengths are known at compile-time are assumed to be of length 1.

Array Indexing: We track all store addresses which correspond to the start of an array. Any indexing operation performed using the starting address of this array as a base is assumed to be in bounds and will return the starting address of the array (essentially, the store address of the first element of the array). This analysis will not result in incorrect dynamic optimizations because accessing an array out of bounds is undefined behavior in C/C++ and incorrect behavior in Fortran. The one exception to this rule is for vtable lookups in which case we do not assume that the array is of length 1.

Struct/Class Indexing: We also track all store addresses which correspond to the first element of an instance of a struct or class. When accessing a member of such an object, the offset is usually compile-time constant, say c from the starting address $\mathcal{C}_a$ of the struct. In this case, we return the cell address at $\mathcal{C}_a + c$. We have never encountered a case where LLVM accesses a member of a struct using a non-constant offset.

Pointer Arithmetic: Apart from the special cases for arrays and structs described above, any other form of pointer arithmetic will trigger an error state. We provide limited support for `inttoptr` and `ptrtoint` instructions. A pattern that is sometimes seen in C++ when dealing with virtual inheritance is for a pointer to an object to be converted to an integer, some amount added to this integer and the result converted back to a pointer. In such cases, we allow the pointer arithmetic to be performed.

Call: A call results in a mapping being added to the environment for every function parameter. This gets updated with the arguments passed to the function at each call-site. Since our analysis is context-insensitive, this results in some imprecision in the analysis. For the kinds of JIT-time optimizations that we perform, this has not proven to be detrimental in practice. Every function is allocated a private call stack in the store. This allows us to simulate pass-by-value semantics during the analysis without introducing spurious aliasing effects.

Analysis Loop

The analysis first allocates space in the store σ for every global variable, compile-time constant, and both statically and dynamically allocated objects. The analysis iterates over all the functions and performs an abstract execution of the instructions until either an error state is triggered or the analysis converges. Once the analysis converges, a summary is generated for each region in the program. Figure 3 is a partial summary for the region in Fig. 1. The status of each program entity is computed using Eq. 1.

Entity	Readers	Writers	Status
`s.curr`	`timestep`	`setup` `timestep`	*Variable*
`s.N1`	`derivative`	`setup`	**Constant**

`s.dF`	`derivative`
	`rhs`
	`output`
		`setup`	**Constant**

`*s.dF`	`derivative`
	`rhs`
	`output`
		`derivative`
		`rhs`
		`setup`
			Variable

`s.F`	`derivative`
	`rhs`
	`output`
		`setup`	**Constant**

`*s.F`	`derivative`
	`rhs`
	`bc`
	`output`
		`derivative`
		`rhs`
		`bc`
		`setup`
			Variable

Fig. 3. Partial summary of analysis results

Error State: There are several conditions that can cause the analysis to reach an error state.

- Loading/storing using an invalid store address $\mathcal{C}_p$.
- Accessing a field of a struct using a non-constant offset from the base.
- Failing to determine the function called at a callsite.
- Failing to find a model for a library function.

Convergence: The analysis converges when no new mappings are added to the environment and no new contents are added to any cell in the store.

Termination: Both ρ and σ grow monotonically; once an abstract object $\mathcal{C}$ is inserted into a cell in the store, it is never removed. The same is true for the environment. In addition, we never perform any arithmetic even on compile-time constants. The result of arithmetic or logical operators is always a scalar of indeterminate value $\mathcal{C}_r$. Since there are only a finite number of object allocation sites in the program (we ignore back-edges in loops), only a finite number of objects are ever allocated in the store. These conditions ensure that the analysis terminates. Since we know that the analysis always terminates, it is guaranteed to always either converge or reach an error state.

5.3 Library Models

Since we need to determine exactly which functions modify a program entity, we need to know about the behavior of those library functions which take a pointer as an argument or return a pointer. In this case, we need to know how the pointer is used by the function and since the code is not available to the program, a model describing the behavior of the function must be supplied. We have currently implemented models for some widely used libraries such as MPI, Cantera, ScaLAPACK, HDF and libc. If the library is compiled using Moya, it will contain a payload composed of the LLVM bitcode for the whole library. This can then be retrieved and the analysis performed on the functions called from the user code.

6 JIT - Time Optimizations

6.1 Function Argument Specialization

For each different set of parameters with which a JIT'ed function is called, Moya will generate a different version of the JIT'ed code with all the dynamic constants reachable from the arguments folded into the code. If the function is called in the future with the same arguments, then the JIT'ed version is reused. If one of the arguments to the function is a pointer and the function is called a second time with the same pointer as an argument, it is safe to reuse the code. This reduces the function calling overhead since we don't have to chase pointers to determine if any state has changed between calls to the function.

6.2 Dynamic Constant Propagation (DCP)

The dynamic constant propagation optimization relies on the regular compiler's constant propagation framework to do most of the work of propagating and folding constants. Figure 4 is a summary of the optimization. It is carried out on an LLVM-IR representation of the function being JIT'ed. Here, Θ is the summary of the mutability analysis that is available to the perform the dynamic optimizations. For each function parameter `param`, we query the analysis results and obtain an abstract object corresponding to it. `param` is an LLVM Value. If the object is a scalar dynamic constant, we replace all uses of `param` in the function with its concrete runtime value, `arg`. If the parameter is a pointer, we call `propagate` for each use of `param`. `propagate` needs an LLVM value (`val`), a runtime value (`rt`) and an abstract object ($\mathcal{C}$). Essentially, propagate does pointer chasing to identify all the dynamic constants that are reachable given a starting pointer value. It does not attempt to perform constant propagation, but merely plugs in the runtime values in the appropriate places in the LLVM-IR and invokes LLVM's constant folding pass. In addition, Moya invokes the default -O2 optimization passes in LLVM, in particular the loop unrolling pass each time any dynamic constants are propagated. This ensures that the maximum number of dynamic constants are uncovered.

```
def dyn_const_prop(f, args):
  for i = 0 to f.get_num_params():
    param = f.params[i]
    𝒞 = Θ[param]
    arg = args[i]
    if typeof(param) is pointer:
      for u in param.uses():
        propagate(u, arg, 𝒞)
    else if is_dynamic_constant(𝒞):
      replace_uses(param, arg)

def propagate(llvm_val, rt, 𝒞):
  if not is_dynamic_constant(𝒞):
    return
  if llvm_val isa load:
    if typeof(var.loaded) is pointer:
      for u in var.uses():
        propagate(u, *conc, Θ[u])
    else:
      replace_uses(llvm_val, rt)
  else if llvm_val isa getelementptr:
    if indices_constant(llvm_val):
      n = calc_offset(llvm_val,rt)
      for u in var.uses():
        propagate(u, rt + n, 𝒞 + n)
```

Fig. 4. Pseudo-code for DCP

6.3 Invariant Load Detection

In cases where a pointer is being loaded inside a loop, the compiler may sometimes be unable to hoist the load outside the loop thereby inhibiting vectorization. This may happen when the compiler is unable to disambiguate between the locations of writes through two pointers present in the loop. The mutability analysis can then be combined with scalar evolution and looking up the actual value of the pointer variable to determine whether or not it is safe to hoist the load instruction out of the loop. This pass, too, relies on the regular's LICM (Loop Invariant Code Motion) pass for the mechanics of hoisting the value.

7 Results

We evaluated Moya on the NAS parallel benchmark suite as well as PlasComCM. All the experiments were run on a desktop computer equipped with dual Intel Xeon E5-2609 processors with 32 GB RAM. All executions were serial (a single MPI process) and each test ran for at least 2 min. In cases where the default inputs to the benchmarks did not result in the program completing before that time, we modified the benchmarks to increase the execution time. In most cases, we increased the number of iterations rather than modify the problem size. For PlasComCM, the input was a scaled-down model of the physical system used in predictive simulation runs.

Program execution statistics were compiled using PAPI [26]. The functions annotated with Moya's `specialize` directive were instrumented at compile-time to call Moya's statistics collection routines on function entry and exit. The same was done for the JIT'ed functions. Note that all the instrumentation is done automatically and without the need for programmer intervention.

To determine the functions to be JIT'ed, we ran each benchmark with a profiler to determine the "hot" functions. We sorted these in descending order of the fraction of the total execution time that was spent in each function. Starting from the top, we proceeded to pick the first n functions until the cumulative execution time of these functions was at least 50% of the total execution time of the application. We added Moya's `specialize` directive to each of these. For PlasComCM, we also consulted the developers who suggested functions whose performance they were unable to improve by hand and suggested that we try JIT'ing them.

To annotate the JIT region, we inspected the code to find the time marching loop that is characteristic of most numerical applications and marked the entire time marching loop as comprising the JIT region. Despite not being familiar with most of the code, this never took us more than a few minutes to find. In most of the code that we inspected, the programmer's comments made this task trivial. Even when comments were unavailable, the code followed a somewhat predictable structure with descriptive function names which simplified this task.

We never modified any executable lines of code in any of the benchmarks or applications. All modifications to the code consisted exclusively of the addition of Moya annotations. Moya is designed to be a drop-in replacement for the GNU compilers. For the most part, we only had to edit the path to the compiler. On occasion, we had to remove compiler flags that Moya does not currently support. In most cases, these were flags to perform static linking which Moya currently does not support. Moya requires all applications to be dynamically linked. We have identified ways to enable static linking but currently, this has not been implemented.

7.1 Compile-Time Static Analysis

Figure 5 shows the execution time of the mutability analysis and the dynamic memory used in the course of this analysis. The memory value is the high water mark as reported by PAPI. We believe that this is an underestimate since it does not seem to include the memory allocated by LLVM for the bitcode on which we are carrying out the analysis. Nevertheless, this suggests that the environment and store do not grow drastically even when dealing with sizeable application code such as PlasComCM. The lines of code reported for each application by counting the total number of lines in all the source files in the application. The last column in the table is the number of iterations that the analysis loop carried out before convergence.

	kLoC	Time(s)	Mem(KB)	Iters
PlasComCM	184	117	319	3
BT	5.2	1.2	443	3
CG	1.1	0.9	579	3
DC	3.1	0.1	39	3
EP	0.3	0.1	67	3
FT	0.8	20	3984	4
LU	0.5	1.2	418	3
MG	1.4	16	6266	4
SP	3.2	1.3	446	3
UA	7.1	1.4	335	4

Fig. 5. Mutability analysis statistics

7.2 PlasComCM

PlasComCM is a combustion simulation application that solves the compressible Navier-Stokes equation written primarily in Fortran90 with some C and C++.

Figure 6 presents some execution statistics collected during execution of PlasComCM. We JIT'ed 5 different functions and obtained a range of speedups up to 1.5. These are purely the speedups in the execution time and do not take into account the dynamic compilation time and launch overheads. The remaining columns in the table are the improvements in the number of load instructions, L2 and L3 cache misses and L1 and L2 instruction cache misses respectively. Each value is the ratio $\frac{v_a}{v_j}$ where v_a is the value without Moya and v_j is the value with Moya performing JIT compilation. As we can see, we generally decrease the number of load instructions in almost all cases. However, the effect on the caches is inconsistent and merits further investigation.

Function	Speedup	Loads	L2/L3	I-cache
strnrt	1.04	2.80	0.76	0.81
euler	1.22	1.00	1.03	0.82
viscousterms	1.04	0.85	1.16	0.87
apply_operator	1.53	1.71	0.84	1.10
modelldv	1.01	1.03	1.35	1.23

Fig. 6. Execution statistics for PlasComCM

The `apply_operator` function in Fig. 6 is the full version of the simplified `derivative` function of Fig. 1. The speedups obtained here are mostly the result of more effective vectorization. In the function, the loop corresponding to the one on line 14 of Fig. 1 is vectorized. However, this loop corresponds to a 5-point stencil and the vectorization is unprofitable. The other loops in the nest are the dimensions of the grid which in this case are all 100. Since the loop bounds are determined to be dynamic constants, their runtime values are folded into the code at JIT-time. The compiler then sees that the innermost loop is short and unrolls it fully. This enables the much longer outer loop to be vectorized.

In the case of `model1dv`, we do not obtain any measurable speedups because the static compiler was able to optimize all of the code effectively. The effect of the JIT-time optimizations was merely to reduce the number of load instructions by folding in the values of the dynamic constants.

Figure 7 lists some of the overheads associated with JIT compilation. The columns are the total JIT compilation time in seconds, the number of different versions of the function that were JIT'ed, the number of calls to the function during execution and the overhead of launching the JIT'ed code. The `apply_operator` function incurred significant compilation overhead and resulted in the largest number of specialized variants being generated. The function is called once in the x, y and z directions for each of 3 grids with an additional order parameter which could be 1 or 2. This results in $3 \times 3 \times 2 = 18$ different versions of the function being generated. This function had the best reuse of all the functions that were JIT'ed. The compilation overheads were overcome after about 10 reuses of the function. All variants of the JIT'ed functions were generated before the end of the first time step. In terms of overall application runtime, the overheads of JIT'ing these functions was overcome after 25 time steps. This does result in a net improvement since a typical production run of PlasComCM would typically involve hundreds or thousands of time steps.

Function	**Compile(s)**	n	**Calls**	**Exec(μs)**
strnrt	0.41	3	60	6
euler	0.76	3	60	9
viscousterms	2.1	3	60	5
apply_operator	19.7	18	5220	5
model1dv	0.57	3	75	10

Fig. 7. Overheads for PlasComCM

7.3 NAS Parallel Benchmarks

The NAS Parallel Benchmarks (NPB) consist of several computational kernels that represent some of the most commonly performed numerical operations and have been hand-optimized. Moreover, the benchmark suite is set up such that the input parameters to the benchmarks are known at compile-time. We did not expect to see any significant improvement as a result of JIT'ing. We sought instead to see if the overheads of JIT'ing could be kept tolerably low in such cases. Figure 8 shows that this is generally the case for the class A benchmarks although we

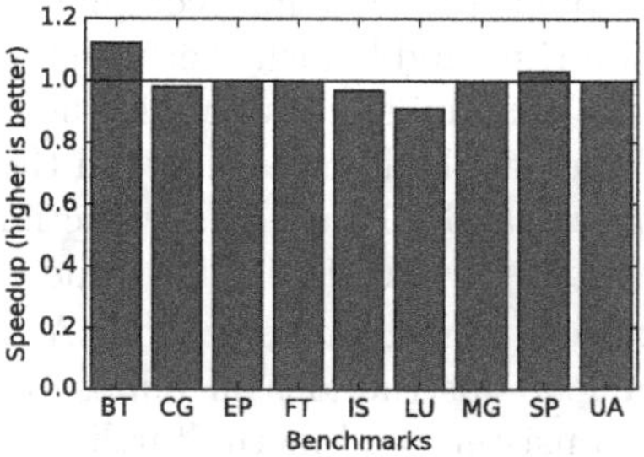

Fig. 8. Overall speedup for NPB

do manage to improve the performance of BT. We omitted the DC benchmark since it performs only I/O.

8 Related Work

JIT compilation is a well-known technique that has been widely used in many different programming languages. It is perhaps best known for its use in the Java Virtual Machine [11,21,25,27,33]. There has also been extensive work discussing the optimizations used in the JVM, some of which are specific to Java and the JVM, [6,14,17–19] and others which are effectively used by the Java's JIT compiler to improve performance [8,9,12]. Recently, the same technique has been used in many different languages such as Haskell [4], Racket [30], Python [1,22, 31], Javascript [15,20] and C# [5]. A common feature of all of these languages is that they start out being interpreted. They tend to have relatively heavy-weight runtime systems which use JIT compilation to improve the performance of "hot" code. The JIT compiler in the JVM is also tightly coupled with the runtime system itself and there is constant communication between the compiler and the runtime system. None of these languages are in widespread use within the HPC community where compiled languages like Fortran, C and C++ are preferred for their superior performance.

DyC [16] was a dialect of C with annotations to support dynamic compilation. These annotations required the programmer to explicitly identify variables and arrays which were to be treated as runtime-constants within a given region of code. Unlike DyC which requires the programmer to explicitly demarcate regions for each variable to be treated as a runtime constant, Moya only requires the programmer to create regions where the JIT compiler should be active. DyC is more flexible since the regions are multiple-entry-multiple-exit and may overlap, whereas Moya's regions are single-entry-single-exit and may not overlap.

`C [28] was another approach to adding dynamic compilation support to C by adding syntactic features to the language. In `C, a ` operator was used to identify arbitrary blocks of code which were to be dynamically compiled. Within these blocks, the `$` operator was used to identify variables which were to be treated as runtime constants within the block being JIT'ed. Since `C adds syntactic features to the language, once a program has been "translated" to `C, it cannot be compiled with any other compiler. However, since Moya uses `pragma`'s, those annotations will simply be ignored by other compilers. We believe that this makes it easier for programmers to retrofit large, legacy code bases with JIT capabilities using Moya and without sacrificing the ability to use other compilers. Since the annotations required are also relatively limited in number, this should not have a significant impact on maintainability.

Some libraries have used JIT internally to accelerate carefully chosen parts of their code, for instance OpenGL [24] and the MPI runtime [29,32].

Profile-guided optimization (PGO) is a technique that is often used in manner similar to this. The disadvantage of PGO is that the profile information is only valid as long as the input data's characteristics do not change. The program also needs to be recompiled to take advantage of the profiled data. While JIT compilation adds a runtime overhead, it is suitable for programs which also dynamically alter their behavior.

Approaches such as Kokkos [13] have been proposed to improve compiler performance by providing abstractions that would allow the programmer to provide guidance which would then perform similar code specializations at compile-time. However, these can drastically increase compilation time since all the specialized code has to be generated regardless of whether or not it will be used in any given execution.

9 Future Work

There are several directions in which this work can be extended. Currently, we do not attempt to identify functions that would benefit from JIT compilation. One approach might be to use the results of the mutability analysis to determine whether the dynamic constants are on a "critical path" that has a strong impact on the compiler's optimization decisions. The speed of the mutability analysis could be improved by computing "summaries" of functions. This could be done for each function independently and the summaries then "composed" to get the final result. This would improve scalability of the analysis. Instead of the current "one-shot" JIT's, we could perform autotuning at runtime by exploring different compilation strategies and options on a function call even if an appropriate version of the function has already been JIT'ed. Instead of auto-tuning being performed ahead of time when moving to a new platform, it could be performed while simultaneously doing "useful" work. Another direction would be to save either the JIT'ed code itself or the sequence of optimizations that were applied to it so that the same JIT'ed code could be used in a subsequent invocation of the program - thereby reducing the JIT overhead even further.

10 Conclusion

With Moya, we have demonstrated how a small number of easy-to-use annotations can be combined with aggressive static analysis to implement efficient JIT compilation for compiled languages. We describe a compile-time object mutability analysis that enables dynamic constant propagation at JIT-time. We have shown that JIT compilation can improve the performance of functions in real-world code and obtained a speedup of as much as 1.5 by enabling the compiler to make optimization decisions that it would not have made in the absence of runtime information. We have also shown that Moya does not adversely affect the performance of codes even when the JIT compiler does not uncover optimizations that the static compiler was unwilling or unable to perform.

References

1. Akeret, J., Gamper, L., Amara, A., Refregier, A.: HOPE: a Python just-in-time compiler for astrophysical computations. Astron. Comput. **10**, 1–8 (2015). https://doi.org/10.1016/j.ascom.2014.12.001
2. Artzi, S., Kiezun, A., Glasser, D., Ernst, M.D.: Combined static and dynamic mutability analysis. In: Proceedings of the Twenty-second IEEE/ACM International Conference on Automated Software Engineering, ASE 2007, pp. 104–113. ACM, New York (2007). https://doi.org/10.1145/1321631.1321649
3. Bailey, D.H., et al.: The NAS parallel benchmarks & Mdash; summary and preliminary results. In: Proceedings of the 1991 ACM/IEEE Conference on Supercomputing, Supercomputing 1991, pp. 158–165. ACM, New York (1991). https://doi.org/10.1145/125826.125925
4. Bauman, S., et al.: Pycket: a tracing JIT for a functional language. SIGPLAN Not. **50**(9), 22–34 (2015). https://doi.org/10.1145/2858949.2784740
5. Bebenita, M., et al.: SPUR: a trace-based JIT compiler for CIL. SIGPLAN Not. **45**(10), 708–725 (2010). https://doi.org/10.1145/1869459.1869517
6. Berndl, M., Hendren, L.: Dynamic profiling and trace cache generation. In: Proceedings of the International Symposium on Code Generation and Optimization: Feedback-Directed and Runtime Optimization, CGO 2003, pp. 276–285. IEEE Computer Society, Washington, DC (2003). http://portal.acm.org/citation.cfm?id=776291
7. Bodony, D.: Accuracy of the simultaneous-approximation-term boundary condition for time-dependent problems. J. Sci. Comput. **43**(1), 118–133 (2010). https://doi.org/10.1007/s10915-010-9347-4
8. Choi, J.D., Gupta, M., Serrano, M., Sreedhar, V.C., Midkiff, S.: Escape analysis for Java. In: Proceedings of the 14th ACM SIGPLAN Conference on Object-Oriented Programming, Systems, Languages, and Applications, OOPSLA 1999, pp. 1–19. ACM, New York (1999). https://doi.org/10.1145/320384.320386
9. Click, C.: Global code motion/global value numbering. SIGPLAN Not. **30**(6), 246–257 (1995). https://doi.org/10.1145/223428.207154
10. Cousot, P., Cousot, R.: Systematic design of program analysis frameworks. In: Proceedings of the 6th ACM SIGACT-SIGPLAN Symposium on Principles of Programming Languages, POPL 1979, pp. 269–282. ACM, New York (1979). https://doi.org/10.1145/567752.567778
11. Cramer, T., Friedman, R., Miller, T., Seberger, D., Wilson, R., Wolczko, M.: Compiling Java just in time. IEEE Micro **17**(3), 36–43 (1997). https://doi.org/10.1109/40.591653
12. Dean, J., Grove, D., Chambers, C.: Optimization of object-oriented programs using static class hierarchy analysis. In: Tokoro, M., Pareschi, R. (eds.) ECOOP 1995. LNCS, vol. 952, pp. 77–101. Springer, Heidelberg (1995). https://doi.org/10.1007/3-540-49538-X_5
13. Edwards, H.C., Trott, C.R., Sunderland, D.: Kokkos: enabling manycore performance portability through polymorphic memory access patterns. J. Parallel Distrib. Comput. **74**(12), 3202–3216 (2014). https://doi.org/10.1016/j.jpdc.2014.07.003. Domain-Specific Languages and High-Level Frameworks for High-Performance Computing

14. Fink, S.J., Qian, F.: Design, implementation and evaluation of adaptive recompilation with on-stack replacement. In: Proceedings of the International Symposium on Code Generation and Optimization: Feedback-Directed and Runtime Optimization, CGO 2003, pp. 241–252. IEEE Computer Society, Washington, DC (2003). http://portal.acm.org/citation.cfm?id=776288
15. Gal, A., et al.: Trace-based Just-in-time type specialization for dynamic languages. SIGPLAN Not. **44**(6), 465–478 (2009). https://doi.org/10.1145/1543135.1542528
16. Grant, B., Mock, M., Philipose, M., Chambers, C., Eggers, S.J.: DyC: an expressive annotation-directed dynamic compiler for C. Theor. Comput. Sci. (2000). http://citeseerx.ist.psu.edu/viewdoc/summary?doi=10.1.1.75.3999
17. Inagaki, T., Komatsu, H., Nakatani, T.: Integrated prepass scheduling for a Java just-in-time compiler on the IA-64 architecture. In: Proceedings of the International Symposium on Code Generation and Optimization: Feedback-Directed and Runtime Optimization, CGO 2003, pp. 159–168. IEEE Computer Society, Washington, DC (2003). http://portal.acm.org/citation.cfm?id=776279
18. Inoue, H.: A trace-based Java JIT compiler for large-scale applications. In: Proceedings of the Sixth ACM Workshop on Virtual Machines and Intermediate Languages, VMIL 2012, pp. 1–2. ACM, New York (2012). https://doi.org/10.1145/2414740.2414742
19. Ishizaki, K., et al.: Design, implementation, and evaluation of optimizations in a JavaTM just-in-time compiler. Concurrency: Pract. Exper. **12**(6), 457–475 (2000). https://doi.org/10.1002/1096-9128
20. Jeon, S., Choi, J.: Reuse of JIT compiled code in JavaScript engine. In: Proceedings of the 27th Annual ACM Symposium on Applied Computing, SAC 2012, pp. 1840–1842. ACM, New York (2012). https://doi.org/10.1145/2245276.2232075
21. Kotzmann, T., Wimmer, C., Mössenböck, H., Rodriguez, T., Russell, K., Cox, D.: Design of the Java HotSpot^{TM}; client compiler for Java 6. ACM Trans. Archit. Code Optim. **5**(1), 1–32 (2008). https://doi.org/10.1145/1369396.1370017
22. Lam, S.K., Pitrou, A., Seibert, S.: Numba: a LLVM-based Python JIT compiler. In: Proceedings of the Second Workshop on the LLVM Compiler Infrastructure in HPC, LLVM 2015. ACM, New York, November 2015. https://doi.org/10.1145/2833157.2833162
23. Lattner, C., Adve, V.: LLVM: a compilation framework for lifelong program analysis & transformation. In: International Symposium on Code Generation and Optimization, CGO 2004, vol. 0, pp. 75–86. IEEE, Los Alamitos, March 2004. https://doi.org/10.1109/cgo.2004.1281665
24. LLVM for OpenGL and other stuff, May 2007. http://llvm.org/devmtg/2007-05/10-Lattner-OpenGL.pdf
25. Maruyama, F., Matsuoka, S., Ogawa, H., Maruyama, N., Shimura, K.: OpenJIT 2: the design and implementation of application framework for JIT compilers. In: Proceedings of the 2001 Symposium on JavaTM Virtual Machine Research and Technology Symposium - Volume 1, JVM 2001, p. 12. USENIX Association, Berkeley (2001). http://portal.acm.org/citation.cfm?id=1267859
26. Mucci, P.J., Browne, S., Deane, C., Ho, G.: PAPI: a portable interface to hardware performance counters. In: In Proceedings of the Department of Defense HPCMP Users Group Conference, pp. 7–10 (1999). http://citeseerx.ist.psu.edu/viewdoc/summary?doi=10.1.1.117.6801
27. Paleczny, M., Vick, C., Click, C.: The Java hotspot^{TM} server compiler. In: Proceedings of the 2001 Symposium on JavaTM Virtual Machine Research and Technology Symposium - Volume 1, JVM 2001, p. 1. USENIX Association, Berkeley. http://portal.acm.org/citation.cfm?id=1267848

28. Poletto, M., Hsieh, W.C., Engler, D.R., Kaashoek, M.F.: C and Tcc: a language and compiler for dynamic code generation. ACM Trans. Program. Lang. Syst. **21**(2), 324–369 (1999). https://doi.org/10.1145/316686.316697
29. Prabhu, T., Gropp, W.: DAME: a runtime-compiled engine for derived datatypes. In: Proceedings of the 22nd European MPI Users' Group Meeting, EuroMPI 2015, pp. 42–52. ACM, New York, September 2015. https://doi.org/10.1145/2802658.2802659
30. Performance in Racket, July 2016. https://docs.racket-lang.org/guide/performance.html
31. Rigo, A.: Representation-based just-in-time specialization and the psyco prototype for Python. In: Proceedings of the 2004 ACM SIGPLAN Symposium on Partial Evaluation and Semantics-Based Program Manipulation, PEPM 2004, pp. 15–26. ACM, New York, August 2004. https://doi.org/10.1145/1014007.1014010
32. Schneider, T., Kjolstad, F., Hoefler, T.: MPI datatype processing using runtime compilation. In: Proceedings of the 20th European MPI Users' Group Meeting, EuroMPI 2013, pp. 19–24. ACM, New York, September 2013. https://doi.org/10.1145/2488551.2488552
33. Suganuma, T., et al.: Overview of the IBM Java just-in-time compiler. IBM Syst. J. **39**(1), 175–193 (2000). https://doi.org/10.1147/sj.391.0175

Polyhedral Optimization of TensorFlow Computation Graphs

Benoît Pradelle, Benoît Meister, Muthu Baskaran(✉), Jonathan Springer, and Richard Lethin

Reservoir Labs, New York, USA
{pradelle,meister,baskaran,springer,lethin}@reservoir.com

Abstract. We present R-Stream·TF, a polyhedral optimization tool for neural network computations. R-Stream·TF transforms computations performed in a neural network graph into C programs suited to the polyhedral representation and uses R-Stream, a polyhedral compiler, to parallelize and optimize the computations performed in the graph. R-Stream·TF can exploit the optimizations available with R-Stream to generate a highly optimized version of the computation graph, specifically mapped to the targeted architecture. During our experiments, R-Stream·TF was able to automatically reach performance levels close to the hand-optimized implementations, demonstrating its utility in porting neural network computations to parallel architectures.

1 Introduction

Deep Convolutional Neural Networks (DCNN) [16], and more generally deep learning, recently reached maturity. Impressive results achieved in recent years demonstrated the technology was ripe for general, practical use. New applications are developed every day, and deep learning is already ubiquitous in our lives. This considerable activity around machine learning is becoming increasingly structured around a few common tools. For instance, Caffe [15], Torch [10], CNTK [27], and TensorFlow [2] are popular frameworks commonly used to develop and exploit neural networks. These frameworks are based on a similar concept: high-level operations such as convolutions and pooling are exposed to the user, who can design networks simply by composing them as operators. The frameworks also empower users by facilitating data preprocessing and streamlining back-propagation for training.

Applications based on neural networks often require strict performance constraints to be enforced, such as when performing interactive tasks. They also require high throughput (bandwidth) such as when performing many queries simultaneously. To minimize the latency and bandwidth required to process an input sample, neural networks frameworks rely on highly optimized implementations. A common approach for speeding up neural network processing consists in building a hand-optimized library of DCNN operators.

While this method significantly improves the performance of the computations, the hand optimization effort is tedious and error-prone. It is also inherently

A. Bhatele et al. (Eds.): ESPT/VPA 2017/2018, LNCS 11027, pp. 74–89, 2019.
https://doi.org/10.1007/978-3-030-17872-7_5

unable to exploit optimization opportunities available by combining successive operations. For instance, an element-wise operation and a convolution can be computed more efficiently if both operations are fused. In order to benefit from these optimization opportunities, several graph-based optimizers have been proposed and are currently being developed. The most representative approach is XLA, a just-in-time compiler for TensorFlow computation graphs. XLA has shown its ability to significantly speed up the computations performed in TensorFlow, but it seems limited to basic pattern-matching optimizations. Only simple cases of fusion and array contraction can be realistically achieved with this method.

Our contribution is to extend and generalize the approach of graph optimizers through polyhedral optimization techniques. Compilers and optimizers based on the polyhedral model can apply powerful code transformations on programs, using a precise mathematical representation of the code.

Polyhedral optimizations encompass fusion and array contraction, but they also subsume any combination of loop fusion/fission, interchange, skewing, and reversals. Data dependencies are exact in the polyhedral model, enabling automatic parallelization and other common memory-oriented optimizations such as loop tiling [14] and data layout transformations [9]. The polyhedral model is most precise on regions with affine constructs [12], which include most of the classical neural network operators.

In this paper, we present R-Stream·TF, a new optimizer for TensorFlow computation graphs. R-Stream·TF emits high-level sequential C code implementing the exact computations performed in the input TensorFlow graph. The generated C code is specific to the graph: it is specialized to the exact tensor shapes and types used as the input and output of every operation. The generated C code is then automatically parallelized and optimized by R-Stream [19], a polyhedral compiler developed by Reservoir Labs. R-Stream optimizes the computation specifically for the target architecture. R-Stream supports numerous targets including common x86 CPUs and GPUs and can generate the code to parallel programming models including OpenMP, CUDA, OpenCL, POSIX threads and task-based runtimes APIs [18,23].

R-Stream·TF extracts and merges TensorFlow operator subgraphs, and lets R-Stream apply a full range of polyhedral optimizations to the underlying computations. Such transformations are specific to the target platform, which can have several levels of parallelism and any combination of caches and scratchpads [22]. The result is a set of highly optimized parallel TensorFlow operators, which are reintegrated into the original TensorFlow computation graph.

The main benefit of our approach is the ability to use the full set of polyhedral optimizations within computation subgraphs. This ability is superior to current approaches based on domain-specific optimizations, since it enables several additional optimizations to be performed automatically on computation graphs. Because the optimizations applied to the graph are both specialized to the graph itself and to the target architecture, R-Stream·TF generates highly optimized code, specifically tailored for the target platform. This makes R-Stream·TF an adequate automatic porting tool, providing an optimized support for TensorFlow computations on new architectures.

The rest of the paper is organized as follows. The design of R-Stream·TF is presented in details in Sect. 2. The tool has been implemented and evaluated on popular DCNNs. The evaluation results are presented in Sect. 3. We compare R-Stream·TF to existing systems in Sect. 5, before concluding in Sect. 6.

2 Design

2.1 Overview

The overall flow of R-Stream·TF, described in Fig. 1, starts with a TensorFlow computation graph and results in an optimized graph with the same semantics. The optimization process is performed in several successive steps. First, optimizable subgraphs of the overall operator graph are identified. Restricting the process to well-structured subgraphs ensures that optimization is possible and tractable. Simple sequential C code is then generated for every identified operator. The sequential source code is sent as-is to R-Stream to be parallelized and optimized. The resulting parallel code is wrapped in a custom C++ TensorFlow operator automatically generated by R-Stream·TF. The operator itself implements the operation API defined by the framework, allowing the optimized code to be seamlessly reintegrated to the TensorFlow computation graph. As a result, R-Stream·TF produces an optimized computation graph based on automatically-generated custom operators. The optimized graph can then be used in lieu of the original graph.

2.2 Subgraph Selection

Polyhedral optimization scales super-linearly in the number of statements, hence practical optimization time constraints somewhat limit the number of nodes in

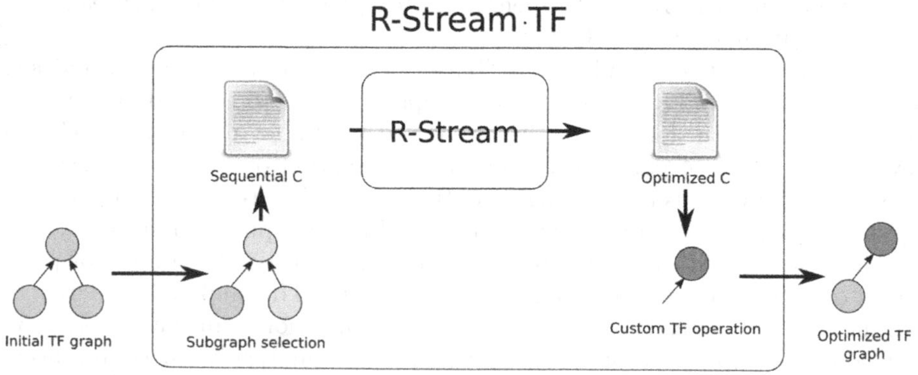

Fig. 1. TensorFlow graphs are converted into simple sequential C code, optimized using the R-Stream compiler, wrapped in a custom TensorFlow operators, and finally stitched back in the computation graph.

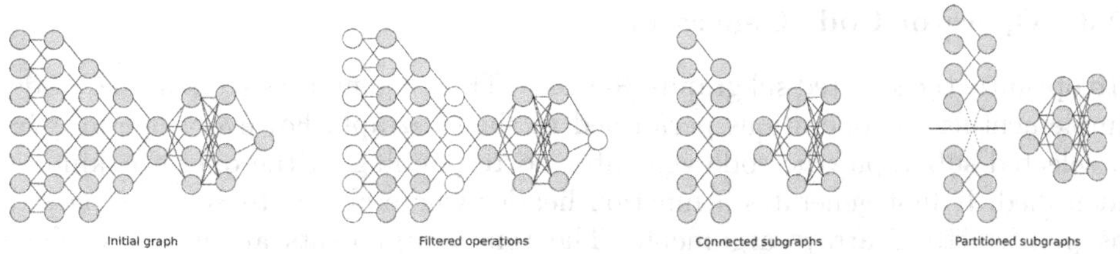

Fig. 2. Connected subgraphs of supported operations are computed first, before partitioning the large subgraphs into smaller ones to improve the optimization scalability.

subgraphs. While this number can be quite large, the number of nodes in current DCNNs is typically larger. In order to ensure that the optimization remains tractable, R-Stream·TF pre-processes the input graph, extracting subgraphs that are optimized independently from each other.

Partitioning operator graphs in order to expose better optimization opportunities and maintain scalability (i.e., tractable optimization times) has been studied many times over, from instruction set synthesis [3] to streaming graphs (with e.g., [1,11]). Optimality of subgraphs is typically defined by the amount of computation and data reuse within the subgraph, and the amount (and weight) of resulting in- and out-edges. In parallel computing frameworks, grain of parallelism and load balancing are also important optimality criteria.

The most impactful constraints are similar in our case. Additionally, code generators may not be available for some operators, which should then not be included in a subgraph to optimize. While we plan to implement more sophisticated subgraph selection algorithms in the future, we meet the proof-of-concept objective of this paper using a simple two-step approach. First, we identify connected subgraphs in the overall computation graph that are exclusively made of operations for which a code generator is available. Second, the connected subgraphs are partitioned when they are estimated to be too large for the optimizer. These steps are illustrated in Fig. 2. The second step is expressed as a balanced k-way partitioning problem, where the objective is to minimize the number of graph edges between two partitions. Edges in the computation graph represent tensors on which the operations are performed. While R-Stream is free to change the data layout in the tensors *within* partitions, transforming the layout of tensors used across several partitions is illegal. Thus, by minimizing the number of edges between the partitions, R-Stream·TF increases data layout optimization opportunities for R-Stream, including array contraction, expansion, and spatial locality optimizations.

R-Stream works from C code, which is generated as the next phase of the R-Stream·TF() optimization process.

2.3 Operator Code Generators

To optimize the selected subgraphs, R-Stream·TF first generates sequential C code implementing the operations performed in the subgraph. For every operator in a selected subgraph, the code generator corresponding to the operator kind is identified. It first generates a function header where all the tensors are passed as pointers to C arrays arguments. The tensor arguments are monomorphic, meaning that if several types are allowed in the TensorFlow graph, they will result in different functions being generated. The body of the generated function implements the operator semantics, generally as a set of loop nests.

2.4 Subgraph Code Generator

Once a function is generated for every operator of a selected subgraph, a subgraph function is also generated. The subgraph function calls the individual subgraph operator functions, materializing the actual subgraph computation. R-Stream·TF currently restricts the subgraphs to be acyclic, simplifying the generation of subgraph functions. Exploiting the acyclic property, the operators in the subgraph are topologically sorted and a sequence of calls to the corresponding operator C function is generated as the subgraph function body. The process is illustrated in Fig. 4. Similarly to the operator functions, the subgraph function accepts as its inputs a pointer to a C array for every tensor used in the computation.

The subgraph function is marked as being a region of interest for R-Stream using a pragma directive. R-Stream is also instructed to inline all the operator functions, which is easily done since their definitions are generated in the same compilation unit. The operator functions along with the subgraph functions of every selected subgraph are generated using the same process and finally sent to R-Stream to be optimized.

2.5 R-Stream Optimization

Using the polyhedral model, R-Stream infers the data dependencies of the input program from its C form. Based on the exact dependence information, R-Stream computes a new schedule for the program statements. The schedule can be seen as a combination of loop fusion, fission, skewing, interchange, and reversal. The scheduler used in R-Stream tries to maximize parallelism while optimizing locality, contiguity, vectorization, and data layout [17,19]. After scheduling, R-Stream performs other important non-affine transformations such as tiling, along with the generation of explicit memory (e.g. scratchpad, virtual scratchpad) management and communication (e.g. DMA) instructions. The optimizations that R-Stream performs are all parameterized by a model of

```
static inline void add1(
  const float (*t_in0)[256],
  const float (*t_in1)[256],
  float (*t_out0)[256])
{
  for (int i = 0; i < 256; ++i) {
    for (int j = 0; j < 256; ++j) {
      t_out0[i][j] = t_in0[i][j] +
        t_in1[i][j];
    }
  }
}

static inline void add2(
  const int (*t_in0),
  const int (*t_in1)[1024],
  int (*t_out0)[1024])
{
  for (int i = 0; i < 1024; ++i) {
    for (int j = 0; j < 1024; ++j) {
      t_out0[i][j] = t_in0[j] +
        t_in1[i][j];
    }
  }
}

static inline void add3(
  const double (*t_in0),
  const double (*t_in1),
  double (*t_out0)[512])
{
  for (int i = 0; i < 512; ++i) {
    for (int j = 0; j < 512; ++j) {
      t_out0[i][j] = t_in0[j] + *t_in1;
    }
  }
}
```

Fig. 3. Three specializations of the element-wise addition. The generated functions have specific data types, data sizes, and broadcasting even though the TensorFlow operator is the same.

the target platform encoded in an XML hierarchical/heterogeneous architecture machine modeling description language. R-Stream then generates output C using "unparsing" techniques that conform to idioms appreciated by downstream or "backend" compilers (e.g., gcc, icc); this enables further backend optimizations such as typical scalar optimizations and the use of vector opcodes.

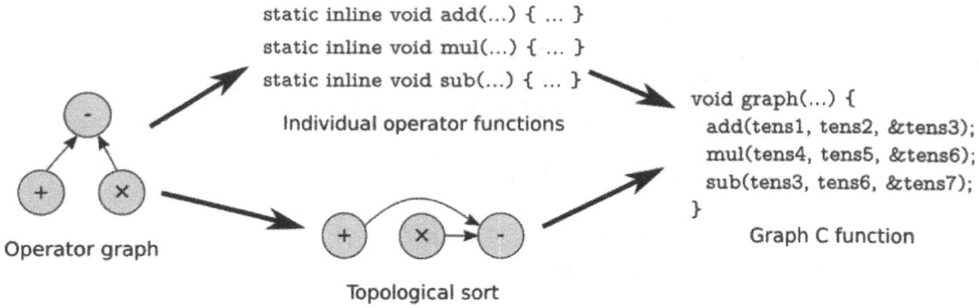

Fig. 4. Subgraph C code generation.

Tensor computing is an excellent match to the polyhedral model.[1] The loop extents and access functions are affine. Working on tensors rather than matrices results in deeper loop nests presents optimization challenges beyond the classical techniques used by library writers and beyond the reach of non-polyhedral classical loop optimizers, but which are very much in scope of a modern polyhedral compiler such as R-Stream.

While it would be straightforward to engineer a translator to go directly from TensorFlow IR to a polyhedral IR (in the case of R-Stream, the Generalized Dependence Graph (GDG)), we chose for this initial prototype the simple path of going through C. The code generators implemented in R-Stream·TF generate C code specifically targeted at the polyhedral model. The generators may produce visually non-intuitive code for some operators, but the code is specifically structured to be easily and immediately raised to the polyhedral representation. In some sense, R-Stream·TF uses a subset of C as an intermediate representation to communicate TensorFlow computations to polyhedral compilers. The code generator also benefit from extensions of the polyhedral model implemented in R-Stream to support more operators. For instance, R-Stream supports data-dependent conditions, which allows operators such as the rectifier activation function to be supported.

[1] Raising generic C codes into a polyhedral representation can be a complex problem, when programmers or library writers have made manual optimizations (e.g., parallelization, tiling, ...) based on domain knowledge which cannot be easily inferred from their program source. Such manual optimizations are often not performance portable (or portable at all) to new platforms, thus their action of performing manual optimization "bakes the code" to that one original target. To re-optimize to a new architecture through the polyhedral model, such manual optimizations often have to be reverted to produce an efficient polyhedral representation of the program. Unknown aliasing and overflowing arithmetic are among the challenges of such "unbaking." With modern compiler tools like R-Stream now available, it would a much more sustainable practice for programmers to express their code originally in a high-level, domain-specific manner.

2.6 TensorFlow Operator

TensorFlow exposes a public C++ API to specify custom operations. R-Stream·TF generates the code implementing the API for every subgraph, in effect generating a custom optimized TensorFlow operator for every selected subgraph.

The generated TensorFlow operator declares itself to the framework, detailing the expected inputs and outputs for the custom operator. The operator also checks and validates its inputs. Although this is not required, generating such guards helps in debugging R-Stream·TF itself and ensures that the user does not change the input specification by transforming the graph after it has been optimized. Finally, the operator performs the required memory allocations for the tensors identified as being temporary or output tensors. Temporary tensors are tensors that do not exist before the operation is run but do not need to be maintained in memory after the tensor execution. Output tensors are created by the operation but are consumed later by other operations in the graph. Both temporary and output tensors are allocated before starting the computation and a pointer to the raw tensor data content is acquired and transmitted to the code optimized by R-Stream. R-Stream·TF reuses tensors as much as possible to limit the number of tensors required at any time during the optimized subgraph execution.

All the custom operators generated by R-Stream·TF are compiled into a shared library. Because the tool implements the TensorFlow API, the generated library can be easily loaded by calling a standard TensorFlow function.

As a final step, R-Stream·TF edits the graph structure by removing the original subgraphs and replacing them by the optimized custom operators. The result is generated as a standard protobuf file which can also be loaded in TensorFlow using the standard API.

2.7 Leveraging Broadcast

TensorFlow automatically expands the input tensors to match the largest one in several operations. This expansion is called *broadcasting* in the TensorFlow terminology and consists of inflating a tensor by duplicating it. Broadcasting is a convenient flexibility allowed by the framework to help the user express operations such as an element-wise addition with a scalar using the general tensor-based element-wise addition operator. R-Stream·TF generates operator functions that account for broadcasting without explicitly copying the data. For instance, an element-wise tensor addition can be generated as an addition with a scalar to match the broadcasting semantics. Broadcasting is one of the several specializations performed when generating the operator code. As illustrated in Fig. 3, the different data types, data sizes, and broadcasting can result in many different variants of the operator functions, which would not be tractable if the code were written by hand but can be easily managed when the code is generated automatically.

3 Experiments

We implemented a prototype of R-Stream·TF and used it to evaluate the potential outcome of our approach. For the sake of simplicity and because of time constraints, our prototype is focused on common x86 processors. The system could benefit from further improvements to support accelerators and other architectures but we left these extensions for future work. In our experiments, we evaluate R-Stream·TF by running it on popular deep neural networks. The time required to perform an inference of the optimized graph has been measured and compared when using different optimizers as well as the default TensorFlow setup.

We first evaluate R-Stream·TF when calling no optimizer to parallelize and optimize the code generated. The goal of this measurement is to determine what performance level can be reached if the graph operators are naively implemented, using their textbook definitions. This is typically the performance that would be reached by an inexperienced developer when porting TensorFlow to a new platform. Next, we evaluate R-Stream·TF with several polyhedral compilers, allowing us to better estimate the range of performance that can be reached by this class of tools and how performance is impacted by the capabilities of each optimizer. Finally, we compare R-Stream·TF to the standard TensorFlow performance. TensorFlow defers the operation optimization to the Eigen library, a collection of highly-optimized kernels. Because a library cannot implement optimized versions of any combination of kernels, the Eigen library is limited to some individual kernels and a few common combinations. On the other hand, the library provides extremely well-optimized implementations for the supported kernels. Hence, the performance reached by TensorFlow can be considered as that of a well-optimized implementation, even though not all the optimizations opportunities are exploited. In order to optimize the graph computations further, TensorFlow also provides XLA, a compiler exploiting operation fusion to improve the performance of the computations. Despite all our efforts, we were not able to have XLA to produce correct results with our experimental setup in a reasonable time, which ruled it out of evaluation.

We ran the experiments on a standard Ubuntu 16.04 system with an Intel Core i7-4600U processor, using the standard binary package of TensorFlow in version 1.2.1. We evaluated R-Stream·TF in different configurations using 3 popular deep learning graphs: Inception versions 3 and 4, and SqueezeDet. We froze the Inception graphs using the learned weights provided by Google, emulating a production-ready setup. The graphs were evaluated when inferring the sample image of Admiral G. Hopper provided with TensorFlow. This image choice allowed us to guarantee the correctness of our setup, since the expected output of the graphs has been published for this input image. Similarly, we used weights provided with SqueezeDet as well as an example image from the KITTI dataset for which the expected result is published. For comparison, we also used PPCG version 0.07 plus all the commits performed in the master branch until June 19, 2017. PPCG was run using the following options: "`--target=c --openmp --tile`". We also evaluated Polly, as provided in LLVM 5.0, as a polyhedral optimizer for the code generated by R-Stream·TF. Polly was run using the following Clang options: "`-mllvm -polly -mllvm -polly-parallel -mllvm -polly-vectorizer=stripmine`".

In the evaluated implementation of R-Stream·TF, the element-wise addition, subtraction, and multiplication, convolutions, and rectifying linear units were optimized. R-Stream·TF can optimize only operations for which a code generator is available and we limited our implementation effort to these common operations. The system can easily be extended with more operations as needed. The effort required to add a new operation is a matter of hours for a single developer, and this can then be used for any input network on any target.

The measured execution times of one inference on the experimental platform are presented in Figs. 5, 6 and 7 for different optimization backends. The execution time of the naive code generated by R-Stream·TF before applying any optimizer corresponds to the "Unoptimized" entry in the figures. The open-source PPCG polyhedral compiler was used to optimize the code generated by R-Stream·TF and is shown as the "PPCG" entry in the figures. Similarly, the code optimized by Polly is shown as "LLVM/Polly" and "R-Stream" is used to represent the entries where R-Stream is used to optimize the code generated by R-Stream·TF. Finally, the "TensorFlow" entry represents the reference execution time using the hand-optimized Eigen library provided with TensorFlow.

The results presented in Figs. 5, 6 and 7 show that a polyhedral compiler can reach a performance level close to that achieved using highly optimized libraries. The execution time reached by the R-Stream optimized code, "R-Stream" in the figures, is significantly lower than that of the unoptimized version, emphasizing

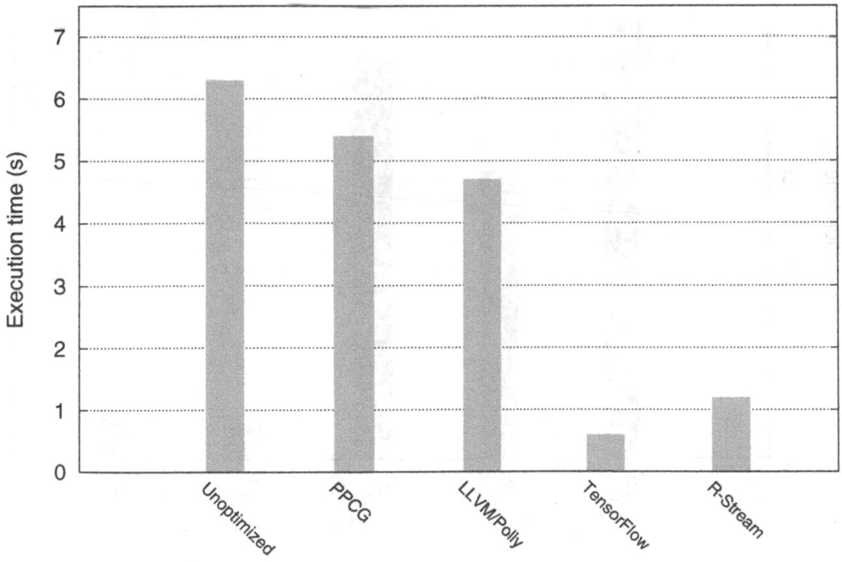

Fig. 5. Execution time of an inference of Inception 3 using different optimization backends.

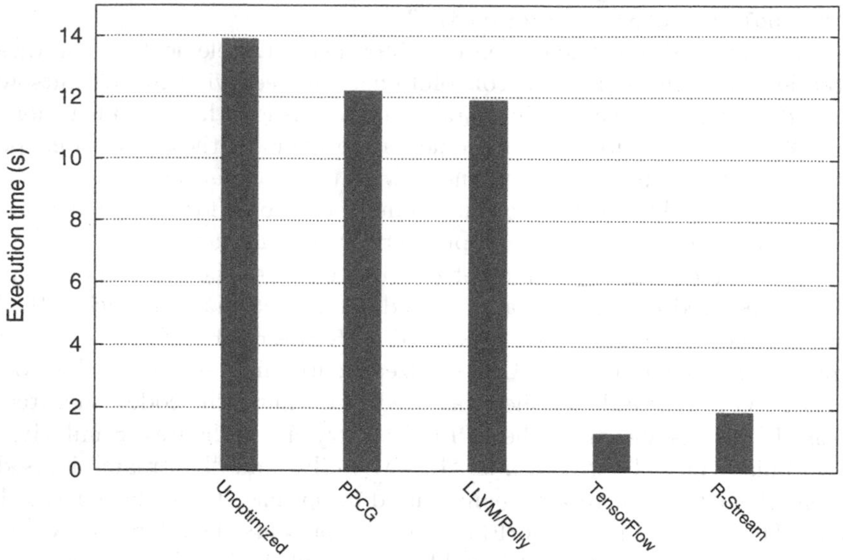

Fig. 6. Execution time of an inference of Inception 4 using different optimization backends.

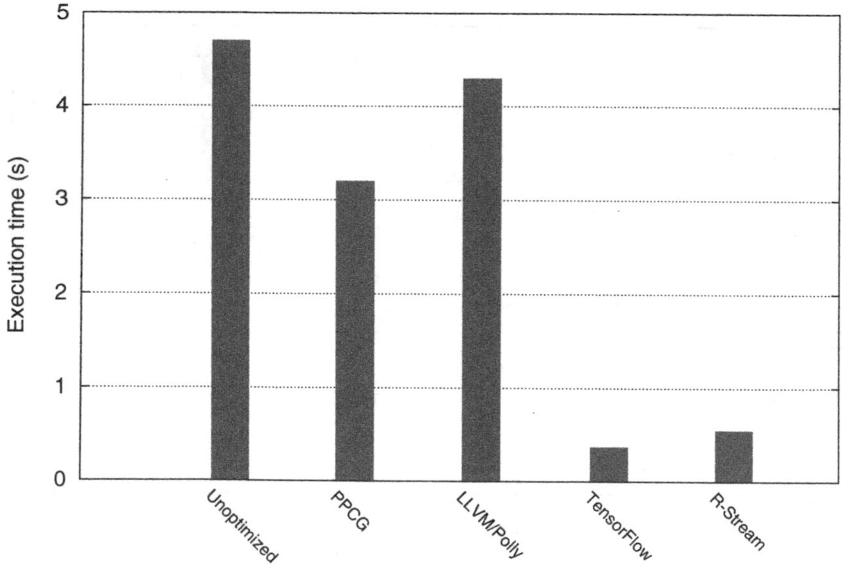

Fig. 7. Execution time of an inference of SqueezeDet using different optimization backends.

the optimization power of the polyhedral compiler. Specifically, R-Stream generates code running about 5× faster in Inception v3, 7× faster in Inception v4, and 12× faster in SqueezeDet, a substantial achievement considering that the experimental platform is a modest dual-core processor. Despite this achievement, the optimized subgraphs still suffer from a 2× slowdown in Inception v3 to a 50% slowdown in SqueezeDet compared to the hand-optimized "TensorFlow" implementation, exposing optimization opportunities currently not exploited by R-Stream. The measured slowdown should be contrasted with the amount of human effort required to produce both codes. In the case of the TensorFlow reference, a significant amount of effort had to be invested to produce the highly optimized libraries used by TensorFlow. Such optimizations are not only complicated to produce and debug, even for expert developers, but they are also not portable, even across different processors of the same family. When a new platform needs to be supported, a new effort has to be initiated by experts, often using different techniques than those used for the other supported platforms. On the other hand, the optimization performed by R-Stream was achieved with no human intervention in a few minutes. Such extreme productivity improvement and the resulting performance level indicate that R-Stream·TF is a useful tool for quickly generating highly optimized implementations of TensorFlow. The optimized code generated by R-Stream·TF can be used as-is on platforms for which no optimized implementations of the kernel libraries used by TensorFlow are available. It can also provide an optimized baseline implementation of TensorFlow which can be progressively replaced by hand-optimized kernels when needed and as the resources become available to perform those optimizations.

All the code optimizations available in R-Stream are enabled when it is used as the optimizer of R-Stream·TF. Even though the individual contribution of each compiler transformation is hard to assess from the optimized code generated, we observed that automatic parallelization and vectorization were the primary contributors to performance. Other optimizations such as loop fusion and code generation optimizations also contribute to the resulting performance improvements.

From the measured execution times, it is also clear that not all the polyhedral optimizers reach the same level of performance. We evaluated three different polyhedral optimizers considered as robust optimizers but the achieved performance varied considerably across optimizers during our experiments. The different levels of performance are due to the different heuristics and designs employed in the tools. For instance, PPCG and Polly both use the scheduling algorithm implemented in the ISL library [25]. On the other hand, R-Stream uses the JPLCVD scheduler [5,17], which exploits a different set of heuristics and techniques to determine the best schedule for a program. Similarly, R-Stream is able to automatically determine relevant tile sizes for the loop nests, while PPCG cannot and falls back to default tile sizes in the absence of further instructions. Such different designs result in different optimization decisions and explain the variation in the performance reached by the various optimizers.

4 Enabled Experiments/Work

With R-Stream·TF many new experiments and future developments are enabled, including:

- Expansion of the set of TensorFlow operators supported.
- Greater exploration of subgraph formation heuristics. R-Stream includes special features for greatly improving the scalability of polyhedral optimization, which may enable subgraphs of large size to be handled, and for more complex architecture targets to be addressed.
- A comparison with XLA and a deeper investigation of the gap with hand code.
- Expansion to additional deep-learning frameworks (Caffe, etc.)
- Addressing the opportunities of sparsity. R-Stream has some ability to optimize code working on sparse matrices and tensors.
- Generating optimized code for training.
- Exploitation of R-Stream's ability to generate code for distributed architectures, GPUs and event-driven task (EDT) dataflow runtimes.
- Application of R-Stream to model and generate code for specialized deep-learning architectures.
- Just-in-time compilation improvements and direct-to-GDG translation.

5 Related Work

Polyhedral optimizations are integrated in most of the mainstream compilers to perform advanced code transformations and improve execution time. For instance, Graphite [21] is a polyhedral optimizer in GCC and Polly [13] is the counterpart for LLVM. Independent polyhedral compilers also exist, though most of them are research projects and tend to become unsupported quickly. Notable polyhedral compilers still maintained are Pluto [7] and PPCG [26]. Most of the polyhedral tools are currently backed by the ISL library [24]. R-Stream [19] is a commercially supported polyhedral compiler with additional capabilities and supported platforms. R-Stream·TF is naturally based on R-Stream but can exploit any optimizer, polyhedral or not, that accepts C files as its input. This flexibility is demonstrated in the experimental section.

R-Stream·TF is essentially a polyhedral compiler for a domain specific language: TensorFlow graphs. Polyhedral optimizers based on DSLs have already been proposed for domains where regular data structures and computations are common [4,20]. R-Stream·TF is however, to the best of our knowledge, the first attempt at performing automatic polyhedral optimizations on neural network computations.

There is currently intense activity around software frameworks oriented towards neural network computations. The high interest in this domain is reflected in the numerous frameworks available, most of them backed by significant companies or organizations. Caffe [15], the Cognitive Toolkit (CNTK) [27],

Torch [10], Theano [6], and TensorFlow [2] are among the most popular frameworks. Interestingly, while all these frameworks compete against each other by providing roughly the same set of capabilities, they are all based on the same design, with an operation graph as their core concept. Such uniformity across all the platforms is doubly beneficial to our approach. First, the ecosystem of frameworks is still unsettled and it is unlikely that all the competing approaches will be maintained in the future. However, since all the popular frameworks are based on the same design, it is likely that the approach implemented in R-Stream·TF will remain relevant. Second, because the frameworks share similar designs, R-Stream·TF could be easily ported to another framework, extending its applicability beyond the sole TensorFlow framework.

Neural network software frameworks are sometimes able to optimize the computation graphs in a holistic way, similarly to what is done in R-Stream·TF. Relevant examples include NNVM in MXNET [8], Intel Nervana Graph, and, closer to our work, the XLA compiler of TensorFlow. The most advanced optimizations available in these tools propagate the constants in the graph, reduce memory usage, and fuse operators. TensorFlow provides a dedicated optimizer, XLA, performing ahead-of-time and JIT optimizations on the graph. XLA relates to R-Stream·TF since both tools have the same goals: specializing the graph code to the specific operation parameters and hardware platform in order to improve the computation performance. However, R-Stream·TF exploits the polyhedral model and all the associated optimization techniques to optimize the computation instead of ad-hoc optimizations specifically designed for the graphs. Using the polyhedral model generalizes the representation of the graph operations present in TensorFlow and significantly extends the set of optimizations that can be performed to the graphs.

6 Conclusion

R-Stream·TF exploits the polyhedral model to optimize TensorFlow computations. The optimizations are performed by an existing polyhedral compiler specifically for a graph and a target architecture and without human intervention. During its evaluation, R-Stream·TF reached performance levels close to that of the hand-optimized code provided with TensorFlow for modern x86_64 processors. Such ability to automatically produce highly-optimized code makes R-Stream·TF an adequate tool for generating an optimized baseline implementation for TensorFlow computations on a new architecture.

Acknowledgment. This research was developed with funding from the Defense Advanced Research Projects Agency (DARPA). The views and conclusions contained in this document are those of the authors and should not be interpreted as representing the official policies, either expressly or implied, of the Defense Advanced Research Projects Agency or the U.S. Government. This document was cleared by DARPA on August 23, 2017. Distribution Statement "A" (Approved for Public Release, Distribution Unlimited).

References

1. Khandekar, R., et al.: COLA: optimizing stream processing applications via graph partitioning. In: Bacon, J.M., Cooper, B.F. (eds.) Middleware 2009. LNCS, vol. 5896, pp. 308–327. Springer, Heidelberg (2009). https://doi.org/10.1007/978-3-642-10445-9_16
2. Abadi, M., et al.: Tensorflow: large-scale machine learning on heterogeneous distributed systems (2015). http://download.tensorflow.org/paper/whitepaper2015.pdf
3. Atasu, K., Pozzi, L., Ienne, P.: Automatic application-specific instruction-set extensions under microarchitectural constraints. In: Proceedings of the 40th Annual Design Automation Conference, pp. 256–261. ACM (2003)
4. Baghdadi, R., et al.: PENCIL: a platform-neutral compute intermediate language for accelerator programming. In: Parallel Architectures and Compilation Techniques (PACT), San Francisco, CA, USA (2015). https://hal.archives-ouvertes.fr/hal-01257236
5. Bastoul, C., et al.: System, methods and apparatus for program optimization for multi-threaded processor architectures, April 2010
6. Bergstra, J., et al.: Theano: a CPU and GPU math compiler in Python (2011)
7. Bondhugula, U., Baskaran, M., Krishnamoorthy, S., Ramanujam, J., Rountev, A., Sadayappan, P.: Automatic transformations for communication-minimized parallelization and locality optimization in the polyhedral model. In: Hendren, L. (ed.) CC 2008. LNCS, vol. 4959, pp. 132–146. Springer, Heidelberg (2008). https://doi.org/10.1007/978-3-540-78791-4_9
8. Chen, T., et al.: MXNet: a flexible and efficient machine learning library for heterogeneous distributed systems. CoRR abs/1512.01274 (2015). http://arxiv.org/abs/1512.01274
9. Clauss, P., Meister, B.: Automatic memory layout transformation to optimize spatial locality in parameterized loop nests. ACM SIGARCH Comput. Archit. News **28**(1), 11–19 (2000)
10. Collobert, R., Kavukcuoglu, K., Farabet, C.: Torch7: a matlab-like environment for machine learning. In: BigLearn, NIPS Workshop No. EPFL-CONF-192376 (2011)
11. Dayarathna, M., Suzumura, T.: Automatic optimization of stream programs via source program operator graph transformations. Distrib. Parallel Databases **31**(4), 543–599 (2013). https://doi.org/10.1007/s10619-013-7130-x
12. Feautrier, P.: Some efficient solutions to the affine scheduling problem. Part I. One-dimensional time. Int. J. Parallel Program. **21**(5), 313–348 (1992). citeseer.ist.psu.edu/feautrier92some.html
13. Grosser, T., Groesslinger, A., Lengauer, C.: Polly-performing polyhedral optimizations on a low-level intermediate representation. Parallel Process. Lett. **22**(04), 1250010 (2012)
14. Irigoin, F., Triolet, R.: Supernode partitioning. In: Proceedings of the 15th ACM SIGPLAN-SIGACT Symposium on Principles of programming languages, pp. 319–329. ACM Press, New York, January 1988
15. Jia, Y., et al.: Caffe: convolutional architecture for fast feature embedding (2014)
16. LeCun, Y., Bottou, L., Bengio, Y., Haffner, P.: Gradient-based learning applied to document recognition. Proc. IEEE **86**(11), 2278–2324 (1998)
17. Lethin, R.A., Leung, A.K., Meister, B.J., Vasilache, N.T.: Methods and apparatus for joint parallelism and locality optimization in source code compilation, September 2009

18. Meister, B., Baskaran, M.M., Pradelle, B., Henretty, T., Lethin, R.: Efficient compilation to event-driven task programs. CoRR abs/1601.05458 (2016). http://arxiv.org/abs/1601.05458
19. Meister, B., Vasilache, N., Wohlford, D., Baskaran, M.M., Leung, A., Lethin, R.: R-stream compiler. In: Padua, D. (ed.) Encyclopedia of Parallel Computing, pp. 1756–1765. Springer, Boston (2011). https://doi.org/10.1007/978-0-387-09766-4
20. Meister, B., et al.: SANE: an array language for sensor applications. In: Proceedings of a Workshop on Domain-Specific Languages and High-Level Frameworks for High Performance Computing, Salt Lake City, UT, USA, November 16 2012
21. Pop, S., et al.: GRAPHITE: loop optimizations based on the polyhedral model for GCC. In: Proceedings of the 4th GCC Developper's Summit, pp. 179–198. Ottawa, Canada, June 2006
22. Pradelle, B., Meister, B., Baskaran, M.M., Konstantinidis, A., Henretty, T., Lethin, R.: Scalable hierarchical polyhedral compilation. In: International Conference on Parallel Processing (ICPP) (2016)
23. Vasilache, N., et al.: A tale of three runtimes. arXiv:1409.1914
24. Verdoolaege, S.: *isl*: an integer set library for the polyhedral model. In: Proceedings of the Third international congress conference on Mathematical software (ICMS 2010), pp. 299–302. ACM Press (2010)
25. Verdoolaege, S., Janssens, G.: Scheduling for PPCG. Technical report, Department of Computer Science, KU Leuven (2017)
26. Verdoolaege, S., Juega, J.C., Cohen, A., Gómez, J.I., Tenllado, C., Catthoor, F.: Polyhedral parallel code generation for CUDA. ACM Trans. Archit. Code Optim. **9**(4), 54:1–54:23 (2013)
27. Yu, D., Yao, K., Zhang, Y.: The computational network toolkit [best of the web]. IEEE Signal Process. Mag. **32**(6), 123–126 (2015)

CAASCADE: A System for Static Analysis of HPC Software Application Portfolios

M. Graham Lopez[1(✉)], Oscar Hernandez[1], Reuben D. Budiardja[2], and Jack C. Wells[2]

[1] Computer Science and Mathematics Division, Oak Ridge National Laboratory, Oak Ridge, TN 37831, USA
{lopezmg,oscar}@ornl.gov

[2] National Center for Computational Sciences, Oak Ridge National Laboratory, Oak Ridge, TN 37831, USA
{reubendb,wellscj}@ornl.gov

Abstract. With the increasing complexity of upcoming HPC systems, so-called "co-design" efforts to develop the hardware and applications in concert for these systems also become more challenging. It is currently difficult to gather information about the usage of programming model features, libraries, and data structure considerations in a quantitative way across a variety of applications, and this information is needed to prioritize development efforts in systems software and hardware optimizations. In this paper we propose CAASCADE, a system that can harvest this information in an automatic way in production HPC environments, and we show some early results from a prototype of the system based on GNU compilers and a MySQL database.

1 Introduction

Heterogeneous architectures and complex system design have been consistent challenges for the high-performance computing (HPC) applications community. For example, in the ongoing CORAL project [4] and Exascale Computing Project (ECP) [10], HPC researchers, U.S. Department of Energy computing facilities,

---

This manuscript has been authored by UT-Battelle, LLC under Contract No. DE-AC05-00OR22725 with the U.S. Department of Energy. The United States Government retains and the publisher, by accepting the article for publication, acknowledges that the United States Government retains a non-exclusive, paid-up, irrevocable, world-wide license to publish or reproduce the published form of this manuscript, or allow others to do so, for United States Government purposes. The Department of Energy will provide public access to these results of federally sponsored research in accordance with the DOE Public Access Plan (http://energy.gov/downloads/doe-public-access-plan). This paper is authored by an employee(s) of the United States Government and is in the public domain. Non-exclusive copying or redistribution is allowed, provided that the article citation is given and the authors and agency are clearly identified as its source.

© Springer Nature Switzerland AG 2019
A. Bhatele et al. (Eds.): ESPT/VPA 2017/2018, LNCS 11027, pp. 90–104, 2019.
https://doi.org/10.1007/978-3-030-17872-7_6

and system builders are engaged in designing the system software layers to tightly couple with both low-level hardware and high-level applications. In order to better inform such efforts, often referred to as "co-design," we have to answer specific questions about how applications are using current HPC architectures with detailed, quantitative data as evidence.

Currently in the HPC community, we have insufficient ways to know in quantitative detail which system software features are required by user applications; we most often rely on single-use, labor-intensive efforts [33], "institutional knowledge", or written survey responses and anecdotal input from developers [15]. This knowledge is tethered to the developers who have intimate knowledge of the codes, and current tools are used on a subset of applications providing either very narrow, application-specific views of the source code and performance traits that are not well-suited for inter-application reasoning or broad summaries that lose the detail needed for research and system design. This absence of quantitative application information at HPC centers leads to intuition-based engineering and is increasingly identified as an HPC community challenge with calls for structured responses emerging within community forums [31].

There are simple questions about the distribution of HPC applications that we cannot answer quickly and accurately in production application environments, like which programming language features, parallelization methods, libraries, and communication APIs are used commonly across HPC applications. These questions become even more urgent for the documentation of application requirements for next generation HPC systems, the planning of long-term computer science research programs to fill capability gaps, and in the execution of scientific applications readiness programs that prepare codes to accomplish large-scale science on upcoming systems. Program characteristics such as data structures layouts, data access patterns, type of parallelism used, profitable compiler optimizations and runtime information, need to be captured in a systematic and transparent way to the user, so that conclusions can be made at an HPC center-wide level.

To provide this currently unavailable information, we propose a method to automate the collection of application program characteristics from compiler-based tools and enable knowledge discovery and feature detection from this data. Since compilers know everything that is necessary about a source code to lower it to a resulting executable on a given architecture, we are working to create a curated database to provide convenient access to information harvested directly from compiler intermediate representations to enable data analytics techniques on application source code to inform ongoing HPC research and co-design activities. These cross-application analyses will lead to a quantitative understanding of the overall HPC application landscape and where high-value opportunities lie for development of system software and tools.

Having the ability to answer the questions similar to those above will enable evidence-based support for the HPC research community, standards committees, and system vendors. Exploring these issues in depth will allow researchers to gain continued and deeper insights into these issues as we co-design applications with upcoming exascale software and hardware architectures as part of ECP. Our community will be better equipped to develop tools, inform hardware development and standards committees, and understand HPC science application needs. Designing HPC systems and vendor engagement will be facilitated by a complete and detailed understanding of real application practices and requirements across the breadth of HPC applications.

In order for this knowledge to be useful in the near and longer-term future, it needs to be both accurately harvested with reliable tools, curated for data quality, and made easily accessible to a variety of users. Rather than relying on one-off research and limited-use implementations, our approach uses as a reference implementation industry-standard tools that are already widely used on HPC platforms and can handle the complexities of all full HPC applications rather than miniapps or only specific applications, while being totally transparent from the user. The GNU Compiler Collection (GCC) is today able to compile the in-production version of most current HPC codes, and it supports both the OpenMP and OpenACC programming models. As the Clang and Flang LLVM front-ends continue to mature on upcoming systems and become adopted by production HPC application users, we envision porting our analysis tools to that toolchain as well. Finally, we have worked with PGI to implement this data extraction in their compiler suite, with the `-Msummary` flag made available in the PGI 17.7 release [7]. We hope to engage with other HPC compiler vendors in the near future and come up with defacto specifications for parallel program static analysis information.

2 Background and Related Work

Various tools have been developed to capture program information, but they are not commonly used for application data collection on production systems because they are either not fully automated (e.g. transparent to the user), have high barriers to entry for users, not able to handle full production application codebases, require significant user intervention (e.g. code restructuring, working with tools experts), and/or they are not available on all platforms.

OpenAnalysis [43] was an attempt to create a database of program analysis that can be reused across compilers or tools. It relied on Open64 [24] and ROSE [36] compiler components, but neither of these are widely used by production applications across HPC centers. The TAU Program Database Toolkit [37] captures program structure and stores it in the PDB format which is used for instrumenting the source code. However, this requires adding extra steps in the build system and parsing the application with PBT front-ends that may require program refactoring. The HPCToolkit [12] hpcstruct component gathers some program traits from the binaries of applications by trying to reconstruct specific constructs like loop nests, however it cannot detect the higher level features of languages due to information loss during lowering.

There have been compiler-based tools with advanced analysis capabilities. Tools such as ROSE [46], Hercules [35], TSF [21] and RTalk [25] store program analysis information with the goal of applying transformation-based recipes that contain static or run-time information of the code. CHiLL, together with Active Harmony [45] focus on parameter selection and compiler heuristics for auto-tuning. The Klonos [26] tool extracts sequences of operators from the intermediate representation of compilers to find similarity between the codes, but the resulting information is difficult to relate back to the source code beyond the procedure functionality. These tools either do not cover the full spectrum of HPC languages or are maintained as research tools not intended to be used in production, and their goal is not to be totally transparent from the user, as they are meant to interact with the user.

The Collective Tuning project [30] aims to create a database of program structure features and find compiler optimizations for performance, power, and code size. The main goal of the now deprecated [8] GCC plugin-based MILEPOST project from cTuning was to collect program features for the purpose of feeding these back to the compiler optimizer, instead of being made understandable for human researcher consumption. However, it was the efforts of cTuning's Interactive Compilation Interface [6] project that contributed to GCC's plugin infrastructure that we now use for CAASCADE.

Dehydra [1] and Treehydra [2] are analysis plugins that expose different GCC intermediate representations intended for simple analyses and "semantic grep" applications. Unfortunately, they have only limited Fortran90 support, and the output hides important application information. Pliny [27] is a project that focuses on detecting and fixing errors in programs, as well as synthesizing reliable code from high-level specifications. It relies on mining information and statistical information and is still in the early research stage and currently doesn't support Fortran. Finally, tools such as XALT/ALTD [13,22], PerfTrack [34], Oxbow/-PADS [41], IPM [29], and HPC system scheduling information provide system environment, linkage information (e.g. for library detection) runtime and performance information that is complementary to application source code features. As discussed below, we intend for CAASCADE to interface closely with these related sources of application information.

3 Design and Methods

The core of CAASCADE consists of: the compiler-based static analysis and the data storage and analytics backend. Information about various aspects of the application source code is harvested directly from the compiler's intermediate representations (IR) and converted into a format that can be ingested into a SQL database or analytic engines such as Apache Spark [47]. CAASCADE produces program information for each compilation unit and inserts the information in the object file. At link time, it then retrieves the program information from every object file and stores this information in the database. A symbol identifier is inserted in the application executable binary to identify it with the program information stored in the database.

3.1 GNU Compiler Plugin Implementation

To prototype the static application analysis, we used the built-in plugin infrastructure [5] from the GNU Compiler Collection (GCC) to extract information directly from the compiler's IR and data structures. There are about thirty plugin callback hooks to trigger plugin execution, that span locations from just before a new translation unit pass is started to the majority of these locations being among the various lowering and optimization passes.

For gfortran, GNU doesn't currently provide any plugin callback in the Fortran front-end. We found it easiest to add our own call-back to the gfortran front-end that triggers right after the processing of a translation unit is completed (after parsing but before any lowering). For the C/C++ front-end as well, we added our own hook into the g++ front-end right after a translation unit has been finalized, and piggy-back onto the translation-unit tree dumper (enabled with the `-fdump-translation-unit` flag to g++), where we reuse the internal tree traversal engine, but insert our own data extraction and processing routines.

By placing our plugin execution carefully within the GCC front-ends, we know that all of the parsing and abstract syntax tree (AST) building has been completed, but lowering has not yet taken place. This approach will also help us store the compiler's internal data structures to communicate across multiple levels of intermediate representation and relate the analysis back to the source code. Currently, we primarily target the AST level IR as it is most directly relatable to the original user-written source code. However, our goal is to enable the extraction of program information and analysis from multiple levels of the intermediate representation while mapping them to the source code.

High-Level Languages. Each translation unit is characterized by the invocation of a GCC language front-end, so to keep track of the proportion of each high-level language being used in an application, we can accumulate statistics about executable statements and data declarations within each translation unit. By working at the AST level, it is possible to eliminate inconsistencies such as comments, whitespace, bracket placement, or line-continuations. Additionally, based on the features that we see in executable statements or declarations and classifying them according to the language standard needed to support those features, we can determine the proportion of each language standard being used and the coverage across those standards. Table 1 shows the information the compiler is collecting about the source code for Fortran applications.

In addition to the metrics above, the plugins collect information regarding variable and data structure information from the application; a list of these metrics is shown in Table 2.

Parallelization Methods. Our plugins understand directives from both OpenMP [39] and OpenACC [42], as well as Message Passing Interface (MPI) [38] library calls. This allows us to easily detect when we are within a parallel directive's lexical extent, and which variables and types are being used in inter-node communication via MPI or directive `data` clauses for transfers between host and discrete accelerator memories. As with the high-level languages, we can also detect the proportion and coverage of each standard being used, based here on matching the directives or calls that are present in the code with those in the specification versions. For understanding directives, we depend on the compiler's native support and so are constrained to versions of OpenMP and OpenACC that have been implemented in GCC. To handle MPI, we treat it as any other library (as discussed below). Table 2 shows the program information we collect about the directives parallelization method.

Table 1. Translation unit and procedure information

Translation unit	Procedures
compiler version	subroutine name
programming language/model	# of exec statements
module/class/typedef	# of loops
main program name	max loop nest depth
line numbers	# call statements
	list of call chains
	# use modules
	total module variables
	list of module variables
	list of module subroutines
	# of symbols
	# symbols in other namespaces
	# of namelists
	# of statements
	classification by statement types
	modules used by subroutine
	classification of statements per standard

Libraries. While there is a practically unlimited number of libraries that could be used in a code, we are interested in common HPC libraries that have high reuse across applications, are critical for an application's performance and portability across HPC architectures, and typically require a large effort (both by the community and hardware vendors) to optimize for various platforms. As a starting point, we chose a sample of numerical (BLAS [14], LAPACK [16], FFTW [28], PETSc [18–20]), communication (MPI [38], SHMEM [23]), and data management (HDF5 [44], ADIOS [11], NetCDF [40]) libraries.

For C/C++, this task is made easier by the necessity of include files which become part of the analyzed translation unit. By descending into recognized include files, symbol names can be gathered that are known to be part of the library, and their usage examined along with the application's declared data representations, for example as type information passed as part of function parameters. However, in the case of Fortran, it is necessary to separately gather, compile, and store information about the libraries of interest, and then compare the information from application compilation to that previously seen during the separate library compilation. For this reason, the source code metadata pertaining to the libraries listed above must be stored along with the data from applications of interest.

Table 2. Data structure and parallelization method information

Variable/Data structure information	Parallelization method information
# variables	# OpenMP directives
# array variables	# statements inside OpenMP
# co-array variables	# OpenMP threadprivate variables
# pointer variables	# OpenMP UDR variables
# contiguous variables	# OpenMP declare target variables
# target variables	# OpenACC directives
# allocatable variables	# statements inside OpenACC
# artificial variables	# OpenACC subroutine
# asynchronous variables	# OpenACC declare create variables
# optional variables	# OpenACC declare copyin variables
# dummy variables	# OpenACC declare deviceptr variables
# protected variables	# OpenACC declare device_resident variables
# volatile variables	# OpenACC declare link variables
# abstract variables	
# implicit type variables	
# in namelist variables	
# external variables	
# parameters	
# common block variables	
# derived types	
# derived types with components	
# derived types with direct components	
# derived types with indirect components	
# derived types with array components	
# derived types with allocatable components	
# derived types with pointer components	
# derived types recursive	

3.2 Database Infrastructure

As compilation proceeds and the plugin gathers data from the IR, this data is stored in an application-independent way so that it is available for queries about the application and its design. The goal is to make the data more accessible than the source code or the raw compiler IR, but flexible enough that it minimizes presuppositions about particular questions that might be asked about an application's implementation.

Application Data. In order to provide the most general representation of the data while making it structured enough that non-compiler experts can explore and use it, we use an SQL database with a normalized schema. The schema holds administrative data about the build platforms and application versions, as well as the source code metadata itself. This enables comparison and differentiation for the data collected depending on the target platforms of the application compilation, e.g. if specialized features are guarded with `#ifdef`'s. Our current version stores a linkage and compile table to store program information. The compiler output from both GNU and PGI is stored in JSON format. The next version of the tool will refine the database schema to the compilation information from both compilers into a single schema.

To ensure support in different HPC environments, we allow several transmission methods to store to the database the results gathered by our plugins. We leverage the XALT [13,22] transmission machinery to easily accomplish this. The most direct way is by making an SQL connection from the compiler plugin itself and inserting the streaming results into the database. The plugins can also create an intermediate JSON file which can be parsed at some later time for consumption by the database. Finally, the plugin can elect to send results via syslog to a logging server which can then be parsed for database storage. The latter two methods are useful if direct database connection is not possible or is undesirable, for example due to security considerations that require the database server to be in a different network enclave, or due to performance considerations by avoiding the higher latency often associated with direct database queries on high-load machines.

Front-End Access. Storing this data in the database also enables advanced queries and post-processing analysis to be performed at a later time in order to gain more insight about the applications. For example, one can get historical perspectives about how data structures and directives in the source code have evolved by looking at the plugin compilation data over time. One can also do queries across different databases about the application (e.g. from a user accounts/project database, a job submission database, an XALT database [13,22], etc.). An inter-source-code analysis across all files for an application can be done to gain an overall understanding of all the data structures and directives used by an application.

Some users may not want to interact directly with SQL queries, so we are building a front-end website that allows the user to get basic insights about the application data. We provide graphical representations for some of the major statistics that are gathered and stored by the system. An example showing language usage, parallelization strategies, and data structure compositions is shown in Fig. 1 for the ACME [17] application.

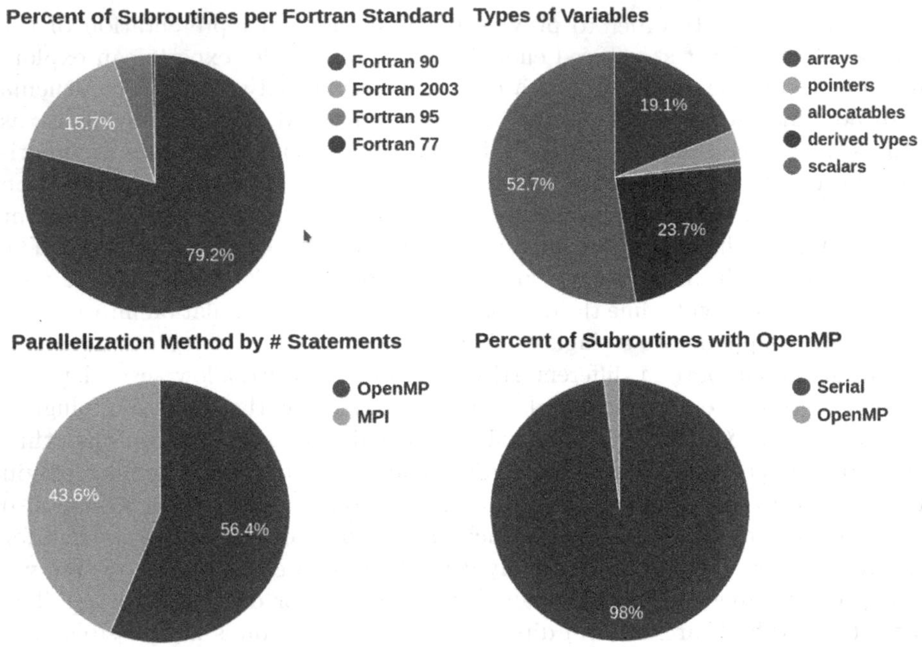

Fig. 1. High-level information such as Fortran language standard (top left), the type of variables (top right), OpenMP and MPI parallelization methods by the number of statements (bottom left), and subroutines with OpenMP pragmas (bottom right) in ACME as collected by our tools.

4 Results

As a prototype of these ideas, we have implemented the compiler-based static analysis in the GCC gfortran and g++ frontends, and through collaboration with PGI in the pgfortran and pgcc frontends as of release 17.7. We have designed an SQL schema as described in Sect. 3.2, which we use in a database alongside the XALT system installed at the Oak Ridge Leadership Computing Facility (OLCF). In the following sections, we demonstrate a sample of some of the basic statistics that can be gathered using these tools on full in-production HPC applications.

We take the Accelerated Climate Modeling for Energy (ACME) [17] as one of the first applications on which we exercised our tools. To make our tools work transparently on the system, we created a simple wrapper for the GCC compiler executables to automatically enable our custom plugin. This avoids having to modify the application build system with specific flags. Our tools also automatically insert the collected compile-time information back into the object files. During linking, a linker wrapper goes through these object files to gather these data using the selected transmission method (see Sect. 3.2).

As a sample of the information that is automatically pre-generated by our front-end website, Fig. 1 shows high-level information from the ACME application such as the Fortran language standard usage in the code, the distribution of the type of variables and parallelization methods (OpenMP and/or MPI).

In Fig. 1, the top left panel shows the relative usage of various Fortran standards, which (combined with specifics on the features used) gives an indication of the support required by compilers for HPC architectures. The lower left panel gives a high-level description of the overall "MPI+X" parallelization scheme being used in this application. While MPI and OpenMP express their respective forms of parallelism differently, this comparison might give an overview of the relative effort being expended on each type of parallelism – in this case, it is essentially equally distributed. The top right and bottom right panels indicate

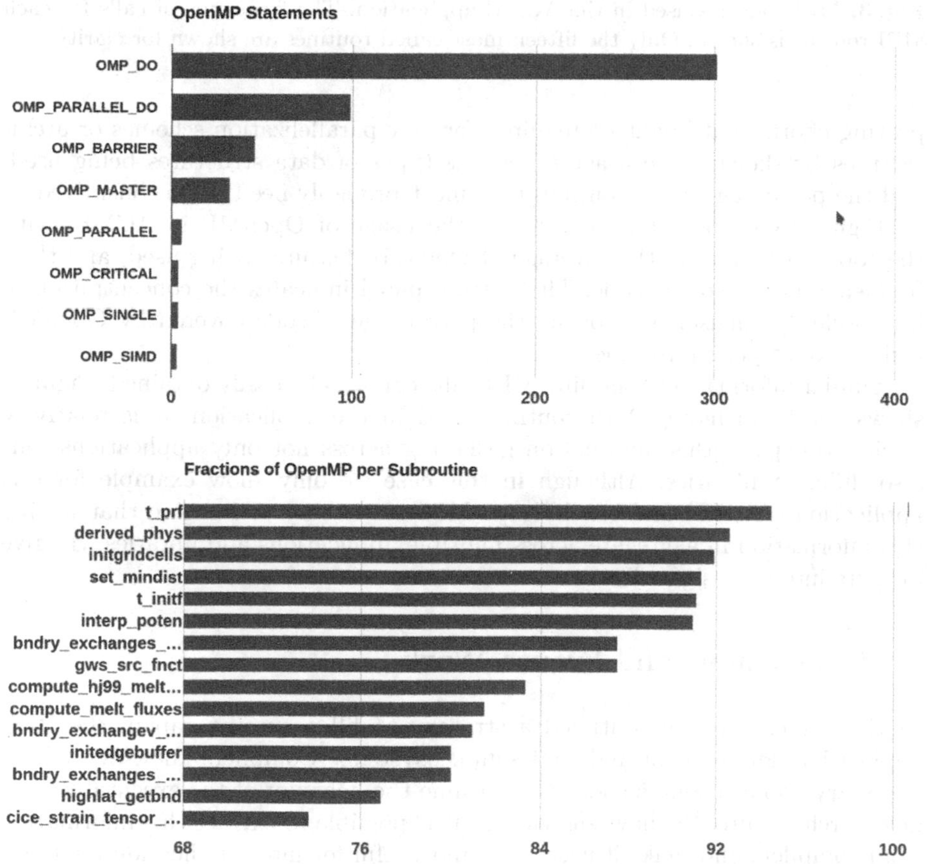

Fig. 2. Summary information about OpenMP usage in the ACME application. The usage of specific OpenMP statements is shown in the top panel, and the proportion of code covered within OpenMP lexical extents is shown per subroutine in the bottom panel. On the bottom panel, only the top fifteen subroutines are shown for clarity.

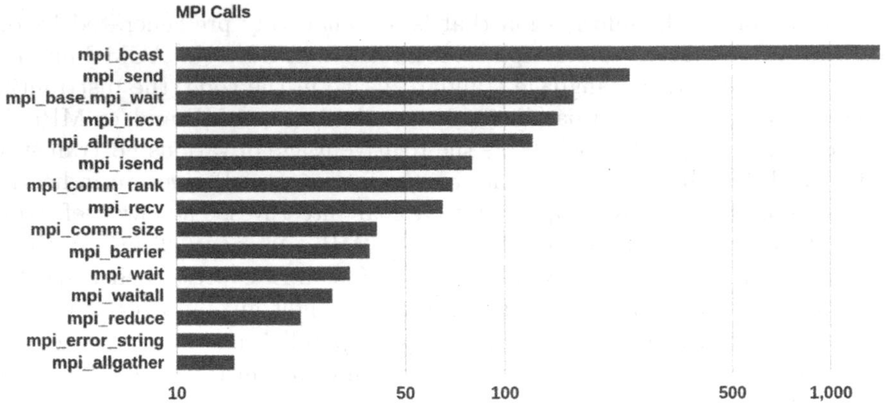

Fig. 3. MPI routines used in the ACME application. The frequency of calls for each MPI routine is shown. Only the fifteen most called routines are shown for clarity.

porting efforts that might be required for new parallelization schemes or architectures by showing the usage of various types of data structures being used, and the percentage of subroutines that most probably need to be considered.

Figure 2 goes one step deeper into the usage of OpenMP in ACME, with the top panel showing the coverage of OpenMP features being used, and their frequency in the source code. The bottom panel indicates the concentration of intranode parallelism by showing the percentage of code covered by OpenMP lexical extent per subroutine.

Similar information regarding MPI calls can also be easily obtained. Figure 3 shows the frequency of MPI routines used in the application. It is relatively trivial to expand this information gathering across not only applications, but also different libraries. Although in this case we only show example for one application (ACME) and one library (MPI), it is easy to imagine that having this information in aggregate across multiple applications and libraries will give insights into co-design efforts.

5 Conclusions and Future Work

In this paper, we have outlined a strategy to fill a current gap in the HPC application development and co-design ecosystems. Compilers know everything necessary about a source code to determine the behavior of the executable on a given architecture. We have shown that it is possible to extract this information from compilers and make it accessible and useful for inter-application analyses. In the near term, we have received requests for this data for use in designing and extending parallel APIs in both programming models and well-known HPC libraries. We also hope that this information will be useful in the upcoming exascale platform designs by shedding light on how application developers have been using the current leadership architectures, as well as prototyping their algorithms on new hardware.

In order to increase the deployment flexibility of the system and decouple the data analysis and storage phases, we envision using the DWARF [3] binary data format, which is an extensible open-standard format for storing information in binaries generated by most modern compilers both proprietary and open-source. DWARF can be used to store the static analysis information together with the generated application binary, which could then be extracted by existing, standard-conforming binary manipulation utilities. This would allow for a portable and standardized way for other compiler implementers (including proprietary and closed-source) to participate in the system.

For maximum coverage, the prototype system as described in this paper is being installed on the Oak Ridge Leadership Computing Facility (OLCF) Titan [32] and early-access Summit [9] systems to automatically gather and store application data at compile time from participating users on an opt-in/out basis. It is necessary to work with early adopters to determine the appropriate level of data anonymization and sanitation before making the data publicly available outside of OLCF. Systems usage and user job information is already being stored in systems like XALT, and we have coupled our SQL schema to be easily queried together with the dynamic linkage and job submission information already being captured by XALT.

Furthermore, coupling detailed yet generalizable information from static analysis and runtime performance analysis will greatly increase the efficacy of both, especially for inter-application statistics. For example, combining hotspot analysis with data structure layout information should lead to optimization opportunities in compilers, runtimes, and programming model design.

Structuring the data in an application- and compiler-agnostic way and storing it in an SQL database that can accommodate flexible queries is essential to servicing previously intractable questions about application source code and programming model usage. However, even more complex data analytics is made possible by using purpose-built frameworks like Apache Spark. Through ongoing collaborations, we are investigating these techniques to answer "fuzzier" questions about topics such as automatic parallel computational motif usage and application evolution over time and hardware architectures.

It is hoped that tools such as the one presented here, when coupled with advanced data analytics techniques, will lay the foundation for future research in sophisticated methods for adapting high-performance applications to various types of architectures, such as using machine learning techniques for porting applications. Additionally, this work will provide better insight into how HPC applications are evolving over time and across disparate architectures, e.g. through quantitative metrics that can be captured as applications transition to exascale platforms.

Acknowledgements. This material is based upon work supported by the U.S. Department of Energy, Office of Science, Office of Advanced Scientific Computing Research, under contract number DE-AC05-00OR22725.

This research used resources of the Oak Ridge Leadership Computing Facility at the Oak Ridge National Laboratory, which is supported by the Office of Science of the U.S. Department of Energy under Contract No. DE-AC05-00OR22725.

Research sponsored by the Laboratory Directed Research and Development Program of Oak Ridge National Laboratory, managed by UT-Battelle, LLC, for the U. S. Department of Energy. The project was sponsored via the LDRD project 8277: "Understanding HPC Applications for Evidence-based Co-design".

References

1. https://developer.mozilla.org/en-US/docs/Archive/Mozilla/Dehydra
2. https://developer.mozilla.org/en-US/docs/Archive/Mozilla/Treehydra
3. http://dwarfstd.org/Dwarf5Std.php
4. CORAL fact sheet. http://www.anl.gov/sites/anl.gov/files/CORAL
5. GNU Compiler Collection (GCC) Internals: Plugins. https://gcc.gnu.org/onlinedocs/gccint/Plugins.html
6. Interactive compilation interface. http://ctuning.org/wiki/index.php/CTools:ICI
7. PGI Compiler & Tools. http://www.pgroup.com/index.htm
8. Reproducing MILEPOST project. https://github.com/ctuning/ck/wiki/Reproducing-MILEPOST-project
9. Summit: scale new heights. Discover new solutions. https://www.olcf.ornl.gov/summit/
10. The Exascale Computing Project. https://exascaleproject.org
11. Abbasi, H., Lofstead, J., Zheng, F., Schwan, K., Wolf, M., Klasky, S.: Extending I/O through high performance data services. In: 2009 IEEE International Conference on Cluster Computing and Workshops, pp. 1–10, August 2009. https://doi.org/10.1109/CLUSTR.2009.5289167
12. Adhianto, L., et al.: HPCTOOLKIT: tools for performance analysis of optimized parallel programs. Concurr. Comput.: Pract. Exp. **22**(6), 685–701 (2010). https://doi.org/10.1002/cpe.1553
13. Agrawal, K., Fahey, M.R., McLay, R., James, D.: User environment tracking and problem detection with XALT. In: Proceedings of the First International Workshop on HPC User Support Tools, HUST 2014, pp. 32–40. IEEE Press, Piscataway (2014). https://doi.org/10.1109/HUST.2014.6
14. Blackford, L.S., et al.: An updated set of basic linear algebra subprograms (BLAS). ACM Trans. Math. Softw. **28**(2), 135–151 (2002). https://doi.org/10.1145/567806.567807
15. Anantharaj, V., Foertter, F., Joubert, W., Wells, J.: Approaching exascale: application requirements for OLCF leadership computing. Oak Ridge Leadership Computing Facility Technical report ORNL/TM-2013/186 (2013)
16. Anderson, E., et al.: LAPACK Users' Guide, 3rd edn. Society for Industrial and Applied Mathematics, Philadelphia (1999)
17. Bader, D.B., et al.: ACME Pre-Release Documentation (2017). http://climatemodeling.science.energy.gov/acme/information-for-collaborators
18. Balay, S., et al.: PETSc Web page (2016). http://www.mcs.anl.gov/petsc
19. Balay, S., et al.: PETSc users manual. Technical report ANL-95/11 - Revision 3.7. Argonne National Laboratory (2016). http://www.mcs.anl.gov/petsc

20. Balay, S., Gropp, W.D., McInnes, L.C., Smith, B.F.: Efficient management of parallelism in object oriented numerical software libraries. In: Arge, E., Bruaset, A.M., Langtangen, H.P. (eds.) Modern Software Tools in Scientific Computing, pp. 163–202. Birkhäuser Press, Boston (1997)
21. Bodin, F., Mével, Y., Quiniou, R.: A user level program transformation tool. In: Proceedings of the 12th International Conference on Supercomputing, pp. 180–187. ACM (1998)
22. Budiardja, R., Fahey, M., McLay, R., Don, P.M., Hadri, B., James, D.: Community use of XALT in its first year in production. In: Proceedings of the Second International Workshop on HPC User Support Tools, HUST 2015, pp. 4:1–4:10. ACM, New York (2015). https://doi.org/10.1145/2834996.2835000
23. Chapman, B., et al.: Introducing OpenSHMEM: SHMEM for the PGAS community. In: Proceedings of the Fourth Conference on Partitioned Global Address Space Programming Model, PGAS 2010, pp. 2:1–2:3. ACM, New York (2010). https://doi.org/10.1145/2020373.2020375
24. Chapman, B., Eachempati, D., Hernandez, O.: Experiences developing the OpenUH compiler and runtime infrastructure. Int. J. Parallel Program. **41**(6), 825–854 (2013). https://doi.org/10.1007/s10766-012-0230-9
25. von Dincklage, D., Diwan, A.: Integrating program analyses with programmer productivity tools. Softw. Pract. Exp. **41**(7), 817–840 (2011). https://doi.org/10.1002/spe.1035
26. Ding, W., Hsu, C.H., Hernandez, O., Chapman, B., Graham, R.: KLONOS: similarity-based planning tool support for porting scientific applications. Concurr. Comput. Pract. Exp. **25**(8), 1072–1088 (2013). https://doi.org/10.1002/cpe.2903
27. Feser, J.K., Chaudhuri, S., Dillig, I.: Synthesizing data structure transformations from input-output examples. SIGPLAN Not. **50**(6), 229–239 (2015). https://doi.org/10.1145/2813885.2737977
28. Frigo, M., Johnson, S.G.: The design and implementation of FFTW3. Proc. IEEE **93**(2), 216–231 (2005). https://doi.org/10.1109/JPROC.2004.840301
29. Fuerlinger, K., Wright, N.J., Skinner, D.: Effective performance measurement at petascale using IPM. In: 2010 IEEE 16th International Conference on Parallel and Distributed Systems, pp. 373–380, December 2010. https://doi.org/10.1109/ICPADS.2010.16
30. Fursin, G., Lokhmotov, A., Plowman, E.: Collective knowledge: towards R&D sustainability. In: Proceedings of the 2016 Conference on Design, Automation & Test in Europe, DATE 2016, pp. 864–869. EDA Consortium, San Jose (2016). http://dl.acm.org/citation.cfm?id=2971808.2972009
31. Gibbs, T.: Accelerate the path to exascale: best practices to acquire and analyze HPC application workload data (2016). http://www.isc-hpc.com/isc16_ap/sessiondetails.htm?t=session&o=328&a=select&ra=personendetails
32. Joubert, W., et al.: Accelerated application development: the ORNL Titan experience. Comput. Electr. Eng. **46**, 123–138 (2015). https://doi.org/10.1016/j.compeleceng.2015.04.008
33. Joubert, W., Su, S.Q.: An analysis of computational workloads for the ORNL Jaguar system. In: Proceedings of the 26th ACM International Conference on Supercomputing, ICS 2012, pp. 247–256. ACM, New York (2012). https://doi.org/10.1145/2304576.2304611

34. Karavanic, K.L., et al.: Integrating database technology with comparison-based parallel performance diagnosis: the PerfTrack performance experiment management tool. In: Proceedings of the 2005 ACM/IEEE Conference on Supercomputing, SC 2005, p. 39. IEEE Computer Society, Washington, DC (2005). https://doi.org/10.1109/SC.2005.36
35. Kartsaklis, C., Hernandez, O., Hsu, C.H., Ilsche, T., Joubert, W., Graham, R.L.: HERCULES: a pattern driven code transformation system. In: 2012 IEEE 26th International Parallel and Distributed Processing Symposium Workshops & PhD Forum, IPDPSW, pp. 574–583. IEEE (2012)
36. Liao, C., Lin, P.H., Quinlan, D.J., Zhao, Y., Shen, X.: Enhancing domain specific language implementations through ontology. In: Proceedings of the 5th International Workshop on Domain-Specific Languages and High-Level Frameworks for High Performance Computing, WOLFHPC 2015, pp. 3:1–3:9. ACM, New York (2015). https://doi.org/10.1145/2830018.2830022
37. Lindlan, K.A., et al.: A tool framework for static and dynamic analysis of object-oriented software with templates. In: ACM/IEEE 2000 Conference on Supercomputing, p. 49, November 2000. https://doi.org/10.1109/SC.2000.10052
38. MPI Forum: MPI: a message-passing interface standard. Technical report. MPI Forum, Knoxville, TN, USA (1994)
39. OpenMP Architecture Review Board: OpenMP application program interface version 4.5, November 2015. http://www.openmp.org/wp-content/uploads/openmp-4.5.pdf
40. Rew, R.K., Davis, G.P., Emmerson, S.: NetCDF user's guide, an interface for data access, version 2.3, April 1993
41. Sreepathi, S., et al.: Application characterization using Oxbow toolkit and PADS infrastructure. In: 2014 Hardware-Software Co-Design for High Performance Computing, pp. 55–63, November 2014. https://doi.org/10.1109/Co-HPC.2014.11
42. OpenACC Standard: OpenACC - directives for accelerators. http://www.openacc-standard.org
43. Strout, M.M., Mellor-Crummey, J., Hovland, P.: Representation-independent program analysis. SIGSOFT Softw. Eng. Notes **31**(1), 67–74 (2005). https://doi.org/10.1145/1108768.1108810
44. The HDF Group: Hierarchical data format version 5 (2000–2017). http://www.hdfgroup.org/HDF5
45. Tiwari, A., Chen, C., Chame, J., Hall, M., Hollingsworth, J.K.: A scalable autotuning framework for compiler optimization. In: IEEE International Symposium on Parallel & Distributed Processing, IPDPS 2009, pp. 1–12. IEEE (2009)
46. Willcock, J.J., Lumsdaine, A., Quinlan, D.J.: Reusable, generic program analyses and transformations. In: Proceedings of the Eighth International Conference on Generative Programming and Component Engineering, GPCE 2009, pp. 5–14. ACM, New York (2009). https://doi.org/10.1145/1621607.1621611
47. Zaharia, M., et al.: Apache spark: a unified engine for big data processing. Commun. ACM **59**(11), 56–65 (2016). https://doi.org/10.1145/2934664

Visual Comparison of Trace Files in Vampir

Matthias Weber[1(✉)], Ronny Brendel[2], Michael Wagner[1,3], Robert Dietrich[1], Ronny Tschüter[1], and Holger Brunst[1]

[1] Technische Universität Dresden, Dresden, Germany
{matthias.weber,robert.dietrich,ronny.tschueter, holger.brunst}@tu-dresden.de
[2] Oak Ridge National Laboratory, Oak Ridge, USA
brendelr@ornl.gov
[3] Barcelona Supercomputing Center, Barcelona, Spain
michael.wagner@bsc.es

Abstract. Comparing data is a key activity of performance analysis. It is required to relate performance results before and after optimizations, while porting to new hardware, and when using new programming models and libraries. While comparing profiles is straightforward, relating detailed trace data remains challenging.

This work introduces the Comparison View. This new view extends the trace visualizer Vampir to enable comparative visual performance analysis. It displays multiple traces in one synchronized view and adds a range of alignment techniques to aid visual inspection. We demonstrate the Comparison View's value in three real-world performance analysis scenarios.

Keywords: Alignment · Comparison · Performance analysis · Tracing · Visualization

1 Introduction

HPC application developers need to leverage the potential performance of modern HPC computing systems. Increasingly complex hardware configurations as well as software systems make achieving this goal ever more challenging. Performance analysis tools aid developers in obtaining better scalability, tracking

This manuscript has been co-authored by UT-Battelle, LLC, under contract DE-AC05-00OR22725 with the US Department of Energy (DOE). The US government retains and the publisher, by accepting the article for publication, acknowledges that the US government retains a nonexclusive, paid-up, irrevocable, worldwide license to publish or reproduce the published form of this manuscript, or allow others to do so, for US government purposes. DOE will provide public access to these results of federally sponsored research in accordance with the DOE Public Access Plan (http://energy.gov/downloads/doe-public-access-plan).

A. Bhatele et al. (Eds.): ESPT/VPA 2017/2018, LNCS 11027, pp. 105–121, 2019.
https://doi.org/10.1007/978-3-030-17872-7_7

down bottlenecks, and in general enable detailed understanding of the performance characteristics of applications.

Performance tools observe metrics about and behavior of a running application and its underlying system. After an execution they present the obtained performance data in text or through visualizations. Investigating application performance typically involves comparing data between multiple application runs, for example with varying number of processing elements, varying inputs, and varying hardware configurations.

Performance data comes in two principal flavors: profiles and traces. Profiles consist of aggregated performance data. For instance a *flat profile* summarizes the number invocations and time spent for each function of an application. Another common form is the *call path profile*. It works similarly, but aggregates information for a function call stack configuration, rather than a function and disregarding its calling context. Comparing two profiles can be achieved by subtracting the values of one profile from the other for each equal function (or call path).

However, the ability of profiles to reveal performance problems is limited. Many performance issues are dynamic in nature, and hard to detect in an aggregated statistic. For example to see if load balance worsens over time, or a performance flaw occurs only occasionally (and is thus averaged out), more detailed performance data is needed.

Traces retain the chronological order of events, where profiles do not. This more fine-grained performance data enables investigating dynamic behavior of applications. However, displaying more data, makes investigating traces more difficult. Comparing two traces is even more challenging, because two runs of the same application can be very different. Possible reasons for this include timing differences, reordered functions, partially removed stacks (due to e.g. function inlining) and changes in dynamic application behavior.

In this work we introduce techniques to improve visual trace comparison. Our contributions are:

- Vampir's [2] *Comparison View*, which displays traces and statistics side by side. It allows manual alignment of multiple traces on one common timescale to simplify visual comparison.
- A heuristic to automatically align traces.
- A case study demonstrating the effectiveness of the *Comparison View* for performance analysis of real-world applications.

All introduced techniques are available starting with the current Vampir and VampirServer releases.

This work is organized as follows: Sect. 2 enumerates related work. Section 3 presents our techniques and implementation. Section 4 shows how the Comparison View aids performance understanding and improvement for three real-world scientific applications. The last section summarizes our contribution and highlights future development directions.

2 Related Work

Comparing performance data is a central activity in performance analysis. Consequently, a wide range of research has been performed on this topic. Solutions range from profile comparison techniques to advanced trace compression and analysis schemes. The developed techniques can serve different purposes. For example clustering algorithms can be used to compress data, automatically categorize it, or aid visualization.

Schulz and de Supinski's [14] present a tool, based on GNU gprof, for comparing profiles between application runs. Song et al. [15] introduce an algebraic framework for comparing profile-based performance data.

PerfExplorer [7] provides a framework for performance data mining. It allows comparing runtime, relative speedup, and efficiency across different sets of profiles.

Weber et al. developed techniques for structural comparison of performance data. They introduced a hierarchical alignment algorithm [17] that compares the structure of two traces. Building on that, they introduced alignment-based comparison metrics [20] to highlight structural and temporal differences between application runs. In subsequent work they developed a structural clustering algorithm [18] that scalably classifies processing elements into groups of similar behavior.

In the context of the performance analysis tool Paraver [13], Llort et al. [11] use object tracking techniques to automatically detect changing performance characteristics between application runs. Knüpfer et al. [9] propose the *Compressed Complete Call Graph* structure for trace data. The technique identifies similarities inside of and between processes to store trace data more efficiently. This compressed storage is able to speed up various analysis operations, as well as reveal repeating patterns in program execution.

Mohror and Karavanic [12] divide applications into segments. Based on the similarity of these segments they compress the traces while retaining as much crucial performance information as possible. Gamblin et al. [4] use an adapted k-means clustering algorithm to scalably compress trace data.

Trace viewers like Vampir [2] and Intel Trace Analyzer [8] provide visual analysis of trace data. Intel Trace Analyzer offers visual comparison of two traces, but lacks the ability to align them. To compare trace it stretches both into the same time frame. This leads to a rather unnatural representation of the trace, making visual comparison challenging. Vampir supports folding timelines [19] to save space and get an aggregate view of multi-processing element activity (e.g. CUDA streams, or OpenMP threads) where appropriate. Edge bundling [1] is a promising technique for aiding visual analysis and comparison of large-scale communication traces.

3 Methodology

This section introduces a new *Comparison View* and its features for visual trace file comparison. The Comparison View integrates all common performance charts of Vampir and adds additional comparison functionality. To enable effective comparison of multiple trace files we couple and synchronize the zoom of the traces. In Vampir the user can *zoom* into regions of a trace to investigate areas in more detail. To compare areas of interest between traces, displayed trace regions need to be freely shiftable in time. This allows for arbitrary alignments of the trace files, and thus, enables visual comparison of user selected areas side by side.

The number of compared trace files is not limited by Vampir. However, Vampir needs to load the complete data of all trace files into main memory. Thus, the amount of available main memory becomes the limiting factor. In order to compare large trace files exceeding the size of typically available memory on workstations, users can employ VampirServer for the comparison. VampirServer runs in parallel on an HPC machine. This component allows to harness the distributed memory of a cluster for the comparison.

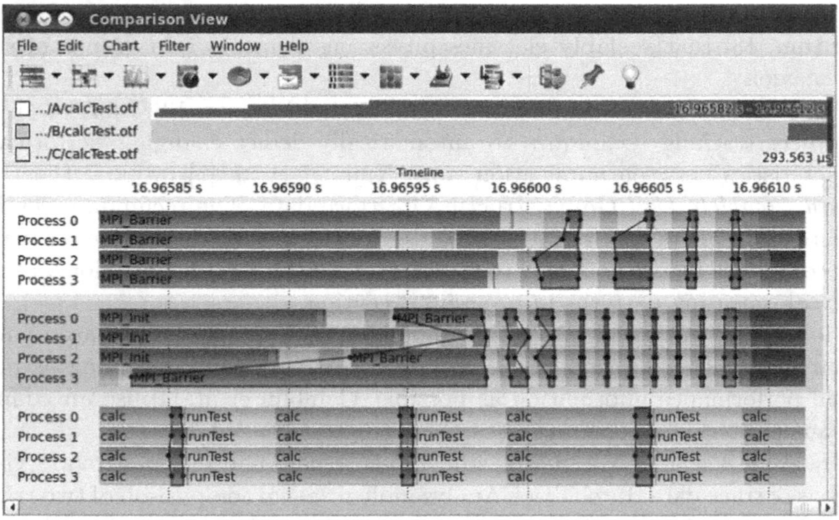

Fig. 1. The Comparison View showing three traces

Figure 1 shows the new *Comparison View*. We use three example trace files to introduce its comparison functionality. The example traces show one test application performing ten iterations of calculations. Each trace, respectively, represents an execution of this application on a different machine.

3.1 Comparing Application Characteristics Using Charts

As indicated by the *Navigation Toolbar*, at the top in Fig. 2, all three trace files are included in the single Comparison View instance. The Navigation Toolbar gives an overview of all open traces and provides an easy access for manipulating

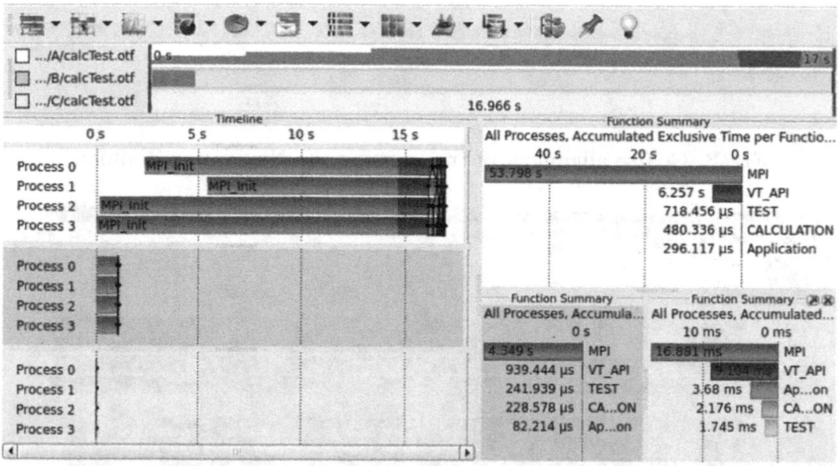

Fig. 2. Open Comparison View

the selected zoom area. The Comparison View provides timeline and statistic charts (common charts of Vampir) for the comparison of performance metrics. Colors in the charts represent different function calls, e.g., MPI calls are shown in red, computations are shown in cyan (in this example). The Comparison View opens one chart instance for each loaded trace file, i.e., one click on the Master Timeline icon opens three Master Timeline charts. In order to distinguish charts between traces, we assign a dedicated background color to all charts belonging to one trace.

As shown in Fig. 2, trace *A* exhibits the largest duration time. The duration of trace *C* is so short that it is barely visible. Zooming into the compute iterations of trace *C* (left side in Fig. 2 at 0 s) would make them visible and allow an detailed inspection. However, due to the coupled zoom, zooming into the area around 0 s would also zoom into the `MPI_Init` phase in trace *A* and *B*. To visually compare the compute iterations between all three traces, they need to be aligned side by side. This necessitates an alignment method for the traces to facilitate a meaningful visual comparison of related areas. We present the available options for trace alignment in the following.

3.2 Aligning Traces Manually

The Comparison View allows to shift individual trace files in time. This enables comparison of areas that did not occur at the same time. In our example the compute iterations need to be aligned prior to visual comparison because the initialization of the application took different times on the three machines.

We provide several ways to shift trace files in time. One option is to directly set the time offset of an individual trace using a context menu. The easiest way to achieve a coarse alignment is to directly drag and drop (using the mouse) the trace in the Navigation Toolbar. Figure 3 shows the compute iterations of all example trace files coarsely aligned.

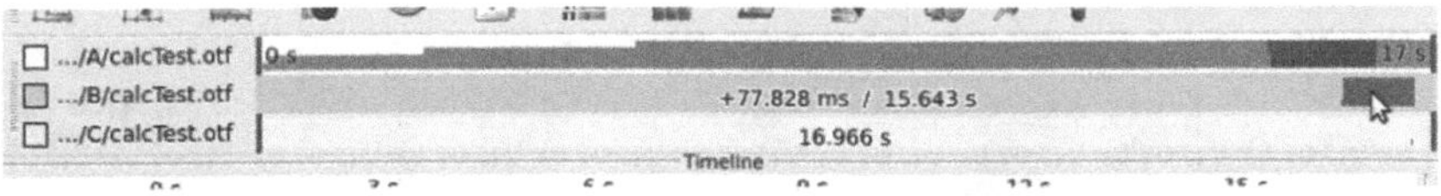

Fig. 3. Coarse alignment of traces using the Navigation Toolbar

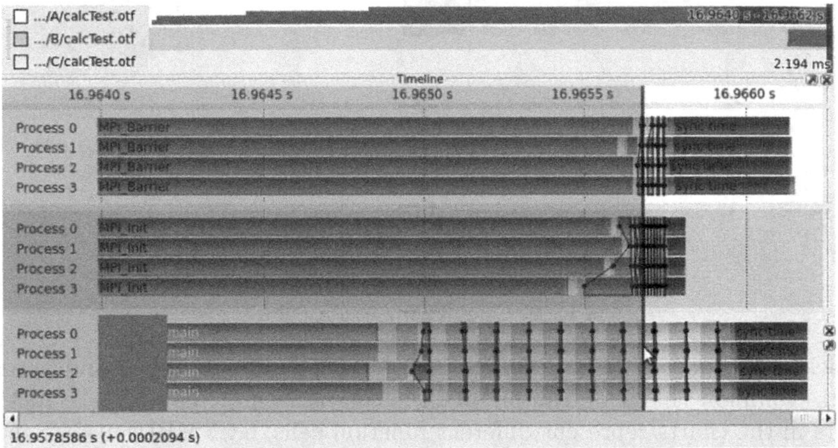

Fig. 4. Fine-grain alignment of traces directly in the Master Timeline

After the coarse shifting the Master Timeline allows a finer alignment directly inside the chart. Therefore, the user can zoom into an area of interest and directly align the traces by dragging with the mouse. Figure 4 depicts the process of dragging trace C to the compute iterations of trace A and B.

As shown in Fig. 4, although the initialization of trace A took the longest, this machine was the fastest in computing the calculations.

3.3 Aligning Traces Automatically Using Predefined Markers

Markers in traces point to particular places of interest in the trace data. These markers are useful for navigation in trace files. For trace file comparison markers are interesting due to their potential to quickly locate places in large trace data sets. They allow to quickly find the same location in multiple trace files.

The *Marker View* in Vampir provides a combined access to all markers contained in the open trace files. Clicking a marker in the Marker View highlights the respective marker in the Master Timeline. Another way to navigate to a marker in the timeline charts is to use the zooming functionality. Therefore, a user first zooms into the desired zooming level. Clicking a marker in the Marker View will then set the timeline chart to the marker position. Thus, the selected marker appears in the center of the timeline chart. Moreover, the Marker View provides two additional ways of navigating with markers. If two markers of one trace are selected, the Comparison View sets the zoom to the according timestamps of the markers. If two markers of different traces are selected, the Comparison View adjusts the time offset between the respective traces and shows the selected markers next to each other, and consequently, aligns both traces at the respective markers.

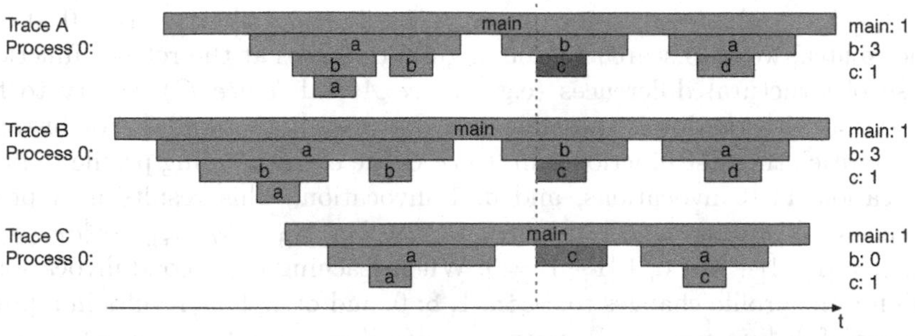

Fig. 5. Example showing the automatic alignment of three processes. Function c (shown in red) in trace A is selected. Our heuristic finds the respective function invocations in trace B and C and aligns all traces at that function. The function invocation profiles for the selected functions (red line) are shown at the right side. (Color figure online)

3.4 Aligning Traces Automatically Using Call Invocation Profiles

In addition to manual alignment we also provide a heuristic that automatically aligns traces. Using this heuristic users can select an interesting function in one trace and have all other traces aligned automatically to that function. This facilitates direct visual comparison by saving the user from manual aligning.

In this section we describe the alignment heuristic using the example shown in Fig. 5. In this example the user selected function `c` of *Process 0* in *Trace A* (marked red in the figure). To align *Trace B* and *Trace C* to that function, we first select the corresponding process in the other traces. Therefore, we search for a process with the name *Process 0* in all open traces[1]. If no exact match is found, we compute the Levenshtein distance [10] between names to find the closest match.

In order to detect the corresponding invocations of function `c` in *Trace B* and *Trace C* we employ an invocation profile based approach. For reference we first generate the function invocation profile for *Trace A*. Therefore, we identify all functions contained in the call stack of the selected function (red line in *Trace A* in the figure). In our example these functions are `main`, `b`, and `c`. Then we traverse *Trace A* and count all occurrences of these functions until we reach the selected function. For *Trace A* this results in the following invocation profile (also shown right of *Trace A* in Fig. 5): `main`: 1 invocation, `b`: 3 invocations, and `c`: 1 invocation.

[1] This simple example contains only one process per trace. However, in parallel applications searching for the selected process is necessary.

For the alignment we then traverse *Process 0* of *Trace B* and *Trace C* and try to match their invocation profiles as good as possible with the profile of *Trace A*. In case of a structurally identical traces (e.g., *Trace A* and *Trace B*), we find the related function with a perfect match between both profiles, i.e., the difference between the invocations of both profiles is zero: $|main_{TraceA} - main_{TraceB}| + |b_{TraceA} - b_{TraceB}| + |c_{TraceA} - c_{TraceB}| = |1-1| + |3-3| + |1-1| = 0$. If both profiles match, we stop searching and align both traces at the related functions. In case of structural differences (e.g., *Trace A* and *Trace C*) we try to find the position with the lowest possible error between both profiles. For instance, when we reach the first function `c` in *Trace C* the corresponding profile is: `main`: 1 invocation, `b`: 0 invocations, and `c`: 1 invocation. This results in a profile difference of 3: $|main_{TraceA} - main_{TraceC}| + |b_{TraceA} - b_{TraceC}| + |c_{TraceA} - c_{TraceC}| = |1-1| + |3-0| + |1-1| = 3$. When reaching the second invocation of function `c` the profile changes to: `main`: 1, `b`: 0, and `c`: 2. This results in a profile difference of 4: $|main_{TraceA} - main_{TraceC}| + |b_{TraceA} - b_{TraceC}| + |c_{TraceA} - c_{TraceC}| = |1-1| + |3-0| + |1-2| = 4$. The second profile exhibits a higher difference to the reference profile than the first profile. Thus, we stop searching and select the first invocation of `c` as related function in *Trace C*.

The comparison of m trace files requires the traversal of m processes. The complexity for the traversal of one process is $\mathcal{O}(n)$ with respect to the number of recorded events (each function invocation consists of one *enter* and one *leave* event) in the related process. Thus, in total the complexity for an alignment of m processes is $\mathcal{O}(m \cdot n)$, assuming maximal n events in each process. In practice, the computation of the heuristic does not introduce any noticeable lag in the visualization of Vampir. Interestingly, the computation of a *Function Summary* (profile view in the figures) in Vampir poses even higher requirements, involving a full traversal of all processes of a trace[2].

This approach improves the usability of the visual comparison. The heuristic exactly aligns structurally equal processes. While not perfect, it is also sufficiently robust to correctly align trace files in many cases of structural differences between processes.

4 Case Study

This section showcases how the comparison view benefits visual performance analysis. Three real-world optimization scenarios demonstrate its wide applicability. *LSMS* analyzes the performance impacts of different hardware on an application. *CloverLeaf* compares several versions of an application executed using different programming models. *Trinity RNA-Seq Assembler* performs a comparative scalability study of an application and detects scalability bottlenecks.

[2] This example is not directly related to the alignment heuristic. It is only mentioned here to contrast the computational requirements of the alignment heuristic with common processing steps in Vampir.

4.1 LSMS – Comparing Performance Between Different Hardware

The Oak Ridge Leadership Computing Facility uses Vampir and its comparison view for visual performance analysis to support porting applications from Titan to Summit. The system employed for early development work is Summitdev.

These new systems bring a number of major changes. Some of them are: Summitdev consists of 20 Power8+ cores and four NVIDIA P100 GPUs per node. One P100 has four times the theoretical DPFLOPS peak performance compared to the Tesla K20X used in Titan. One node has four GPUs instead of one for Titan. The system supports CUDA MPS, which allows sharing GPUs between multiple processes.

To explore how these differences affect the CORAL benchmark code LSMS [3] visual performance analysis is vital. Figure 6 shows an LSMS run on 80 Titan vs 20 Summitdev nodes. The total number of graphics cards for both is 80.

The vastly faster GPUs and the fact that each GPU has at most five CPU threads paired (20 divided by 4), in comparison to 16 on Titan, cause the GPU-accelerated function `zblock_lu` to speed up, while the non-GPU-enabled function `buildKKRMatrix` gains in relative execution time. Thus to further improve LSMS's performance, `buildKKRMatrix` is the new prime function to investigate.

To compare iterations in detail developers use the alignment functionality, shown in Fig. 7.

To gauge whether CUDA MPS can speed up LSMS, we run it with varying numbers of threads and processes per node (Fig. 8). The first run has four MPI processes with four threads each. The second one has five threads each. The third and fourth runs are 8×2, and 16×1, i.e. two and four processes share one GPU. Strictly, LSMS is most resource-efficient if the total number of threads and processes divides the number of simulated atoms evenly. But, it turns out using all 20 cores in a four by five setup is faster than the other variants, although it adds occasional waiting time on the "left-over" threads. Note that 8 or 16 processes cannot evenly use 20 cores with the same number of threads per process. Another interesting observation is that the increase in MPI waiting time (more red in the green and cyan timelines) is negated by better GPU utilization.

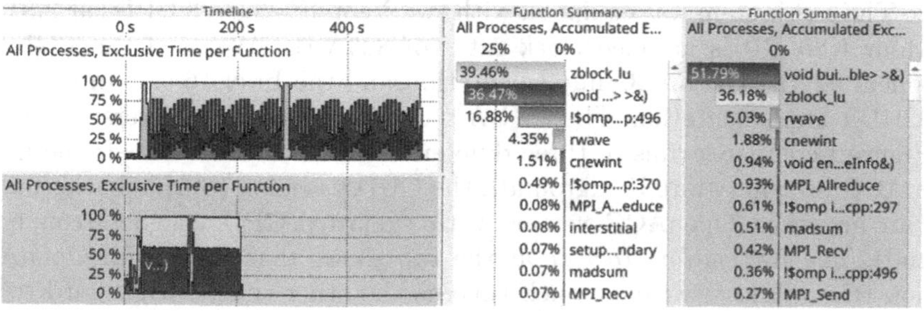

Fig. 6. Overview of a 80-GPU LSMS run on Titan (white background) and Summitdev (blue). The timeline display is on the left. Profiles are on the right. (Color figure online)

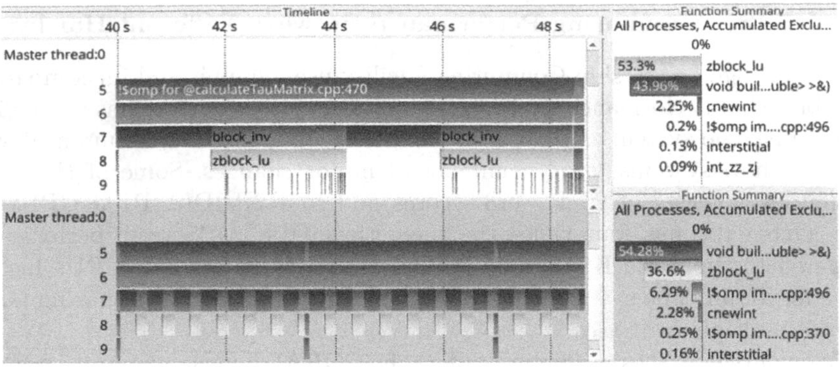

Fig. 7. Detailed comparison of one iteration on Titan vs roughly 2.5 on Summitdev

Summarizing our findings, GPU MPS uses the GPU more efficiently. But not using four cores per node negates this advantage.

The comparison view highly improves visual comparative analysis. With its help, we are able to gain a deeper understanding of LSMS's changing performance characteristics while transitioning to Summit.

4.2 CloverLeaf – Comparing Performance Between Programming Models

CloverLeaf is a hydrodynamics mini-app, which solves the compressible Euler equations on a Cartesian grid with an explicit, second-order accurate method [6]. It is composed of small execution kernels, which simplifies the implementation with different programming models. To accelerate the computation, the grid can be split into parts and processed on multiple MPI processes, threads, and target devices, which however requires a halo exchange and thus, data transfers.

This paper compares the CUDA and the OpenACC implementation[3] on an NVIDIA K80 GPU as target device. We ran all experiments with two MPI processes, a fixed grid size of 1920 × 960 cells, and a fixed number of 87 time steps. The test system was equipped with two Xeon E5-2680v3 CPUs at 2.5 GHz and four K80 GPUs at fixed clock rates of 823 MHz. We used the PGI 17.7 compilers for the OpenACC implementation and the Intel 16.0.2 compilers for the CUDA implementation. The CUDA toolkit was installed in version 8.0.44.

Figure 9 compares runs of three different versions of CloverLeaf: the initial OpenACC version (white background), the CUDA version (purple background), and an improved OpenACC version with exclusive GPU usage (green background). The *Navigation Toolbar* at the top shows that the initial OpenACC version takes almost twice as much time as the other runs, with regard to the computation phase. A closer look into the execution exposes that it uses the

[3] Available at http://uk-mac.github.io/CloverLeaf/, last accessed 26 September 2017.

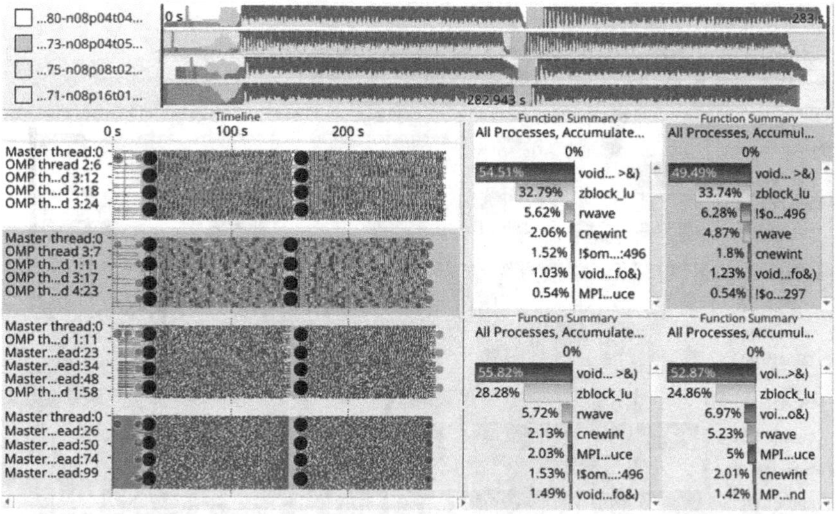

Fig. 8. Exploratory comparison of different process vs thread setups. White: 4 processes times 4 threads per node. Blue: 4 processes times 5 threads. Green: 8 times 2. Cyan: 16 times 1. (Color figure online)

default offloading device on both MPI processes, which results in resource contention with an MPI imbalance as further symptom. CUDA kernels, launched by one MPI process, delay the kernel execution from the other process. Some CUDA kernels, such as `pdv_kernel_80_gpu`, run concurrently on the GPU as they do not fully utilize all compute resources. In the CUDA version and the fixed OpenACC version, both MPI processes use one GPU exclusively, which prevents resource contention and keeps the MPI imbalance negligible. Although the CUDA version is comparatively fast, considering the total runtime, it reveals optimization potential in the selected program phase. Costly `cudaMalloc` and `cudaFree` calls, invoked by thrust library routines, could be avoided, especially as they are nonexistent in the OpenACC implementations.

The automatic alignment of traces facilitates the review of small code changes. Figure 10 shows the effect of an optimization in the halo exchange of the OpenACC version. The traces have been aligned at function `update_halo`. The first optimization avoids two unnecessary host-to-device transfers per `pack kernel`, indicated by the two missing black lines in the optimized version (purple background). The second optimization replaces synchronous offloading of multiple successive CUDA kernels or data transfers with asynchronous equivalents and a collective synchronization. The effect is obvious for a set of successive kernels, which update the halo on the GPU. They are executed one after another, without the kernel trigger overhead in between. The same optimization has been applied for the `pack kernel` and its following device-to-host transfer.

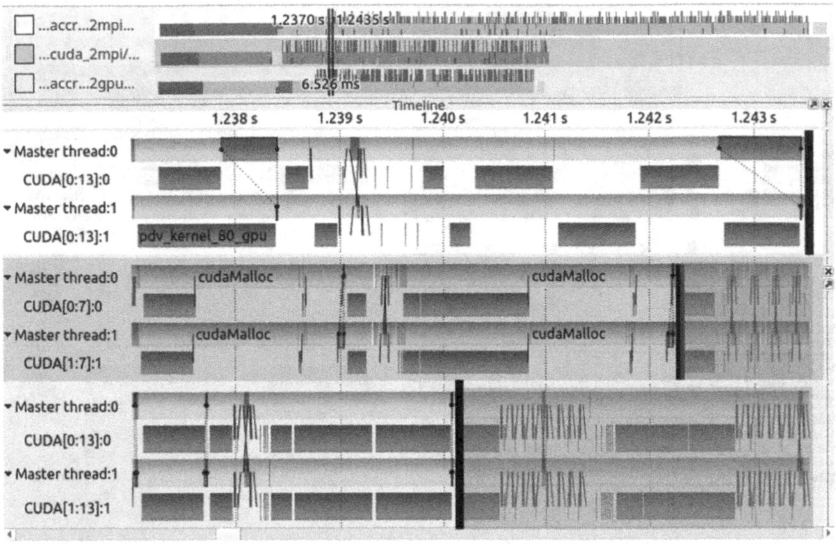

Fig. 9. Comparison of different CloverLeaf implementations: initial OpenACC (top), CUDA (middle), and improved OpenACC (bottom). (Color figure online)

The comparison view helps porting applications to new programming APIs. It allows users to spot runtime and structural differences, which finally helps in detecting individual weak spots of implementations. Eventually, comparing traces is useful to validate code optimizations.

4.3 Trinity RNA-Seq Assembler – Comparing Performance Between Different Process Numbers

In this section we highlight our efforts to analyze and optimize the RNA-Seq assembler Trinity with the help of the Comparison View [16]. Trinity [5] is a software framework for accurate de novo reconstruction of transcriptomes from RNA-Seq data. Trinity is a pipeline of up to 27 individual components in different programming and script languages, including C++, Java, Perl, and system binaries, which are invoked by the main Trinity perl script. The pipeline consists of three stages: first, *Inchworm* assembles RNA-seq data into sequence contigs, second, *Chrysalis* bundles the Inchworm contigs and constructs complete de Bruijn graphs for each cluster, and, third, *Butterfly* processes the individual graphs in parallel and computes the final assembly.

Our analysis results refer to the release version 2.0.6, while many of our optimizations were included in the release version 2.1.1. One of the main performance issues that was identified is the poor intra-node scaling of the `GraphFromFasta` module. `GraphFromFasta` is a key part of the *Chrysalis* stage that clusters the Inchworm contigs and constructs complete de Bruijn graphs for each cluster.

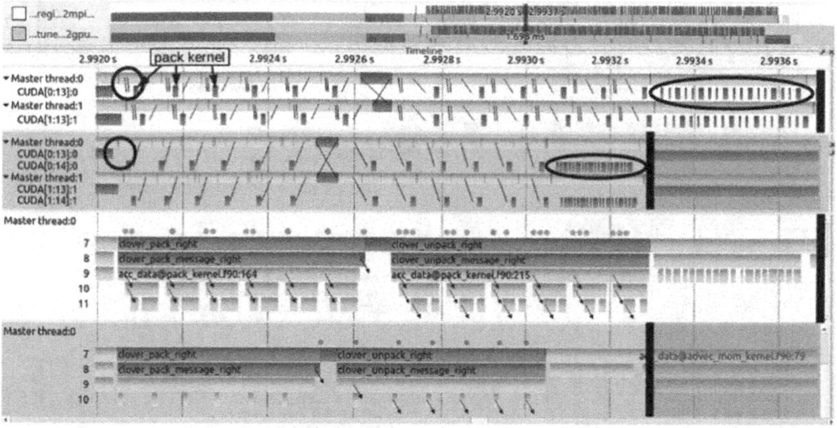

Fig. 10. Validation of code optimizations for the CloverLeaf OpenACC port (Color figure online)

The intra-node parallelism using OpenMP showed very poor scalability by achieving a speed up of only 2.27 with a full 16-core node in comparison to the version with only one core [16]. To further investigate this issue we analyzed the parallel intra-node behavior. We recorded application traces with 1, 2, 4, 8, and 16 OpenMP threads using manual instrumentation of code regions in the main loop. Figure 11 shows the recorded behavior in comparison for 1, 2, 4, 8, and 16 threads from top to bottom with white, red, yellow, green, and blue background, respectively. The left side depicts the active code regions over time on the horizontal axis and the executing threads on the vertical axis. The summarized overview on the right side presents the accumulated runtime over all threads for each code region.

The comparison view in Fig. 11 reveals that the work load in the first part of `GraphFromFasta` increases nearly linearly with the number of OpenMP threads. Consequently, there is practically no parallel speed up with more than two threads. We identified the root cause for this behavior being the frequent creation and destruction of string stream objects within an inner loop of the massively called function `is_simple`. The string stream creation is internally locked by a mutex, which produces excessive wait time since all threads simultaneously created the string stream objects with a very high frequency. This is visible by the increasing amount of time spent in the code region marked `stringstreams`, from about 25 s with one thread to 260 s with 16 threads.

Further investigation showed that the string stream creation can be moved out of the inner loop by creating the string stream object before the loop and only clearing the string streams in the inner loop. Consequently, we were able to avoid the serialization in this critical section.

This optimization leads to a substantial increase in parallel performance and, therefore, a remarkable reduced runtime for the first part of `GraphFromFasta`.

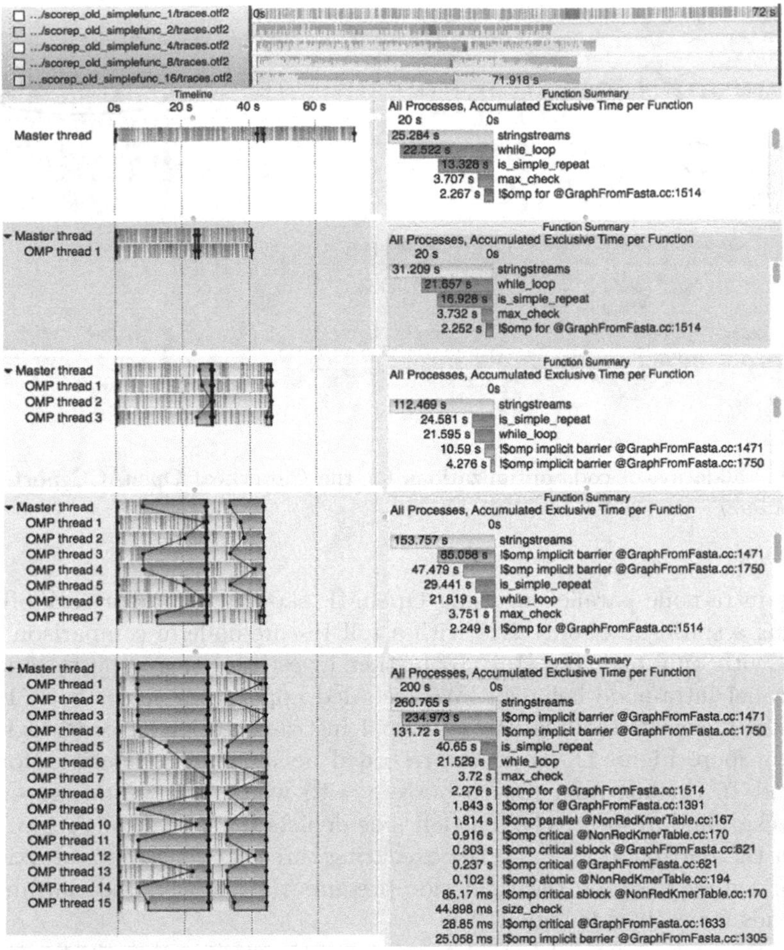

Fig. 11. Resource utilization of original Trinity 2.0.6 version (Color figure online)

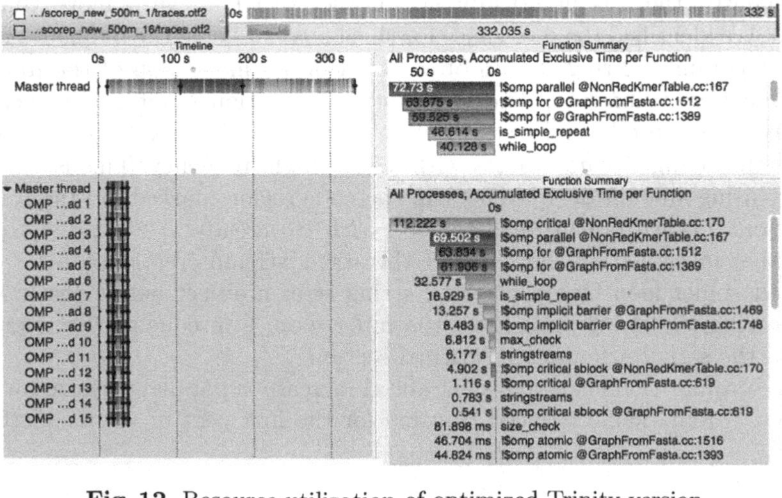

Fig. 12. Resource utilization of optimized Trinity version

In addition to the better scaling, the serial runtime is reduced, as well; for the analyzed test data set, the serial runtime decreases from 72 s to 5 s. Figure 12 shows the improved scaling of the optimized version. The parallel speed up is increased to 8.9 instead of 2.3 with the unoptimized version.

During the analysis of Trinity the comparison functionality was pivotal in understanding the parallel, intra-node behavior of the `GraphFromFasta` module and in identifying and omitting the root causes of poor parallel scalability. Equipped with this knowledge, we were able to introduce modifications resulting in a speedup of 3.9 in the intra-node performance of the `GraphFromFasta` module and in combination with other optimizations a 22 % improvement in overall run time.

5 Conclusions

This work introduces features for visual trace comparison in Vampir. Our contributions enable simultaneous inspection of multiple traces in a synchronized *Comparison View*. This view is already available in current Vampir and VampirServer releases. It greatly simplifies analyzing application performance for, i.a., different input data sets, software versions, processing element setups and hardware architectures.

We present three methods for synchronizing the zoom of multiple traces. Users can align traces manually, automatically using predefined markers, and via a heuristic that aligns according to the call profile. The latter method works well even if the traces have diverging structure.

Three use cases demonstrate the wide applicability of the Comparison View for performance analysis of real-world applications and highlight its benefits for detailed visual comparison of performance data.

In this work we focus on visual comparison and structural alignment of multiple traces. We intend to use this work as a basis for enhanced analysis approaches which automatically analyze structural and temporal differences.

Acknowledgments. This research used resources of the Oak Ridge Leadership Computing Facility at Oak Ridge National Laboratory, which is supported by the Office of Science of the Department of Energy under Contract DE-AC05-00OR22725.

References

1. Brendel, R., Heyde, M., Brunst, H., Hilbrich, T., Weber, M.: Edge bundling for visualizing communication behavior. In: Proceedings of the 3rd International Workshop on Visual Performance Analysis, pp. 1–8. IEEE Press (2016)
2. Brunst, H., Weber, M.: Custom hot spot analysis of HPC software with the vampir performance tool suite. In: Cheptsov, A., Brinkmann, S., Gracia, J., Resch, M., Nagel, W. (eds.) Tools for High Performance Computing, pp. 95–114. Springer, Heidelberg (2012). https://doi.org/10.1007/978-3-642-37349-7_7

3. Eisenbach, M., Nicholson, D.M., Rusanu, A., Brown, G.: First principles calculation of finite temperature magnetism in fe and fe3c. J. Appl. Phys. **109**(7), 07E138 (2011)
4. Gamblin, T., de Supinski, B.R., Schulz, M., Fowler, R., Reed, D.A.: Clustering performance data efficiently at massive scales. In: Proceedings of the 24th ACM International Conference on Supercomputing, ICS 2010, pp. 243–252. ACM, New York (2010)
5. Grabherr, M.G., et al.: Full-length transcriptome assembly from RNA-Seq data without a reference genome. Nat. Biotechnol. **29**(7), 644–652 (2011)
6. Herdman, J.A., et al.: Accelerating hydrocodes with OpenACC, OpenCL and CUDA. In: SC Companion: High Performance Computing, Networking Storage and Analysis, pp. 465–471 (2012)
7. Huck, K.A., Malony, A.D., Shende, S., Morris, A.: Scalable, automated performance analysis with TAU and PerfExplorer. In: Proceedings of the 14th Conference on Parallel Computing (ParCo 2007), pp. 629–636 (2007)
8. Intel Trace Analyzer and Collector, November 2015. http://software.intel.com/en-us/articles/intel-trace-analyzer/
9. Knüpfer, A., Voigt, B., Nagel, W.E., Mix, H.: Visualization of repetitive patterns in event traces. In: Kågström, B., Elmroth, E., Dongarra, J., Waśniewski, J. (eds.) PARA 2006. LNCS, vol. 4699, pp. 430–439. Springer, Heidelberg (2007). https://doi.org/10.1007/978-3-540-75755-9_52
10. Levenshtein, V.I.: Binary codes capable of correcting deletions, insertions, and reversals. Sov. Phys. Dokl. **10**(8), 707–710 (1966)
11. Llort, G., Servat, H., González, J., Giménez, J., Labarta, J.: On the usefulness of object tracking techniques in performance analysis. In: Proceedings of SC13: International Conference for High Performance Computing, Networking, Storage and Analysis, SC 2013, pp. 29:1–29:11. ACM, New York (2013)
12. Mohror, K., Karavanic, K.L.: Evaluating similarity-based trace reduction techniques for scalable performance analysis. In: Proceedings of the Conference on High Performance Computing Networking, Storage and Analysis, p. 55. ACM (2009)
13. Pillet, V., Labarta, J., Cortes, T., Girona, S.: PARAVER: a tool to visualize and analyze parallel code. In: Proceedings of WoTUG-18: Transputer and occam Developments, pp. 17–31. March 1995
14. Schulz, M., de Supinski, B.R.: Practical differential profiling. In: Kermarrec, A.-M., Bougé, L., Priol, T. (eds.) Euro-Par 2007. LNCS, vol. 4641, pp. 97–106. Springer, Heidelberg (2007). https://doi.org/10.1007/978-3-540-74466-5_12
15. Song, F., Wolf, F., Bhatia, N., Dongarra, J., Moore, S.: An algebra for cross-experiment performance analysis. In: Proceedings of the 2004 International Conference on Parallel Processing, ICPP 2004, pp. 63–72. IEEE Computer Society, Washington (2004)
16. Wagner, M., Fulton, B., Henschel, R.: Performance optimization for the trinity RNA-Seq assembler. In: Knüpfer, A., Hilbrich, T., Niethammer, C., Gracia, J., Nagel, W.E., Resch, M.M. (eds.) Tools for High Performance Computing 2015, pp. 29–40. Springer, Cham (2016). https://doi.org/10.1007/978-3-319-39589-0_3
17. Weber, M., Brendel, R., Brunst, H.: Trace file comparison with a hierarchical sequence alignment algorithm. In: Proceedings of the 2012 IEEE 10th International Symposium on Parallel and Distributed Processing with Applications, ISPA 2012, pp. 247–254. IEEE Computer Society, Washington, July 2012

18. Weber, M., Brendel, R., Hilbrich, T., Mohror, K., Schulz, M., Brunst, H.: Structural clustering: a new approach to support performance analysis at scale. In: Proceedings of the 30th IEEE International Parallel and Distributed Processing Symposium (IPDPS), pp. 484–493. IEEE Computer Society, May 2016
19. Weber, M., Geisler, R., Brunst, H., Nagel, W.E.: Folding methods for event timelines in performance analysis. In: Proceedings of the 29th IEEE International Parallel and Distributed Processing Symposium Workshops (IPDPSW), pp. 205–214. IEEE Computer Society, May 2015
20. Weber, M., Mohror, K., Schulz, M., de Supinski, B.R., Brunst, H., Nagel, W.E.: Alignment-based metrics for trace comparison. In: Wolf, F., Mohr, B., an Mey, D. (eds.) Euro-Par 2013. LNCS, vol. 8097, pp. 29–40. Springer, Heidelberg (2013). https://doi.org/10.1007/978-3-642-40047-6_6

ESPT 2018

Understanding the Scalability of Molecular Simulation Using Empirical Performance Modeling

Sergei Shudler[1(✉)], Jadran Vrabec[2], and Felix Wolf[3]

[1] Argonne National Laboratory, Lemont, IL 60439, USA
sshudler@anl.gov

[2] Thermodynamics and Process Engineering, Technical University Berlin, 10587 Berlin, Germany
vrabec@tu-berlin.de

[3] Laboratory for Parallel Programming, Technical University Darmstadt, 64289 Darmstadt, Germany
wolf@cs.tu-darmstadt.de

Abstract. Molecular dynamics (MD) simulation allows for the study of static and dynamic properties of molecular ensembles at various molecular scales, from monatomics to macromolecules such as proteins and nucleic acids. It has applications in biology, materials science, biochemistry, and biophysics. Recent developments in simulation techniques spurred the emergence of the computational molecular engineering (CME) field, which focuses specifically on the needs of industrial users in engineering. Within CME, the simulation code *ms2* allows users to calculate thermodynamic properties of bulk fluids. It is a parallel code that aims to scale the temporal range of the simulation while keeping the execution time minimal. In this paper, we use empirical performance modeling to study the impact of simulation parameters on the execution time. Our approach is a systematic workflow that can be used as a blueprint in other fields that aim to scale their simulation codes. We show that the generated models can help users better understand how to scale the simulation with minimal increase in execution time.

Keywords: Molecular dynamics · Performance modeling · Parallel programming

1 Introduction

Molecular dynamics simulation is a fundamental approach for understanding the behavior of matter at the molecular level. In physics, molecular dynamics is used to study the behavior and interactions between single atoms. In biomedical research, scientists simulate macromolecules such as proteins and viruses to better understand cell structures in organisms, as well as to design better medical

A. Bhatele et al. (Eds.): ESPT/VPA 2017/2018, LNCS 11027, pp. 125–143, 2019.
https://doi.org/10.1007/978-3-030-17872-7_8

drugs. In chemistry and chemical engineering, molecular simulations are used to understand and predict thermodynamic properties of fluid mixtures.

Some of the well-known molecular simulation packages are LAMMPS [7,22], NAMD [8,11], and GROMACS [6,9]. Although all these codes are based on the same principle, they have different aims and target different scientific fields. LAMMPS stands for Large-scale Atomic/Molecular Massively Parallel Simulator and is a versatile code designed to be easily modified or extended with new functionality. It supports both solid-state materials (e.g., metals) as well as soft matter (e.g., biomolecules and polymers). The primary objective of LAMMPS is providing a platform for further research in molecular simulation. NAMD stands for Nanoscale Molecular Dynamics and is implemented in Charm++ [19]. It is specifically designed to simulate large biomolecular systems such as viruses. Similar to NAMD, GROMACS (GROningen MAchine for Chemical Simulations) is designed to simulate biomolecular structures such as proteins, lipids, and nucleic acids. This code is most often used for simulation of protein folding. One notable example is the *Folding@home* [5] project, which is a massively distributed computing effort that exploits the idle time of processing elements of personal computers owned by a large group of volunteers worldwide.

To support chemical engineering needs, recent advances in simulation techniques of fluids ushered in a new field of Computational Molecular Engineering (CME). It falls under the category of simulation-based engineering and aims to adapt existing simulation techniques, optimized for soft matter physics, to the requirements of the chemical and process engineering industry [17]. Rather than providing scientific insight, the goal of CME is to provide a systematic approach to replace experiments that are otherwise too complex, hazardous, or expensive.

LAMMPS, NAMD, and GROMACS, albeit powerful and flexible, focus in most cases on scaling the size of the molecular system rather then the simulation time. On the other hand, chemical engineering in general and thermodynamics in particular have more benefit from longer running simulations. Furthermore, industrial applications require a proportional increase both in size of the system and simulation time.

One of the simulation packages in CME is *ms2* (molecular simulation: 2nd generation) [15,16,23]. It is aimed at industrial users and samples the full set of thermodynamic properties of bulk fluids. Since these properties can reliably be calculated from a relatively smaller number of molecules (i.e., the order of 10^4), *ms2* is not designed for larger molecular systems. The challenge, therefore, is to keep the execution time (i.e., time-to-solution) of *ms2* low as various other parameters of the simulation increase.

In this paper, we use empirical performance modeling to understand the impact of simulation parameters on the execution time of *ms2*. Empirical performance modeling produces human-readable performance models from real measurements. It has been extensively studied before [12,13,24,25], but in this work, we focus on specific challenges related to modeling the performance of a CME code. The produced models can help users select appropriate input values for the simulation such that the execution time stays within potential constraints. The workflow we provide can also help developers optimize individual computational procedures during simulation. We make the following specific contributions:

- Systematic and reliable workflow that can be used as a blue-print in performance engineering efforts of simulation codes in other fields
- Identification of pitfalls in the process of producing measurements for empirical modeling
- Exhaustive set of two-parameter and three-parameter models of execution time for the *ms2* application

The remainder of the paper is organized as follows. Section 2 provides a brief overview of the design of *ms2*. Next, Sect. 3 discusses the modeling methodology in detail. In Sect. 4, we describe the experimental setup for evaluating the methodology, and then provide a detailed analysis of the results in Sect. 5. Finally, we review related work in Sect. 6, before drawing conclusions in Sect. 7.

2 ms2 Application

The *ms2* simulation application offers a choice between two fundamental molecular simulation techniques, namely, Monte-Carlo (MC) and Molecular Dynamics (MD) [15,16,23]. The MC technique investigates the behavior of molecular ensembles stochastically. In other words, during each iteration the MC technique displaces molecules in the volume randomly, such that the probability of accepting a displacement is chosen in a way that allows obtaining a representative set of configurations. By repeating this step a large number of times, the MC technique generates a Markov chain of configurations. From this chain, static (i.e., time-independent) thermodynamic properties of the simulated molecular ensembles can be obtained. The MD technique, on the other hand, relies on the numerical solution of Newton's equations of motion. In each time step, the technique evaluates intermolecular interactions (i.e., forces and torques) that are then used to determine the spatial displacement of all molecules during the time step. Each time step results in a new configuration. Ordered chronologically, the sequence of configurations represents an approximation of the molecular propagation process such that both static and dynamic thermodynamic properties can be calculated.

Although MC is more limited in terms of accessible thermodynamic properties, it is a technique that can be parallelized easily (i.e., embarrassingly-parallel problem) since each process can generate an independent Markov chain and all chains have to be gathered only once at the end of the simulation run. To parallelize the MD technique, on the other hand, one has to parallelize the interaction calculation. For this purpose, *ms2* relies on force decomposition as proposed by Plimpton [22]. Instead of traditional domain decomposition, the interaction matrix is rearranged such that the interacting molecules are almost equally distributed in the matrix. Assuming n is the number of molecules and p is the number of processes, each process is responsible for $\frac{n}{p}$ columns of the interaction matrix. Figure 1 presents a schematic of this interaction matrix. Each gray cell

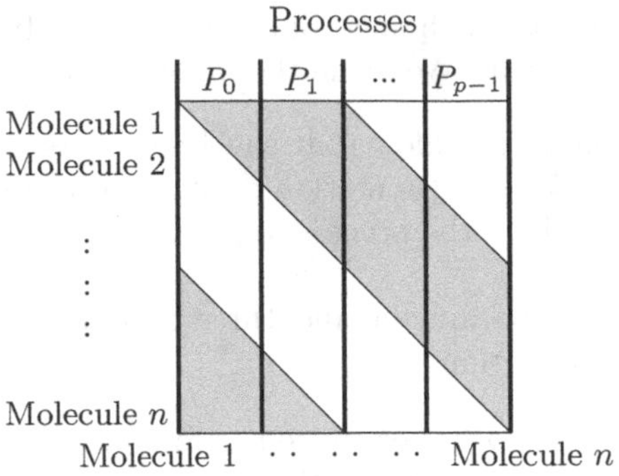

Fig. 1. Parallelization in *ms2* using force decomposition. The shaded area shows the pair interactions that have to be calculated for the simulation to proceed. Vertical black lines delimit the range of molecules for which a single process calculates the interactions.

represents an interaction between a pair of molecules that has to calculated for the simulation to proceed to the next time step. The assumption is that each process stores all molecule data (coordinates, momenta, etc.) locally. However, each process calculates only the interaction for a subgroup of molecules—exactly the group of molecules delimited by the black vertical lines in the figure. In this way, the work load is distributed almost equally between the processes. The root process then reduces all the resulting interaction components to sum up the molecular forces exerted on each individual molecule. For both MC and MD parallelization, the *ms2* application uses MPI [15]. Specifically, the MPI collective operations Barrier, Bcast, Reduce, and Allreduce are employed.

3 Methodology

In this section, we describe the methodology to produce performance models for the execution time of *ms2*. In general, the methodology follows the practice established by earlier studies. Specifically, we draw upon past experience in modeling the isoefficiency functions of task-based applications [25].

Figure 2 provides an overview of our methodology. In general, we can identify three separate phases: selecting parameters, benchmarking, and empirical modeling. Code instrumentation is an optional step that should be included if the aim is to produce models and derive predictions for specific parts of the code rather than the simulation as a whole. The subsections below cover the phases in the workflow in more detail.

3.1 Simulation Parameters

The *ms2* application has a group of parameters that characterize the simulation scenario. The most important parameters identify the type of the simulated

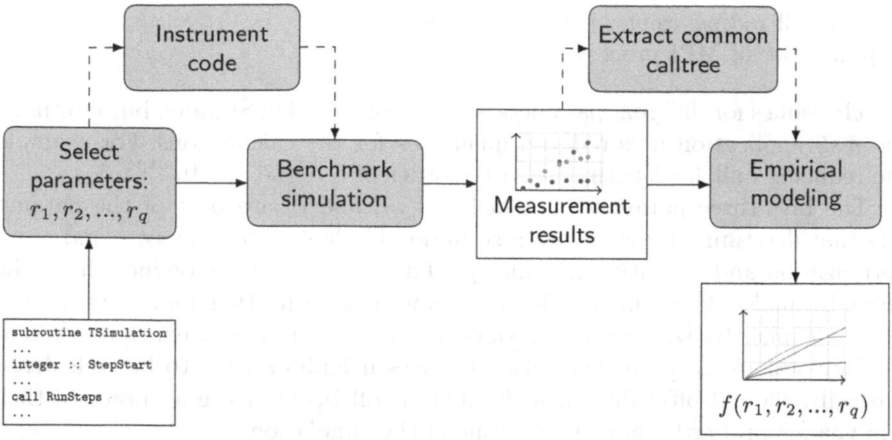

Fig. 2. Modeling workflow.

molecule (i.e., a molecular model), the number of molecules, density (or the simulated volume), temperature, and the number of time steps.

To accurately describe the interaction between molecules, *ms2* uses potential functions that describe different interaction types. Each molecular model specifies the placement of an *interaction site* on the molecule and the type of this site. A Lennard-Jones (LJ) site represents dispersive and repulsive interactions, while point charge (PC), point dipole (PD), and point quadrupole (PQ) sites represent electrostatic interactions. The complexity of molecular models depends on the molecules they represent. A simple Ar (argon) atom has only a single LJ site. A more complex CO_2 (carbon dioxide) molecule consists of three LJ sites and one PQ site. A $(CH_3)_2CO$ (acetone) molecule, however, has four LJ sites, one PD site, and one PQ site. *ms2* calculates the interaction forces between pairs of the same type of sites. For example, the interaction between two CO_2 molecules will be a combination of nine interactions between the LJ sites (three sites in each molecule equals nine different pairs) and one interaction between the PQ sites.

Using appropriate interaction sites in a molecular model is crucial for obtaining correct thermodynamic properties. However, from a computational point of view, the difference between calculating the interaction between any of the different sites is small. Furthermore, the calculation does not depend on any other simulation parameter. A far more important factor is the total number of sites in a molecule, since the computation time of molecule interaction grows quadratically with the number of sites of each type.

Following an analysis of the *ms2* design, we identified the group of parameters that should be considered for modeling the execution time of *ms2* (i.e., independent variables in our modeling):

- n: number of molecules in the simulation; range: 10^3–10^4
- m: number of interaction sites; range: 1–8
- d: density of the fluid; range: 0.001–0.9 (in reduced units σ^{-3})

- c: cut-off radius; range: 1–10 (in reduced units σ)
- p: number of MPI processes

The values for different parameters can be provided in SI units, but internally, the *ms2* application uses reduced quantities for the calculations. For example, the reducing unit for length σ is on the order of 3 Å (i.e., $3 \cdot 10^{-10}$ m).

The first three parameters, namely, n, m, and d, are part of the parameters that determine the simulation scenario. The last two, namely, c and p, are optimization and execution parameters. The cut-off radius c defines the radius around a molecule within which the interactions with other molecules are calculated explicitly. Decreasing c results in less computational effort to evaluate the interactions for each molecule, since less neighbors have to be considered. Basically, the cut-off radius provides a trade-off between the accuracy of thermodynamic properties and the runtime of the simulation.

To simplify benchmarking and modeling, we used synthetic molecular models with m LJ sites. Each such model is comparable to a model of a real molecule with the same number of interaction sites m, independent of the site type.Therefore, performance models based only LJ sites (synthetic molecules) are a viable proxy for performance models based on ensembles of real molecules. The advantage of the former is the ease of generating synthetic molecular models. The LJ sites in the synthetic molecule were placed at the vertices of a regular polygon with m edges and an edge $s = 0.1$ Å. This allowed us to conveniently generate molecular models for arbitrary values of m. If the center of the polygon was at (0, 0), then the coordinates (x_i, y_i) of vertex i are given by (k is the circumradius from the center of the polygon to one of the vertices):

$$r = \frac{s}{2\sin(\frac{\pi}{m})}$$

$$x_i = r \cdot \cos(2\pi \frac{i}{m})$$

$$y_i = r \cdot \sin(2\pi \frac{i}{m})$$

The list of parameters above is not exhaustive. Additional parameters of *ms2* are the specified boundary conditions (i.e., simulated ensemble type), the length and the number of time steps, frequency of writing results and errors to a disk, temperature, and so on. Some of these parameters, such as temperature, have little influence on the computational cost. The number of time steps influences the execution time, but the relation is simply linear such that this parameter does not have to be considered in the modeling process. The same rationale also applies to other parameters omitted from the list above.

3.2 Benchmarking

Once the group of independent parameters has been identified, we can move to the benchmarking phase. However, one optional step before benchmarking is instrumentation. By instrumenting the relevant regions of the code (i.e., functions, kernels, or code blocks), one can produce a model for each region. In this way, for example, we can obtain a model for the execution time of a single time step in *ms2*. Whether such high-resolution modeling is needed depends on the application and the analysis goals. In the *ms2* case, a model for a single time step makes little sense, since a simulation with a single time step is useless. The aim of the simulation is to simulate an evolving environment of molecules. Nevertheless, we ran benchmarks with both an instrumented and an uninstrumented version of *ms2* to evaluate our workflow. We used Score-P [20] for the instrumentation since it integrates easily with the Extra-P [4] modeling tool (discussed in the next subsection) and provides flexible instrumentation approaches. In other words, one can either automatically instrument all of the regions in the code or manually instrument just the most relevant ones.

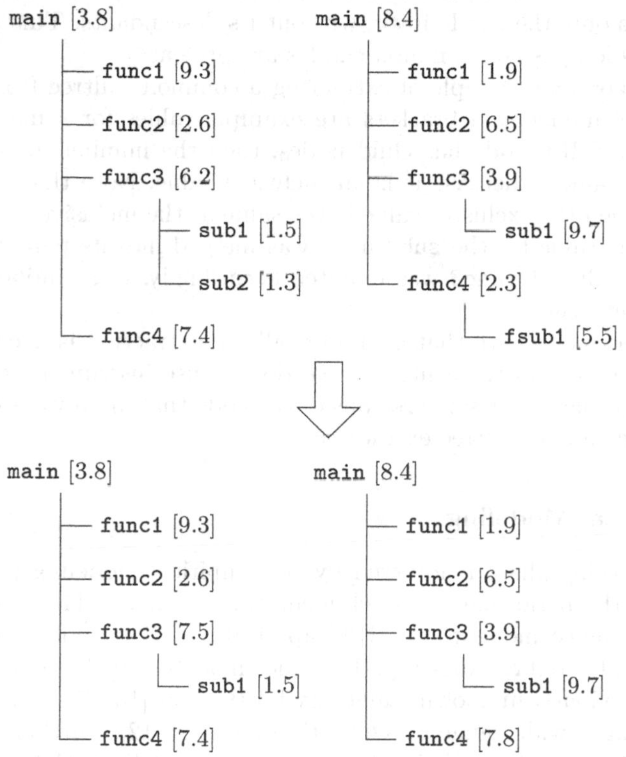

Fig. 3. Common calltree extraction from two different trees (top). The two trees at the bottom have a common structure.

During the execution of an instrumented application Score-P creates a calltree, where the root node is the first (main) function called and each new node (i.e., *cnode*) represents a called subfunction. An edge between nodes represents a caller-callee relation. Once the application terminates, Score-P writes a performance profile to disk. Each profile is a CUBE [2] file that contains performance data arranged in three dimensions—metrics, calltree (cnodes), and system (processes/threads). Basically, there is a measurement value for each combination of (metric, cnode, process/thread). When Extra-P is used to generate a model of the execution time from these data, it collapses the system dimension by taking the maximum value and generates a separate model for each cnode. Therefore, it is important to ensure that the calltree structure is similar across all of the data used for modeling. Since the application is executed with different values for independent parameters, differences in calltrees are inevitable. To extract a common calltree, we used the `cube_commoncalltree` utility provided with CUBE. This utility looks for cnodes that do not appear in every calltree and then merges them into the parent cnode by adding the inclusive value of performance data of the child cnode to the parent's exclusive value. An inclusive value is a sum of values for the cnode itself and all of its descendants, whereas an exclusive value includes only the cnode itself, without its descendants. This computation is repeated as long as non-common cnodes are present.

Figure 3 shows an example of extracting a common calltree from two different trees. The numbers in brackets are example values for some metric (e.g., execution time). If a node has child nodes, then the number in the bracket is the exclusive value, otherwise it is an inclusive value. Note that if a node has no children, then the exclusive value is the same as the inclusive one. The figure shows that the value for the `sub2` node was merged into its parent `func3`, and the exclusive value of `func3` was updated accordingly. In a similar way, `fsub1` was merged into `func4`.

It is important to note that common calltree extraction is necessary only if all code regions are instrumented. If we do not use instrumentation at all or manually instrument just some regions of the code that are always executed, we can skip the common calltree extraction.

3.3 Empirical Modeling

The benchmarking phase is followed by the empirical modeling phase. Specifically, we use the performance-model generator in Extra-P [4], a tool for automated performance modeling of HPC applications. The model generator has already shown to confirm known performance models of real applications as well as discover previously unknown scalability bottlenecks [13, 27], and has also been validated using a wide range of synthetic functions [12]. Furthermore, specific usage examples include modeling the performance of OpenMP constructs [18] and the isoefficiency functions of task-based programs [25].

A multi-parameter model aims to capture how a number of independent parameters, such as process count, problem size, and algorithmic parameters, influence a target metric, such as runtime, floating-point operations, and so on. The key concept of the modeling approach in Extra-P is the *performance model normal form* (PMNF) for multiple parameters [12]:

$$f(r_1, r_2, ..., r_q) = \sum_{k=1}^{n} c_k \cdot \prod_{l=1}^{q} r_l^{i_{k_l}} \cdot \log^{j_{k_l}}(r_l) \quad (1)$$

In this form, parameters r_l are represented by q combinations of monomials and logarithms, which are summed up in n different terms to form the model. The exponents i_{k_l} and j_{k_l} are chosen from sets $I, J \subset \mathbb{Q}$, respectively. Essentially, these sets define the scope of all possible terms. Consider, for example, $n = 3$, $q = 2$, and $I = \{0, 0.25, 0.5\}$, $J = \{0, 1\}$. In this case, the search space for possible terms would be $\{1, \log(r), r^{0.25}, r^{0.25}\log(r), r^{0.5}, r^{0.5}\log(r)\}$, and an example model could be: $f(r_1, r_2) = c_1 + c_2 \cdot r_1^{0.5} + c_3 \cdot r_1^{0.25} r_2^{0.25} \log(r_2)$.

The generator requires a set of measurements as input whose precise nature depends on the scaling objective (e.g., number of processes vs. input size, weak vs. strong). As a rule of thumb, it needs at least five different settings for each independent parameter. For example, if there is only a single parameter, such as the number of processes, we need to benchmark the application with five different values of this parameter. If there are two or more parameters, we need to benchmark the application for each combination of parameter values. This means at least 5^q measurements are required for q parameters. Each such measurement has to be repeated a number of times to obtain a statistically significant result. If k repetitions are required, the application has to be executed $k \cdot 5^q$ times. Figure 4 shows typical benchmarking results for two parameters. In this case, the number of MPI processes p and the number of molecules n were varied. The points represent parameter combinations for which execution times were measured. There are six different values for each parameter, which means that there are 36 combinations. Each of the 36 points represents a median value of $k = 10$ repetitions.

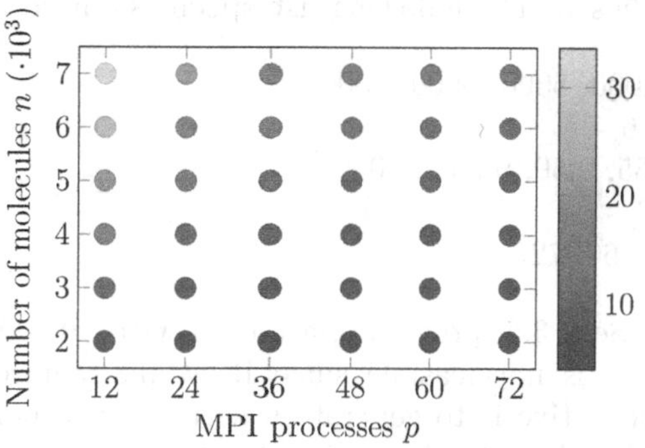

Fig. 4. Typical benchmark results for two parameters; in this case, the number of MPI processes p and the number of molecules n were varied. The color of each point represents the execution time in seconds. (Color figure online)

The modeling technique in Extra-P is based on an iterative modeling refinement process that stops when $\bar{R}^2$—the adjusted coefficient of determination—cannot be improved any further. The adjusted coefficient of determination is a standard statistical fit factor $\in [0,1]$ such that a value of 1 indicates a perfect fit. Since even small increases in n and q can lead to a prohibitively large search space of possible terms, the technique employs a heuristic that reduces the number of candidate models. Specifically, the search space of possible terms is generated from the best single parameter models for each individual parameter. This leads to a smaller number of candidate models, which greatly reduces the time for finding the best fitting model, but still retains a high degree of accuracy [12].

4 Experimental Setup

We performed our evaluation on Hazel Hen, a Cray XC40 system at the High Performance Computing Center Stuttgart (HLRS). The system has 7712 compute nodes with the Aries interconnect fabric and Dragonfly topology. Each node comprises two Intel Xeon E5-2680 v3 processors with 12 cores each and 128 GB of memory. In other words, there are 24 cores per node and more than 5 GB of memory per core on Hazel Hen.

The *ms2* application uses OpenMP to parallelize the calculation of interactions in each process. A performance audit of *ms2*, performed as part of the Performance Optimisation and Productivity project [3], suggested that the optimal number of OpenMP threads is four (i.e., four cores are used by one process). Following this observation, we used four OpenMP threads in all of our benchmarks. Consequently, there were six MPI processes per node.

4.1 Parameter Values

For each independent parameter discussed in Sect. 3.1, at least five different values have to be chosen. The following list specifies our choices:

- n: 2000, 3000, 4000, 5000, 6000, 7000
- m: 1, 2, 3, 4, 5, 6
- d: 0.05, 0.20, 0.35, 0.50, 0.65, 0.80
- c: 1, 2, 3, 4, 5, 6
- p: 12, 24, 36, 48, 60, 72

As discussed in Sect. 3.3, producing a model with all independent variables (e.g., $T(n, m, d, c, p)$) is not feasible since it would require at least 5^5 measurements. The alternative is to generate a series of two-parameter and three-parameter models that describe the application behavior and allow us to produce useful time predictions. For example, we can generate models $T(n, p)$, $T(n, m)$, $T(n, m, p)$, and so on. In each case, however, we vary only a subset of two or three parameters. The values for the other parameters have to remain constant throughout the benchmarking phase of each particular model. For example, if one runs benchmarks to generate the model $T(n, p)$, the values for m, d, and c have to remain constant.

4.2 Measurements Variability

Earlier studies showed that applications that run on Cray XC40 might experience a high degree of variability in execution time and performance [10,14,28]. The reason is that Cray XC40 uses the Dragonfly topology. It is a high-radix, low-diameter network that utilizes shared links and is designed to improve bandwidth and reduce packet latency. Furthermore, it uses adaptive routing and random node placement, both of which can alleviate congestion and achieve better load-balancing. However, the combination of these characteristics makes each application highly susceptible to the behavior of other applications that are being executed at the same time. In other words, a communication-intensive application can cause performance degradation in less-intensive applications executed concurrently.

Table 1. Variability (i.e., coefficient of variation (CV)) of measurements for generating the model $T(n, p)$. The columns specify values for the time step number and cut-off radius, as well as whether the code was instrumented and a compact placement (CP) of nodes was used.

Time steps	Cut-off	Instr.	CP	CV
3,000	2.0			3.3%
3,000	2.0	✓		13.5%
30,000	2.0			10.5%
3,000	4.0			6.2%
3,000	4.0	✓		58.7%
40,000	4.0	✓		26.6%
40,000	4.0	✓	✓	8.3%

For empirical modeling, the execution of the application for any combination of parameter values has to be repeated k times (see Sect. 3.3). In our evaluation, we set $k = 10$, and sometimes $k = 5$ to reduce the total time to obtain the measurements. The purpose of these repetitions was to increase the statistical significance of the measurements. However, a high degree of variability between repetitions indicates a high level of noise, which makes modeling far less accurate [13].

Table 1 shows how various factors influence the variability of the measurements. In this case, the measurements were performed to generate the model $T(n, p)$, which means repeated executions for different combinations of parameter values for n and p. Variability was measured as the coefficient of variance (CV) between the repetitions for each combination of values. The CV is defined as the ratio of the standard deviation to the mean and shows the extent of samples variability in relation to the mean.

The two leftmost columns in Table 1 specify the values for the number of time steps and the cut-off radius, respectively. The column *Instr* specifies whether the

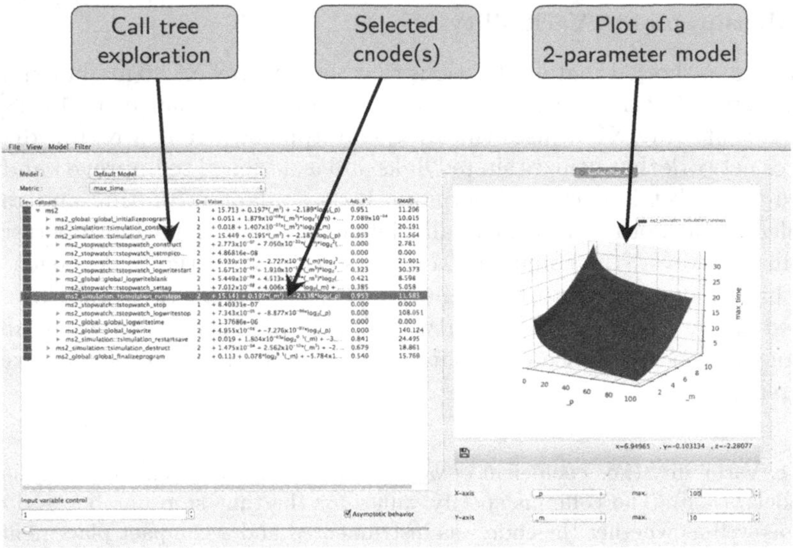

Fig. 5. Graphical user interface of Extra-P.

code was fully instrumented and column *CP* specifies whether the nodes were placed compactly in the machine, that is on the same blade and in the same chassis. The table indicates that increasing the number of time steps increases the variability. It also shows that fully instrumenting the code increases the variability as well. However, one factor which helps reduce the CV is placing the nodes physically together. These observations can be explained by the Dragonfly topology studies [10,14,28] and the low intensity of communication in *ms2* [15]. The longer the *ms2* code runs, the more time it is under the influence of other communication-heavy applications on the machine, which causes the variability to increase. This is also the reason why placing the nodes together reduces the variability—only local communication links are used in such cases. Unfortunately, this placement mode is not generally available on Hazel Hen as it has a negative effect on the utilization of the system.

Full instrumentation has a minimal perturbation in terms of performance, but has a significant effect on the variability. One likely explanation is that code instrumentation uses more communication to collate some of the measured data while the program runs. As discussed earlier, full instrumentation is not needed to model the total simulation time. Consequently, to reduce the variability we ran uninstrumented code with 3,000 time steps and cut-off radius of 2.0 (when it is not a parameter in the model).

5 Result Analysis

In this section, we discuss the results of our evaluation. As described above, we chose to focus on the execution time of full simulations rather than the execution

Table 2. 2-parameter models for the execution time of the *ms2* application.

Model	Fixed parameters	Model	$\bar{R}^2$
$T(n,m)$	$d = 0.84$, $c = 2.0$, $p = 72$	$4.41 + 8.03 \cdot 10^{-5} \cdot m \cdot n \cdot \log n$	0.99
$T(p,m)$	$n = 4{,}000$, $d = 0.84$, $c = 2.0$	$6.6 + 3.21 \cdot m^2 - 0.42 \cdot m^2 \cdot \log p$	0.92
$T(p,d)$	$n = 4{,}000$, $m = 1$, $c = 2.0$	$20.67 - 2.2 \cdot \log p$	0.88
$T(p,c)$	$n = 4{,}000$, $m = 1$, $d = 0.84$	$33.83 + 0.05 \cdot c^3 - 4.89 \cdot \log p$	0.79
$T(n,c)$	$m = 1$, $d = 0.84$, $p = 36$	$-0.99 + 0.06 \cdot c^3 + 1.81 \cdot 10^{-5} \cdot \log^2 n$	0.95
$T(m,c)$	$n = 4{,}000$, $d = 0.84$, $p = 36$	$-23.49 + 10.09 \cdot m + 0.22 \cdot c^3 \cdot m$	0.95

Table 3. 3-parameter models for the execution time of the *ms2* application.

Model	Fixed parameters	Model	$\bar{R}^2$
$T(p,n,m)$	$d = 0.84$, $c = 2.0$	$62.28 + 2.03 \cdot 10^{-8} \cdot m^2 \cdot n^{1.5} \cdot \log^2 n - 9.63 \cdot \log p$	0.83
$T(n,m,c)$	$d = 0.84$, $p = 72$	$9.24 + 5.71 \cdot 10^{-6} \cdot n \cdot \log n \cdot c^2 \cdot \log c \cdot m$	0.88

time of individual steps, so that there was no need for full instrumentation of the code. Nevertheless, Sect. 3 provides a detailed description of how the workflow can support full instrumentation for later analysis of *ms2* or other codes. To complete the discussion on full instrumentation, we briefly present the Extra-P graphical user interface (GUI) that allows users to analyze the model at each cnode. Figure 5 shows a screenshot of the Extra-P window. The left part is divided into two areas. The upper area has a dropdown box that shows the selected metric (e.g., time, visits, etc.) and allows users to choose a different metric. The lower area contains the calltree with a model for each cnode and fit factors such as $\bar{R}^2$ (adjusted coefficient of determination) besides each model. By clicking on any one of the cnodes, the plot of the corresponding model is displayed in the right part of the Extra-P window. The figure shows an example plot for a two-parameter model $T(p,m)$. It is a three-dimensional surface where the vertical axis is the time dimension.

The Extra-P GUI provides a convenient way to explore and compare multiple models from the same calltree. However, when no instrumentation is involved, Extra-P provides a programmatic interface to produce models directly from the measurement results. We used this interface in our evaluation and produced a set of models summarized in Tables 2 and 3. The leftmost column specifies the independent parameters in each model and the following column specifies the values of the parameters that were fixed in each case. The second column from the right shows the two-parameter and three-parameter models produced by Extra-P and the rightmost column specifies the adjusted coefficient of determination.

Unsurprisingly, the model $T(p,m)$ shows that the execution time increases in quadratic proportion to the number of interaction sites m. Furthermore, all models with the cut-off radius c as an independent parameter show that the time increases in cubic proportion to c. This is because every increase in the cut-off

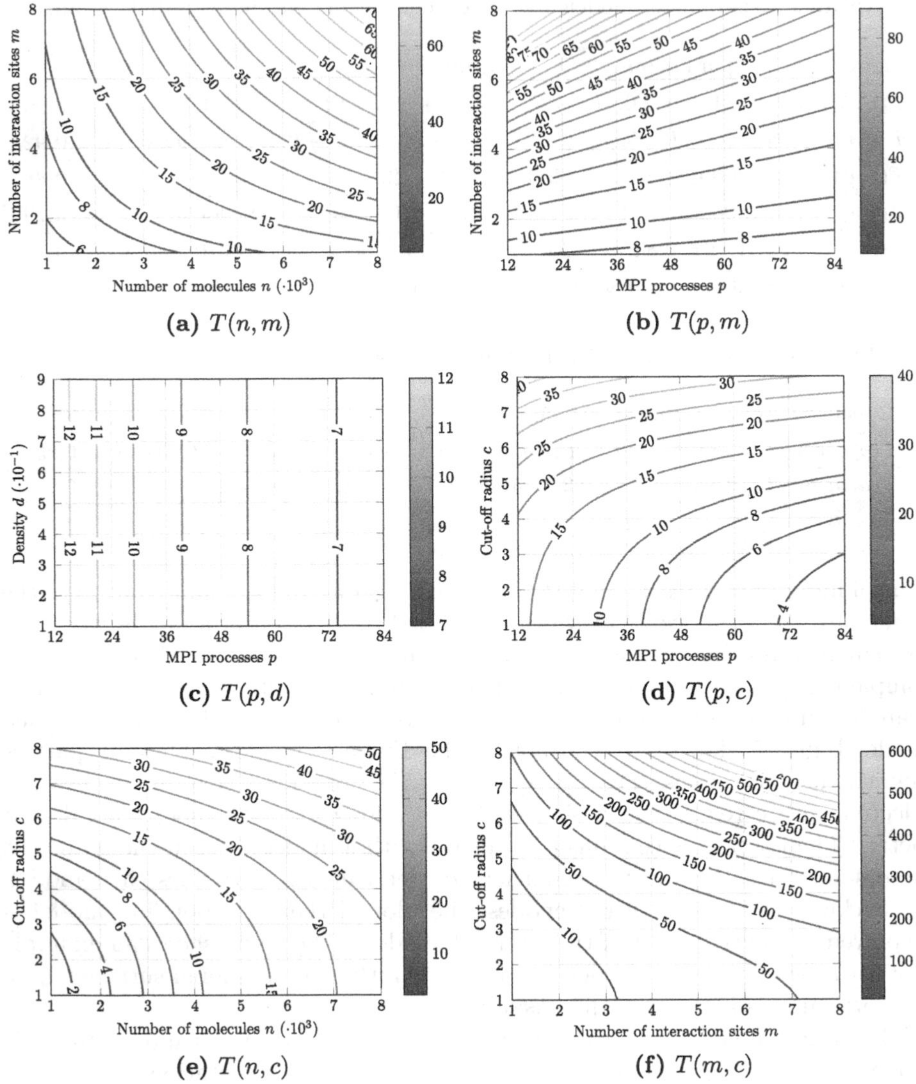

Fig. 6. Contour lines of the plots for 2-parameter models of the *ms2* execution time. All times are in seconds.

radius leads to a cubic increase in the cut-off volume around each particle, which also means a cubic increase in the number of particles in the cut-off sphere. These results confirm our expectations about the factors that influence the simulation. Although m depends on the simulated fluid and cannot be reduced without breaking the simulation, the cut-off radius c is an important optimization factor and should be as minimal as the simulation goals permit.

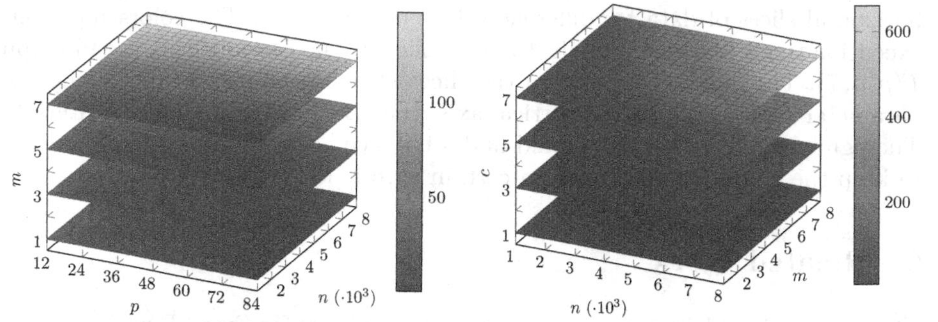

(a) $T(p, n, m)$ (b) $T(n, m, c)$

Fig. 7. Stacked plots of 3-parameter models of the *ms2* execution time. All times are in seconds.

The model $T(p, d)$ has no terms with density d, which suggests that increasing d has a minimal or no effect on the execution time at all. This is surprising since increasing the density leads to a linear increase in the number of particles in the cut-off sphere. One reasonable explanation is that not all the molecules in the cut-off sphere are taken into the account during the interaction calculation. The interaction matrix, discussed in Sect. 2, is arranged in a way that makes each process calculate only part of the interactions. Therefore, additional interaction calculations that are caused by a higher number of molecules in the cut-off sphere are distributed evenly between the processes leading only to a slight increase in the wallclock time of the simulation.

Furthermore, all models containing the number of processes p clearly show that increasing p leads to just a logarithmic improvement in the execution time. Although an increase in the number of processes means less interactions have to calculated by each single process, the cost of communication (i.e., MPI collective operations) still increases. This suggests that to achieve shorter execution time, we might look at changing other parameters rather than p.

Figure 6 depicts the plots of two-parameter models from Table 2 as contour lines. The label on each line specifies the time value along that line. The shape of the lines and their density provide a visual cue as to how fast the execution time increases and which parameter has more impact on this increase. Furthermore, each contour line shows how both parameters have to be increased so that the execution time remains constant. Figures 6b and d, for example, show that increasing p reduces the execution time. However, the shape of the contour lines in these figures is different. For higher p values, increasing c leads to faster increase in the runtime in Fig. 6b compared to equivalent increase of m in Fig. 6d. As another example, Figs. 6e and f show that the impact of increasing both m and c is much more severe than increasing n and c at the same time.

Figure 7 depicts three-parameter models from Table 3, namely, $T(p, n, m)$ and $T(n, m, c)$. As these functions are four-dimensional entities it is not straightforward to visualize them. The figure shows 3 axes—one for each parameter—and horizontal slices of data for different values of the z axis. The colors represent execution times. For example, the topmost slice in Fig. 7a represents the function $T(p, n, 7)$. The differences between the slices show the impact of increasing the parameter represented by the vertical axis, that is m in Fig. 7a and c in Fig. 7b. The figures suggest that one should find a balance between different parameters to keep the execution time under a certain threshold.

6 Related Work

The empirical modeling approach that forms the basis for Extra-P was first proposed by Calotoiu et al. [13] in the context of identifying scalability bugs. A scalability bug is a part of the program in which scaling behavior is unintentionally poor. In this study, the authors produced scaling models of execution time as a function of the MPI process count, but no other independent parameters were considered. In another study, Vogel et al. [27] used both Score-P and Extra-P to analyze the scalability of the whole UG4 framework, which simulates drug diffusion through the human skin. The authors showed that Extra-P was able to produce over 10,000 models—spanning the whole calltree—in less than a minute. Each model was a scaling model of execution time as a function of the number of MPI processes. These studies had only one independent parameter and did not have to overcome pitfalls that arise when dealing with multiple parameters.

The capability to produce empirical models with multiple parameters was introduced by Calotoiu et al. [12]. This functionality is based on a number of important heuristics that make the approach feasible in practice. The authors performed their evaluation using a number of scientific codes that were executed on a Blue Gene/Q system. They produced multi-parameter models of execution time and floating point operations. In the present study, we go one step further and provide a systematic workflow that can be readily applied in performance engineering of simulation codes.

Shudler et al. [24] proposed a framework, based on empirical modeling, for validating performance expectations of HPC libraries. The framework targets both developers and users, and provides a systematic method that allows, with as little effort as possible, to evaluate whether the observed behavior corresponds to the expected behavior. The authors focused on scaling models with one independent parameter, namely, the number of MPI processes. The benefits of this framework for performance engineering inspired the methodology developed in this work. Furthermore, past experience of Shudler et al. [25] in modeling the isoefficiency functions of task-based applications [25] provided important guiding points for designing the present workflow.

Singh et al. [26] and Marathe et al. [21] used machine learning techniques to model the effects of various input parameters on the performance of scientific codes. The authors showed that some of these techniques can handle a large parameter space without the costs associated with our methodology. However, machine learning techniques are inherently black-box, meaning that users can use the models to obtain predictions, but the models themselves provide little insight. We use a transparent technique that produces human-readable models, which indeed can provide additional insights.

7 Conclusion

In this paper, we propose a versatile methodology for understanding the performance of simulation codes in particular and scientific codes in general. It is based on a systematic workflow for producing empirical performance models. Empirical performance modeling is a proven technique for automated generation of performance models from the results of code benchmarking. Using our methodology, we generated two-parameter and three-parameter models for the execution time of *ms2*, a molecular dynamics code for studying thermodynamic properties of bulk fluids. The models provide insight on the impact of various parameters on the execution time. They also show in which situations the impact is compounded, for example, increasing both the number of interaction sites and the cut-off radius leads to a much higher increase in execution time.

Besides providing insight, the generated performance models are analytical expressions that can be used to calculate the execution time for given parameter values. In other words, the models allow us to predict the performance of the application. This capability was employed in the TaLPas project [1], which aims to provide a solution for fast and robust simulation of many, potentially dependent particle systems in a distributed environment. Specifically, performance prediction is used to support a purpose-built scheduler in the process of finding optimal execution configurations for individual simulation runs.

The study also identifies potential pitfalls in the workflow and provides suggestions for overcoming them. Specifically, we discuss the necessity of extracting a common calltree from performance profiles, and also provide guidelines for performing the benchmarking. Furthermore, we highlight the influence of various factors on the variability of the measurements and the importance of reducing it to obtain accurate models.

Acknowledgements. This work was supported by the German Research Foundation (DFG) through the Program Performance Engineering for Scientific Software and the ExtraPeak project, by the German Federal Ministry of Education and Research (BMBF) through the TaLPas project under Grant No. 01IH16008D, and by the US Department of Energy through the PRIMA-X project under Grant No. DE-SC0015524. The authors would like to thank the partners of the TaLPas project for fruitful discussions. Finally, the authors would also like express their gratitude to the High Performance Computing Center Stuttgart (HLRS) and the University Computing Center (Hochschulrechenzentrum) of Technische Universität Darmstadt for providing access to machines Hazel Hen and Lichtenberg, respectively.

References

1. BMBF project TaLPas - Task-based Load Balancing and Auto-tuning in Particle Simulations. https://wr.informatik.uni-hamburg.de/research/projects/talpas/start. Accessed 22 May 2018
2. Cube 4.x series. http://www.scalasca.org/software/cube-4.x/download.html. Accessed 22 May 2018
3. European Union's Horizon 2020 project POP - Performance Optimisation and Productivity. https://pop-coe.eu. Accessed 25 June 2018
4. Extra-P – Automated Performance-modeling Tool. http://www.scalasca.org/software/extra-p. Accessed 22 May 2018
5. Folding@home. https://foldingathome.org/. Accessed 04 July 2018
6. GROMACS: Molecular Dynamics Package. http://www.gromacs.org/. Accessed 03 July 2018
7. LAMMPS: Molecular Dynamics Simulator. http://lammps.sandia.gov/. Accessed 03 July 2018
8. NAMD: Scalable Molecular Dynamics. http://www.ks.uiuc.edu/Research/namd/. Accessed 03 July 2018
9. Berendsen, H., van der Spoel, D., van Drunen, R.: GROMACS: a message-passing parallel molecular dynamics implementation. Comput. Phys. Commun. **91**(1), 43–56 (1995). https://doi.org/10.1016/0010-4655(95)00042-E
10. Bhatele, A., Jain, N., Livnat, Y., Pascucci, V., Bremer, P.T.: Analyzing network health and congestion in dragonfly-based supercomputers. In: Proceedings of the 30th IEEE International Parallel & Distributed Processing Symposium (IPDPS), pp. 93–102. IEEE Computer Society, May 2016. https://doi.org/10.1109/IPDPS.2016.123
11. Phillips, J.C., et al.: Scalable molecular dynamics with NAMD. J. Comput. Chem. **26**(16), 1781–1802 (2005). https://doi.org/10.1002/jcc.20289
12. Calotoiu, A., et al.: Fast multi-parameter performance modeling. In: Proceedings of the IEEE International Conference on Cluster Computing (CLUSTER), pp. 1–10. IEEE, September 2016. https://doi.org/10.1109/CLUSTER.2016.57
13. Calotoiu, A., Hoefler, T., Poke, M., Wolf, F.: Using automated performance modeling to find scalability bugs in complex codes. In: Proceedings of the ACM/IEEE Conference on Supercomputing (SC), pp. 45:1–45:12. ACM, November 2013. https://doi.org/10.1145/2503210.2503277
14. Chunduri, S., et al.: Run-to-run Variability on Xeon Phi based cray XC systems. In: Proceedings of the ACM/IEEE Conference on Supercomputing (SC), pp. 52:1–52:13. ACM, November 2017. https://doi.org/10.1145/3126908.3126926
15. Deublein, S., et al.: *ms*2: a molecular simulation tool for thermodynamic properties. Comput. Phys. Commun. **182**(11), 2350–2367 (2011). https://doi.org/10.1016/j.cpc.2011.04.026
16. Glass, C.W., et al.: *ms*2: a molecular simulation tool for thermodynamic properties, new version release. Comput. Phys. Commun. **185**(12), 3302–3306 (2014). https://doi.org/10.1016/j.cpc.2014.07.012
17. Horsch, M., Niethammer, C., Vrabec, J., Hasse, H.: Computational molecular engineering as an emerging technology in process engineering. Methods Appl. Inform. Inf. Technol. **55**(3), 97–101 (2013). https://doi.org/10.1524/itit.2013.0013
18. Iwainsky, C., et al.: How many threads will be too many? On the scalability of OpenMP implementations. In: Träff, J.L., Hunold, S., Versaci, F. (eds.) Euro-Par 2015. LNCS, vol. 9233, pp. 451–463. Springer, Heidelberg (2015). https://doi.org/10.1007/978-3-662-48096-0_35

19. Kale, L.V., Krishnan, S.: CHARM++: a portable concurrent object oriented system based on C++. In: Proceedings of the 8th Annual Conference on Object-Oriented Programming Systems, Languages, and Applications (OOPSLA), pp. 91–108. ACM (1993). https://doi.org/10.1145/165854.165874
20. Knüpfer, A., et al.: Score-P - a joint performance measurement run-time infrastructure for periscope, scalasca, TAU, and vampir. In: Brunst, H., Müller, M., Nagel, W., Resch, M. (eds.) Tools for High Performance Computing, pp. 79–91. Springer, Heidelberg (2011). https://doi.org/10.1007/978-3-642-31476-6_7
21. Marathe, A., et al.: Performance modeling under resource constraints using deep transfer learning. In: Proceedings of the International Conference for High Performance Computing, Networking, Storage and Analysis, SC 2017, pp. 31:1–31:12. ACM (2017). https://doi.org/10.1145/3126908.3126969
22. Plimpton, S.: Fast parallel algorithms for short-range molecular dynamics. J. Comput. Phys. **117**(1), 1–19 (1995). https://doi.org/10.1006/jcph.1995.1039
23. Rutkai, G., et al.: *ms*2: a molecular simulation tool for thermodynamic properties, release 3.0. Comput. Phys. Commun. **221**, 343–351 (2017). https://doi.org/10.1016/j.cpc.2017.07.025
24. Shudler, S., Calotoiu, A., Hoefler, T., Strube, A., Wolf, F.: Exascaling your library: will your implementation meet your expectations? In: Proceedings of the 29th ACM International Conference on Supercomputing (ICS), pp. 165–175. ACM, June 2015. https://doi.org/10.1145/2751205.2751216
25. Shudler, S., Calotoiu, A., Hoefler, T., Wolf, F.: Isoefficiency in practice: configuring and understanding the performance of task-based applications. In: Proceedings of the 22nd ACM SIGPLAN Symposium on Principles and Practice of Parallel Programming (PPoPP), pp. 131–143. ACM, February 2017. https://doi.org/10.1145/3018743.3018770
26. Singh, K., İpek, E., McKee, S.A., de Supinski, B.R., Schulz, M., Caruana, R.: Predicting parallel application performance via machine learning approaches: research articles. Concurr. Comput.: Pract. Exper. **19**(17), 2219–2235 (2007). https://doi.org/10.1002/cpe.1171
27. Vogel, A., et al.: 10,000 performance models per minute – scalability of the UG4 simulation framework. In: Träff, J.L., Hunold, S., Versaci, F. (eds.) Euro-Par 2015. LNCS, vol. 9233, pp. 519–531. Springer, Heidelberg (2015). https://doi.org/10.1007/978-3-662-48096-0_40
28. Yang, X., Jenkins, J., Mubarak, M., Ross, R.B., Lan, Z.: Watch out for the bully!: job interference study on dragonfly network. In: Proceedings of the ACM/IEEE Conference on Supercomputing (SC), pp. 64:1–64:11. IEEE Press (2016). https://doi.org/10.1109/SC.2016.63

Advanced Event-Sampling Support for PAPI

Forrest Smith and Vincent M. Weaver(✉)

University of Maine, Orono, ME 04469, USA
{forrest.smith,vincent.weaver}@maine.edu

Abstract. The PAPI performance library is a widely used tool for gathering performance data from running applications. Modern processors support advanced sampling interfaces, such as Intel's Precise Event Based Sampling (PEBS) and AMD's Instruction Based Sampling (IBS). The current PAPI sampling interface predates the existence of these interfaces and only provides simple instruction-pointer based samples.

We propose a new, improved, sampling interface that provides support for the extended sampling information available on modern hardware. We extend the PAPI interface to add a new `PAPI_sample_init` call that uses the Linux `perf_event` interface to access the extra sample information. A pointer to these samples is returned to the user, who can either decode them on the fly, or write them to disk for later analysis.

By providing extended sampling information, this new PAPI interface allows advanced performance analysis and optimization that was previously not possible. This will greatly enhance the ability to optimize software in modern extreme-scale programming environments.

1 Introduction

When conducting performance analysis, the easiest type of data to collect is total, aggregate results. This includes information such as the total number of cycles a program ran, the total number of cache misses that occurred, and the total wall clock time. While all of this information is of interest, often more detail is wanted: *what* function takes the most cycles, *which* data structure causes the cache misses, *why* is the code taking so long to run.

The most straightforward way to get this detailed information is via *sampling*; to periodically interrupt the program's execution and gather machine state about what it is happening at the time of the interruption. Overall program behavior can be extrapolated based on these representative samples. There is a tradeoff between overhead and accuracy: a higher sample rate leads to more accurate results, but if you sample *too* frequently you will add overhead that can interfere with the results being measured. Some of this overhead can be mitigated if the sampling is done in hardware rather than in software.

A. Bhatele et al. (Eds.): ESPT/VPA 2017/2018, LNCS 11027, pp. 144–161, 2019.
https://doi.org/10.1007/978-3-030-17872-7_9

1.1 Hardware Performance Counters

Most modern processors support hardware performance counters; these counters are internal to the system and increment when certain architectural events occur. Total aggregate counts can be gathered by starting the counters at the beginning of the code of interest, and stopping them afterward. Traditionally these counters are found in CPUs, but their use has expanded to other pieces of hardware such as the disk, network, and memory systems.

Typically there are only a handful of counters available, often in the range from two to eight (though this varies by vendor, architecture, and processor generation). The counters are typically between 32 and 64 bits in size. Each counter can measure an event, chosen from a large list (potentially hundreds on some architectures [4,13]).

Usually the counters can be configured to trigger a hardware interrupt if the register overflows. This can be used to notice and account for large counts generated by frequent events; if the counter overflows multiple times between readings it would not be possible to determine the exact count. The overflow mechanism is also useful for sampling. An event can be set to overflow periodically, for example, every 100,000 cycles. Once the interrupt triggers, the operating system interrupt handler takes over and can construct a sample that includes additional useful information, such as where the instruction pointer is currently located. If your CPU lacks performance counter overflow interrupt support, sampling can still be done by using some other regular interrupt source (such as a periodic timer). However usually the performance counters are used for this purpose if they are available.

1.2 Advanced Sampling

While you can learn a lot about a program by gathering instruction pointer samples, there is a lot more to program behavior than just instruction traces. Recent processors from Intel and AMD support more advanced sampling modes. These allow gathering extra information on an overflow, such as detailed cache miss and cache latency values.

The sampling features are grouped together under a large number of processor features with sometimes confusing acronyms. The more well known are Intel's Precise Event Based Sampling (PEBS) and AMD's Instruction Based Sampling (IBS). There are a few common sampling related interfaces:

- **Sampled Profiling** – traditional sampling, as defined previously. A periodic interrupt is used to sample the instruction pointer and any other info that can be easily obtained, such as register values. Most CPUs can do this purely in hardware or can emulate it in software (by using some sort of timer).
- **Low-latency Sampling** – instead of having periodic interrupts and manually gather program state, some hardware allows automatically sampling multiple times to a dedicated memory buffer without any operating system (interrupt) involvement. This has lower latency than traditional interrupt-based sampling. Intel PEBS does this.

- **Hardware Profiling** – at regular intervals the CPU is interrupted and detailed information about the current instruction is logged. Often the actual instruction logged is randomly chosen after a certain trigger point. AMD IBS and Intel PEBS do this.
- **Extra CPU State** – PEBS and IBS log additional CPU state that cannot be obtained in software from the operating system. This includes register state, kernel register state (if the interrupt happened in the kernel), branch predictor outcome, instruction latencies, sources of cache misses, etc.
- **Low-skid Interrupts** – One issue with measurements involving interrupts is "skid": once an overflow interrupt happens, it takes a CPU (especially modern complex out-of-order designs) some amount of time to stop the processor and pinpoint exactly which instruction was active at time of the overflow. Often there is an offset between the instruction indicated versus the one causing the interrupt (this offset is called the skid). PEBS and IBS provide support for low-skid sampling, at the expense of some additional time overhead.
- **Last Branch Sampling** – The hardware keeps track of the last branches taken, and allows generating call stacks. Intel Last Branch Record (LBR) allows this.
- **Processor Trace** – The CPU logs to a buffer details on all instructions being executed (although usually this is filtered, as the raw data stream can be huge otherwise). Intel Processor Trace and ARM CoreSight are examples of this.

Ideally all of these types of sample data could be easily returned to the user through a straightforward interface.

1.3 Software Interfaces

Hardware counter accesses are privileged by the hardware, so usually the operating system is responsible for enforcing access. On Linux this is done by the `perf_event` [10] subsystem. Over the years Linux has gradually added support for the more advanced sampling modes. Directly accessing these results from userspace involves using the `perf_event` interface which is complicated to set up and use [33]. Most users instead opt to use the `perf` command-line tool which abstracts away some of the low-level interface.

PAPI [26] is a portable, cross-platform library for accessing hardware performance counters. Many higher-level tools, such as VAMPIR [19] and HPCToolkit [1] build on PAPI. PAPI has supported simple event sampling for a long time, but has lacked the ability to gather advanced samples from modern processors. In this paper we describe the existing PAPI support for sampling, and how we plan to add support for the more advanced hardware sampling interfaces supported by perf_event.

2 Hardware Sampling Interfaces

As with general performance counter support, sampling interfaces are not part of any x86 standard and thus have completely different implementations between vendors. What follows is a quick overview of support found on recent processors.

2.1 Intel x86_64

Intel processors introduced performance counter support with the original Pentium processor. Since the beginning they have supported hardware interrupt on counter overflow, allowing sampled profiling. More advanced sampling interfaces began appearing starting with the Pentium 4 processor.

Intel Precise Event-Based Sampling (PEBS). Recent Intel chips support Precise Event Based Sampling (PEBS), as described in Chapter 18 of the Intel 64 and IA-32 Architectures Software Developer's Manual (Volume 3) [13]. PEBS support originated in Pentium 4 and Core architectures. It is available on all subsequent Core-derived processors as well as some Atom models.

Only a subset of events can be used as PEBS events, and sometimes only a certain counter slot can be used. A suitable Data Store (DS) area must be set up in memory; samples will be directly written to this area without any operating system involvement. When PEBS is enabled for an event, the PEBS circuitry is armed when the counter overflows. The next instruction that triggers this event had a record with sample information written out to the DS area. The DS area can be configured to generate an interrupt when full (or nearing being full) so that multiple samples worth of data can be queued up and processed at once by the operating system, reducing overall overhead.

The information that can be recorded on a PEBS sample varies by architecture but can include:

- trap vs fault (whether the event recorded is the next or the current one),
- a full set of processor registers (in addition to the instruction pointer),
- store latency data,
- transactional memory data
- TSC value, and
- the counter value.

Nehalem processors add more features. Now you can record load latency information: the latency in cycles from first dispatch to final retirement of the instruction. When enabled, load instructions are randomly chosen to accumulate the load latency info. The value recorded is the latency for the last randomly tagged event, not necessarily the one that triggered the PEBS operation. The information gathered includes the Data Linear Address (usually the same as the virtual address of value being loaded), latency value, and data source (which indicates what part of the cache memory hierarchy was involved with returning the loaded value).

Sandybridge processors add more PEBS features, and enable PEBS for more events. In addition to loads, now store instructions can also be measured (but this is limited in some ways, including not being able to get latency values). Additional info is returned on whether loads hit in the TLB. Precise store support is added, where information is returned on the very next store rather than a randomly selected one. Sandybridge also adds support for low-skid measurement via the Precise Distribution of Instructions Retired (PDIR) interface. It notices when an overflow interrupt is about to happen and prepares for it and enters a slower high-accuracy mode that allows it to exactly determine which instruction caused the overflow.

With Haswell precise store was replaced by Data Linear Address Profiling (DataLA); the full linear (virtual) destination address of the load or store is stored in the sample. Additionally information on whether the access hit in the closest level of cache is stored. The eventing instruction pointer (the address of the instruction that caused PEBS to trigger) is also recorded. Finally, various transactional memory related sample types were added.

Skylake processors add a field for recording the TSC timestamp value from when that event occurred, and adds additional front-end events (iTLB and iCache misses).

PEBS support was originally designed for desktop and server chips, but some of the Atom class chips also have support for PEBS. On Goldmont Atom chips, PEBS records can be recorded for all events. However for non-precise events there is no guarantee about what instruction actually generates the sample. Other information recorded includes the time stamp counter (TSC) and info on which event caused the overflow (if multiple are enabled). Reduced skid and linear address support is also available.

Intel Last Branch Record (LBR). Starting with the Pentium 4 most Intel hardware supports logging a trace of the last branches that were executed via the Last Branch Record (LBR) interface. Full details can be found in Chapter 17 of the Vol3b documentation. The number of branches recorded varies from 4 up to 32. The LBR record contains detailed information about the branch, such as the last location branched from, the last location branched to, and whether the branch was predicted correctly or not. This is not strictly a sampling feature, but the data is recorded to MSR registers and under Linux is reported via the perf_event interface.

Intel Branch Trace Store (BTS). Intel processors can also support the Branch Trace Store (BTS), where the last N branch records can be written out to a circular buffer called the Debug Store (DS) which should not be confused with the PEBS Data Store. This feature lets you track the branch behavior of your program, but is known to slow down program execution when enabled.

Nehalem chips added the ability to filter based on branch type. Haswell supports call-stack recording, where you can configure it to record the branches in a LIFO setup (i.e. when you return from a function call, the branches that have happened since the initial call to the function are backed off). This allows generating a call stack more easily especially with programming languages that have deep call trees. Skylake changes the format a bit, and includes transactional memory info as well as cycle counts. It has 32 entries now and can capture length of time spent in a basic block with the TSC time. Atom Goldmont allows you to obtain the number of cycles since last branch.

Intel Resource Director Technology (RDT). The Intel Resource Director Technology (RDT) is available on server machines, Haswell Xeon E5 v3 and newer. It supports a number of technologies. Cache Monitoring Technology (CMT) can measure cache occupancy of program in last level cache. Memory bandwidth monitoring (MBM) [14] can monitor memory bandwidth between cache levels. You can assign a resource monitoring ID (RMID) to a task, processor, or group of processors and monitor them.

On Xeon E5 v4 processors (Broadwell) RDT also supports cache allocation technology (CAT) and code data prioritization (CDP). This allows one to give hints on how much cache a program should be allowed to use.

Some machines have Cache Quality-of-service Monitoring (CQM) but it is not documented, and while Linux has some initial support for it, it was later removed.

Intel Processor Trace (PT). Intel Processor Trace (PT) [18] lets you record program execution traces. The first implementation is control flow tracing and can log enough information to give an exact program flow trace. It can also generate basic block vectors and trace power events. It aims for less than 5% overhead, and records latency info. It can reconstruct program flow by recording the taken/not-taken path of conditional branches. There is a possibly related technology called Intel Architectural Event Trace (AET) but information on how to use this is not publicly released.

2.2 AMD x86_64

AMD processors support simple sampling using hardware interrupts on counter overflow. Recent processors also support some more advanced sampling interfaces, but not quite as many nor as varied as supported by Intel.

AMD Instruction Based Sampling (IBS). AMD chips support Instruction Based Sampling (IBS), which is described in the various BIOS and Kernel Development Guides [2,3] as well as in some research papers [6,7].

IBS was introduced with Barcelona (fam10h) to aid in creating low-skid profiles. It selects a random instruction or micro operation (uop) and records information, generating an interrupt when completed. There are two types of sample: one that happens on instruction fetch (involving TLB and instruction cache behavior) and one that happens on instruction execution.

For instruction fetch the following information is logged:

- if the fetch was completed or aborted,
- number of cycles spent on the fetch,
- if the fetch hit in the caches and TLB, and
- the linear/physical address corresponding to the fetch.

For instruction execution the following is logged:

- if only one micro-op of the instruction can be tagged,
- branch status of the instruction,
- linear/physical address of instruction,
- linear/physical address of load/store destination,
- data cache statistics (hit or not, latency),
- clocks from tag until retire,
- clocks from execution until retire, and
- DRAM and MMIO source info.

Unlike PEBS these values aren't stored in a memory buffer, but in a set of MSRs. Only one record can be pending at a time. Only three events are supported: cycles, cycles:p, and uops.

2.3 Other Processors

Most other modern processors support performance counters, and again most of these support simple sampling via counter-overflow interrupt (although notably various ARM based platforms might not, such as the original ARM1176 Raspberry Pi systems).

Support for more advanced sampling is not as widespread as it is on x86. ARM has no PEBS or IBS equivalent, but it does have something similar to Processor Trace called CoreSight. Newer 64-bit ARM models optionally support the Statistical Profiling Extension (SPE) [5]; perf_event added support for this with Linux 4.15.

The IBM s390 class of machines has a sampling facility as part of the CPU Measurement Facility [12] that will write samples into a buffer that will trigger an interrupt when full.

3 Software Interface for Sampling

Advanced hardware sampling interfaces are complex and vendor specific. Some of this complexity can be abstracted away by the operating system (in our case we will assume the OS is Linux). On Linux the `perf_event` interface used for accessing regular hardware performance counters is also used for accessing sample data. This interface itself is complex and hard to use, so we develop the PAPI library which is yet another layer of abstraction on top of `perf_event`. This allows existing users of PAPI to gain access to the sampling interface using familiar PAPI interfaces, without needing to majorly restructure their code.

3.1 Linux perf_event Interface

Access to performance counter registers requires supervisor or privileged access to the hardware, in order to initialize the model-specific registers (MSRs) and set up the sampling memory buffers. Because of this the operating system is usually responsible for the interface. In addition access to the underlying hardware might be further restricted for security reasons. A clever user can monitor in detail what a system is doing based on fine grained performance information, and this can leak information. This was once considered a mostly theoretical attack, such as being able to reverse engineer encryption happening on other cores by monitoring cycle or cache miss counts; this has recently become a much more critical worry with the advent of the Meltdown and Spectre vulnerabilities [22].

The standard performance counter interface provided by Linux is known as `perf_event` and the primary way of accessing it is the `perf_event_open()` system call [33]. This system call is used to configure and open a performance counter event; it is a complex call with over forty interacting parameters. The system call returns a file descriptor which can be used to control and access the event. Values can be read with the `read()` system call, and memory can be set up with `mmap()` that allows both sampling to a circular buffer as well as gathering additional information about the event. Various `ioctl()` calls are used to start and stop the events. Advanced features, such as event scheduling, event multiplexing, and save/restore on context switch are all provided by the interface.

Linux perf_event supports most of the advanced hardware sampling interfaces described in Sect. 2.

perf_event Sampled Profiling. As long as your system supports overflow interrupts you can do statistical sampling with perf_event. You can specify the event, the frequency, and a whole host of other options. On overflow, a user-specified signal handler can be called that your code can use to find the register state, including instruction pointer location.

perf_event Low-Latency Sampling. The perf_event interface can provide access to low-latency sampling, which is gathering multiple samples into a buffer without program intervention. The samples are gathered until a watermark threshold is crossed, and only then will your program be interrupted to let it know that the buffer is full and ready to be processed. There is still some operating system overhead involved, as some events need to be handled in the kernel even if userspace code is not bothered. When using an interface such as Intel PEBS even this can be avoided, as the hardware can store PEBS records to a memory buffer directly without any operating system involvement at all.

By default perf_event does not support low-latency sampling, and instead runs in "single-entry" mode. This is because the perf records require some values that only the OS can provide, such as pid/tid. It is possible to enable the N-entry PEBS mode if you are willing to sacrifice some features: you must use a fixed period, no timestamp if pre-Skylake, the PEBS buffer flushed on context-switches, and no LBR [8].

perf_event Extra Processor State. Linux perf_event supports returning a large amount of data with each sample. Some of the sample types are extended with PEBS data when available. Currently any of the following can be dumped into a sample by perf:

- PERF_SAMPLE_IP – instruction pointer
- PERF_SAMPLE_TID – thread ID
- PERF_SAMPLE_TIME – a timestamp
- PERF_SAMPLE_ADDR – effective address
- PERF_SAMPLE_READ – counts for all events in group
- PERF_SAMPLE_CALLCHAIN – callchain info
- PERF_SAMPLE_ID – a unique id for the group leader
- PERF_SAMPLE_CPU – current CPU
- PERF_SAMPLE_PERIOD – current sampling period
- PERF_SAMPLE_STREAM_ID – another unique ID
- PERF_SAMPLE_RAW – raw data (PMU specific).
  On IBS this contains the raw MSR dumps which include the below (and other) info:
  - Fetch: Randomize event enabled, TLB miss, TLB size, icache miss, fetch addresses
  - Execute: address, microcode, branch fused, branch predicted, cache hit, offcore (northbridge) source, tlb latency, memory width, l2 cache miss, load or store, TLB stats, alignment, branch target access, physical address
- PERF_SAMPLE_BRANCH_STACK – branch stack from LBR
- PERF_SAMPLE_REGS_USER – current user level register state.
- PERF_SAMPLE_STACK_USER – user stack, to allow stack unwinding (useful for call traces)
- PERF_SAMPLE_WEIGHT – for PEBS this is the cycle time
- PERF_SAMPLE_DATA_SRC – this is the PEBS cache miss hierarchy info
- PERF_SAMPLE_IDENTIFIER – another unique ID, but in a fixed location
- PERF_SAMPLE_TRANSACTION – has to do with Intel TSX transactional memory
- PERF_SAMPLE_REGS_INTR – current register state at interrupt, can be in userspace. If PEBS enabled and a precise event is being measured then the registers here are the ones gathered by PEBS.

Note that the PEBS weight and data source data can be hard to interpret and often gives non-intuitive results, such as it reporting a cache miss taking more cycles to complete than an L3 cache miss. This is (at least in part) because the cycles count can take into account other things going on in the chip unrelated to the memory hierarchy.

perf_event Low-Skid Interrupts. The perf_event interface supports various levels of low-skid measurements on an event. This is enabled via the *precise_ip* field, which is indicated in both perf and PAPI by putting `:p` values on the end of events (`:p`, `:pp`, `:ppp`). Only a subset of events support precise reporting, and it varies by processor model.

The following precise settings are supported:

- Level 0 – an event can have arbitrary skid
- Level 1 – request constant skid
- Level 2 – request zero skid (but the processor might not always be able to deliver)
- Level 3 – require zero skid (or equivalent, such as "randomization to avoid shadowing effects").

On Intel chips, PEBS support gives you level 1 of precise events, LBR and PEBS format v2 gives you level 2 (IP Fixup), and PEBS precise distribution support gives you level 3. Note Level 2 support uses the LBR for accuracy, so it might not be able if you are also attempting to use LBR for branch sampling.

On AMD machines precise IP is supported through the IBS interface. Both Level 1 and Level 2 are supported. Only three events are supported, cpu-cycles, cycles, and uops. Previously you needed to specify you want to run system wide `-a` not just per-task to do this (which often requires root) but on a recent machines this is no longer necessary.

perf_evet Branch Sampling. This info can be gathered with the raw perf_event PERF_SAMPLE_BRANCH_STACK option. It can report the last N branches (16 on recent machines), the address and target, and whether it was properly predicted. On some machines you can filter by branch type.

The related Branch Trace Store functionality has its own PMU driver and uses a special AUX area of the mmap buffer which is mostly independent from the normal sample buffer. It can return branches, their ip, their target, and whether they were a branch hit or miss.

Other, Non-sampling Interfaces. Intel Processor Trace is a whole tracing subsystem, and does much more than sampling [16]. It uses the AUX mmap buffer just like BTS does.

3.2 PAPI Library Interface

The PAPI performance library [26] is a cross-platform library designed to allow access to performance counters on a wide variety of machines. On current Linux machines PAPI uses the perf_event interface. We will briefly describe the old sampling methods available in PAPI prior to the forthcoming 6.0 release expected in 2019.

PAPI Statistical Sampling. The current PAPI interface used when sampling is `PAPI_overflow()`. There are two key parameters: an overflow threshold and a signal handler. Once the event in question hits the threshold, the hardware triggers an overflow interrupt which is then passed by the operating system to the Linux system handler. It is up to the user to do something useful in the signal handler (such as read out the instruction pointer value) before returning. PAPI does not support returning info besides the instruction pointer, although in theory the register state can also be manually gathered from the signal context on Linux. Currently it is not possible to get the advanced sample info (kernel register state, latencies, branch predictor outcome, cache hierarchy extra info, etc.)

```
int PAPI_overflow(int EventSet, int EventCode,
                  int threshold, int flags,
                  PAPI_overflow_handler_t handler);
```

The signal handler looks like:

```
typedef void (*PAPI_overflow_handler_t)
                  (int EventSet, void *address,
                  long long overflow_vector, void *context);
```

PAPI_profil(). There are two legacy PAPI sampling interfaces, `PAPI_profil()` and `PAPI_sprofil()`, which are meant to provide interfaces compatible with the UNIX "profil" system call.

```
int PAPI_profil(void *buf, unsigned bufsiz,
        caddr_t offset, unsigned scale,
        int EventSet, int EventCode,
        int threshold, int flags);

int PAPI_sprofil( PAPI_sprofil_t *prof,
        int profcnt, int EventSet,
        int EventCode, int threshold, int flags );
```

A range of addresses to watch is given, and then there is a regular overflow which stops, notes the instruction pointer, and then increments the value in a set of "bins". This can be used to generate a profile of where the code has been executing. This interface is not as widely used as the much more popular `PAPI_overflow()`.

PAPI Low-Skid Interrupts. PAPI currently support perf_event low skid interrupts. To do this you use the `PAPI_add_named_event()` interface and when specifying the event name include one of the `:p` suffixes to indicate you want a more precise event.

4 Related Work

Other interfaces besides PAPI offer ways to read hardware performance counters. Many of these interfaces also support sampling.

4.1 Existing Profiling Tools

Profil. On some UNIX implementations there is a `profil()` system call that will periodically interrupt program execution and generate a profile histogram. Linux does not support this system call, although the C library implements it in software via a timer that triggers every 10 ms. PAPI has existing code to emulate this interface. While profiles can be generated, no advanced sampling information is available.

gprof. gprof lets you instrument your program at compile time (with the `-pg` compiler option) and then at run time it will report how long each function was called and how much time was spent in it. This allows sampling at the function-call level. This is a bit intrusive overhead-wise, and requires you have access to the source code.

Valgrind. Valgrind [27] does dynamic-binary instrumentation. One of its tools is "callgrind" which will instrument basic blocks on the fly and allow creating profiles which can be viewed with the "callgrind_annotate" tool. It also has "cachegrind" which runs the code through a cache simulator. The primary downside to Valgrind and similar tools is the slowdown which ranges from 10–100x slower than natively running.

4.2 NUMA Profiling

numap [31] presents an API for gathering sampled data for use when analyzing NUMA systems. First `init_samp_session()` is called to specify threads to be profiled. Then `samp_read_start()` called to setup the mmap buffer. The code of interest happens. Then `samp_read_stop()` called to stop sampling. Finally the results printed with `print_rd()` which decodes the binary blob returned by the kernel. It is also possible to get the data results directly. The data of interest is mostly the PEBS data: instruction pointer of the instruction, address of the load/store, "weight" which is the number of cycles, and data_src which is the part of the hierarchy causing the result. The primary downside of this, at least to PAPI users, is that it is a separate tool and not integrated into the PAPI interface.

Memphis [25] is a tool that talks to the AMD IBS registers directly via a kernel module in order to gather the extended sample information. MemProf [20] is another AMD IBS-based NUMA memory profiler. Again, neither of these is integrated into the PAPI infrastructure.

4.3 GPU Profiling

Some GPU hardware supports profiling interfaces too, specifically recent NVIDIA devices [30]. For MAXWELL GPUs and CUDA 7.5 you can use CUPTI to create a sampling data structure `PC_SAMPLING_ACTIVITY`, `SOURCE_LOCATOR`, and `KERNEL_ACTIVITY`. To use the Activity API you initialize, register callbacks, enable the activities, and set the sample rate. While useful for analyzing GPU code, in our work we are more concerned with the advanced sampling interfaces provided on modern CPUs.

4.4 Other Tools with Sampling Interfaces

LIKWID [32] is a hardware performance measurement interface that is capable of reading performance counters on supported x86 processors. Using the likwid-perfctr command with the -t option, the user can measure performance results from LIKWID at a specified time interval. The interface recommends using an interval no smaller than 100 ms, otherwise the results are considered invalid. Achieving fine-grained sampling results from the LIKWID interface is not possible due to this constraint. LIKWID does not support PEBS as it is a userspace tool and cannot setup the kernel buffers needed to hold the PEBS records.

HPCToolkit [1] is a large suite of tools for analyzing the performance of multithreaded applications. It can be used for anything from a home computer to a super computer. HPCToolkit interfaces directly with PAPI to read hardware performance counters and gather samples. The samples do not contain the extra data that is available from PEBS events; they are merely counter readings using the `PAPI_overflow()` code.

4.5 Other Proposed PAPI Sampling Interfaces

Lopez, Moore, and Weaver [24] were the first to propose an enhanced sampling interface for PAPI that gathered the PEBS cache latency values. Their sampling interface is similar to the one that we propose in this paper. Their proposed interface was never implemented and remained a proof of concept. They used raw perf_event calls to show it was possible to measure both single thread and multithreaded applications. They were successfully able to gather STREAM sample results using OpenMP with eight threads.

5 Proposed Advanced PAPI Sampling API

It is not possible to retrofit the existing `PAPI_overflow()` method of gathering samples to handle extended sample information in a backwards compatible way.

We propose two new enhanced interfaces. One stays true to the historical cross-platform layer-of-abstraction nature of PAPI, but only provides limited information. The other acts as a thin layer on top of the perf_event interface that provides all sampling info, but is very Linux specific.

5.1 Abstracted Interface

This interface attempts to provide access specifically to the cache latency values that can be found in PAPI. This is the most requested feature, and in theory can be made cross-platform although currently only Intel PEBS provides this information.

This interface involves a `PAPI_sample_init()` call shown in Fig. 1 which internally inside of PAPI will take the event selected and set up a sampling buffer. Once the buffer is full, PAPI will gather the data and create an array of sample data that will be passed back to the user.

```
struct sample_struct {
        uint64_t        type;
        uint64_t        instruction_address;
        uint64_t        memory_access_address;
        uint64_t        cache_access_type;
        uint64_t        latency;
};

int     PAPI_sample_init(int EventSet, int EventCode,
        long long sample_period, long long buffer_size,
        PAPI_overflow_handler_t handler);

typedef void (*PAPI_overflow_handler_t)
        (int EventSet, void *sample_struct,
        long long num_samples);
```

Fig. 1. Proposed abstract interface

5.2 Direct perf_event Interface

This option for the interface does not try to abstract away the samples. It operates on the assumption that most HPC work happens on Linux kernels via the perf_event interface and as much information as possible provided by this interface should be passed back to PAPI if requested. While this is the most powerful interface, it requires a lot of internal `perf_event` knowledge. The example interface is shown in Fig. 2.

```
int     PAPI_sample_init(int EventSet, int EventCode,
        long long sample_period, long long buffer_size,
        struct perf_event_attr *attr,
        PAPI_overflow_handler_t handler);

typedef void (*PAPI_sample_handler_t)
        (int EventSet, void *buffer_address);
```

Fig. 2. Proposed perf_event interface

This interface provides a pointer to the raw perf_event mmap() sample buffer, and it is up to the user code to interpret this and get the samples out. For performance reasons, the Linux kernel enforces a rule that to gather PEBS-type sample data, each individual core needs to have its own `mmap()` buffer. Currently it is up to the user to open one event per core as needed, but we are planning an interface to simplify this.

Existing PAPI code using `PAPI_overflow()` can be used with few changes. You still need to create an eventset, add an event (note: only some events are capable of providing extra sampling information). Then initialize sampling using the proposed interface. Finally, start/stop events as per normal.

When a threshold is crossed and a sample is gathered, PAPI will activate the signal handler that was set up by the user. It is then up to the user to access the `mmap()` buffer and do something useful with the contents before returning.

In PAPI we provide two sample programs: one writes out the raw sample data to disk for later analysis, and one that prints out the sample results on the fly.

The low level changes required to PAPI are mostly about making sure the mmap() buffers get set up properly. A lot of the hard work involving internal PAPI management of mmap() buffers was already done when fast rdpmc read support was added [23]. The PAPI code manages setting up the mmap()s and making sure that the events are opened properly.

The types of sample information available can be found in the perf_event_open manpage [33]. For PEBS latency information use one specifies `PERF_SAMPLE_IP | PERF_SAMPLE_WEIGHT | PERF_SAMPLE_DATA_SRC` which asks for the instruction pointer, the weight (latency) and the source of data. For IBS events one would ask for PERF_SAMPLE_RAW and you have to parse the IBS values yourself.

Limitations of this Interface. The primary limitation of this proposed interface is how Linux-centric it is. PAPI is in theory supposed to be platform agnostic. In addition the samples are in the raw perf_event sample record format which requires the users to have some non-trivial code to decode the results.

Another concern is how to remain forward compatible. As Intel adds more features to PEBS how can we return those too without requiring tools to be recompiled.

Unsupported Sample Types. The perf_event interface returns most sample data through the mmap() interface, so anything supported by perf_event can be gathered that way. This means results such as LBR records can also be obtained through this interface.

Some values, such as Intel BTS and Intel Processor Trace, use an additional, auxiliary, mmap() buffer to store the results. PAPI currently does not support gathering data via that mechanism.

Data Format. Once the user signal handler is called, the program can read out the samples in the mmap() buffer and interpret them. There are two straightforward ways to deal with the data. One is to immediately write it to disk, interpreting it offline. The other is to decode and act on the results immediately. Both methods of gathering data will require some sort of library to interpret the fields in the samples. We provide examples that do both types of analysis, but this code is currently not part of PAPI, but separate code to be included in the analysis routines.

For the save to disk case, there is a standard on-disk format for perf records, the a `perf.data` file [9,17,28]. Programs that write out data in this format can then be analyzed by other compatible perf tools. There are various existing tools that can parse raw `perf.data` files:

- pmu-tools parser [15],
- quipper C++ parser (part of chromiumos-wide-profiling),
- gooda [21], and
- flame graphs [11].

6 Preliminary Results

We have been developing the advanced PAPI sampling interface on a number of machines, with the primary testing happening on an Intel Skylake machine with four cores. The test machine is running Linux 4.4.0-127-generic and our primary benchmark is a PAPI instrumented version 2.2 of the High-Performance Linpack (HPL) benchmark [29]. Samples have been recorded and verified for all PEBS events in the Skylake, Haswell, and Broadwell architectures.

Figure 3 shows results gathered on a Skylake machine when using sample types PERF_SAMPLE_IP, PERF_SAMPLE_READ, and PERF_SAMPLE_CPU. The native FRONTEND_RETIRED.L1I_MISS event was used, which counts instruction cache misses. Each sample contains the value of the performance counter, which can be seen next to "Value:". The samples also record the CPU on which the event is occur ING and the instruction pointer at the time of the event. The samples were collected with a sample period of 10000. Two captured samples are shown; it is a multithreaded benchmark and it can be seen that the samples were gathered from two different cores. In this example, the raw data is gathered in a signal handler and this is parsed and printed each time a signal occurs.

Figure 4 shows results gathered on a Haswell machine that include cache latency and source results. These were gathered using the event:
MEM_TRANS_RETIRED:LATENCY_ABOVE_THRESHOLD
and the sample type:
PERF_SAMPLE_IP | PERF_SAMPLE_WEIGHT | PERF_SAMPLE_DATA_SRC.

```
PERF_RECORD_SAMPLE [91], MISC=2
(PERF_RECORD_MISC_USER), Size=64
PERF_SAMPLE_IP, IP: 7f9b5f1bc439
PERF_SAMPLE_CPU, cpu: 2  res 0
PERF_SAMPLE_READ, read_format
Number: 1
enabled: 4827080
running: 4827080
Value: 10000 id: 2084

PERF_RECORD_SAMPLE [91], MISC=2
(PERF_RECORD_MISC_USER), Size=64
PERF_SAMPLE_IP, IP: 7f9b6f03b7fc
PERF_SAMPLE_CPU, cpu: 7  res 0
PERF_SAMPLE_READ, read_format
Number: 1
enabled: 12203500
running: 4517409
Value: 10001 id: 2089
```

Fig. 3. Example advanced sampling, with IP, CPU, and READ samples shown.

```
PERF_RECORD_SAMPLE [c001],
MISC=16386
PERF_SAMPLE_IP, IP: 55fb7799a730
PERF_SAMPLE_WEIGHT, Weight: 48
PERF_SAMPLE_DATA_SRC,
Raw: 668100842
Load Hit L3 cache No snoop
Hit Level 1
TLB Level 2 TLB Hardware walker

PERF_RECORD_SAMPLE [c001],
MISC=16386
PERF_SAMPLE_IP, IP: 55fb7799a730
PERF_SAMPLE_WEIGHT, Weight: 67
PERF_SAMPLE_DATA_SRC,
Raw: 668100842
Load Hit L3 cache No snoop
Hit Level 1
TLB Level 2 TLB Hardware walker
```

Fig. 4. Example of advanced sampling, with IP, WEIGHT, and DATA_SRC samples. The weight indicates the latency of the sampled instruction.

7 Conclusion and Future Work

We have designed an improved sampling interface for PAPI. It integrates advanced sampling support into the PAPI interface while abstracting away some of the difficulty of using the perf_event_open sampling interface. We provide code that can be used to parse samples found in the mmap() buffer which is not a trivial task.

The interface is currently under test for architectures other than Broadwell, Haswell and Skylake. Once testing is completed, the interface will be included and released with the upcoming 6.0 PAPI release.

By adding extended sampling support to PAPI we have opened new avenues for code analysis that will greatly aid users trying to optimize for performance in current and future extreme-scale systems.

Acknowledgment. This work was supported by the National Science Foundation under Grant No. SSI-1450122.

References

1. Adhianto, L., et al.: HPCToolkit: tools for performance analysis of optimized parallel programs. Concurrency Comput.: Practice Exp. **22**(6), 685–701 (2010)
2. Advanced Micro Devices: BIOS and Kernel Developer's Guide (BKDG) For AMD Family 15h Models 00h–0Fh Processors, January 2013
3. Advanced Micro Devices: BIOS and Kernel Developer's Guide (BKDG) For AMD Family 15h Models 30h–3Fh Processors, March 2014
4. AMD: AMD Family 15h Processor BIOS and Kernel Developer Guide (2011)
5. ARM: ARM Architecture Reference Manual Supplement Statistical Profiling Extension, for ARMv8-A (2017)
6. Drongowski, P., Yu, L., Swehosky, F., Suthikulpanit, S., Richter, R.: Incorporating instruction-based sampling into AMD CodeAnalyst. In: Proceedings of IEEE International Symposium on Performance Analysis of Systems and Software, pp. 119–120, March 2010
7. Drongowski, P.: Instruction-Based Sampling: A New Performance Analysis Technique for AMD Family 10h Processors. Advanced Micro Devices, Inc. (2007)
8. Eranian, S.: Linux perf_events status update. In: Scalable Tools Workshop, August 2016
9. Fässler, U., Nowak, A.: Perf file format. Technical report, CERN Openlab, September 2011
10. Gleixner, T., Molnar, I.: Performance counters for Linux (2009)
11. Gregg, B.: FlameGraphs. http://www.brendangregg.com/FlameGraphs/cpuflamegraphs.html
12. IBM: Linux on Z and LinuxONE: Device Drivers, Features, and Commands (2018)
13. Intel Corporation: Intel® 64 and IA-32 Architectures Software Developer's Manual Volume 3: System Programming Guide, June 2015
14. Juvva, K.: Memory bandwidth monitoring in Linux for HPC applications. In: Linux Con North America 2015, August 2015
15. Kleen, A.: Intel PMU profiling tools. https://github.com/andikleen/pmu-tools

16. Kleen, A.: Adding processor trace support to Linux. Linux Weekly News (2015). https://lwn.net/Articles/648154/
17. Kleen, A.: perf.data file format specification draft (2015). https://lwn.net/Articles/644919/
18. Kleen, A., Strong, B.: Intel®processor trace on Linux. In: Tracing Summit 2015 (2015)
19. Knüpfer, A., et al.: The Vampir performance analysis tool-set. In: Resch, M., Keller, R., Himmler, V., Krammer, B., Schulz, A. (eds.) Tools for High Performance Computing, pp. 139–155. Springer, Heidelberg (2008). https://doi.org/10.1007/978-3-540-68564-7_9
20. Lachaize, R., Lepers, B., Quéma, V.: Memprof: a memory profiler for NUMA multicore systems. In: USENIX Annual Technical Conference, June 2012
21. Levinthal, D.: Gooda PMU event analysis package. https://github.com/David-Levinthal/gooda
22. Lipp, M., et al.: Meltdown. ArXiv e-prints, January 2018
23. Liu, Y., Weaver, V.: Enhancing PAPI with low-overhead rdpmc reads. In: Proceedings of the 6th Workshop on Extreme-Scale Programming Tools, November 2017
24. Lopez, I., Moore, S., Weaver, V.: A prototype sampling interface for PAPI. In: Extreme Science Engineering Discovery Environment Conference, July 2015
25. McCurdy, C., Vetter, J.: Finding and fixing NUMA-related performance problems on multi-core platforms. In: Proceedings of IEEE International Symposium on Performance Analysis of Systems and Software, pp. 87–96, March 2010
26. Mucci, P.J., Browne, S., Deane, C., Ho, G.: PAPI: a portable interface to hardware performance counters. In: Proceedings of Department of Defense HPCMP User Group Conference, June 1999
27. Nethercote, N., Seward, J.: Valgrind: a framework for heavyweight dynamic binary instrumentation. In: Proceedings of ACM SIGPLAN Conference on Programming Language Design and Implementation, pp. 89–100, June 2007
28. Olsa, J.: Perf & CTF. In: Tracing Summit 2014 (2014)
29. Petitet, A., Whaley, R., Dongarra, J., Cleary, A., Luszczek, P.: HPL – a portable implementation of the high-performance linpack benchmark for distributed-memory computers. Innovative Computing Laboratory, Computer Science Department, University of Tennessee, v2.2, December 2017. http://www.netlib.org/benchmark/hpl/
30. Ragate, S.: GPU PC sampling utility. Technical report, Innovative Computing Lab, University of Tennessee (2015)
31. Selva, M., Morel, L., Marquet, K.: numap: a portable library for low level memory profiling. Technical report RR-8879, INRIA, March 2016
32. Treibig, J., Hager, G., Wellein, G.: LIKWID: a lightweight performance-oriented tool suite for x86 multicore environments. In: Proceedings of the First International Workshop on Parallel Software Tools and Tool Infrastructures, September 2010
33. Weaver, V.: perf_event_open manual page. In: Kerrisk, M. (ed.) Linux Programmer's Manual, February 2018

PARLOT: Efficient Whole-Program Call Tracing for HPC Applications

Saeed Taheri[1], Sindhu Devale[2], Ganesh Gopalakrishnan[1(✉)], and Martin Burtscher[2(✉)]

[1] School of Computing, University of Utah, Salt Lake City, UT, USA
{staheri,ganesh}@cs.utah.edu

[2] Department of Computer Science, Texas State University, San Marcos, TX, USA
sindhu.devale@gmail.com
burtscher@cs.txstate.edu

Abstract. The complexity of HPC software and hardware is quickly increasing. As a consequence, the need for efficient execution tracing to gain insight into HPC application behavior is steadily growing. Unfortunately, available tools either do not produce traces with enough detail or incur large overheads. An efficient tracing method that overcomes the tradeoff between maximum information and minimum overhead is therefore urgently needed. This paper presents such a method and tool, called ParLoT, with the following key features. (1) It describes a technique that makes low-overhead on-the-fly compression of whole-program call traces feasible. (2) It presents a new, efficient, incremental trace-compression approach that reduces the trace volume dynamically, which lowers not only the needed bandwidth but also the tracing overhead. (3) It collects all caller/callee relations, call frequencies, call stacks, as well as the full trace of all calls and returns executed by each thread, including in library code. (4) It works on top of existing dynamic binary instrumentation tools, thus requiring neither source-code modifications nor recompilation. (5) It supports program analysis and debugging at the thread, thread-group, and program level. This paper establishes that comparable capabilities are currently unavailable. Our experiments with the NAS parallel benchmarks running on the Comet supercomputer with up to 1,024 cores show that ParLoT can collect whole-program function-call traces at an average tracing bandwidth of just 56 kB/s per core.

Keywords: Tracing · HPC · Data compression · Incremental compression

1 Introduction

Understanding and debugging HPC programs is time-consuming for the user and computationally inefficient. This is especially true when one has to track control flow in terms of function calls and returns that may span library and system codes. Traditional software engineering quality assurance methods are often

A. Bhatele et al. (Eds.): ESPT/VPA 2017/2018, LNCS 11027, pp. 162–184, 2019.
https://doi.org/10.1007/978-3-030-17872-7_10

inapplicable to HPC where concurrency combined with large problem scales and sophisticated domain-specific math can make programming very challenging. For example, it took months for scientists to debug an MPI laser-plasma interaction code [12].

HPC bugs may be a combination of both flawed program logic and unspecified or illegal interactions between various concurrency models (e.g., PThreads, MPI, OpenMP, etc.) that coexist in most large applications [12]. Moreover, HPC software tends to consume vast amounts of CPU time and hardware resources. Reproducing bugs by rerunning the application is therefore expensive and undesirable. A natural and field-proven approach for debugging is to capture detailed execution traces and compare the traces against corresponding traces from previous (stable) runs [2,26]. A *key requirement* is to do this collection *as efficiently as possible* and in *as general and comprehensive a manner* as possible.

Existing tools in this space do not meet our criteria for efficiency and generality. The highly acclaimed STAT [2] tool has helped isolate bugs based on building equivalence classes of MPI processes and spotting outliers. We would like to go beyond the capabilities offered by STAT and support the collection of *whole-program* traces that can then be employed by a gamut of back-end tools. Also, STAT is usually brought into the picture when a failure (e.g., a deadlock or hang) is encountered. We would like to move toward an "always on" collection regime, as we cannot anticipate when a failure will occur – or, more importantly, *whether the failure will be reproducible.* There are no reported debugging studies on using STAT in continuous collection ("always on") mode. In CSTG [26], the collection is orchestrated by the user around chosen collection points and employs heavy-weight unix `backtrace` calls. These again are different from ParLoT, where collection points would not be a priori chosen.

The thrust of the work in this paper is to avoid many of the drawbacks of existing tracing-based tools. We are interested in avoiding source-code modifications and recompilation—thus making binary instrumentation-based tools the only practical and widely deployable option. We also believe in the value of creating tools that are *portable across a wide variety of platforms.*

Our goal is to use *compression* for trace aggregation and to offer a generic and low-overhead tracing method that (1) collects dynamic call information during execution (all function calls and returns) for debugging, performance evaluation, phase detection [27], etc., (2) has low overhead, (3) and requires little tracing bandwidth. *Providing all these features in a single tool that operates based on binary instrumentation is an unsolved problem.* In this paper, we describe a new tracing approach that fulfills these requirements, which we implemented in our proof-of-concept ParLoT tool.

With ParLoT, users can easily build a host of post-processors to examine executions from many vantage points. For instance, they can write post-processors to detect unexpected (or "outlier") executions. If needed, they can drill down and detect abnormal behaviors *even in the runtime and support library stack* such as MPI-level activities. In HPC, it is well-known (especially on newer machines) that bugs are often due to broken libraries (MPI, OpenMP), a broken runtime, or OS-level activities. Having a single low-overhead tool that can "X-ray" an application to this depth is a goal met by ParLoT—a unique feature in today's tool eco-system.

To further motivate the need for whole-program function call traces, consider the expression `f()+g()`. In C, there is no sequence point associated with the + operator [24]. If these function calls have inadvertent side-effects causing failure, it is important to know in which order `f()` and `g()` were invoked—something that is easy to discern using ParLoT's traces. One may be concerned that such a tool introduces excessive execution slowdown. ParLoT goes to great lengths to minimize these overheads to a level that we believe most users will find acceptable. The mindset is to *"pay a little upfront to dramatically reduce the number of overall debug iterations"*.

As proof of concept, we gathered preliminary results from using the ParLoT tracing mechanism to compare different runs. We injected various bugs into the MPI-related functions of ILCS [4], a parallelization framework for iterative local searches. We ran ParLoT on top of executions of buggy and bug-free versions of ILCS and collected traces. Since ParLoT's traces maintain the order of the function calls, we were able to split the traces at multiple points of interest and to feed different chunks of traces to a Concept Lattice data structure [10,11]. Having the totally ordered sequence of function calls of the whole program for each active process/thread enabled us to quickly narrow down the search space to locate the cause of the abnormal behavior in the buggy version of ILCS.

This paper does not pursue debugging per se but rather a thorough benchmarking of ParLoT. It makes the following main contributions:

- It introduces a new tracing approach that makes it possible to capture the whole-program call-return, call-stack, call-graph, and call-frequency information, including all library calls, for every thread and process of HPC applications at low overhead in both space and time.
- It describes a new incremental data compression algorithm to drastically reduce the required tracing bandwidth, thus enabling the collection of whole-program traces, which would be infeasible without on-the-fly compression.
- It presents ParLoT, a proof-of-concept tool that implements our compression-based low-overhead tracing approach. ParLoT is capable of instrumenting x86 applications at the binary level (regardless of the source language used) to collect whole-program call traces.

The remainder of this paper is organized as follows. Section 2 introduces the basic ideas and infrastructure behind ParLoT and other tracing tools. Section 3 describes the design of ParLoT in detail. Sections 4 and 5 present our evaluation of different aspects of ParLoT and compare it with a similar tool. Section 6 concludes the paper with a summary and future work.

2 Background and Related Work

Recording a log of events during the execution of an application is essential for better understanding the program behavior and, in case of a failure, to locate the problem. Recording this type of information requires instrumentation of the program either at the source-code or the binary-code level. Instrumenting the source code by adding extra libraries and statements to collect the desired information is easy for developers. However, doing so modifies the code and requires recompilation, often involving multiple different tools and complex hierarchies of makefiles and libraries, which can make this approach cumbersome and frustrating for users. Instrumenting an executable at the binary level using a tool is typically easier, faster, and less error prone for most users. Moreover, binary instrumentation is language independent, portable to any system that has the appropriate instrumentation tool installed, and provides machine-level insight into the behavior of the application.

2.1 Binary Instrumentation

Executables can be instrumented *statically*, where the additional code is inserted into the binary before execution, which results in a persistent modified executable, or *dynamically*, where the modification of the executable is not permanent. In dynamic binary instrumentation, code behavior can be monitored at runtime, making it possible to handle dynamically-generated and self-modifying code. Furthermore, it may be feasible to attach the instrumentation to a running process, which is particularly useful for long-running applications and infinite loops.

Many different tools for investigating application behavior have been designed on top of such Dynamic Binary Instrumentation (DBI) frameworks. For instance, Dyninst [19] provides a dynamic instrumentation API that gives developers the ability to measure various performance aspects. It is used in tools like Open-SpeedShop [29] and TAU [30] as well as correctness debuggers like STAT [2]. Moreover, VampirTrace [16] uses it to provide a library for collecting program execution logs.

Valgrind [23] is a shadow-value DBI framework that keeps a copy of every register and memory location. It provides developers with the ability to instrument system calls and instructions. Error detectors such as Memcheck [22] and call-graph generators like CALLGRIND [33] are built upon Valgrind.[1]

We implemented PARLOT on top of PIN [18], a DBI framework for the IA-32, x86-64, and MIC instruction-set architectures for creating dynamic program analysis tools. There is also version of PIN available for the ARM architecture [13]. PARLOT mutates PIN to trace the entry (call) and exit (return) of every executed function. Note that our tracing and compression approaches can equally be implemented on top of other instrumentation tools. For example, PMaC [32] is a DBI tool for the PowerPC/AIX architecture upon which PARLOT could also be based.

[1] Given the absence of tools similar to PARLOT, we employ CALLGRIND as a "close-enough" tool in our comparisons elaborated in Sect. 4.3. In this capacity, CALLGRIND is similar to PARLOT(M), a variant of PARLOT that only collects traces from the `main` image. We perform such comparison to have an idea of how we fare with respect to one other tool. In Sect. 5, we also present a self-assessment of PARLOT separately.

2.2 Efficient Tracing

When dealing with large-scale parallel programs, any attempt to capture reasonably frequent events will result in a vast amount of data. Moreover, transferring and storing the data will incur significant overhead. For example, collecting just one byte of information per executed instruction yields on the order of a gigabyte of data per second on a single high-end core. Storing the resulting multi-gigabyte traces from many cores can be a challenge, even on today's large hard disks.

Hence, to be able to capture whole-program call traces, we need a way to decrease the space and runtime overhead. *Compression* can encode the generated data using a smaller number of bits, help reduce the amount of data movement across the memory hierarchy, and lower storage and network demands. Although the encoded data will later have to be decoded for analysis, compressing them during tracing enables the collection of *whole-program* traces.

The use of compression by itself is not new. Various performance evaluation tools [1,17,30] already employ compression during the collection of performance analysis data. Tools such as ScalaTrace [25] also exploit the repetitive nature of time-step simulations [8]. Aguilar et al. [1] proposed a lossy compression mechanism using the Nami library [9] for online MPI tracing. Mohror and Karavanic [20] investigated similarity-based trace reduction techniques to store and analyze traces at scale.

Many performance and debugging tools for HPC applications [2,21] rely on mechanisms such as MRNet [28] to accelerate the collection and aggregation of traces based on an overlay network to overcome the challenge of massive data movement and analysis. However, our experiments show that, due to the high compression ratio of ParLoT traces, such mechanisms for data movement and aggregation may be unnecessary.

The novelty offered by ParLoT lies in the combination of compression speed, efficacy, and low timing jitter made possible by its *incremental* lossless compression algorithm, which is described in Sect. 3. It immediately compresses all traced information while the application is running, that is, ParLoT does not record the uncompressed trace in memory. As a result, just a few kilobytes of data need to be written out per thread and per second, thus requiring only a small fraction of the disk or network bandwidth. The traces are decompressed later when they are read for offline analysis. From the decompressed full function-call trace, the complete call-graph, call-frequency, and caller-callee information can be extracted. This can be done at the granularity of a thread, a group of threads, or the whole application. We now elaborate on the design of ParLoT that makes these innovations possible.

3 Design of ParLoT

Our experimental results in Sect. 5 highlight why *compression* is essential to make our approach work. We used ParLoT to record a unique 16-bit identifier for every function call and return. Tracing just this small amount of information without compression when running the Mantevo miniapps [14] on Stampede 1

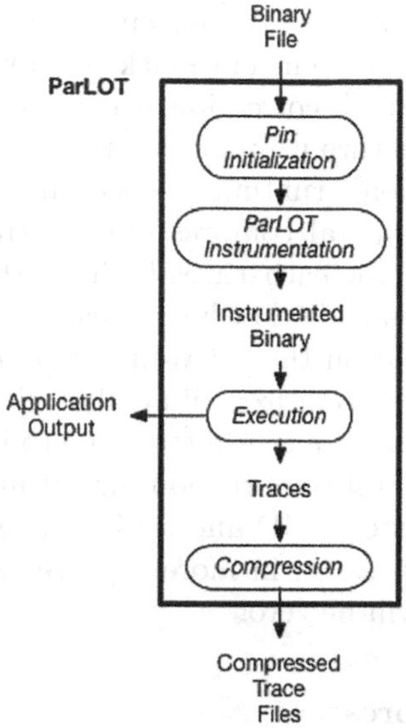

Fig. 1. Overview of ParLoT

resulted in about 2 MB/s of data per core on average. Extrapolating this value to all 102,400 cores of Stampede 1 (not counting the accelerators) yields 205 GB/s of trace data, which exceeds the Lustre filesystem's parallel write performance of 150 GB/s. Enabling ParLoT's compression algorithm reduced the emitted trace data by a factor of 100 on average, a ratio that is quite stable w.r.t scaling, making it possible to trace full-scale programs while leaving over 98% of the I/O bandwidth to the application. Therefore, ParLoT should also work for codes with higher bandwidth requirements than the ones we tested.

Figure 1 provides a general overview of ParLoT's workflow. Basic blocks within program executables are *dynamically* instrumented before being executed. The collected data are compressed on-the-fly at runtime.

3.1 Tracing Operation

ParLoT uses the PIN API as its instrumentation mechanism to gather traces. In particular, it instructs PIN to instrument every thread launch and termination in the application as well as every function entry and exit. The thread-launch instrumentation code initializes the per-thread tracing variables and opens a file into which the trace data from that thread will be written. The thread-termination code finalizes any ongoing compression, flushes out any remaining entries, and closes the trace file. ParLoT assigns every static function in each image (main program and all libraries) a unique unsigned 16-bit ID, which it records in a separate file together with the image and function name. This file allows the trace reader to map IDs back to function-name/image pairs.

For every function *entry*, PARLOT executes extra code that has access to the thread ID, function ID, and current stack-pointer (SP) value. Based on the SP value, it performs call-stack correction if necessary (see Sect. 3.4), adds the new function to a data structure it maintains that holds the call stack (which is separate from the application's runtime stack), and emits the function ID into the trace file via an incremental compression algorithm (see Sect. 3.2). All of this is done independently for each thread. Similarly, for every function *exit*, PARLOT also executes extra code that has access to the thread ID, function ID, and current SP value. Based on the SP value, it performs call-stack correction if necessary, removes the function from its call-stack data structure, and emits the reserved function ID of zero into the trace file to indicate an exit. As before, this is done via an incremental compression algorithm. We use zero for all exits rather than emitting the function ID and a bit to specify whether it is an entry or exit because using zeros results in more compressible output. This way, half of the values in the trace will be zero.

3.2 Incremental Compression

PARLOT immediately compresses the traced information even before it is written to memory. It does, however, keep a sliding window (circular buffer) of the most recent uncompressed trace events, which is needed by the compressor. It compresses each function ID before the next function ID is known. The conventional approach would be to first record uncompressed function IDs in a buffer and later compress the whole buffer once it fills up. However, this makes the processing time very non-uniform. Whereas almost all function IDs can be recorded very quickly since they just have to be written to the buffer, processing a function ID that happens to fill the buffer takes a long time as it triggers the compression of the entire buffer. This results in sporadic blocking of threads during which time they make no progress towards executing the application code. Initial experiments revealed that such behavior can be detrimental when one thread is polling data from another thread that is currently blocked due to compression. For example, we observed a several order of magnitude increase in entry/exit events of an internal MPI library function when using block-based compression.

To remedy this situation, the compressor must operate incrementally, i.e., each piece of trace data must be compressed when it is generated, without buffering it first, to ensure that there is never a long-latency compression delay. Few existing compression algorithms have been implemented in such a manner because it is more difficult to code up and probably a little slower. Nevertheless, we were able to implement our algorithm (discussed next) in this way so that each trace event is compressed with similar latency.

3.3 Compression Algorithm

We used the CRUSHER framework [5–7, 34] to automatically synthesize an effective and fast lossless compression algorithm for our traces. CRUSHER is based on a library of data transformations extracted from various compression algorithms. It combines these transformations in all possible ways to generate algorithm candidates, which it then evaluates on a set of training data. We gathered uncompressed traces from some of the Mantevo miniapps [14] for this purpose. This evaluation revealed that a particular word-level Lempel-Ziv (LZ) transformation followed by a byte-level Zero-Elimination (ZE) transformation works well. In other words, ParLoT's trace entries, which are two-byte words, are first transformed using LZ. The output is interpreted as a sequence of bytes, which is transformed using ZE for further compression. The output of ZE is written to secondary storage.

LZ implements a variant of the LZ77 algorithm [35]. It uses a 4096-entry hash table to identify the most recent prior occurrence of the current value in the trace. Then it checks whether the three values immediately before that location match the three trace entries just before the current location. If they do not, the current trace entry is emitted and LZ advances to the next entry. If the three values match, LZ counts how many values following the current value match the values following that location. The length of the matching substring is emitted and LZ advances by that many values. Note that all of this is done incrementally. The history of previous trace entries available to LZ for finding matches is maintained in a 64k-entry circular buffer.

ZE emits a bitmap in which each bit represents one input byte. The bits indicate whether the corresponding bytes are zero or not. Following each eight-bit bitmap, ZE emits the non-zero bytes.

As mentioned above, we had to implement the two transformations incrementally to minimize the maximum latency. This required breaking them up into multiple pieces. Depending on the state the compressor is in when the next trace entry needs to be processed, the appropriate piece of code is executed and the state updated. If the LZ code produces an output, which it only does some of the time, then the appropriate piece of the ZE code is executed in a similar manner.

3.4 PIN and Call-Stack Correction

To be able to decode the trace, i.e., to correctly associate each exit with the function entry it belongs to, our trace reader maintains an identical call-stack data structure. Unfortunately, and as pointed out in the PIN documentation [15], it is not always possible to identify all function exits. For example, in optimized code, a function's instructions may be inlined and interleaved with the caller's instructions, making it sometimes infeasible for PIN to identify the exit. As a consequence, we have to ensure that ParLoT works correctly even when PIN misses an exit. This is why the SP values are needed.

During tracing, ParLoT not only records the function IDs in its call stack but also the associated SP values. This enables it to detect missing exits and to correct the call stack accordingly. Whenever a function is entered, it checks if there is at least one entry in the call stack and, if so, whether its SP value is higher than that of the current SP. If it is lower, we must have missed at least one exit since the runtime stack grows downwards (the SP value decreases with every function entry and increases with every exit). If a missing exit is detected in this manner, ParLoT pops the top element from its call stack and emits a zero to indicate a function exit. It repeats this procedure until the stack is empty or its top entry has a sufficiently high SP value. The same call-stack correction technique is applied for every function exit whose SP value is inconsistent. Note that the SP values are only used for this purpose and are not included in the compressed trace.

The result is an internally consistent trace of function entry and exit events, meaning that parsing the trace will yield a correct call stack. This is essential so that the trace can be decoded properly. Moreover, it means that the trace includes exits that truly happened in the application but that were missed by PIN. Note, however, that our call-stack correction is a best-effort approach and may, in rare cases, temporarily not reflect what the application actually did. For example, this can happen for functions that do not create a frame on the runtime stack. When implementing ParLoT on top of another DBI framework, call-stack correction may not be needed, resulting in even lower ParLoT overhead.

4 Evaluation Methodology

4.1 Benchmarks and System

We performed our evaluations on the MPI-based NAS Parallel Benchmarks (NPB) [3]. NPB includes four inputs sizes. To keep the runtimes reasonable, we show results for the class B (small-medium) and class C (medium-large) inputs.

We compiled the NPB codes with the mpicc and mpif77 wrappers of MVAPICH 2.2.1, which are based on icc/ifort 14.0.2 using the prescribed -g and -O1 optimization flags. Quick tests showed that higher optimization levels do not significantly improve the performance.

We ran all experiments on Comet at the San Diego Supercomputer Center [31], whose filesystem is NFS and Lustre. Comet has 1944 compute nodes, each of which has dual-socket Intel Xeon E5-2680 v3 processors with a total of 28 cores (14 per socket) and 128 GB of main memory. Note that we only used 16 cores per node as many of the NPB programs require a core count that is a power of two. To study the scaling behavior, we ran experiments on 1, 4, 16 and 64 compute nodes, i.e., on up to 1024 cores.

4.2 Metrics

We use the following metrics to quantify and compare the performance of the tracing tools. Unless otherwise noted, all results are based on the median of three identical experiments.

- The **tracing overhead** is the runtime of the target application when it is being traced divided by the runtime of the same application without tracing. This lower-is-better ratio measures by how much the tracing (and the compression when enabled) slows down the target application.
- The **tracing bandwidth** is the size of the trace information divided by the application runtime. To make the results easier to compare, we generally list the tracing bandwidth per core, i.e., the tracing bandwidth divided by the number of cores used. This lower-is-better metric is expressed in kilobytes per second (kB/s) per core. It specifies the average needed bandwidth to record the trace data.
- The **compression ratio** is the size of the uncompressed trace divided by the size of the generated (compressed) trace. This higher-is-better ratio measures the factor by which the compression reduces the trace size. In other words, without compression, the tracing bandwidth would be higher by this factor.

4.3 Tracing Tools

We compare our PARLOT tool, implemented on top of PIN 3.5, with CALLGRIND 3.13. PARLOT was compiled with gcc 4.9.2 using PIN's make system and CALLGRIND with Valgrind's make system. We created the following versions of PARLOT to evaluate different aspects of its design.

- **PARLOT(M)** is the normal PARLOT tool configured to only collect function-call traces from the main image of the application.
- **PARLOT(A)** is the normal PARLOT tool configured to collect function-call traces from all images of the application, including library function calls.
- **PIN-INIT** is a crippled version of PARLOT from which the tracing code has been removed. The purpose of PIN-INIT is to see how much of the overhead is due to PIN.
- **PARLOT-NC** is the normal PARLOT tool but with compression disabled. It writes out the captured data in uncompressed form. The purpose of PARLOT-NC is to show the performance impact of the compression.

It proved surprisingly difficult to find a tool that is similar to PARLOT because there appear to be no other tools that generate whole program call traces. In the end, we settled on CALLGRIND as the most similar tool we could find and used it for our comparisons. CALLGRIND is based on the Valgrind DBI tool. It collects function-call graphs combined with performance data to show the user what portion of the execution time has been spent in each function.

Each CALLGRIND trace file contains a sequence of function names (or their code) plus numerical data for each function on its caller-callee relationship with other functions. Moreover, it contains cost information for each function in terms of how many machine instructions it read. This information is collected using hardware performance counters. The format of the file is plain ASCII text. Interestingly, all numerical values are expressed relative to previous values, i.e., they are delta (or difference) encoded. This simple form of compression is enabled by default in CALLGRIND.

We believe the information traced by CALLGRIND is reasonably similar to the information traced by PARLOT(M). Whereas CALLGRIND's traces include performance data that PARLOT does not capture, PARLOT records the whole-program call trace, which CALLGRIND does not capture. The full function-call trace is a strict superset of the call-graph information that CALLGRIND records because the call graph can be extracted from the function-call trace but not vice versa. In particular, CALLGRIND cannot recreate the order of the function calls a thread made whereas PARLOT can.

Table 1. Overhead added by each tool

Input	Tool	# Nodes	bt	cg	ep	ft	is	lu	mg	sp	GM
B	PARLOT(M)	1	1.6	1.8	2.6	2.1	2.5	1.3	2.5	1.3	1.9
		4	1.8	1.9	1.9	1.7	1.8	1.8	1.5	1.7	1.8
		16	2.2	2.6	2.0	1.9	1.8	2.7	2.4	2.2	2.2
		64	2.1	2.2	2.4	2.0	4.3	4.4	2.0	2.1	2.5
		AVG	1.9	2.1	2.2	1.9	2.6	2.6	2.1	1.8	**2.1**
	PARLOT(A)	1	1.8	2.7	4.2	2.8	4.2	1.7	4.8	1.7	2.8
		4	2.6	3.1	3.4	2.8	3.0	2.8	2.8	2.7	2.9
		16	3.5	4.2	3.4	2.9	2.8	4.3	4.5	3.7	3.6
		64	3.1	3.3	3.8	3.0	5.4	4.7	3.2	3.3	3.7
		AVG	2.8	3.3	3.7	2.9	3.9	3.4	3.8	2.8	**3.2**
	CALLGRIND	1	8.6	6.0	8.9	10.1	2.5	7.5	3.3	6.6	6.1
		4	6.0	3.6	2.9	3.5	1.5	5.2	1.2	5.8	3.2
		16	4.3	3.3	2.2	2.2	1.7	4.6	1.8	4.3	2.8
		64	2.3	2.0	1.7	2.1	4.1	4.0	1.5	2.5	2.3
		AVG	5.3	3.7	3.9	4.5	2.4	5.3	2.0	4.8	**3.6**
C	PARLOT(M)	1	1.4	1.3	2.5	1.9	2.3	1.1	1.7	1.1	1.6
		4	1.6	1.7	1.8	1.6	1.7	1.3	1.8	1.4	1.6
		16	1.8	2.4	2.5	1.5	1.8	2.2	2.4	1.8	2.0
		64	2.2	2.7	2.4	1.6	4.5	3.4	2.4	2.2	2.6
		AVG	1.8	2.0	2.3	1.7	2.6	2.0	2.1	1.6	**1.9**
	PARLOT(A)	1	1.5	1.6	3.2	2.0	2.8	1.2	2.5	1. 2	1.9
		4	1.9	2.4	2.6	2.1	2.6	1.7	3.1	1.7	2.2
		16	2.7	3.5	4.1	2.1	2.8	3.2	4.0	2.5	3.0
		64	3.6	4.1	4.2	2.2	5.5	4.4	4.2	3.0	3.8
		AVG	2.4	2.9	3.5	2.1	3.4	2.6	3.5	2.1	**2.7**
	CALLGRIND	1	8.5	4.4	13.2	13.1	3.3	7.9	5.9	5.1	6.9
		4	8.7	4.5	4.8	6.4	1.7	6.4	2.8	6.3	4.6
		16	6.9	3.9	3.1	2.8	1.8	6.4	2.1	6.1	3.7
		64	4.4	3.5	2.1	2.5	4.2	5.2	2.1	3.8	3.3
		AVG	7.1	4.1	5.8	6.2	2.8	6.5	3.2	5.3	**4.6**

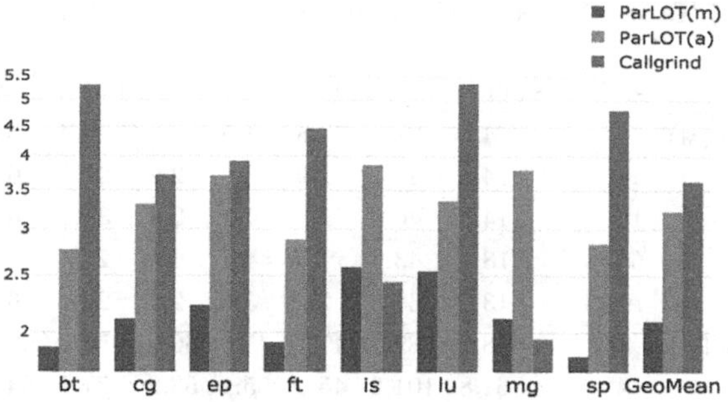

Fig. 2. Average tracing overhead on the NPB applications - Input B

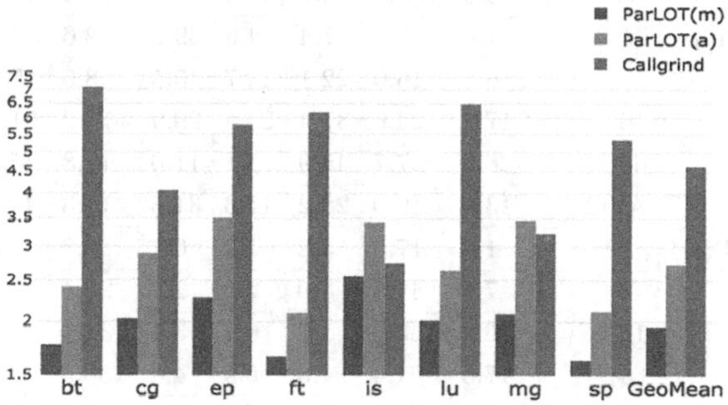

Fig. 3. Average tracing overhead on the NPB applications - Input C

5 Results

5.1 Tracing Overhead

Table 1 shows the tracing overhead of PARLOT(M), PARLOT(A), and CALLGRIND on each application of the NPB benchmark suite for different node counts. The last column of the table lists the geometric mean over all eight programs. The AVG rows show the average over the four node counts.

On average, both PARLOT(M) and PARLOT(A) outperform CALLGRIND. The bolded numbers in Table 1 for input C show that the average overhead is 1.94 for PARLOT(M), 2.73 for PARLOT(A), and 4.63 for CALLGRIND. Figures 2 and 3 show these results in visual form.

The key takeaway point is that the overhead of PARLOT is roughly a factor of two to three, which we believe users may be willing to accept, for example, if it helps them debug their applications. This is promising especially when considering how detailed the collected trace information is and that most of the overhead is due to PIN (see Sect. 5.4). Note that PARLOT's overhead is typically lower than that of CALLGRIND, which collects less information.

The overhead of PARLOT increases as we scale the applications to more compute nodes. However, the increase is quite small. Going from 16 to 1024

Table 2. Required bandwidth per core (kB/s)

Input	Tool	# Nodes	bt	cg	ep	ft	is	lu	mg	sp	GM
B	ParLoT(m)	1	4.7	21.9	3.8	1.5	0.8	2.4	5.6	5.4	3.7
		4	14.3	41.1	1.9	3.5	2.2	21.5	6.5	15.9	8.1
		16	14.3	46.6	1.5	4.9	3.4	31.8	6.5	18.6	9.4
		64	18.6	43.6	1.3	4.6	4.5	27.1	5.6	29.6	9.9
		AVG	13.0	38.3	2.1	3.6	2.7	20.7	6.1	17.4	**7.8**
	ParLoT(a)	1	48.7	89.4	47.2	45.6	60.0	53.6	60.8	54.3	56.2
		4	61.8	101.2	45.2	55.1	53.2	71.1	54.9	73.6	62.7
		16	74.0	116.9	47.4	48.9	47.8	100.9	55.8	84.6	68.0
		64	81.8	110.2	44.2	48.0	37.8	100.3	52.7	99.9	66.5
		AVG	66.6	104.4	46.0	49.4	49.7	81.5	56.0	78.1	**63.3**
	Callgrind	1	1.6	7.7	7.4	4.6	39.5	2.6	34.4	2.7	6.7
		4	6.5	16.0	22.1	15.7	45.5	8.6	45.5	7.8	16.3
		16	17.2	24.6	37.4	23.8	29.9	16.2	51.5	15.8	24.9
		64	26.8	27.7	45.9	25.1	11.0	17.8	45.3	20.2	25.0
		AVG	13.0	19.0	28.2	17.3	31.5	11.3	44.2	11.6	**18.2**
C	ParLoT(m)	1	1.8	17.0	5.2	1.2	0.7	0.8	3.6	1.4	2.2
		4	7.5	44.9	3.0	2.5	2.1	20.1	7.1	13.7	7.6
		16	16.3	55.0	1.8	6.1	3.4	34.1	7.2	20.7	10.7
		64	17.5	61.4	1.3	5.9	4.4	38.3	5.6	26.1	10.9
		AVG	10.8	44.6	2.8	3.9	2.7	23.3	5.9	15.5	**7.8**
	ParLoT(a)	1	17.8	53.4	26.3	20.9	48.3	25.3	52.6	19.5	30.0
		4	51.8	95.8	36.8	43.8	51.4	58.4	54.2	65.8	55.2
		16	75.4	121.0	44.3	61.4	46.9	101.1	56.5	101.3	71.4
		64	80.6	135.2	43.5	46.3	37.1	117.9	54.1	99.0	69.0
		AVG	56.4	101.4	37.7	43.1	45.9	75.7	54.3	71.4	**56.4**
	Callgrind	1	0.4	3.1	2.0	1.1	14.6	0.7	7.0	0.8	1.9
		4	1.8	8.9	7.7	4.5	31.7	2.8	21.0	2.8	6.4
		16	6.0	15.8	22.9	10.8	26.5	7.5	39.1	7.0	13.7
		64	14.3	19.6	35.8	12.2	11.1	11.9	40.7	12.8	17.4
		AVG	5.6	11.8	17.1	7.1	21.0	5.7	26.9	5.8	**9.8**

cores, a 64-fold increase in parallelism, only increases the average overhead by between 1.3- and 2.1-fold. In contrast, Callgrind's overhead decreases with increasing node count, making it more scalable. Having said that, Callgrind's overhead is larger for the C inputs whereas ParLoT's overhead is larger for the smaller B inputs. In other words, ParLoT scales better to larger inputs than Callgrind.

ParLoT's scaling behavior can be explained by correlating it with the expected function-call frequency. When distributing a fixed problem size over more cores, each core receives less work. As a consequence, less time is spent in the functions that process the work, resulting in more function calls per time

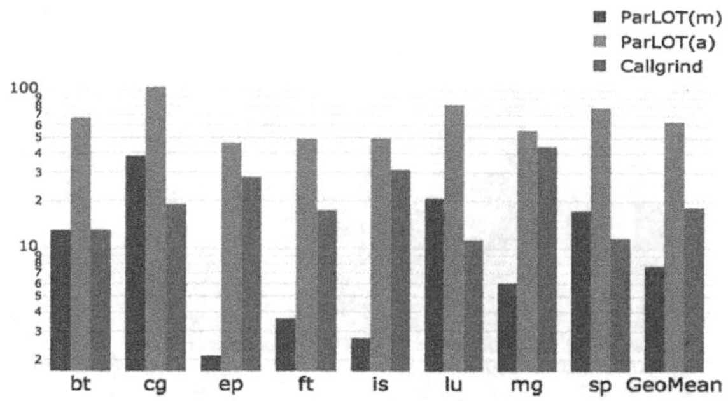

Fig. 4. Average required bandwidth per core (kB/s) on the NPB applications - Input B

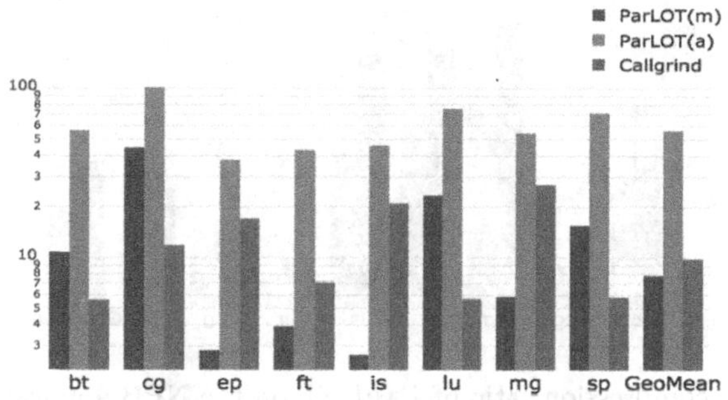

Fig. 5. Average required bandwidth per core (kB/s) on the NPB applications - Input C

unit, which causes more work for PARLOT. In contrast, when distributing a larger problem size over the same number of cores, each core receives more work. Hence, more time is spent in the functions that process the work, resulting in fewer function calls per time unit, which causes less work for PARLOT and therefore less tracing overhead. Hence, we believe PARLOT's overhead to be even lower on long-running inputs, which is where our tracing technique is needed the most.

In summary, PARLOT's overhead is in the single digits for all evaluated applications and configurations, including for 1024-core runs. It appears to scale reasonably to larger node counts and well to larger problem sizes.

5.2 Required Bandwidth

Table 2, Figs. 4 and 5 show how much trace bandwidth each tool requires during the application execution. On average, PARLOT(M) requires less bandwidth than CALLGRIND, especially for smaller inputs. PARLOT(A)'s bandwidth is much higher as it collects call information from all images and not just the main image like PARLOT(M) does.

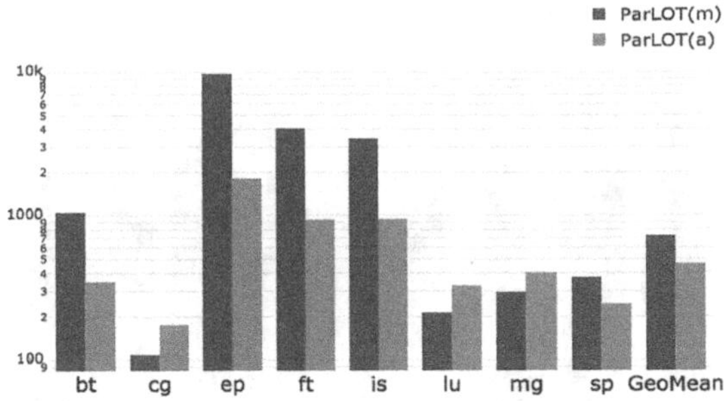

Fig. 6. Average compression ratio of ParLoT on the NPB applications - Input B

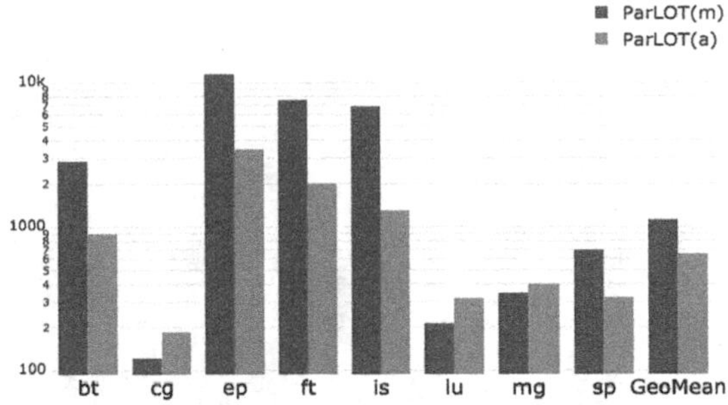

Fig. 7. Average compression ratio of ParLoT on the NPB applications - Input C

We see that the required bandwidth for different input sizes of the NPB applications are almost equal in ParLoT. According to the NPB documentation, the number of iterations for inputs B and C are the same for all applications. They only differ in the number of elements or the grid size. It is clear that the required bandwidth of ParLoT is independent of the problem size, unlike Callgrind, where the input size has a linear impact on the results.

5.3 Compression Ratio

Table 3 shows the compression ratios for all configurations and inputs. On average, ParLoT stores between half a kilobyte and a kilobyte of trace information in a single byte. We observe that the average compression ratio for ParLoT(a) on input C is 644.3, and its corresponding required bandwidth from Table 2 is 56.4 kB/s. This means ParLoT can collect **more than 36 MB** worth of data per core per second while only needing 56 kB/s of the system bandwidth, *leaving the rest of the available bandwidth to the application.* In comparison, Callgrind collects **less than 100 kB** of data but still adds more overhead compared to either ParLoT(a) or ParLoT(m). The average amount of trace data that can be collected by ParLoT(a) is **360x** (85x for ParLoT(m)) larger than that for Callgrind. In the best observed case, the compression ratio of

ParLoT exceeds 21000. This is particularly impressive because it was achieved with relatively low overhead and incremental on-the-fly compression. Generally, the compression ratios of ParLoT(M) are higher than those of ParLoT(A) because the variety of distinct function calls on the main image is smaller than when tracing all images, thus compression performs better on ParLoT(M). Also by looking at Figs. 4, 5, 6 and 7, we find EP to have the highest compression ratio of the NPB applications. At the same time, it has the minimum required bandwidth. The opposite is true for CG, which exhibits the lowest compression ratio and the highest required bandwidth. CG is a conjugate gradient method with irregular memory accesses and communications whereas EP is an embarrassingly parallel random number generator. CG's whole-program trace contains a larger number of distinct calls and more complex patterns than that of EP, thus resulting in a higher bandwidth and lower compression ratio.

ParLoT's compression mechanism works better on larger input sizes because larger inputs tend to result in longer streams of similar function calls (e.g., a call that is made for every processed element).

Table 3. Compression ratio

Input	Tool	# Nodes	bt	cg	ep	ft	is	lu	mg	sp	GM
B	ParLoT(M)	1	3 035.9	94.4	12 456.2	12 173.5	9 718.4	167.7	99.1	878.3	1 255.2
		4	586.6	82.5	10 368.4	1 737.1	909.2	140.3	255.0	338.2	559.4
		16	346.7	113.3	8 563.9	1 077.4	1 200.6	179.0	387.6	123.0	496.8
		64	252.2	147.8	7 611.0	1 122.6	1 908.0	366.8	437.3	152.9	591.1
		AVG	1 055.4	109.5	9 749.9	4 027.6	3 434.0	213.5	294.7	373.1	**725.6**
	ParLoT(A)	1	514.5	137.4	3 335.8	1 226.7	543.2	314.6	260.9	303.9	500.2
		4	315.7	137.2	1 266.9	436.2	316.2	287.3	329.6	199.7	330.7
		16	226.9	181.6	1 246.7	1 026.5	927.1	299.3	469.3	171.5	430.4
		64	329.2	247.3	1 394.1	1 043.9	1 984.6	410.3	548.5	307.2	597.6
		AVG	346.6	175.9	1 810.9	933.3	942.8	327.9	402.1	245.6	**464.7**
C	ParLoT(M)	1	8 619.0	111.2	13 068.0	21 335.6	21 856.5	350.0	247.4	1 977.4	2 371.4
		4	1 910.6	110.5	12 418.7	6 520.3	2 256.6	112.8	268.0	472.7	928.2
		16	580.8	133.2	11 017.4	1 239.3	1 347.9	164.5	396.9	143.1	582.8
		64	322.8	131.9	9 155.0	1 065.1	1 896.3	223.7	465.7	168.9	585.7
		AVG	2 858.3	121.7	11 414.7	7 540.1	6 839.3	212.7	344.5	690.5	**1117.0**
	ParLoT(A)	1	2 579.4	181.8	7 377.0	5 143.1	1 520.4	408.2	314.8	650.7	1 107.4
		4	448.6	161.3	3 194.6	1 062.9	527.3	274.7	319.4	237.4	477.4
		16	285.1	185.7	1 765.5	588.9	1 106.3	273.6	467.4	141.7	426.9
		64	290.0	214.7	1 512.9	1 237.3	2 038.7	329.0	496.2	270.8	565.8
		AVG	900.8	185.9	3 462.5	2 008.1	1 298.2	321.4	399.4	325.2	**644.4**

5.4 Overheads

Table 4 presents the average overhead added to each application for different versions of ParLoT. Last rows of each section of this table present the geometric mean. This information captures how much each phase of ParLoT slows down the native execution.

Table 4. Tracing overhead of versions of ParLoT- Input B

Input: B	Nodes :	1			4			16			64		
	Detail Tools:	Pin-Init	ParLoT	ParLoT-NC	Pin-Init	ParLoT	ParLoT-NC	Pin-Init	ParLoT	ParLoT-NC	Pin-Init	ParLoT	ParLoT-NC
Main	bt	1.5	1.5	5.6	1.7	1.7	5.0	2.1	2.1	5.0	1.8	2.1	3.5
	cg	1.7	1.8	2.3	1.8	1.8	2.6	2.7	2.5	4.4	2.3	2.1	4.6
	ep	2.9	2.6	20.4	1.9	1.8	5.3	2.4	1.9	3.0	2.6	2.3	2.6
	ft	1.8	2.1	6.1	1.7	1.7	2.7	2.0	1.8	2.2	2.1	1.9	2.1
	is	2.4	2.4	4.8	1.7	1.7	2.0	2.1	1.7	1.8	4.5	4.3	5.7
	lu	1.3	1.3	1.4	1.7	1.7	2.2	2.7	2.7	3.6	3.0	4.3	6.1
	mg	2.5	2.5	2.7	1.5	1.5	1.5	2.6	2.4	2.6	1.9	1.9	1.8
	sp	1.3	1.3	2.4	1.7	1.7	3.5	2.1	2.1	2.3	1.9	2.0	2.5
	GM	1.8	1.9	4.1	1.7	1.7	2.9	2.3	2.1	3.0	2.4	2.5	3.3
All	bt	1.7	1.8	6.1	2.3	2.5	6.1	3.2	3.5	9.0	2.8	3.1	7.5
	cg	2.6	2.7	3.8	2.8	3.0	4.4	4.0	4.2	11.3	3.3	3.2	10.3
	ep	4.3	4.1	22.2	3.1	3.4	7.1	3.1	3.3	4.5	4.1	3.8	4.1
	ft	2.8	2.7	6.8	2.6	2.7	3.8	2.8	2.9	3.6	3.1	3.0	3.5
	is	4.4	4.2	7.0	2.8	2.9	3.4	2.9	2.8	3.2	5.3	5.4	8.8
	lu	1.7	1.7	2.3	2.5	2.7	4.8	3.9	4.3	10.4	4.4	4.6	23.4
	mg	4.8	4.7	5.3	2.5	2.7	3.0	4.3	4.4	5.2	2.7	3.1	3.2
	sp	1.7	1.7	3.0	2.4	2.6	5.0	3.2	3.6	5.6	2.7	3.3	11.6
	GM	2.7	2.7	5.5	2.6	2.8	4.5	3.4	3.6	6.0	3.5	3.6	7.4

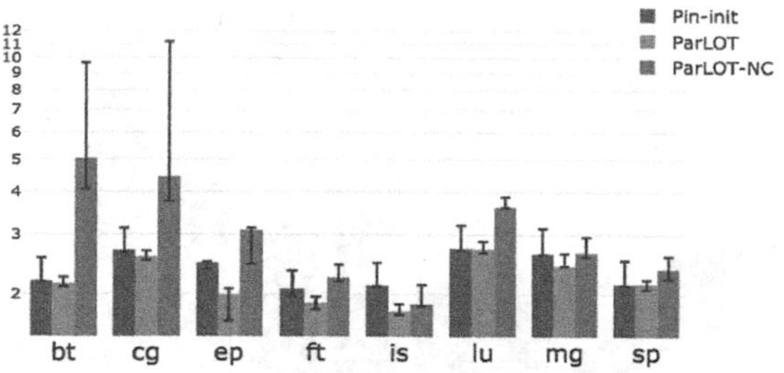

Fig. 8. Variability of ParLoT(m) overhead on 16 nodes - Input B

In general, one expects the following inequality to hold: the overhead of Pin-Init should be less than that of ParLoT, which should be less than that of ParLoT-NC. This is not always the case because of the non-deterministic runtimes of the applications. In fact, the variability across three runs of each experiment is shown in Fig. 8 where we present the minimum, maximum and median overheads. These overheads are for input size B and 16 nodes. This variability explains the seeming inconsistencies in Table 4.

On average, Pin-Init adds an overhead of 3.28 and ParLoT(a) adds an overhead of 3.42. This means that **almost 96% of ParLoT(a)'s overhead is due to PIN**. The results of ParLoT(m) and other inputs follow the same pattern as shown in Figs. 11 and 12. The overhead that ParLoT (excluding the overhead of Pin-Init) *adds* to the applications is very small. If we were to switch to a different instrumentation tool that is not as general as PIN but more lightweight, the overhead would potentially reduce drastically.

5.5 Compression Impact

Figures 9 and 10 show the overhead breakdown of ParLoT-NC, which illustrate the impact of compression. They also highlight the importance of incorporating compression directly in the tracing tool. On average, ParLoT-NC slows down the application execution almost **2x** more than ParLoT(a). The average overhead across Table 4 for ParLoT(a) is **3.4**. The corresponding factor for ParLoT-NC is **6.6**. The numbers of ParLoT(m) and input C follow the same pattern. For example, ParLoT-NC slows down the application execution almost **1.66x** more than ParLoT(m).

Clearly, compression not only lowers the storage requirement but also the overhead. This is important as it shows that the extra computation to perform the compression is more than amortized by the reduction in the amount of data that need to be written out.

This result validates our approach and highlights that incremental, on-the-fly compression is likely essential to make whole-program tracing possible at low overhead.

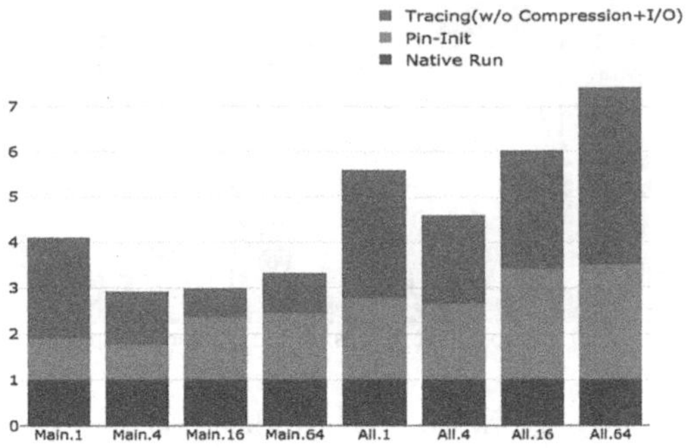

Fig. 9. ParLoT-NC tracing overhead breakdown - Input B

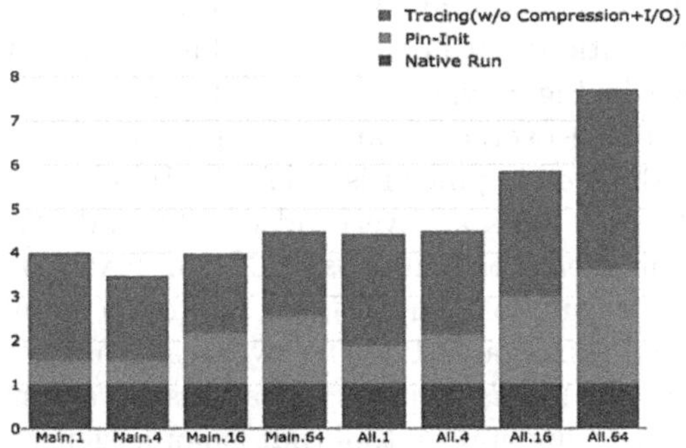

Fig. 10. ParLoT-NC tracing overhead breakdown - Input C

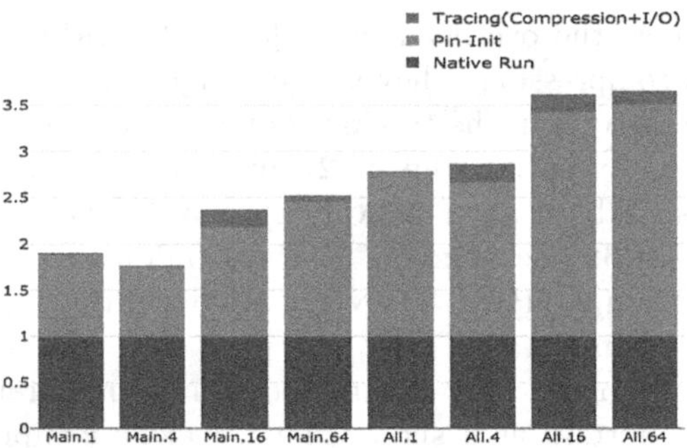

Fig. 11. Tracing overhead breakdown - Input B

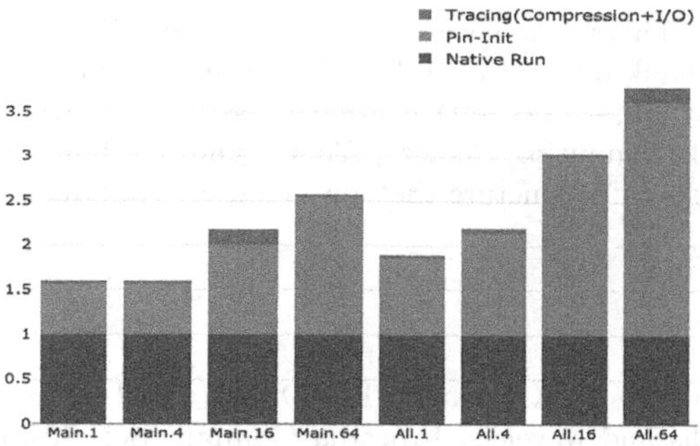

Fig. 12. Tracing overhead breakdown - Input C

6 Discussion and Conclusion

In this paper, we present ParLoT, a portable low overhead dynamic binary instrumentation-based whole-program tracing approach that can support a variety of dynamic program analyses, including debugging. Key properties of ParLoT include its on-the-fly trace collection and compression that reduces timing jitter, I/O bandwidth, and storage requirements to such a degree that whole-program call/return traces can be collected efficiently even at scale.

We evaluate various versions of ParLoT created by disabling/enabling compression, not collecting any traces, etc. In order to provide an intuitive comparison against a well known tool, we also compare ParLoT to Callgrind. Our metrics include the tracing overhead, required bandwidth, achieved compression ratio, initialization overhead, and the overall impact of compression. Detailed evaluations on the NAS parallel benchmarks running on up to 1024 cores establish the merit of our tool and our design decisions. ParLoT can collect more than 36 MB worth of data per core per second while only needing 56 kB/s of bandwidth and slowing down the application by 2.7x on average. These results are highly promising in terms of supporting whole program tracing and debugging, in particular when considering that most of the overhead is due to the DBI tool and not ParLoT.

The traces collected by ParLoT cut through the entire stack of heterogeneous (MPI, OpenMP, PThreads) calls. This permits a designer to project these traces onto specific APIs of interest during program analysis, visualization, and debugging.

A number of improvements to ParLoT remain to be made. These include allowing users to selectively trace at specific interfaces: doing so can further increase compression efficiency by reducing the variety of function calls to be handled by the compressor. We also discuss the need to bring down initialization overheads, i.e., by switching to a less general-purpose DBI tool.

Acknowledgment. This research was supported by the NSF Award CCF 1439002 and CCF 1817073. We thank our colleague Dr. Hari Sundar from the University of Utah who provided insight and expertise that greatly assisted the research. We also thank the Texas Advanced Computing Center (TACC) and the San Diego Supercomputer Center (SDSC) for the infrastructure they provided for running our experiments.

References

1. Aguilar, X., Fürlinger, K., Laure, E.: Online MPI trace compression using event flow graphs and wavelets. Procedia Comput. Sci. **80**(Supp. C), 1497–1506 (2016). https://doi.org/10.1016/j.procs.2016.05.471. http://www.sciencedirect.com/science/article/pii/S1877050916309565. International Conference on Computational Science 2016, ICCS 2016, 6-8 June 2016, San Diego, California, USA
2. Arnold, D.C., Ahn, D.H., de Supinski, B.R., Lee, G.L., Miller, B.P., Schulz, M.: Stack trace analysis for large scale debugging. In: Proceedings of the International Parallel and Distributed Processing Symposium (IPDPS), pp. 1–10 (2007)
3. Bailey, D.H., et al.: The NAS parallel benchmarks— summary and preliminary results. In: Proceedings of the 1991 ACM/IEEE Conference on Supercomputing, Supercomputing 1991, pp. 158–165. ACM, New York (1991). https://doi.org/10.1145/125826.125925
4. Burtscher, M., Rabeti, H.: A scalable heterogeneous parallelization framework for iterative local searches. In: 2013 IEEE 27th International Symposium on Parallel and Distributed Processing, pp. 1289–1298, May 2013. https://doi.org/10.1109/IPDPS.2013.27
5. Burtscher, M., Mukka, H., Yang, A., Hesaaraki, F.: Real-time synthesis of compression algorithms for scientific data. In: Proceedings of the International Conference for High Performance Computing, Networking, Storage and Analysis, SC 2016, pp. 23:1–23:12. IEEE Press, Piscataway, NJ, USA (2016). http://dl.acm.org/citation.cfm?id=3014904.3014935
6. Claggett, S., Azimi, S., Burtscher, M.: SPDP: an automatically synthesized lossless compression algorithm for floating-point data. In: 2018 Data Compression Conference (2018)
7. Coplin, J., Yang, A., Poppe, A., Burtscher, M.: Increasing telemetry throughput using customized and adaptive data compression. In: AIAA SPACE and Astronautics Forum and Exposition (2016)
8. Freitag, F., Caubet, J., Labarta, J.: On the scalability of tracing mechanisms. In: Monien, B., Feldmann, R. (eds.) Euro-Par 2002. LNCS, vol. 2400, pp. 97–104. Springer, Heidelberg (2002). https://doi.org/10.1007/3-540-45706-2_10
9. Gamblin, T., de Supinski, B.R., Schulz, M., Fowler, R., Reed, D.A.: Scalable load-balance measurement for SPMD codes. In: Proceedings of the 2008 ACM/IEEE Conference on Supercomputing, SC 2008, pp. 1–12, November 2008. https://doi.org/10.1109/SC.2008.5222553
10. Ganter, B., Wille, R.: Formal Concept Analysis: Mathematical Foundations, 1st edn. Springer, Secaucus (1997). https://doi.org/10.1007/978-3-642-59830-2
11. Godin, R., Missaoui, R., Alaoui, H.: Incremental concept formation algorithms based on Galois (concept) lattices. Comput. Intell. **11**(2), 246–267
12. Gopalakrishnan, G., et al.: Report of the HPC correctness summit, 25–26 January 2017, Washington, DC. CoRR abs/1705.07478 (2017). http://arxiv.org/abs/1705.07478

13. Hazelwood, K., Klauser, A.: A dynamic binary instrumentation engine for the ARM architecture. In: Proceedings of the 2006 International Conference on Compilers, Architecture and Synthesis for Embedded Systems, CASES 2006, pp. 261–270. ACM, New York (2006). https://doi.org/10.1145/1176760.1176793
14. Heroux, M.A., et al.: Improving performance via mini-applications. Sandia National Laboratories, Technical report SAND2009-5574 3 (2009)
15. Intel: Pin, a dynamic binary instrumentation. https://software.intel.com/en-us/articles/pin-a-dynamic-binary-instrumentation-tool
16. Jurenz, M., Brendel, R., Knüpfer, A., Müller, M., Nagel, W.E.: Memory allocation tracing with VampirTrace. In: Shi, Y., van Albada, G.D., Dongarra, J., Sloot, P.M.A. (eds.) ICCS 2007. LNCS, vol. 4488, pp. 839–846. Springer, Heidelberg (2007). https://doi.org/10.1007/978-3-540-72586-2_118
17. Knüpfer, A., et al.: Score-P: a joint performance measurement run-time infrastructure for Periscope, Scalasca, Tau, and Vampir. In: Brunst, H., Müller, M., Nagel, W., Resch, M. (eds.) Tools for High Performance Computing 2011, pp. 79–91. Springer, Heidelberg (2011). https://doi.org/10.1007/978-3-642-31476-6_7
18. Luk, C.K., et al.: Pin: building customized program analysis tools with dynamic instrumentation. In: Proceedings of the 2005 ACM SIGPLAN Conference on Programming Language Design and Implementation, PLDI 2005, pp. 190–200. ACM, New York (2005). https://doi.org/10.1145/1065010.1065034
19. Miller, B.P., et al.: The Paradyn parallel performance measurement tool. IEEE Comput. **28**(11), 37–46 (1995). https://doi.org/10.1109/2.471178
20. Mohror, K., Karavanic, K.L.: Evaluating similarity-based trace reduction techniques for scalable performance analysis. In: Proceedings of the Conference on High Performance Computing Networking, Storage and Analysis, SC 2009, pp. 55:1–55:12. ACM, New York (2009). https://doi.org/10.1145/1654059.1654115
21. Nataraj, A., Malony, A., Morris, A., Arnold, D.C., Miller, B.: A framework for scalable, parallel performance monitoring **22**, 720–735 (2009)
22. Nethercote, N., Seward, J.: How to shadow every byte of memory used by a program. In: Proceedings of the 3rd International Conference on Virtual Execution Environments, VEE 2007, pp. 65–74. ACM, New York (2007)
23. Nethercote, N., Seward, J.: Valgrind: a program supervision framework. Electr. Notes Theor. Comput. Sci. **89**(2), 44–66 (2003). https://doi.org/10.1016/S1571-0661(04)81042-9
24. Network, Microsoft, Docs: C sequence points. https://msdn.microsoft.com/en-us/library/azk8zbxd.aspx
25. Noeth, M., Ratn, P., Mueller, F., Schulz, M., de Supinski, B.R.: ScalaTrace: scalable compression and replay of communication traces for high-performance computing. J. Parallel Distrib. Comput. **69**(8), 696–710 (2009). https://doi.org/10.1016/j.jpdc.2008.09.001. Best Paper Awards: 21st International Parallel and Distributed Processing Symposium (IPDPS 2007)
26. de Oliveira, D.C.B., Rakamarić, Z., Gopalakrishnan, G., Humphrey, A., Meng, Q., Berzins, M.: Systematic debugging of concurrent systems using Coalesced Stack Trace Graphs. In: Brodman, J., Tu, P. (eds.) LCPC 2014. LNCS, vol. 8967, pp. 317–331. Springer, Cham (2015). https://doi.org/10.1007/978-3-319-17473-0_21. http://www.sci.utah.edu/publications/Oli2014a/OliveiraLCPC2014.pdf
27. Ratanaworabhan, P., Burtscher, M.: Program phase detection based on critical basic block transitions. In: ISPASS 2008 - IEEE International Symposium on Performance Analysis of Systems and software, pp. 11–21, April 2008. https://doi.org/10.1109/ISPASS.2008.4510734

28. Roth, P.C., Arnold, D.C., Miller, B.P.: MRNet: a software-based multicast/reduction network for scalable tools. In: 2003 ACM/IEEE Conference Supercomputing, p. 21, November 2003. https://doi.org/10.1145/1048935.1050172
29. Schulz, M., Galarowicz, J., Maghrak, D., Hachfeld, W., Montoya, D., Cranford, S.: Open | SpeedShop: an open source infrastructure for parallel performance analysis. Sci. Prog. **16**(2–3), 105–121 (2008). https://doi.org/10.3233/SPR-2008-0256
30. Shende, S.S., Malony, A.D.: The TAU parallel performance system. Int. J. High Perform. Comput. Appl. **20**, 287–311 (2006). https://doi.org/10.1177/1094342006064482. http://portal.acm.org/citation.cfm?id=1125980.1125982
31. Strande, S.M., et al.: Comet: Tales from the Long Tail: Two Years in and 10,000 users later. In: Proceedings of the Practice and Experience in Advanced Research Computing 2017 on Sustainability, Success and Impact, PEARC 2017, pp. 38:1–38:7. ACM, New York (2017). https://doi.org/10.1145/3093338.3093383
32. Tikir, M.M., Laurenzano, M., Carrington, L., Snavely, A.: PMaC binary instrumentation library for PowerPC/AIX. In: Workshop on Binary Instrumentation and Applications (2006)
33. Weidendorfer, J.: Sequential performance analysis with Callgrind and KCachegrind. In: Resch, M., Keller, R., Himmler, V., Krammer, B., Schulz, A. (eds.) Tools for High Performance Computing, pp. 93–113. Springer, Heidelberg (2008). https://doi.org/10.1007/978-3-540-68564-7_7
34. Yang, A., Mukka, H., Hesaaraki, F., Burtscher, M.: MPC: a massively parallel compression algorithm for scientific data. In: 2015 IEEE International Conference on Cluster Computing, pp. 381–389, September 2015. https://doi.org/10.1109/CLUSTER.2015.59
35. Ziv, J., Lempel, A.: A universal algorithm for sequential data compression. IEEE Trans. Inf. Theor. **23**(3), 337–343 (2006). https://doi.org/10.1109/TIT.1977.1055714

Gotcha: An Function-Wrapping Interface for HPC Tools

David Poliakoff(✉) and Matt LeGendre(✉)

Lawrence Livermore National Laboratory, Livermore, USA
{poliakoff1,legendre1}@llnl.gov

Abstract. This paper introduces Gotcha, a function wrapping interface and library for HPC tools. Many HPC tools, and performance analysis tools in particular, rely on function wrapping to integrate with applications. But existing mechanisms, such as LD_PRELOAD on Linux, have limitations that lead to tool instability and complexity. Gotcha addresses the limitations in existing mechanisms, provides a programmable interface for HPC tools to manage function wrapping, and supports function wrapping across multiple tools. In addition, this paper introduces the idea of interface-independent function wrapping, which makes it possible for tools to wrap arbitrary application functions.

Keywords: HPC · Tools · Dynamic linking

1 Introduction

Function wrapping is an important enabling technology behind many HPC tools, including performance analysis tools [1,2,4,7,9,15], correctness tools [5,12], and debuggers [3]. Tools use function wrapping as a mechanism to hook into a target application that they're operating on. Function wrapping allows them to replace some set of functions in the target application with a set of tool-provided versions of those functions. For example, a performance analysis tool might use function wrapping around an application's IO functions and replace them with tool versions that trigger a stopwatch timer around every call. Debuggers like TotalView use function wrapping to wrap the malloc and free family of functions and build a model of an application's heap usage, which lets them automatically identify certain classes of bugs. Typically tools add function wrappers that maintain the original function's semantics. But some tools use function wrapping to change semantics, such as the cram [11] tool that intercepts MPI functions and changes communicator usage to "cram" multiple MPI jobs into a single run.

Tools typically implement function wrapping on Linux with LD_PRELOAD, which is a library injection capability implemented by the GNU dynamic linker. When LD_PRELOAD injects a library into a target process, the injected library's functions will intercept calls that would have gone to the application's equivalently-named functions. This provides the underlying mechanism that tools can build function wrapping on top of. However, there are many

A. Bhatele et al. (Eds.): ESPT/VPA 2017/2018, LNCS 11027, pp. 185–197, 2019.
https://doi.org/10.1007/978-3-030-17872-7_11

drawbacks to building function wrapping on top of LD_PRELOAD, including ABI compatibility, multi-tool compatibility, lack of flexibility, and an enforced workflow on tool. We discuss these issues in detail in Sect. 2. While tools have managed to accommodate many of LD_PRELOAD's limitations, the infrastructure to do so is fragile and, in the author's experience supporting tools at a large HPC center, some the most common source of tool failures in production.

This paper describes a new approach for function wrapping, which we implemented in new tool infrastructure called Gotcha. Rather than provide low-level mechanisms like LD_PRELOAD that function wrapping can be built on, Gotcha raises the level of abstraction and provides a high-level API focused on function wrapping. Concepts like multi-tool compatibility and managing sets of wrappers are first-class concepts in the API and are easy for tools to get right. Gotcha implements function wrapping using a distinct mechanism from LD_PRELOAD (rewriting of the dynamic linker's GOT tables at runtime, which is discussed in Sect. 3), so it does not inherit the fundamental drawbacks of LD_PRELOAD.

Additionally, Gotcha broadens the types of function wrapping available to tools. Classical function wrapping involves a tool developer writing a specific wrapper function that is injected around a matching target function (e.g., a tool function MPI_Send_wrapper is designed to only wrap MPI_Send and nothing else). Gotcha introduces the option of using interface-independent wrappers, which can be wrapped around arbitrary exported functions in the application. These wrappers are less powerful than traditional wrappers–they don't see function arguments and can't easily change semantics, but they can be used in more situations. A performance tool could, for example, use interface-independent wrappers to intercept every function call into an arbitrary dynamic library to provide per-library timings.

Section 2 of this paper provides technical background on dynamic linking and libraries, which is important for understanding the mechanisms behind Gotcha. It also discusses related work in other function wrapping technologies, including binary instrumentation mechanisms and other tool components. Section 3 discusses both the high-level abstractions and ideas in Gotcha, and the implementation behind them. Section 4 describes some of the use cases that motivated Gotcha. Finally, Sect. 5 describes the performance overheads observed in Gotcha.

2 Background and Related Work

To understand how Gotcha and related tools implement function wrapping it is necessary to understand a bit about dynamic linking. This section provides a brief explanation of how dynamic libraries reference symbols, and it describes how related tools use and implement dynamic linking.

2.1 Background

This background on dynamic linking is intentionally simplified. Drepper [8] provides a more complete explanation of dynamic linking on System V operating systems (which includes Linux).

Shared libraries and executables in a dynamically-linked process are known as DSOs (Dynamic Shared Objects). DSOs usually depend on other DSOs, and may themselves be dependents. For example, an executable may depend on libmpi.so. DSOs also have exported and imported symbols, which are technically referred as defined and undefined symbols. Imported symbols are mapped to exported symbols that have the same name. For example, and an executable may import the MPI_Init symbol, and libmpi.so may export that same symbol. There is no direct relationship between a formal DSO dependency and imported/exported symbols. The executable could import the MPI_Init symbol from libtool.so, even when the executable does not depend on libtool.so.

Dynamically-linked processes on Linux all have a special DSO known as the dynamic linker, or ld.so. The dynamic linker is responsible for mapping imported symbols to exported symbols. This could, in theory, be a many-to-many mapping, since multiple DSOs may export a symbol that is imported by multiple DSOs. But the GNU dynamic linker uses a deterministic mapping algorithm that typically matches all imported symbols to a single matching exported symbol (excepting for certain corner cases). It does this by ordering all DSOs into a consistent list, and searching that list from front-to-back for the first instance of an exported symbol. All imported symbols will thus be matched to the first-found exported symbol (there is a common misconception that weak symbols impact this algorithm, but the GNU dynamic linker ignores weak symbols in its default configuration).

The dynamic linker implements this mapping using the GOT (Global Offset Table). The GOT is a table of pointers present in each DSO where each table entry corresponds to an imported symbol. GOT entries for function symbols are function pointers, while GOT entries for data symbols are data pointers. When the dynamic linker matches an imported symbol to an exported symbol, it updates the GOT entry corresponding to the imported symbol with the address of the exported symbol. For example, when an executable wants to call MPI_Init it can look in its MPI_Init GOT entry to get a pointer to an exported MPI_Init function. There are many other tables and data structures used in dynamic linking, such as the PLT, which are not described here for simplicity.

This first-found algorithm is the basis for implementing function wrapping with LD_PRELOAD. LD_PRELOAD is an environment variable that injects a new library into the front of the library search list. When the dynamic linker searches for an exported MPI_Init, for example, it could find one in the front of the library list in the LD_PRELOADed libtool.so, and all calls to MPI_Init will be redirected to libtool.so. The tool could still call the original MPI_Init by invoking an aliased name for the function or looking it up with a dlsym call into the dynamic linker.

2.2 Related Work

Most tools implement function wrapping using the previously described LD_PRELOAD mechanism. But LD_PRELOAD has numerous disadvantages that cause problems in tools. Specifically, LD_PRELOAD:

- requires tools to provide all wrappings up front in a pre-built library. There is no way to change wrappings in response to tool or application actions.
- frequently causes ABI-related bugs. Since LD_PRELOAD injects libraries independent of the normal linking system it does not come with the normal protections. A tool builder could build libtool.so against libmpi.so version 1.2, and application could be built against the incompatible libmpi.so version 1.3. If libtool.so is LD_PRELOADed into this application it would at best produce undefined symbol errors, and at worse cause crashes or undefined application behavior.
- does not provide a way for multiple tools to work together to wrap the same functions. Only one tool can win the dynamic linker's first-found algorithm.

Despite these disadvantages LD_PRELOAD remains a popular mechanism for function wrapping in HPC tools. The HPCToolkit [4] project maintains libmonitor.so, which is also used by OpenSpeedShop [9]. Libmonitor contains function wrappers for routines typically monitored by performance analysis tools. Other tools can add their own custom implementations in these wrappers, then inject libmonitor.so with LD_PRELOAD.

The MPI wrapper generator tool [10] provides a language for generating tool wrappers around MPI routines. The output of the MPI wrapper generator is source code that can be compiled into a shared library and LD_PRELOADed into an application. Both libmonitor and the MPI wrapper generator make it easier to write function wrappers, but they still depend on LD_PRELOAD and inherit its limitations.

A way to implement function wrapping without LD_PRELOAD is with binary instrumentation tools. Tools like DyninstAPI [6] can directly rewrite the machine code in a running process or on-disk DSO to insert function wrappers. The DyninstAPI interface for function wrapping takes a reference to a function that should be wrapped, a reference to a wrapper function, and a symbol that should be rewritten to refer to the original wrappee. The tool could, for example, wrap a tool_MPI_Init function around libmpi.so's MPI_Init, and make the new symbol orig_MPI_Init point at libmpi.so's MPI_Init. DyninstAPI's implementation is strictly more powerful at function wrapping than Gotcha's implementation. It can wrap internal functions that are not exported from a library. However, that power comes at the expense of relying on a significantly more heavy-weight software stack that adds both software complexity and high runtime overheads to safely analyze and modify binaries. The DyninstAPI function wrapping model also does not include support for stacking multiple tools or address the ABI issues that are also in LD_PRELOAD.

It is also possible for software components to export wrapping interfaces that tools can leverage. The under-discussion QMPI [14] interface for the MPI standard adds function-pointer-based callbacks to every MPI routine. Tools can register functions to receive those callbacks and modify or monitor the parameters to MPI routines. This essentially provides the same functionality as traditionally function wrapping. As of mid-2018 the proposed QMPI standard has many aspects in common with Gotcha's interface, including stacking tools and abstractions for handling sets of wrappers.

3 Gotcha Abstractions and Implementation

Gotcha provides a high-level interface for specifying function wrapping. Unlike LD_PRELOAD, Gotcha provides a programmable API for enabling function wrapping. Tools can change how or what they wrap based on external parameters, such as application or tool state. Tools can use the Gotcha API to change wrappings part-way through a process's execution. Also unlike LD_PRELOAD, wrapper functions need not be loaded via environment variable. They can be added to an application with the traditional linker, which can perform its normal safety checks and not introduce additional ABI problems.

Gotcha is designed to make it easy to wrap any exported function, with simple abstractions for both inserting wrappers and calling the original function. Tools can manage wrapping as sets, either inserting or removing groups of wrappers at once.

3.1 Gotcha Wrapping Abstraction

Wrapping a function with Gotcha requires three things: the name of the function being wrapped (the wrappee), a wrapper function, and a handle for referencing the wrappee from the wrapper. Gotcha's interface centers around a user-provided table with this triple. That table can be filled in by the user and passed to Gotcha, which activates the wrappings.

Figure 1 shows a simple program that uses Gotcha to wrap MPI_Init. Error handling has been excluded for brevity. The bindings table could hold multiple function wrappings, through this example only shows one. After passing this table to `gotcha_wrap` (along with the table size and a tool name) then every call to MPI_Init will be redirected to the MPI_Init_wrapper. That wrapper can get a pointer to the original MPI_Init through the `gotcha_get_wrappee` function and the `handle` that was associated with this wrapping.

Gotcha implements these wrappings by translating these wrapping table into manipulations of the running process's GOT tables. As described in Sect. 2, the GOT is a table of function pointers used to link imported symbols and exported symbols. Gotcha looks up the GOT tables in each DSO and rewrites select entries to point at wrapper functions. In this example every GOT table entry that imports MPI_Init will be rewritten to contain the address of MPI_Init_wrapper. The address of the exported MPI_Init symbol is returned from `gotcha_get_wrappee` so that the wrapper can still call the original function. Thus any calls which would have gone to the original function instead go to the wrapper, and the wrapper can ask Gotcha for the original function.

Figure 1 shows the `gotcha_wrap` function being called from main, but this is only for brevity. Tools may find it useful to call `gotcha_wrap` from a library constructor or tool initialization routine.

```
#include "gotcha/gotcha.h"
#include <mpi.h>
#include <stdio.h>

gotcha_handle_t handle;
gotcha_binding_t bindings[] = {
  { "MPI_Init", MPI_Init_wrapper, &handle }
}

int MPI_Init_wrapper(int *argc, char ***argv) {
  int result;
  int (*orig_mpi_init)(int *, char ***);

  printf("In MPI_Init_wrapper\n");
  orig_mpi_init = gotcha_get_wrappee(handle);
  result = orig_mpi_init(argc, argv);
  printf("MPI_init returning %d\n", result);
  return result;
}

int main(int argc, char *argv[]) {
  gotcha_wrap(bindings, 1, "mytoolname");
  MPI_Init(&argc, &argv);
  return 0;
}
```

Fig. 1. Gotcha wrapping example

3.2 Multi-tool Support

Sometimes multiple tools want to wrap the same function. For example, the Cram [11] tool may want to wrap MPI calls to rewrite communication operations, and TAU [15] may want to wrap them for performance analysis. LD_PRELOAD cannot handle this situation since its first-found algorithm allows only one tool to create wrappings (though software intermediate layers, such as P^nMPI [13], handle this with a layer that dispatches wrappings between tools).

Gotcha manages multiple tools by stacking wrappers from different tools on top of each other. It orders these stacked wrappers via a priority system. Tools register an integer priority with Gotcha, which is used to determine which tool is called first. Tools with a lower integer priority are placed innermost in a stack of wrappers. If, for example, Cram registers as a priority 10 tool with Gotcha, and TAU as a priority 50, then when MPI_Send is called Gotcha will first route control to the TAU wrapper. When the TAU wrapper calls the next layer, via `gotcha_get_wrappee`, it will transfer control to the Cram wrappers. The Cram wrappers will eventually call the real MPI_Send function.

Under this interface tools can stack multiple wrappings without being aware of each other. Negotiating the correct priorities for different tools is outside the technical scope of Gotcha, and is perhaps best left to the HPC tools community members that adopt Gotcha. For some tools the ordering of wrappings may not make a difference, though in the above example the order between TAU and Cram determines whether TAU is measuring performance of one Cram job, or all of the Cram jobs.

3.3 Interface-Independent Wrapping

LD_PRELOAD-based function wrapping requires a tool developer to write wrappers that exactly match the signature of the function they are wrapping, since the wrapper must receive and copy arguments to the wrappee. This allows tools to inspect or modify function arguments in wrappers, but prevents them wrapping arbitrary functions. A tool could not wrap MPI_Send with an arbitrary wrapper with a different signature, as this would lead to lost information about MPI_Sends arguments.

This restricts which functions a tool can wrap. A tool developer can only write wrappers for functions where they understand the signature (such as standardized MPI or IO functions). A tool developer cannot wrap arbitrary application functions, even though they may not care about the signature in its wrapper. However, the fundamental operations in many wrappers might not care about the interface of the function being wrapped. A performance tool may, for example, just want trigger a stopwatch-style timer around all calls into a math library to build per-library profiles. It does not need to understand the arguments passed to sqrt to do this.

Gotcha solves this problem by providing an option for interface-independent wrappers. Instead of traditional wrappers that are responsible for generating a call to a wrappee, interface-independent wrappers provide a pair of pre-wrapper and post-wrapper functions that are bracketed around the wrappee. The pre-wrapper function gets control before the wrappee executes. After the pre-wrapper function returns, control is transferred to the wrappee with its original function arguments intact. When the wrappee returns the post-wrapper is called, which returns to the original calling site.

Figure 2 shows an example of interface-independent wrapping (which is known as sigfree wrapping in the Gotcha API). The example puts interface-independent wrappings around MPI_Init. Note that the wrappers do not match the signature of MPI_Init. The same wrappers can be placed around any arbitrary function. The opaque parameter is a mechanism for passing per-call information from the pre-wrapper to the post-wrapper. One use for this mechanism is to wrap all functions exported from an arbitrary library by iterating over the library's exported symbols and building a gotcha_sigfree_binding_t table customized to that library.

Gotcha implements interface-independent wrapping by rewriting the application's GOT tables to point at an assembly-language trampoline. The trampoline receives control immediately after a call to a wrapped function, and its major operations could be summarized as:

```
#include "gotcha/gotcha.h"
#include <mpi.h>
#include <stdio.h>

gotcha_handle_t MPI_Send_handle;
gotcha_sigfree_binding_t bindings[] = {
  { "MPI_Init", pre_wrap, post_wrap, &handle }
}

void pre_wrap(gotcha_wrappee_handle_t handle,
              void **opaque)
{
  printf("pre-call for function %s\n",
         gotcha_get_wrappee_name(handle));
}

void post_wrap(gotcha_wrappee_handle_t handle,
               void *opaque)
{
  printf("post-call for function %s\n",
         gotcha_get_wrappee_name(handle));
}

int main(int argc, char *argv[]) {
  gotcha_sigfree_wrap(bindings, 1, "mytoolname");
  MPI_Init(&argc, &argv);
  return 0;
}
```

Fig. 2. Interface-independent wrapping example

1. Save the values of all registers used for parameter passing onto the stack.
2. Save the original return address of to a per-thread side stack.
3. Call the pre-wrapper.
4. Restore the value of the registers used for parameter passing, and re-align the stack to its original height.
5. Call the wrappee.
6. Save the values of all registers used to pass return values.
7. Call the post-wrapper
8. Restore the values of the registers used to pass return values.
9. Restore and return to the original return address.

Gotcha implements interface-independent wrapping on both x86_64 and ppc64.

4 Use Cases

Gotcha was primarily motivated by limitations in the existing function wrapping technology, LD_PRELOAD. This section describes two use cases that Gotcha enables, Caliper and our Generic MPI Wrappers. For Caliper, Gotcha provides flexible function wrapping needed to support tighter application/tool integration. For the Generic MPI Wrappers, Gotcha provides a mechanism to make existing performance analysis tools more robust.

4.1 Caliper

Caliper is a program annotation interface, which developers can use to label parts of their application such as functions, loops, broad code regions, or data. Performance analysis tools can be plugged into Caliper and subscribe to a trace or aggregated view of those annotations. By measuring certain performance metrics associated with an annotation, Caliper can relate performance information to user-labeled parts of an application. Unlike traditional performance analysis tools, Caliper is meant to be tightly integrated with an application. Applications make calls into Caliper API and link with the caliper library. Similar to how a math library might provide an application with matrix multiplication capabilities, the Caliper library provides an application with performance analysis capabilities.

Traditional LD_PRELOAD-based function wrapping was not appropriate for Caliper. Users decide what metrics Caliper should measure via command line switches or input decks, which are interpreted after an LD_PRELOAD environment variable could be set. If a user asks Caliper to measure MPI performance, it is already too late to insert MPI wrappers. As an initial work-around, Caliper always exported its own MPI wrappers. If the Caliper library was found before the MPI library in the dynamic-linker's first-found algorithm, then Caliper would intercept all MPI calls and implement wrapping, but this was not reliable.

Gotcha reliably solves this problem by letting Caliper manage function wrappings via an API. When an application asks Caliper to measure MPI or threading operations, Caliper can generate an appropriate `gotcha_wrap` call that enables the operation. Caliper no longer needs to concern itself with link orders and can now turn on wrappings only when requested.

Gotcha's multi-tool support is also beneficial to Caliper. Since Caliper is part of an application, it can be configured to be always-on with every application invocation. Since Caliper uses Gotcha and thus supports multi-tool, it's now possible to run Caliper alongside other function-wrapping based tools (which are likely non-performance analysis tools, such as Cram).

4.2 Generic MPI Wrapper

A common user-workflow error in HPC tools is to mix a tool and application that are each built with incompatible MPI libraries. This happens because tools are frequently built and deployed by HPC-center staff, while applications are typically built by end-users. For example, someone supporting tools for an HPC center may install OpenSpeedShop built against mvapich 2.2, while an end-user may build their application against mvapich 2.0. Constant values and function ABIs may change between MPI releases, and trying to mix them can result in unstable applications.

Most performance analysis tools have tried to take some approach to resolving this problem. OpenSpeedShop builds its MPI components against every MPI implementation found at build time, then lets the user set an environment variable that picks one at runtime. The MAP performance analysis tool from Allinea rebuilds its MPI components every time MAP is run, using the MPICC environment variable. The HPCToolkit tool from Rice University limits its MPI wrapping to a few critical functions that it knows how to safely wrap in every MPI implementation. These approaches all rely on the end-user getting an environment variable set correctly or limit tool capability.

Gotcha allowed us to build a demonstration of Generic MPI Wrappers. At tool build time the tool finds every MPI implementation installed on the system. The MPI wrapper generator [10] creates a MPI wrapper C file that is re-compiled against each MPI installation. These are linked into a single library. None of the wrapper routines are exported, so it is safe to put them all into the same library without naming conflicts. The tool can insert this omni-MPI library into the application using its normal mechanisms. Gotcha then inspects which MPI library is actually loaded by the application at runtime, and it enables just the set of wrappers that correspond with that library.

This approach still requires the tool deployer to point the tool at every MPI on a system, but since the people deploying tools and the people deploying MPI installations are typically HPC-center staff, this is manageable. The end-users do not need to set specific environment variables to run the tool, which should significantly improve tool stability. Further, if something goes wrong and Gotcha does not have compiled wrappers that correspond to the loaded MPI library, the tool can explicitly see this at runtime and print a reasonable error message rather than binding incompatible functions and seeing what happens.

5 Performance/Results

In practice Gotcha performs comparably to LD_PRELOAD. We ran two performance experiments to show this. First, we measured how Gotcha scales when the `gotcha_wrap` call modifies processes with large numbers of libraries. Second, we measured how much runtime overhead Gotcha introduces with each wrapper.

Our large binary scaling tests are shown in Fig. 3. We created an artificial test that could be configured to load a massive numbers of libraries (significantly more than any application we have encountered). Each library contains symbol references to every other library (so the number of symbol references increases quadratically with library count). Gotcha was asked to wrap every function in the test. Since the Gotcha implementation iterates over each library and each reference, so we expect (and observed) that `gotcha_wrap` time would increase linearly with the total number of symbol references in test. Since we were concerned with per-library overheads, Fig. 3 normalizes the total runtime to time-per-reference.

Ideally, Fig. 3 would be flat. However, it shows a significantly higher time-per-reference for tests with small library counts. We believe this is because those tests ran fairly quickly, and the constant overheads of Gotcha initialization are increasing the time-per-reference.

For the largest test the total `gotcha_wrap` time took about 22 s. This represents a one-time cost on process start-up and is on an unrealistically-sized binary, though we would still like to optimize this. In practice, we have not seen notable `gotcha_wrap` time on traditionally-sized binaries.

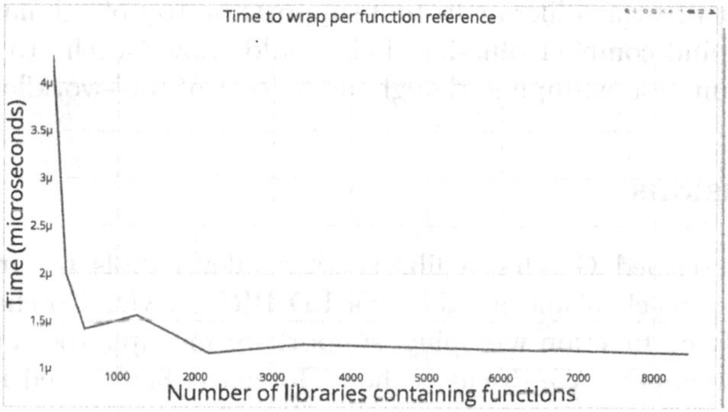

Fig. 3. Impact of application size on `gotcha_wrap` time

Our second test measured the overhead Gotcha imposes per-wrapper. Generally, the operations done inside the wrapper (e.g., walking a call stack) dominate tool overheads. The Gotcha-imposed overheads involve function-call overheads and a memory reference to lookup the wrappee. These are typically only observable in artificial test cases. To verify this we measured an empty wrapper around the getpid call. We measured time to call getpid normally, getpid wrapped by LD_PRELOAD, and getpid wrapped by Gotcha. To reach enough time to make the measurements relevant, we made 2.5 billion calls to getpid.

The unwrapped version took 7.64 s, the LD_PRELOAD version took 11.44 s, and the Gotcha version 16.78 s. The Gotcha to LD_PRELOAD comparison is unsurprising, LD_PRELOAD wrappers tends to have direct calls to the wrappee function, where Gotcha does an indirect lookup of the wrappee for multi-tool support. The time difference between LD_PRELOAD and the normal getpid call is the time to execute an empty function wrapper.

To verify that Gotcha did not have unexpected performance problems compared to LD_PRELOAD, we modified the Gotcha tool to cache its lookup of the wrappee (which would break multi-tool support in normal usage). Overhead dropped to 11.45 s, in line with LD_PRELOAD.

This test shows Gotcha as introducing a wrapper overhead of 6.7 ns per call. In practice tools wrap heavyweight functions like MPI_Send or malloc and perform complicated tool operations that dwarf this wrapper cost.

6 Future Work

Gotcha currently supports x86_64 and PPC64 binaries. We would like to extend Gotcha to also support ARM systems.

Additionally, Gotcha only supports dynamically-linked binaries. The mechanism behind gotcha will not work in statically-linked binaries or on functions internal to a library. Wrapping these functions requires either binary rewriting or compiler-assisted wrapping. It may be possible to implement the gotcha interface, along with features like multi-tool support, on top of a binary rewriter or as a driver behind compiler plug-ins. This would allow Gotcha to support more binaries and function wrapping, though at the cost of tool-workflow complexity.

7 Conclusions

This paper described Gotcha, a library that allows tools to wrap functions. Unlike existing mechanisms like Linux's LD_PRELOAD, Gotcha provides an API for specifying function wrapping, support for multiple tools, and interface-independent wrappers. We discussed how Gotcha is being used in higher-level tools, such as Caliper and we presented resulting show that Gotcha introduces only minimal overheads to function wrapping.

Disclaimer and Auspices

This document was prepared as an account of work sponsored by an agency of the United States government. Neither the United States government nor Lawrence Livermore National Security, LLC, nor any of their employees makes any warranty, expressed or implied, or assumes any legal liability or responsibility for the accuracy, completeness, or usefulness of any information, apparatus, product, or process disclosed, or represents that its use would not infringe privately owned rights. Reference herein to any specific commercial product, process, or service by trade name, trademark, manufacturer, or otherwise does not necessarily constitute or imply its endorsement, recommendation, or favoring by the United States government or Lawrence Livermore National Security, LLC. The views and opinions of authors expressed herein do not necessarily state or reflect those of the United States government or Lawrence Livermore National Security, LLC, and shall not be used for advertising or product endorsement purposes. Lawrence Livermore National Laboratory is operated by Lawrence Livermore National Security, LLC, for the U.S. Department of Energy, National Nuclear Security Administration under Contract DE–AC52–07NA27344. LLNL–CONF–756831.

References

1. Arm map. https://www.arm.com/products/development-tools/server-and-hpc/forge/map
2. mpiP. http://mpip.sourceforge.net
3. Totalview for HPC. https://www.roguewave.com/products-services/totalview
4. Adhianto, L., et al.: HPCTOOLKIT: tools for performance analysis of optimized parallel programs. Concurrency Comput. Pract. Experience **22**(6), 685–701 (2010). https://doi.org/10.1002/cpe.v22:6. http://hpctoolkit.org
5. Atzeni, S., et al.: Archer: effectively spotting data races in large OpenMP applications. In: 2016 IEEE International Parallel and Distributed Processing Symposium (IPDPS), pp. 53–62, May 2016. https://doi.org/10.1109/IPDPS.2016.68
6. Bernat, A.R., Miller, B.P.: Anywhere, any-time binary instrumentation. In: Proceedings of the 10th ACM SIGPLAN-SIGSOFT Workshop on Program Analysis for Software Tools, PASTE 2011, pp. 9–16. ACM, New York (2011). https://doi.org/10.1145/2024569.2024572
7. Carns, P., et al.: Understanding and improving computational science storage access through continuous characterization. Trans. Storage **7**(3), 8:1–8:26 (2011). https://doi.org/10.1145/2027066.2027068
8. Drepper, U.: How to write shared libraries. https://www.akkadia.org/drepper/dsohowto.pdf
9. Galarowiz, J.: Open—speedshop. https://openspeedshop.org
10. Gamblin, T.: MPI wrapper generator, for writing PMPI tool libraries. https://github.com/LLNL/wrap
11. Gyllenhaal, J., Gamblin, T., Bertsch, A., Musselman, R.: Enabling high job throughput for uncertainty quantification on BG/Q. In: IBM HPC Systems Scientific Computing User Group, (ScicomP 2014) (2014)
12. Protze, J., Hilbrich, T., Schulz, M., de Supinski, B.R., Nagel, W.E., Mueller, M.S.: MPI runtime error detection with must: a scalable and crash-safe approach. In: 2014 43rd International Conference on Parallel Processing Workshops, pp. 206–215, September 2014. https://doi.org/10.1109/ICPPW.2014.37
13. Schulz, M., de Supinski, B.R.: PNMPI tools: a whole lot greater than the sum of their parts. In: Proceedings of the 2007 ACM/IEEE Conference on Supercomputing, SC 2007, pp. 1–10, November 2007. https://doi.org/10.1145/1362622.1362663
14. Schulz, M.: Extending and updating the tool interfaces in MPI: a request for feedback. In: Scalable Tools Workshop 2018 (2018)
15. Shende, S.S., Malony, A.D.: The TAU parallel performance system. Int. J. High Perform. Comput. Appl. **20**(2), 287–311 (2006). https://doi.org/10.1177/1094342006064482

References

[illegible]

VPA 2017

Projecting Performance Data over Simulation Geometry Using SOSflow and ALPINE

Chad Wood[1(✉)], Matthew Larsen[2], Alfredo Gimenez[2], Kevin Huck[1], Cyrus Harrison[2], Todd Gamblin[2], and Allen Malony[1]

[1] University of Oregon, Eugene, OR 97403-1212, USA
{cdw,khuck,malony}@cs.uoregon.edu

[2] Lawrence Livermore National Laboratory, Livermore, CA, USA
{larsen30,gimenez1,harrison37,gamblin2}@llnl.gov

Abstract. The performance of HPC simulation codes is often tied to their simulated domains; e.g., properties of the input decks, boundaries of the underlying meshes, and parallel decomposition of the simulation space. A variety of research efforts have demonstrated the utility of projecting performance data onto the simulation geometry to enable analysis of these kinds of performance problems. However, current methods to do so are largely ad-hoc and limited in terms of extensibility and scalability. Furthermore, few methods enable this projection online, resulting in large storage and processing requirements for offline analysis. We present a general, extensible, and scalable solution for in-situ (online) visualization of performance data projected onto the underlying geometry of simulation codes. Our solution employs the scalable observation system SOSflow with the in-situ visualization framework ALPINE to automatically extract simulation geometry and stream aggregated performance metrics to respective locations within the geometry at runtime. Our system decouples the resources and mechanisms to collect, aggregate, project, and visualize the resulting data, thus mitigating overhead and enabling online analysis at large scales. Furthermore, our method requires minimal user input and modification of existing code, enabling general and widespread adoption.

Keywords: SOS · SOSflow · Alpine · HPC · Performance · Visualization · In situ

1 Introduction

Projecting application and performance data onto the scientific domain allows for the behavior of a code to be perceived in terms of the organization of the work it is doing, rather than the organization of its source code. This perspective can be especially helpful [19] for domain scientists developing aspects of a simulation

A. Bhatele et al. (Eds.): ESPT/VPA 2017/2018, LNCS 11027, pp. 201–218, 2019.
https://doi.org/10.1007/978-3-030-17872-7_12

primarily for its scientific utility, though it can also be useful for any HPC developer engaged with the general maintenance requirements of a large and complicated codebase [18].

There have been practical challenges to providing these opportunities for insight. Extracting the spatial descriptions from an application traditionally has relied on hand-instrumenting codes to couple a simulation's geometry with some explicitly defined performance metrics. Performance tool wrappers and direct source-instrumentation need to be configurable so that users can disable their invasive presence during large production runs. Because it involves changes to the source code of an application, enabling or disabling the manual instrumentation of a code often involves full recompilation of a software stack. Insights gained by the domain projection are limited to what was selected a priori for contextualization with geometry.

Without an efficient runtime service providing an integrated context for multiple sources of performance information, it is difficult to combine performance observations across several components during a run. Further limiting the value of the entire exercise, performance data collected outside of a runtime service must wait to be correlated and projected over a simulation's geometry during post-mortem analysis. Projections that are produced offline cannot be used for application steering, online parameter tuning, or other runtime interactions that include a human in the feedback loop. Scalability for offline projections also becomes a concern, as the potentially large amount of performance data and simulation geometry produced and operated over in a massively parallel cluster now must be integrated and rendered either from a single point or within an entirely different allocation.

The overhead of manually instrumenting large complex codes to extract meaningful geometries for use in performance analysis, combined with the limited value of offline correlation of a fixed number of metrics, naturally limited the usage of scientific domain projections for gaining HPC workflow performance insights.

1.1 Research Contributions

This paper describes the use of SOSflow [20] and ALPINE to overcome many prior limitations to projecting performance into the scientific domain. The methods used to produce our results can be implemented in other frameworks, though SOSflow and ALPINE, discussed in detail in later sections, are generalized and intentionally engineered to deliver solutions of the type presented here. This research effort achieved the following:

- Eliminate the need to manually capture geometry for performance data projections of ALPINE-enabled workflows
- Provide online observation of performance data projected over evolving geometries and metrics
- Facilitate interactive selection of one or many performance metrics and rendering parameters, adding dynamism to projections

- Enable simultaneous online projections from a common data source
- In situ performance visualization architecture supporting both current and future-scale systems

2 Related Work

Husain and Gimenez's work on Mitos [7] and MemAxes [6] is motivated similarly to ours. Mitos provides an integration API for combining information from multiple sources into a coherent memoized set for analysis and visualization, and MemAxes projects correlated information across domains to explore the origins of observed performance. SOSflow is being used in our research as an integration API, but takes a different optimization path by providing a general-purpose in situ (online) runtime.

Caliper by Boehme et al. [3] extracts performance data during execution in ways that serve a variety of uses, in much the same way our efforts here are oriented. Caliper's flexible data aggregation [4] model can be used to filter metrics in situ, allowing for tractable volumes of performance data to be made available for projections. Both ALPINE and Caliper provide direct services to users, also serving as integration points for user-configurable services at run time. Caliper is capable of deep introspection on the behavior of a program in execution, yet is able to be easily disabled for production runs that require no introspection and want to minimize instrumentation overhead. ALPINE allows for visualization filters to be compiled separately from a user's application and then introduced into, or removed from, an HPC code's visualization pipeline with a simple edit to that workflow's ALPINE configuration file. More tools like Caliper and ALPINE, featuring well-defined integration points, are essential for the wider availability of cross-domain performance understanding. SOSflow does not collect source-level performance metrics directly, but rather brings that data from tools like Caliper into a holistic online context with information from other libraries, performance tools, and perspectives.

BoxFish [8] also demonstrated the value of visualizing projections when interpreting performance data, adding a useful hierarchical data model for combining visualizations and interacting with data.

SOSflow's flexible model for multi-source online data collection and analysis provides performance exploration opportunities using both new and existing HPC tools.

3 SOSflow

SOSflow provides a lightweight, scalable, and programmable framework for observation, introspection, feedback, and control of HPC applications. The Scalable Observation System (SOS) performance model used by SOSflow allows a broad set of in situ (online) capabilities including remote method invocation, data analysis, and visualization. SOSflow can couple together multiple sources of data, such as application components and operating environment measures, with multiple software libraries and performance tools. These features combined to efficiently create holistic views of workflow performance at runtime, uniting node-local and distributed resources and perspectives. SOSflow can be used for a variety of purposes:

- Aggregation of application and performance data at runtime
- Providing holistic view of multi-component distributed scientific workflows
- Coordinating in situ operations with global analytics
- Synthesizing application and system metrics with scientific data for deeper performance understanding
- Extending the functionality of existing HPC codes using in situ resources
- Resource management, load balancing, online performance tuning, etc.

To better understand the role played by SOSflow, it is useful to examine its architecture. SOSflow is composed of four major components:

- **sosd** : Daemons
- **libsos** : Client Library
- **pub/sql** : Data
- **sosa** : Analytics & Feedback

These components work together to provide extensive runtime capabilities to developers, administrators, and application end-users. SOSflow runs within a user's allocation, and does not require elevated privileges for any of its features.

3.1 SOSflow Daemons

Online functionality of SOSflow is enabled by the presence of a user-space daemon. This daemon operates completely independently from any applications, and does not connect into or utilize any application data channels for SOSflow communications. The SOSflow daemons are launched from within a job script, before the user's applications are initialized. These daemons discover and communicate amongst each other across node boundaries within a user's allocation. When crossing node boundaries, SOSflow uses the machine's high-speed communication fabric. Inter-node communication may use either **MPI** or **EVPath** as needed, allowing for flexibility when configuring its deployment to various HPC environments.

The traditional deployment of SOSflow will have a single daemon instance running in situ for each node that a user's applications will be executing on (Fig. 1). This daemon is called the **listener**. Additional resources can be allocated in support of the SOSflow runtime as-needed to support scaling and to minimize perturbation of application performance. One or more nodes are usually added to the user's allocation to host SOSflow **aggregator** daemons that combine the information that is being collected from the in situ daemons. These aggregator daemons are useful for providing holistic unified views at runtime, especially in service to online analytics modules. Because they have more work to do than the in situ listener daemons, and also are a useful place to host analytics modules, it is advisable to place aggregation targets on their own dedicated node[s], co-located with online analytics codes.

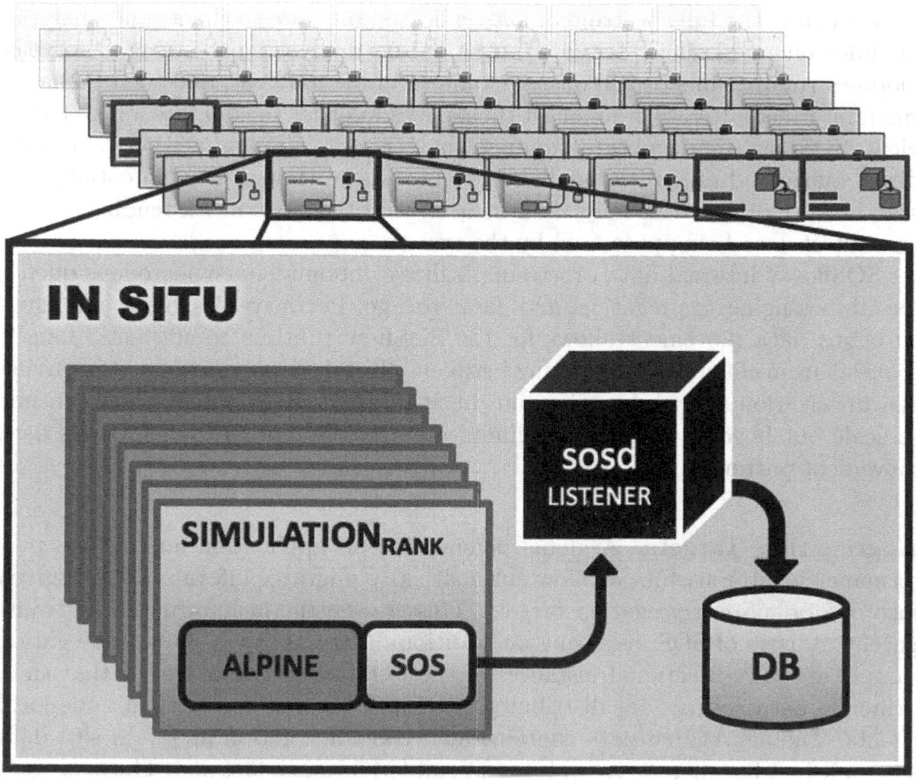

Fig. 1. SOSflow's lightweight daemon runs on each node.

In Situ. Data coming from SOSflow clients moves into the in situ daemon across a light-weight local socket connection. Any software that connects in to the SOSflow runtime can be thought of as a client. Clients connect only to the daemon that is running on their same node. No client connections are made across node boundaries, and no special permissions are required to use SOSflow, as the system considers the SOSflow runtime to be merely another part of a user's workflow.

The in situ listener daemon offers the complete functionality of the SOSflow runtime, including online query and delivery of results, feedback, or application steering messages. At startup, the daemon creates an in-memory data store with a file-based mirror in a user-defined location. Listeners asynchronously store all data that they receive into this store. The file-based mirror is ideal for offline analysis and archival. The local data store can be queried and updated via the SOSflow API, with all information moving over the daemon's socket, avoiding dependence on filesystem synchronization or centralized metadata services.

Providing the full spectrum of data collected on node to clients and analytics modules on node allows for distributed online analytics processing. Analytics modules running in situ can observe a manageable data set, and then exchange small intermediate results amongst themselves in order to compute a final global view. SOSflow also supports running analytics at the aggregation points for direct query and analysis of global or enclave data, though it is potentially less scalable to perform centrally than in a distributed fashion, depending on the amount of data being processed by the system.

SOSflow's internal data processing utilizes unbounded asynchronous queues for all messaging, aggregation, and data storage. Pervasive design around asynchronous data movement allows for the SOSflow runtime to efficiently handle requests from clients and messaging between off-node daemons without incurring synchronization delays. Asynchronous in situ design allows the SOSflow runtime to scale out beyond the practical limits imposed by globally synchronous data movement patterns.

Aggregation Targets. A global perspective on application and system performance is often useful. SOSflow automatically migrates information it is given into one or more aggregation targets. This movement of information is transparent to users of SOS, requiring no additional work on their part. Aggregation targets are fully-functional instances of the SOSflow daemon, except that their principle data sources are distributed listener daemons rather than node-local clients. The aggregated data contains identical information as the in situ data stores, it just has more of it, and it is assembled into one location. The aggregate daemons are useful for performing online analysis or information visualization that needs to include information from multiple nodes (Fig. 2).

SOSflow is not a publish-subscribe system in the traditional sense, but uses a more scalable push-and-pull model. Everything sent into the system will automatically migrate to aggregation points unless it is explicitly tagged as being node-only. Requests for information from SOSflow are ad hoc and the scope of the request is constrained by the location where the request is targeted: in situ queries are resolved against the in situ database, aggregate queries are resolved against the aggregate database. If tagged node-only information is potentially useful for offline analysis or archival, the in situ data stores can be collected at the end of a job script, and their contents can be filtered for that node-only information, which can be simply concatenated together with the aggregate database[s] into a complete image of all data. Each value published to SOSflow is tagged with a globally unique identifier (GUID). This allows SOSflow data from multiple sources to be mixed together while preserving its provenance and preventing data duplication or namespace collision.

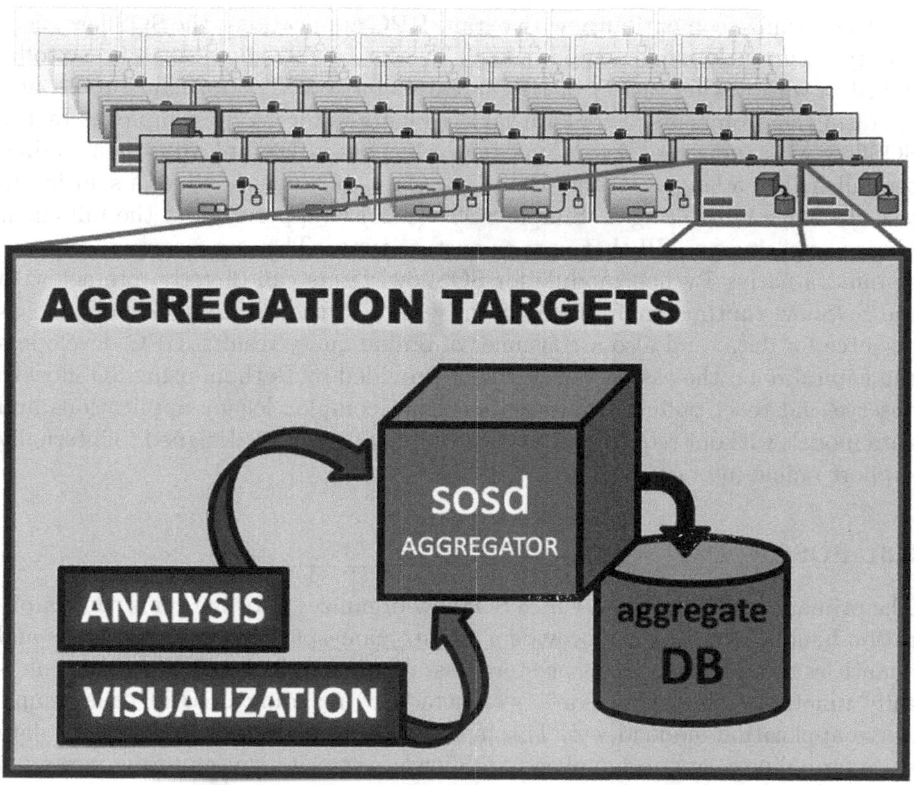

Fig. 2. Co-located aggregation, analysis, and visualization.

3.2 SOSflow Client Library

Clients can directly interface with the SOSflow runtime system by calling a library of functions (libsos) through a standardized API. Applications can also transparently become clients of SOS by utilizing libraries and performance tools which interact with SOSflow on their behalf. All communication between the SOSflow library and daemon are transparent to users. Users do not need to write any socket code or introduce any state or additional complexity to their own code.

Information sent through the libsos API is copied into internal data structures, and can be freed or destroyed by the user after the SOSflow API function returns. Data provided to the API is published up to the in situ daemon with an explicit API call, allowing developers to control the frequency of interactions with the runtime environment. It also allows the user to register callback functions that can be triggered and provided data by user-defined analytics function, creating an end-to-end system for both monitoring as well as feedback and control.

To maximize compatibility with extant HPC applications, the SOSflow client library is currently implemented in C99. The use of C99 allows the library to be linked in with a wide variety of HPC application codes, performance tools, and operating environments. There are various custom object types employed by the SOSflow API, and these custom types can add a layer of complexity when binding the full API to a language other than C or C++. SOSflow provides a solution to this challenge by offering a "Simple SOS" (ssos) wrapper around the full client library, exposing an API that uses no custom types. The ssos wrapper was used to build a native Python module for SOSflow. Users can directly interact with the SOSflow runtime environment from within Python scripts, acting both as a source for data, and also a consumer of online query results. HPC developers can capitalize on the ease of development provided by Python, using SOSflow to observe and react online to information from complex legacy applications and data models without requiring that those applications be redesigned to internally support online interactivity.

3.3 SOSflow Data

The primary concept around which SOSflow organizes information is the "publication handle" (pub). Pubs provide a private namespace where many types and quantities of information can be stored as a key/value pair. SOSflow automatically annotates values with a variety of metadata, including a GUID, timestamps, origin application, node id, etc. This metadata is available in the persistent data store for online query and analysis. SOSflow's metadata is useful for a variety of purposes:

- Performance analysis
- Provenance of captured values for detection of source-specific patterns of behavior, failing hardware, etc.
- Interpolating values contributed from multiple source applications or nodes
- Re-examining data after it has been gathered, but organizing the data by metrics other than those originally used when it was gathered

A complete history of changes to every value is retained within the daemon's persistent data store (Fig. 3). This allows for the changing state of an application or its environment to be explored at arbitrary points in its evolution. When a key is re-used to store some new information that has not yet been transmitted to the in situ daemon, the client library enqueues it up as a snapshot of that value, preserving all associated metadata alongside the historical value. The next time the client publishes to the daemon, current new values and all enqueued historical values are transmitted.

SOSflow is built on a model of a global information space. Aggregate data stores are guaranteed to provide eventual consistency with the data stores of the in situ daemons that are targeting them. SOSflow's use of continuous but asynchronous movement of information through the runtime system does not allow for strict quality-of-service guarantees about the timeliness of information

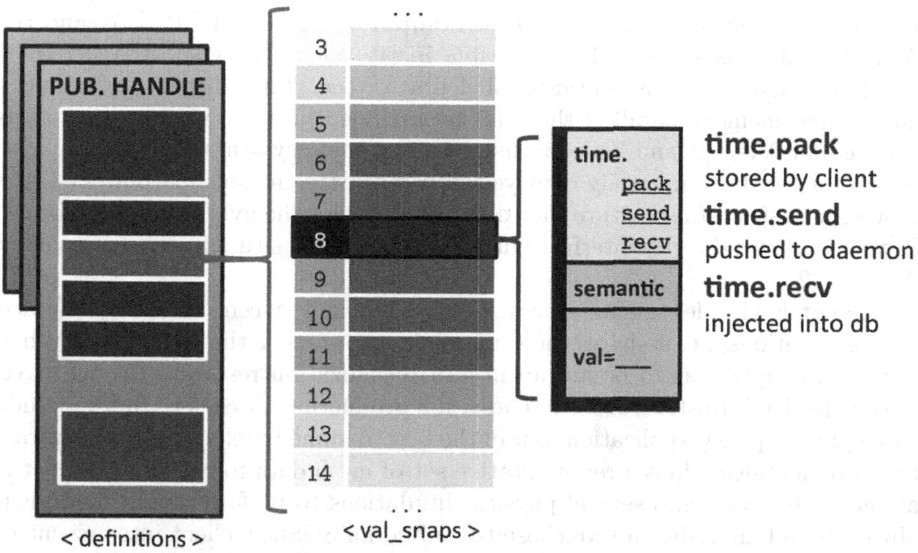

Fig. 3. Each update is stored with its unique metadata, such as timestamps.

being available for analysis. This design constraint reflects the reality of future-scale HPC architectures and the need to eliminate dependence on synchronous behavior to correlate context. SOSflow conserves contextual metadata when values are added inside the client library. This metadata is used during aggregation and query resolution to compose the asynchronously-transported data according to its original synchronous creation. The vicissitudes of asynchronous data migration strategies at scale become entirely transparent to the user.

SOSflow does not require the use of a domain-specific language when pushing values into its API. Pubs are self-defining through use: When a new key is used to pack a value into a pub, the schema is automatically updated to reflect the name and the type of that value. When the schema of a pub changes, the changes are automatically announced to the in situ daemon the next time the client publishes data to it. Once processed and injected into SOSflow's data store, values and their metadata are accessible via standardized SQL queries. SOSflow's online resolution of SQL queries provides a high-degree of programmability and online adaptivity to users. SQL views are built into the data store that mask off the internal schemas and provide results organized intuitively for grouping by application rank, node, time series, etc.

SOSflow uses the ALPINE in situ visualization infrastructure described below to collect simulation geometry that it correlates with performance data.

4 ALPINE Ascent

ALPINE is a project that aims to build an in situ visualization infrastructure and analysis targeting leading edge supercomputers. ALPINE is part of the

U.S. Department of Energy's Exascale Computing Project (ECP) [15], and the ALPINE effort is supported by multiple institutions. The goal of ALPINE is two fold. First, create a hybrid-parallel library (i.e., both distributed-memory and shared-memory parallel) that can be included in other visualization tools such as ParaView [2] and VisIt [5] thus creating an ecosystem where new hybrid-parallel algorithms are easily deployed into downstream tools. Second, create a flyweight in situ infrastructure that directly leverages the hybrid-parallel library. In this work, we directly interface with the ALPINE in situ infrastructure called Ascent [12].

Ascent is the descendant of Strawman [13], and Ascent is tightly-coupled with simulations, i.e. it shares the same node resources as the simulation. While Strawman's goal was to bootstrap in situ visualization research, the ALPINE Ascent in situ infrastructure is intended for production. Ascent includes include three physics proxy-applications out of the box to immediately provide the infrastructure and algorithms a representative set of mesh data to consume. Ascent is already integrated into several physics simulations to perform traditional visualization and analysis, and we chose to embed an SOSflow client into Ascent to eliminate the need for additional manual integration of SOSflow with Ascent-equipped simulations. Ascent uses the Conduit [10] data exchange library to marshal mesh data from simulations into Ascent. Conduit provides a flexible hierarchical model for describing mesh data, using a simple set of conventions for describing meshes including structured, unstructured, and higher order element meshes [11]. Once the simulation describes the mesh data, it publishes the data into Ascent for visualization purposes. Ascent relays the mesh data to SOSflow in the manner described below. In addition to the mesh data, we can easily add performance data that is associated with each MPI rank. Coupling the performance data with the mesh geometry provides a natural way to generate an aggregate data set to visualize the performance data mapped to the spatial region each MPI rank is responsible for.

Ascent includes Flow, a simple dataflow library based on the Python dataflow library within VisIt, to control the execution of visualization filters. The input to Flow is the simulation mesh data, and Ascent adds visualization filters (e.g., contours and thresholding) to create visualizations. Everything within Flow is a filter that can have multiple inputs and a single output of generic types. The flexibility of Flow allows for user defined filters, compiled outside of Ascent, to be easily inserted into the dataflow, and when the dataflow network executes, custom filters have access to all of the simulation mesh data published to Ascent. We leverage the flexibility of Flow to create an SOSflow filter that is inserted at runtime. The SOSflow filter uses the data published by the simulation to extract the spatial extents being operated over by each MPI rank along, with any performance data provided. Next, we publish that data to SOSflow, and then Ascent's visualization filters execute as usual.

5 Experiments

5.1 Evaluation Platform

All results were obtained by running online queries against the SOSflow runtime's aggregation targets (Fig. 2) using SOSflow's built-in Python API. The results of these queries were used to create Vtk [17] geometry files. These files were used as input for the VisIt visualization tool, which we invoked from within the allocation to interactively explore the performance projections.

5.2 Experiment Setup

The experiments performed had the following purposes:

- **Validation** : Demonstrate the coupling of SOSflow with ALPINE and its ability to extract geometry from simulations transparently.
- **Introspection** : Examine the overhead incurred by including the SOSflow geometry extraction filter in an ALPINE Ascent visualization pipeline.

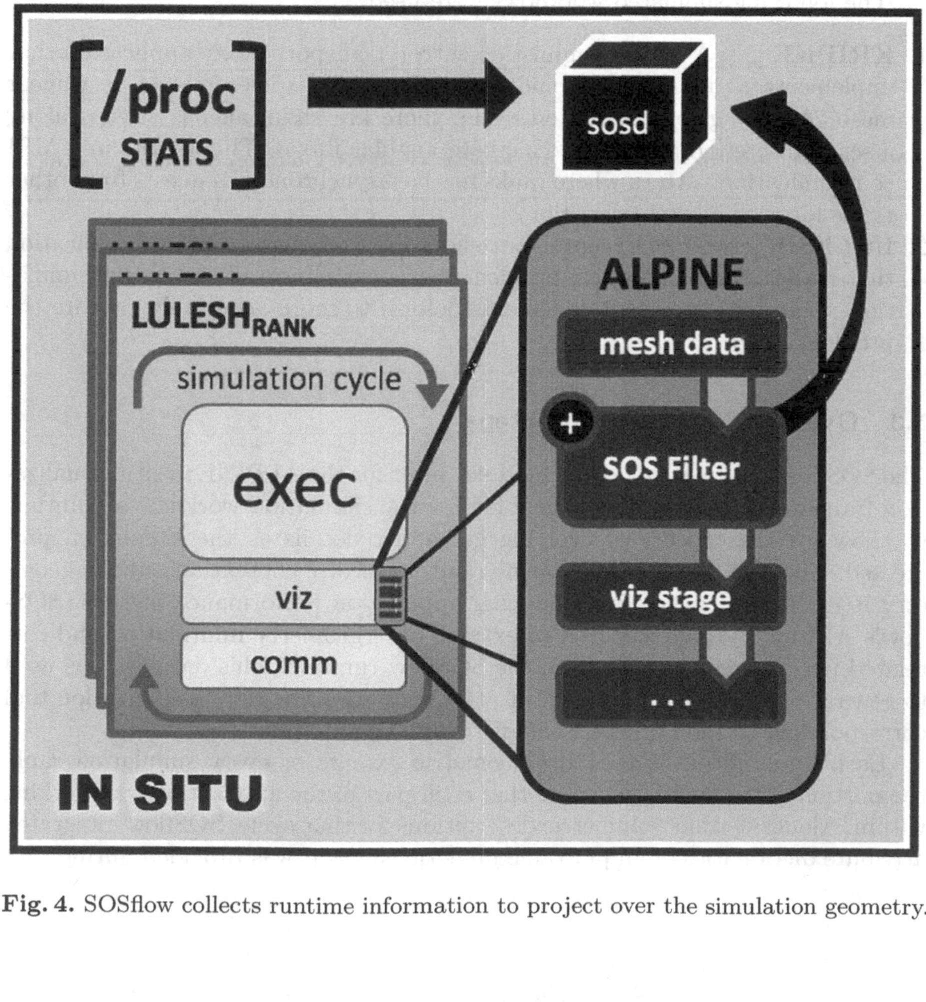

Fig. 4. SOSflow collects runtime information to project over the simulation geometry.

ALPINE's Ascent library was used to build a filter module outfitted with SOSflow, and this filter was used for online geometry extraction (Fig. 4). ALPINE's JSON configuration file describing the connectivity of the in situ visualization pipeline was modified to insert the SOSflow-equipped geometry extraction filter. The SOSflow implementation used to conduct these experiments is general-purpose and was not tailored to the specific deployment environment or the simulations observed. The study was conducted on two machines, the details of which are included here—

1. **Quartz** : A 2,634-node Penguin supercomputer at Lawrence Livermore National Laboratory (LLNL). Intel Xeon E5-2695 processors provide 36 cores/node. Each node offers 128 GB of memory and nodes are connected via Intel OmniPath.
2. **Catalyst** : A Cray CS300 supercomputer at LLNL. Each of the 324 nodes is outfitted with 128 GB of memory and 2x Intel Xeon E5-2695v2 2.40 GHz 12-core CPUs. Catalyst nodes transport data to each other using a QLogic InfiniBand QDR interconnect.

The following simulated workflows were used—

1. **KRIPKE** [9] : A 3D deterministic neutron transport proxy application that implements a distributed-memory parallel sweep solver over a rectilinear mesh. At any given simulation cycle, there are simultaneous sweeps along a set of discrete directions to calculate angular fluxes. This results in a MPI communication pattern where ranks receive asynchronous requests from other ranks for each discrete direction.
2. **LULESH** [1] : A 3D Lagrangian shock hydrodynamics proxy application that models Sedov blast test problem over a curvilinear mesh. As the simulation progresses, hexahedral elements deform to more accurately capture the problem state.

5.3 Overview of Processing Steps

The SOSflow runtime provided a modular filter for the ALPINE in situ visualization framework. This filter was enabled for the simulation workflow at runtime to allow for the capture of evolving geometric details as the simulation progressed. The SOSflow runtime daemon automatically contextualized the geometry it received alongside the changing application performance metrics. SOSflow's API for Python was used to extract both geometry information and correlated performance metrics from the SOSflow runtime. This data set was used to generate sequences of input files to the VisIt scientific data visualization tool corresponding to the cycle of a the distributed simulation.

Each input file contained the geometric extents of every simulation rank, the portion of the simulated space that each part of the application was working within. Alongside that volumetric descriptions for that cycle, SOSflow integrated attribute dictionaries of all plottable numeric values it was provided during that cycle, grouped by simulation rank. Performance metrics could then be interactively selected and combined in VisIt with customizable plots, presenting an application rank's state and activity incident to its simulation effort, projected over the relevant spatial extent.

5.4 Evaluation of Geometry Extraction

Our experiments were validated by comparing aggregated data to data manually captured at the source during test runs. Furthermore, geometry aggregated by ALPINE's Ascent SOSflow filter was rendered and visually compared with other visualizations of the simulation. Projections were inspected to observe the simulation's expected deforming of geometry (LULESH) or algorithm-dependent workload imbalances (KRIPKE). Performance metrics can be correlated in SQL queries to the correct geometric regions by various redundant means such as pub handle GUID, origin PID or MPI rank, simulation cycle, host node name, SOSflow publish frame, and value creation timestamps. Aggregated performance metrics projected over the simulation regions were compared to metrics reported locally, and required to be identical for each region and simulation cycle.

5.5 Evaluation of Overhead

Millisecond-resolution timers were added to the per-cycle *execute* method of the SOSflow Alpine geometry extraction filter. Each rank tracked the amount of time it spent extracting its geometry, packing the geometry into an SOSflow pub handle, and transmitting it to the runtime daemon. Every cycle's individual time cost was computed and transmitted to SOSflow, as well as a running total of the time that Alpine had spent in the SOSflow filter. From a region outside the timers, the timer values were packed into the same SOSflow publication handle used for the geometric data. Timer values were transmitted at the end of the following cycle, alongside that cycle's geometry. The additional transmission cost of these two timer values once per simulation cycle had no perceivable impact on the performance they were measuring.

6 Results

Geometry was successfully extracted (Figs. 5, 6, 7, and 8) with minimal overhead from simulations run at a variety of scales from 2 to 33 nodes. The side-by-side introspection of the behavior of KRIPKE (Fig. 5) are a good example of the value this system provides to developers. The amount of work loops and the backlog of requests for computation are correlated negatively, with ranks operating in the center of the simulation space getting through less loops of work per cycle, since they are required to service data requests in more directions than the ranks simulating the corners regions. The directionality of energy waves moving through he simulated space can also be observed, with more work piling up where multiple waves are converging. A developer can quickly assess the behavior of their distributed algorithm by checking for hot-spots and workload imbalances in the space being simulated.

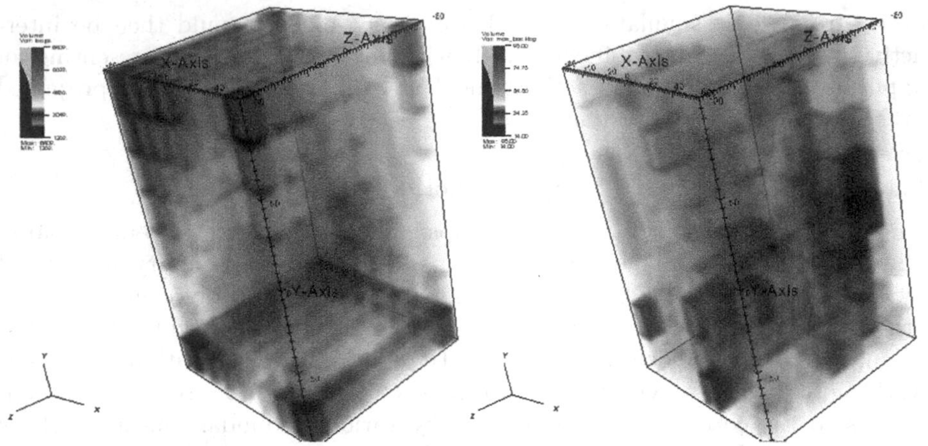

Fig. 5. Loops (left) and maximum backlog (right) from one cycle of 512 KRIPKE ranks distributed to 32 nodes.

6.1 Geometry Extraction and Performance Data Projection

Aggregated simulation geometry was a precise match with the geometry manually recorded within applications, across all runs. After aggregation and performance data projection, geometry from all simulation ranks combined to create a contiguous space without gaps or overlapping regions, representative of the simulated space subdivided by MPI rank.

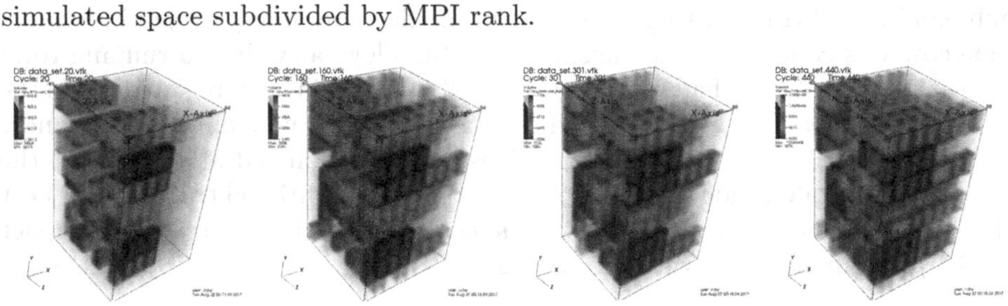

Fig. 6. Cumulative user CPU ticks during 440 cycles of 512 KRIPKE ranks on 32 nodes.

6.2 Overhead

The inclusion of the ALPINE Ascent filter module for SOSflow had no observable impact on overall application execution time, being significantly less than variance observed between experimental runs both with and without the filter. The filter module is executed at the end of each simulation cycle, from the first iteration through to the simulation conclusion. Manual instrumentation was added to the SOSflow filter to measure the time spent inside the filter's *execute* method, where all simulation geometry and performance metrics were gathered for our study.

When gathering *only the simulation geometry*, filter execution never exceeded 2ms per simulation cycle. We collected performance information for our projections by reading from the /proc/[pid] files of each rank. These readings were made from within the SOSflow filter, and published to SOSflow alongside the collected geometry. Collecting 31 system metrics and application counters added additional overhead, but the filter time but did not exceed 4ms for any of the projections shown in this paper. The filter's execution time was logged as a performance metric alongside the other in situ performance data, and is visualized for LULESH in Fig. 7.

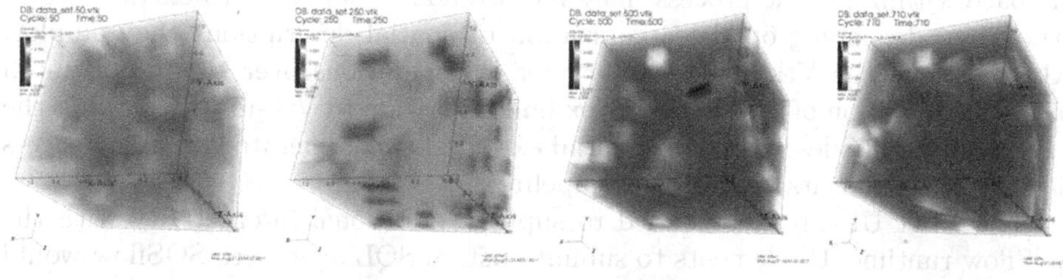

Fig. 7. Filter execution (1–4 ms) over 710 LULESH cycles.

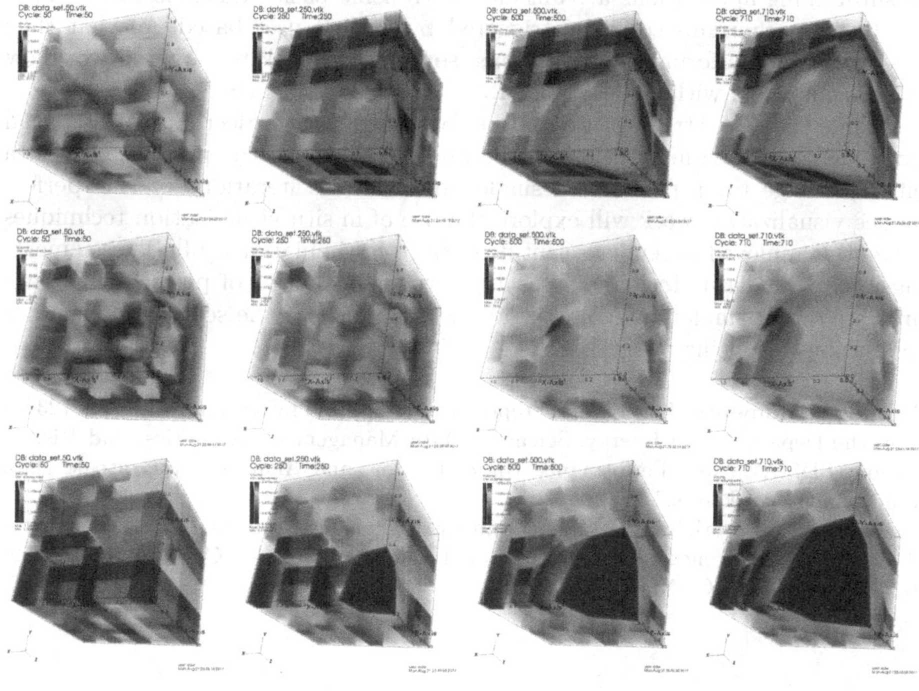

Fig. 8. Many metrics can be projected from one run. Here we see (top to bottom) user CPU ticks, system CPU ticks, and bytes read during 710 cycles of 512 LULESH ranks distributed across 32 nodes.

7 Conclusion

Services from both SOSflow and ALPINE were successfully integrated to provide a scalable in situ (online) geometry extraction and performance data projection capability.

7.1 Future Work

Workflows that use the ALPINE framework but have complex irregular meshes, feature overlapping "halo regions", or that operate over non-continuous regions of space within a single process, may require additional effort to extract geometry from, depending on the organization of spatial descriptions they employ. ALPINE uses the Vtk-m [16] library for its operations over simulation mesh data. The addition of a general convex hull algorithm to Vtk-m will simplify the task of uniformly describing any spatial extent[s] being operated on by a process using ALPINE for its visualization pipeline.

The VisIt UI can be extended to support additional interactivity with the SOSflow runtime. UI elements to submit custom SQL queries to SOSflow would enhance the online data exploration utility of VisIt. SOSflow's interactive code steering mechanisms allow for feedback messages and payloads to be delivered to subscribing applications at runtime. With some basic additions to the VisIt UI, these mechanisms could be triggered by a VisIt user based on what they observe in the performance projections, sending feedback to targeted workflow components from within the VisIt UI.

While the geometry capture and performance data projection in this initial work has a scalable in situ design, the final rendering of the performance data into an image takes place on a single node. Future iterations of this performance visualization work will explore the use of in situ visualization techniques currently employed to render scientific data from simulations [14]. These emerging in situ rendering technologies will allow for live views of performance data projected over simulation geometry at the furthest extreme scales to which our simulations are being pressed.

Acknowledgements. The research report was supported by a grant (DE-SC0012381) from the Department of Energy, Scientific Data Management, Analytics, and Visualization (SDMAV), for "Performance Understanding and Analysis for Exascale Data Management Workflows."

Part of this work was performed under the auspices of the U.S. Department of Energy by Lawrence Livermore National Laboratory under Contract DE-AC52-07NA27344 (LLNL-CONF-737874).

References

1. Hydrodynamics Challenge Problem, Lawrence Livermore National Laboratory. Technical report LLNL-TR-490254
2. Ahrens, J., Geveci, B., Law, C.: ParaView: an end-user tool for large data visualization. In: The Visualization Handbook, vol. 717 (2005)
3. Boehme, D., et al.: Caliper: performance introspection for HPC software stacks. In: International Conference for High Performance Computing, Networking, Storage and Analysis, SC 2016, pp. 550–560. IEEE (2016)
4. Böhme, D., Beckingsdale, D., Schulz, M.: Flexible data aggregation for performance profiling. In: IEEE Cluster (2017)
5. Childs, H., et al.: VisIt: an end-user tool for visualizing and analyzing very large data. In: High Performance Visualization-Enabling Extreme-Scale Scientific Insight, pp. 357–372. CRC Press/Francis-Taylor Group (2012)
6. Gimenez, A.A., et al.: MemAxes: visualization and analytics for characterizing complex memory performance behaviors. IEEE Trans. Vis. Comput. Graph. **24**, 2180–2193 (2017)
7. Husain, B., Giménez, A., Levine, J.A., Gamblin, T., Bremer, P.T.: Relating memory performance data to application domain data using an integration API. In: Proceedings of the 2nd Workshop on Visual Performance Analysis, p. 5. ACM (2015)
8. Isaacs, K.E., Landge, A.G., Gamblin, T., Bremer, P.T., Pascucci, V., Hamann, B.: Exploring performance data with boxfish. In: 2012 SC Companion: High Performance Computing, Networking, Storage and Analysis (SCC), pp. 1380–1381. IEEE (2012)
9. Kunen, A., Bailey, T., Brown, P.: KRIPKE-a massively parallel transport mini-app. Technical report, Lawrence Livermore National Laboratory (LLNL), Livermore, CA (2015)
10. Laboratory, L.L.N.: Conduit: simplified data exchange for HPC simulations (2017). https://software.llnl.gov/conduit/
11. Laboratory, L.L.N.: Conduit: simplified data exchange for HPC simulations - conduit blueprint (2017). https://software.llnl.gov/conduit/blueprint.html
12. Larsen, M., et al.: The alpine in situ infrastructure: ascending from the ashes of strawman. In: Proceedings of the In Situ Infrastructures for Enabling Extreme-Scale Analysis and Visualization Workshop, ISAV2017. ACM, New York (2017)
13. Larsen, M., Brugger, E., Childs, H., Eliot, J., Griffin, K., Harrison, C.: Strawman: a batch in situ visualization and analysis infrastructure for multi-physics simulation codes. In: Proceedings of the First Workshop on In Situ Infrastructures for Enabling Extreme-Scale Analysis and Visualization, ISAV2015, pp. 30–35. ACM, New York (2015). https://doi.org/10.1145/2828612.2828625
14. Larsen, M., Harrison, C., Kress, J., Pugmire, D., Meredith, J.S., Childs, H.: Performance modeling of in situ rendering. In: Proceedings of the International Conference for High Performance Computing, Networking, Storage and Analysis, p. 24. IEEE Press (2016)
15. Messina, P.: The exascale computing project. Comput. Sci. Eng. **19**(3), 63–67 (2017)
16. Moreland, K., et al.: Vtk-m: accelerating the visualization toolkit for massively threaded architectures. IEEE Comput. Graph. Appl. **36**(3), 48–58 (2016)
17. Schroeder, W.J., Lorensen, B., Martin, K.: The Visualization Toolkit: An Object-oriented Approach to 3D Graphics. Kitware, New York (2004)

18. Schulz, M., et al.: A flexible data model to support multi-domain performance analysis. In: Niethammer, C., Gracia, J., Knüpfer, A., Resch, M.M., Nagel, W.E. (eds.) Tools for High Performance Computing 2014, pp. 211–229. Springer, Cham (2015). https://doi.org/10.1007/978-3-319-16012-2_10
19. Schulz, M., Levine, J.A., Bremer, P.T., Gamblin, T., Pascucci, V.: Interpreting performance data across intuitive domains. In: 2011 International Conference on Parallel Processing (ICPP), pp. 206–215. IEEE (2011)
20. Wood, C., et al.: A scalable observation system for introspection and in situ analytics. In: Proceedings of the 5th Workshop on Extreme-Scale Programming Tools, pp. 42–49. IEEE Press (2016)

Visualizing, Measuring, and Tuning Adaptive MPI Parameters

Matthias Diener(✉), Sam White, and Laxmikant V. Kale

University of Illinois at Urbana-Champaign, Urbana, USA
{mdiener,white67,kale}@illinois.edu

Abstract. Adaptive MPI (AMPI) is an advanced MPI runtime environment that offers several features over traditional MPI runtimes, which can lead to a better utilization of the underlying hardware platform and therefore higher performance. These features are overdecomposition through virtualization, and load balancing via rank migration. Choosing which of these features to use, and finding the optimal parameters for them is a challenging task however, since different applications and systems may require different options. Furthermore, there is a lack of information about the impact of each option. In this paper, we present a new visualization of AMPI in its companion Projections tool, which depicts the operation of an MPI application and details the impact of the different AMPI features on its resource usage. We show how these visualizations can help to improve the efficiency and execution time of an MPI application. Applying optimizations indicated by the performance analysis to two MPI-based applications results in performance improvements of up 18% from overdecomposition and load balancing.

Keywords: MPI · Load balancing · AMPI · Migration · Overdecomposition

1 Introduction

Improving the performance of parallel applications that are based on the MPI programming model is an important aspect of High-Performance Computing. Compared to traditional MPI runtimes, Adaptive MPI (AMPI) [6] offers several advanced, unique features, the most important of which are: *overdecomposition through virtualization* and *load balancing through rank migration*. These features can be used to improve performance portability of MPI-based applications. AMPI itself is implemented on top of the Charm++ runtime system [1,10] and makes use of several of its features, including support for migration of threads, comprehensive scheduling and load balancing frameworks, and optimized communication within and between cluster nodes.

The key difference between AMPI and most other MPI implementations is that AMPI virtualizes ranks as lightweight, migratable user-level threads (instead of operating system processes). The Charm++ runtime system can

A. Bhatele et al. (Eds.): ESPT/VPA 2017/2018, LNCS 11027, pp. 219–230, 2019.
https://doi.org/10.1007/978-3-030-17872-7_13

schedule multiple virtual ranks per core based on message delivery, to overlap communication and computation and to enable a more fine-grained decomposition of work. This *overdecomposition* can also help with cache and NUMA locality, since smaller subdomains of a problem might fit more easily into caches.

The AMPI runtime also provides support for *migrating ranks* between address spaces at runtime, both within a cluster node and between separate nodes. This feature can be used for the purposes of load balancing or fault tolerance, among others. Charm++ contains many different load balancing strategies that can be selected by the user or automatically [18], resulting in substantial performance gains for many parallel applications [4, 9].

These load balancing strategies are based on actual measurement of load information at runtime, and on migrating computations from heavily loaded to lightly loaded Processing Elements (PEs, Charm++'s terminology for OS processes). Figures 1 and 2 illustrate overdecomposition and rank migration in AMPI. The only changes necessary to existing MPI applications to run them on AMPI with virtualization and migration are related to privatizing global and static variables to AMPI's user-level threads [6]. All AMPI programs are valid MPI programs, besides any calls they might contain to AMPI's several extension APIs.

Using AMPI's high-level features efficiently is not straightforward, however. Users of MPI applications running on AMPI need to determine whether an application can benefit from each feature, as well as the optimal configuration (such as degree of overdecomposition and load balancing frequency) of each feature. Previously, the impact of these features could only be observed indirectly, by running an application with various parameters and observing its execution time. It was therefore difficult to determine the best configuration without extensive experiments, to understand application performance, as well as to explain the reasons for possible performance gains.

In this paper, we present the additions to AMPI and Projections that enable detailed performance analysis of applications running on AMPI, covering both normal MPI operations as well as AMPI's additions to the standard. With these

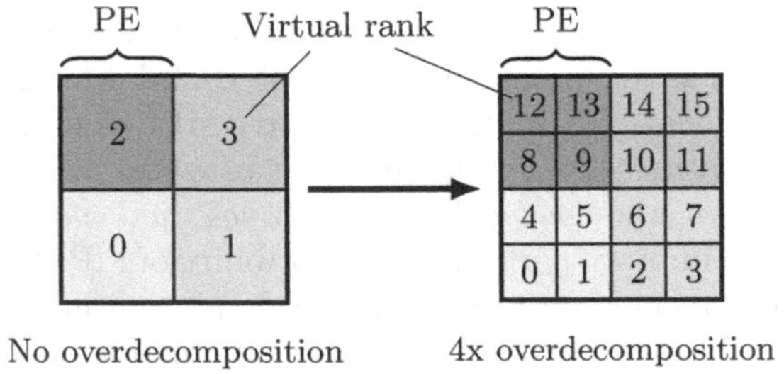

Fig. 1. Overdecomposition in AMPI. Colors indicate different PEs. The working set of a virtual rank in the *no overdecomposition* case might not fit into the cache, but it might fit in the *4x overdecomposition* case. (Color figure online)

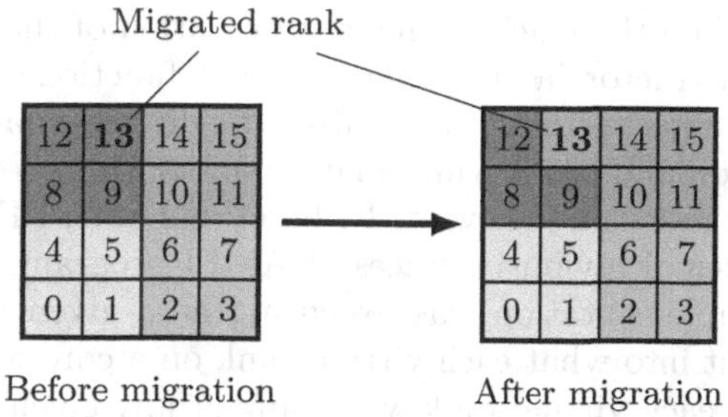

Fig. 2. Rank migration in AMPI. Colors indicate different PEs. Rank 13 is migrating from one PE to another. (Color figure online)

additions, it is possible to better understand the operation of an MPI-based application and its performance characteristics. Our tool can point out possible inefficiencies, their solutions, and can be used to evaluate and compare performance improvements.

In the second part of the paper (Sect. 3), we show how the information provided by AMPI and Projections can be used to optimize the performance of two MPI-based applications, LULESH [11,12] and PIC from the Intel Parallel Research Kernel suite [24]. Our results show that the performance analysis with the help of our additions to AMPI/Projections enabled us to achieve performance improvements of up to 18% from overdecomposition and load balancing. Furthermore, we show that performance gains are highly dependent on the characteristics of the application, such that different applications require using different AMPI features with different parameters.

2 Visualizing AMPI with Projections

This section briefly discusses how the operation of an MPI application running on top of AMPI is traced for visualization, and presents the main visualizations available to the application user in the Projections tool.

2.1 Implementation

Tracing and trace visualization in Charm++ and Projections is built around storing trace events in log files. Prior to version 6.8.0 of Charm++/AMPI, no special support for AMPI events was available, such that only events related to Charm++ were traced.

AMPI. In order to implement tracing of events in AMPI, we extended the support for *bracketed events* in the tracing framework in Charm++. Bracketed events are events that have a duration, that is, a starting time and end time. For every AMPI API function (standard MPI functions as well as AMPI extensions), an object is created on the stack as the first operation of that function. As part of the object's constructor, a time stamp of the function entry is stored. On function exit, this object is destroyed automatically, calculating the total time spent in the function and storing information about this event in the trace file. Information stored includes the event ID, function name, PE, virtual rank, and duration of the event. Previously, traces of AMPI programs only showed what task the AMPI implementation was executing at a given time on each core, providing no insight into what each virtual rank on a core was executing. Now, users can see what each virtual rank was doing at any given time.

Such an implementation via a stack-allocated object simplifies the support in AMPI, as well as seamlessly supporting nested events. The tracing framework itself is not limited to MPI, a user application can register and trace their own events in addition to the MPI functions. Furthermore, an application can also request more fine-grained traces by dynamically enabling and disabling tracing at runtime, via the `AMPI_Trace_begin()` and `AMPI_Trace_end()` functions.

Enabling tracing in Charm++ and AMPI applications has generally a negligible execution time overhead. For the applications discussed in this paper, the measured overhead was typically less than 3% of the total execution time. Trace files are kept in memory and are flushed to disk periodically and at the end of execution in a compressed format.

Projections. The Projections tool reads and evaluates the trace files after the execution of a Charm++ or AMPI application. We extended it with support for displaying virtual ranks for bracketed events, such that a user can see which rank has executed which MPI function. Furthermore, support was added to determine when and where virtual ranks are migrated, by showing the virtual rank numbers for traced events. As in Charm++ traces, MPI functions are grouped by color, such that it is easy to follow the operation of collective functions.

2.2 Visualizations

In the example in this section, we use an MPI application running on four Processing Elements (PEs) and eight virtual ranks (VPs) to illustrate the visualizations. Figure 3 depicts the visualization before the extensions described in this paper were applied, as presented in the original AMPI paper [6]. In the figure, a user can see that the application is running on four PEs and the percentage of time this PE was busy (that is, not blocked while waiting for communication, for example). This percentage is shown below each PE (left number in the parentheses). Furthermore, the figure illustrates at which times each PE was idle (in white) and busy (in red). Not presented in this figure are the virtual ranks of the application, and which operations they are performing.

Figures 4 and 5 depict the visualizations with the changes described in this paper. In addition to the information presented before, now the virtual ranks and the PE they are executing on are shown (two virtual ranks per PE in this example), as well as the operations the ranks perform, giving a detailed view of

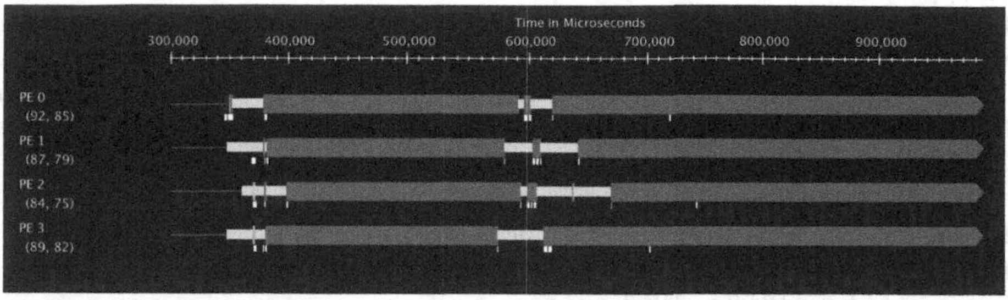

Fig. 3. Previous visualization of AMPI in Projections, as presented in the original AMPI paper [6]. The x-axis depicts time, while the y-axis shows the various processing elements (PE). Visible are the four processing elements, busy percentages (left value below each PE label), idle times (in white), and busy times (in red). Not visible are virtual ranks (two per PE), rank migrations, and which operation each rank is performing. (Color figure online)

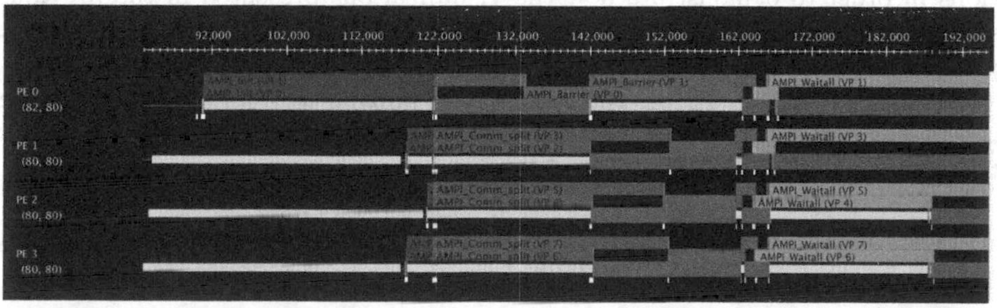

Fig. 4. New visualization of AMPI. In addition to the information shown in Fig. 3, virtual ranks (VPs) are depicted (including on which PE they are executing), as well as the operation performed by each rank.

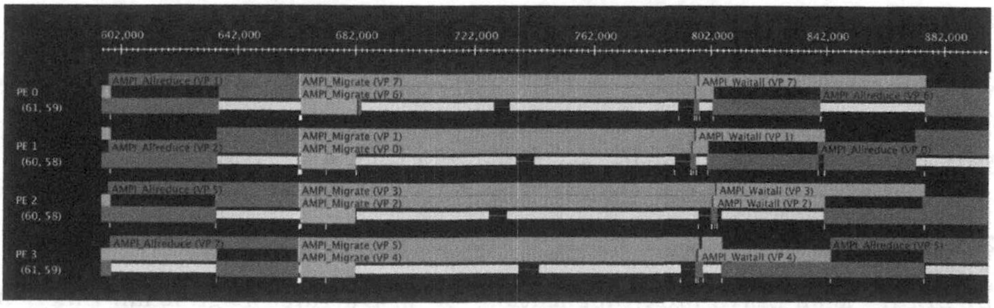

Fig. 5. Visualizing migrations in AMPI. The MPI extension *AMPI_Migrate()* shows where each rank is migrated. For example, VP 1 is migrated from PE 0 to PE 1.

an application's behavior. For example, in Fig. 4, it is possible to see that at the time between 142 ms and 162 ms, PE 0 was idle since both virtual ranks running on that PE (VP 0 and VP 1) were waiting in an `MPI_Barrier`. Starting at about 167 ms, PE 0 is busy with the execution of VP 0, while VP 1 is performing an `MPI_Waitall` operation. This shows how the overdecomposition can help reduce idle time.

In Fig. 5, the operation of a migration operation in AMPI is depicted. By looking the `AMPI_Migrate` event, a user can see which virtual ranks were migrated, and to which PE they were migrated to. In the example shown, VP 1 is migrated from PE 0 to PE 1.

Additional information that is provided by Projections, but not shown in the figures, are statistics related to the number of different events and the time spent for each event, among others.

3 Application Case Studies

This section presents two case studies using two different MPI-based applications in order to demonstrate how the visualizations presented in the previous section can help users and developers of MPI applications to optimize application performance and performance portability.

In this section, we discuss the overall load imbalance of an application using the average busy time and the *percent imbalance* metric λ [21], calculated over the busy time of all PEs using the following equation:

$$\lambda = \left(\frac{max(L)}{avg(L)} - 1 \right) \times 100\% \tag{1}$$

In the equation, L is a vector of the busy times of all PEs. If $\lambda = 0$, the application is perfectly balanced, while higher values of λ indicate increasing amounts of imbalance. The maximum value of λ with 8 PEs and possible values of 0–100 is 700%.

To keep the presentation of the visualizations at a reasonable size, we restrict them in this section to 8 PEs. Results are qualitatively similar to much higher numbers of PEs for both applications presented here.

For the performance experiments, we execute the applications on a system with an Intel Xeon E5-2680 v2 CPU (10-core, 2.8 GHz, SMT disabled) and 64 GByte of DDR3 main memory. The software environment consists of CentOS 7 with Linux kernel 2.6.32, gcc 4.8.2, and Charm++/AMPI 6.8.0.

3.1 LULESH

LULESH[1] is an LLNL proxy application for unstructured Lagrangian-Eulerian shock hydrodynamics [11,12]. We use the MPI implementation of LULESH 2.0 in the experiments.

[1] https://codesign.llnl.gov/lulesh.php.

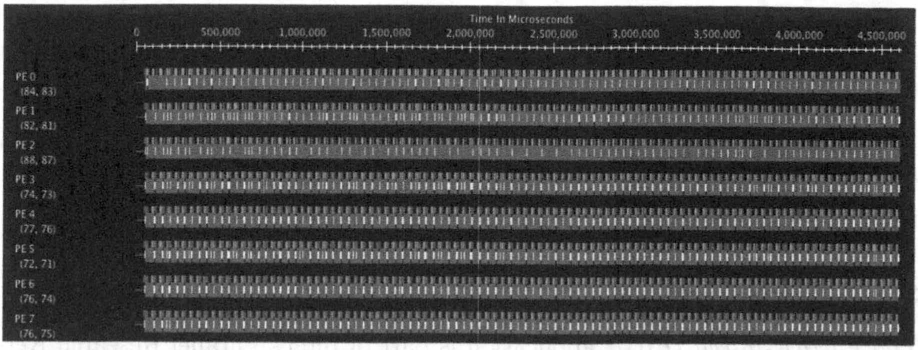

Fig. 6. Baseline execution of LULESH with neither overdecomposition nor load balancing.

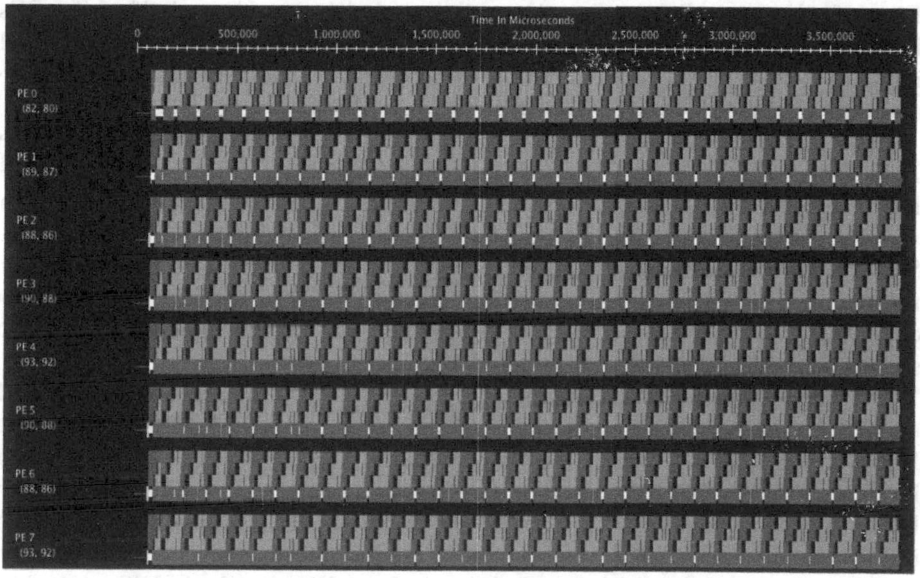

Fig. 7. Execution of LULESH with 3.4x overdecomposition (8 PEs, 27 virtual ranks) and no load balancing.

Figure 6 depicts the operation of LULESH with 8 PEs/ranks, no overdecomposition and no load balancing. As can be seen from the figure, the application is not imbalanced, with similar busy times and load distribution among all PEs. The average busy percentage is 78.6%, with an imbalance of $\lambda = 11.9\%$. Due to the low busy percentage, this application may benefit from overdecomposition. On the other hand, load balancing appears not to be profitable due to the low imbalance.

Figure 7 shows the performance graph of LULESH with a 3.4x overdecomposition (27 virtual ranks running on 8 PEs). As we expected, the busy time of all PEs is increased substantially in this scenario, reaching an average of 89.1%, while also improving the load balance of the application slightly ($\lambda = 4.3\%$).

The impact of these improvements can be seen on the execution time, which was reduced from 4.61 s in the baseline experiment to 3.85 s with overdecomposition (~16% improvement).

3.2 Particle-in-cell

The *Particle-in-cell (PIC)*[2] application is part of Intel's Parallel Research Kernels [24]. We used version 2.17 of the AMPI implementation of PIC.

Figure 8 shows the performance behavior of the PIC application baseline, with 8 PEs/ranks and no load balancing. Several things need to be noted here. First of all, the application is substantially imbalanced. About half of the PEs have a significantly lower busy time than the other half, leading to an overall imbalance of $\lambda = 22.5\%$. Furthermore, since some of the PEs are idle for large amounts of time, the overall busy time is only 75.6%.

The first natural step to fix this behavior is to balance the load between the PEs. For this, we use AMPI's load balancing feature, specifically the RefineLB load balancer mechanism, which has shown good load balancing results with a reasonable overhead [2]. The result of this experiment is presented in Fig. 9. Since overdecomposition is required for load balancing, we selected the smallest reasonable degree of overdecomposition (2x, 16 virtual ranks on 8 PEs) for this experiment. Note that in order to reduce the size of the figures, we are not showing the individual virtual ranks in Figs. 9 and 10.

As can be seen in Fig. 9, the RefineLB load balancer is able to balance the load among the PEs successfully, resulting in an overall imbalance of only $\lambda = 7.3\%$. However, although the work is better distributed, the average busy time (77.4%) increases only slightly compared to the baseline execution, despite the slightly higher overdecomposition. Therefore, we can not expect significant performance improvements compared to the baseline. This is confirmed by the measurement of the execution time, which is reduced only from 3.96 s in the baseline to 3.94 s with load balancing.

The relatively high idle time of the load balanced version indicates that this application can benefit from overdecomposition in addition to load balancing. This intuition is verified with an experiment that uses a 6x overdecomposition (48 virtual ranks on 8 PEs) in addition to RefineLB. The results of this experiment is shown in Fig. 10. Here, we can see that busy time has increased drastically, with an average of 92.4%. Furthermore, the application is also more balanced ($\lambda = 1.7\%$). These improvements lead to a total execution time of 3.26 s, about 18% less than in the baseline version of PIC.

[2] https://github.com/ParRes/Kernels.

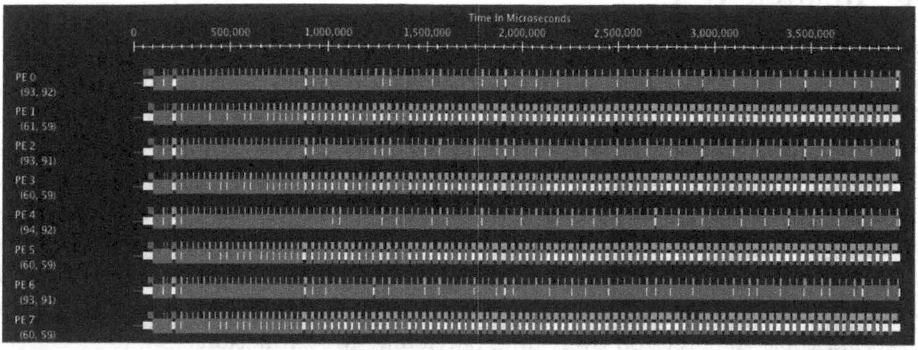

Fig. 8. Baseline execution of PIC with neither overdecomposition nor load balancing.

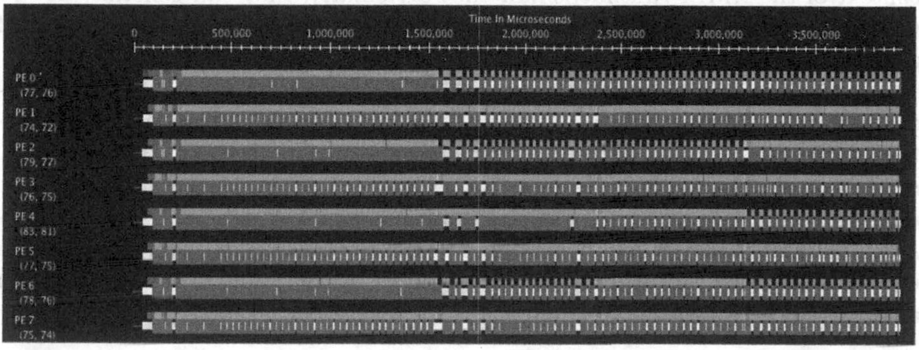

Fig. 9. Execution of PIC with load balancing (RefineLB) and 2x overdecomposition (8 PEs, 16 virtual ranks).

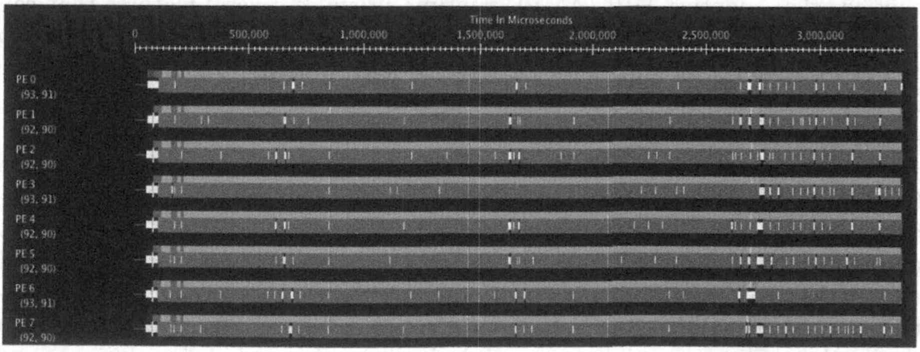

Fig. 10. Execution of PIC with load balancing (RefineLB) and 6x overdecomposition (8 PEs, 48 virtual ranks).

4 Related Work

Several prior tools exist to help with visualizing and understanding MPI application performance. These tools include Totalview [5], Allinea Map and DDT [17], Vampir [14]/Vampirtrace [20], Score-P [15], the HPCToolkit [3], Jumpshot [26], and Marmot [16]. Some of these tools provide visualizations of an application's MPI behavior that are very similar to the visualizations discussed in this paper.

Many proposed techniques exist for monitoring communication in MPI applications [23,25,27]. Tracing itself, as well as storing and analyzing large trace files, is a significant challenge [27]. Since a tracing API is directly integrated in Charm++/AMPI, the tracing overhead can be substantially lower than in external tools that rely on overriding particular MPI functions.

Other tools perform automatic detection of inefficiencies in certain MPI functions (such as send and receive) [22]. However, as these tools are not aware of AMPI's features that go beyond the MPI standard, their applicability in the context of the AMPI runtime is limited. Particularly, they can generally not be used for overdecomposition or migration, as they have no knowledge of virtual ranks.

Many performance analysis tools for MPI use the Profiling MPI (PMPI) standard [13,19], which provides a coarse-grained way to override standard MPI functions with custom versions that can be used for tracing, analysis, and visualization. More recently, the MPI_T interface [7,8] was added to the MPI standard [19]. It allows more fine-grained access to performance counters provided by the environment. Currently, AMPI does not support PMPI or MPI_T, but an implementation is planned for the near future. With such support, AMPI could expose information about overdecomposition and migrations to other external tools.

5 Conclusions

Adapting MPI applications to the underlying hardware platform and guaranteeing performance portability on different systems is a challenging task. In this context, the Adaptive MPI (AMPI) runtime provides several features that can help with this task, the two most important of which are *overdecomposition through virtualization* and *load balancing through rank migration*. Correct usage of these features requires a deep understanding of the application performance, as well as information about inefficient behavior displayed by the application.

In this paper, we presented extensions to the Projections tool to help with the performance analysis of applications running on AMPI. We added tracing capabilities to AMPI, covering standard MPI functions and AMPI's extensions, and added their visualization to Projections. Furthermore, we extended AMPI and Projections to support visualization of virtual ranks as well as rank migrations at runtime. With our extensions, Projections can be used to understand application behavior, point out possible inefficiencies and their solutions, and evaluate improvements in load balance, overdecomposition, and performance. We applied this analysis to two MPI-based applications, and achieved improvements of 16%–18% with overdecomposition and/or load balancing.

The changes discussed in this paper have been integrated into version 6.8.0 of Charm++/AMPI, and are available online[3]. Projections is available at the same location. For the future, we intend to integrate support for PMPI and MPI_T into AMPI in order to better support traditional performance analysis tools. Furthermore, we want to improve how rank migrations are displayed in Projections, and implement automatic suggestions for performance improvements in AMPI and Projections.

Acknowledgments. This paper is based in part upon work supported by the Department of Energy, National Nuclear Security Administration, under Award Number DE-NA0002374.

References

1. Acun, B., et al.: Parallel programming with migratable objects: Charm++ in practice. In: SC (2014). https://doi.org/10.1109/SC.2014.58
2. Acun, B., Kale, L.V.: Mitigating processor variation through dynamic load balancing. In: 2016 IEEE International Parallel and Distributed Processing Symposium Workshops, pp. 1073–1076. IEEE (2016)
3. Adhianto, L., et al.: HPCToolkit: tools for performance analysis of optimized parallel programs. Concurr. Comput.: Pract. Exp. **22**(6), 685–701 (2010). https://doi.org/10.1002/cpe.1553
4. Bhandarkar, M., Kalé, L.V., de Sturler, E., Hoeflinger, J.: Adaptive load balancing for MPI programs. In: Alexandrov, V.N., Dongarra, J.J., Juliano, B.A., Renner, R.S., Tan, C.J.K. (eds.) ICCS 2001. LNCS, vol. 2074, pp. 108–117. Springer, Heidelberg (2001). https://doi.org/10.1007/3-540-45718-6_13
5. Gottbrath, C.: Automation assisted debugging on the Cray with TotalView. In: Proceedings of Cray User Group (2011)
6. Huang, C., Lawlor, O., Kalé, L.V.: Adaptive MPI. In: Rauchwerger, L. (ed.) LCPC 2003. LNCS, vol. 2958, pp. 306–322. Springer, Heidelberg (2004). https://doi.org/10.1007/978-3-540-24644-2_20
7. Islam, T., Mohror, K., Schulz, M.: Exploring the capabilities of the new MPI_T interface. In: Proceedings of the 21st European MPI Users' Group Meeting, p. 91. ACM (2014)
8. Islam, T., Mohror, K., Schulz, M.: Exploring the MPI tool information interface: features and capabilities. Int. J. High Perform. Comput. Appl., pp. 212–222. (2016). https://doi.org/10.1177/1094342015600507
9. Jeannot, E., Meneses, E., Mercier, G., Tessier, F., Zheng, G.: Communication and topology-aware load balancing in Charm++ with TreeMatch. In: 2013 IEEE International Conference on Cluster Computing, CLUSTER, pp. 1–8. IEEE (2013)
10. Kale, L.V., Krishnan, S.: CHARM++: a portable concurrent object oriented system based on C++. In: Conference on Object-Oriented Programming Systems, Languages, and Applications, OOPSLA, pp. 91–108 (1993)
11. Karlin, I., et al.: Exploring traditional and emerging parallel programming models using a proxy application. In: 27th IEEE International Parallel & Distributed Processing Symposium, IEEE IPDPS 2013, Boston, USA, May 2013

[3] https://charm.cs.illinois.edu/software.

12. Karlin, I., Keasler, J., Neely, R.: Lulesh 2.0 updates and changes. Technical report LLNL-TR-641973, August 2013
13. Karrels, E., Lusk, E.: Performance analysis of MPI programs. In: Environments and Tools for Parallel Scientific Computing, pp. 195–200 (1994)
14. Knüpfer, A., et al.: The Vampir performance analysis tool-set. In: Resch, M., Keller, R., Himmler, V., Krammer, B., Schulz, A. (eds.) Tools for High Performance Computing, pp. 139–155. Springer, Heidelberg (2008). https://doi.org/10.1007/978-3-540-68564-7_9
15. Knüpfer, A., et al.: Score-P: a joint performance measurement run-time infrastructure for periscope, Scalasca, TAU, and Vampir. In: Brunst, H., Müller, M., Nagel, W., Resch, M. (eds.) Tools for High Performance Computing, pp. 79–91. Springer, Heidelberg (2012). https://doi.org/10.1007/978-3-642-31476-6_7
16. Krammer, B., Bidmon, K., Müller, M.S., Resch, M.M.: MARMOT: an MPI analysis and checking tool. In: Advances in Parallel Computing, vol. 13, pp. 493–500 (2004)
17. Lecomber, D., Wohlschlegel, P.: Debugging at scale with Allinea DDT. In: Cheptsov, A., Brinkmann, S., Gracia, J., Resch, M., Nagel, W. (eds.) Tools for High Performance Computing, pp. 3–12. Springer, Heidelberg (2013). https://doi.org/10.1007/978-3-642-37349-7_1
18. Menon, H., Chandrasekar, K., Kale, L.V.: POSTER: automated load balancer selection based on application characteristics. In: Proceedings of the 22nd ACM SIGPLAN Symposium on Principles and Practice of Parallel Programming, pp. 447–448. ACM (2017)
19. Message Passing Interface Forum: MPI: A Message-Passing Interface Standard (Version 3.0). Technical report (2012)
20. Müller, M.S., et al.: Developing scalable applications with Vampir, VampirServer and VampirTrace. In: PARCO, vol. 15, pp. 637–644 (2007)
21. Pearce, O., Gamblin, T., de Supinski, B.R., Schulz, M., Amato, N.M.: Quantifying the effectiveness of load balance algorithms. In: ACM International Conference on Supercomputing, ICS, pp. 185–194 (2012). https://doi.org/10.1145/2304576.2304601
22. Vetter, J.: Performance analysis of distributed applications using automatic classification of communication inefficiencies. In: Proceedings of the 14th International Conference on Supercomputing, pp. 245–254. ACM (2000)
23. Vetter, J.: Dynamic statistical profiling of communication activity in distributed applications. In: Proceedings of the 2002 ACM SIGMETRICS International Conference on Measurement and Modeling of Computer Systems, SIGMETRICS 2002, pp. 240–250. ACM, New York (2002). https://doi.org/10.1145/511334.511364
24. Van der Wijngaart, R.F., Mattson, T.G.: The parallel research kernels. In: 2014 IEEE High Performance Extreme Computing Conference, HPEC, pp. 1–6. IEEE (2014)
25. Wu, C.E., et al.: From trace generation to visualization: a performance framework for distributed parallel systems. In: Proceedings of the 2000 ACM/IEEE Conference on Supercomputing, SC 2000. IEEE Computer Society, Washington, DC (2000). http://dl.acm.org/citation.cfm?id=370049.370458
26. Zaki, O., Lusk, E., Gropp, W., Swider, D.: Toward scalable performance visualization with Jumpshot. Int. J. High Perform. Comput. Appl. **13**(3), 277–288 (1999)
27. Zhai, J., Sheng, T., He, J.: Efficiently acquiring communication traces for large-scale parallel applications. IEEE Trans. Parallel Distrib. Syst. (TPDS) **22**(11), 1862–1870 (2011). https://doi.org/10.1109/TPDS.2011.49

VPA 2018

Visual Analytics Challenges in Analyzing Calling Context Trees

Alexandre Bergel[1], Abhinav Bhatele[2(✉)], David Boehme[2], Patrick Gralka[3], Kevin Griffin[2], Marc-André Hermanns[5,6], Dušan Okanović[4], Olga Pearce[2], and Tom Vierjahn[5,7,8]

[1] Department of Computer Science, University of Chile, Santiago, Chile
abergel@dcc.uchile.cl
[2] Lawrence Livermore National Laboratory, Livermore, CA, USA
{bhatele,boehme3,griffin28,olga}@llnl.gov
[3] Visualization Research Center, University of Stuttgart, Stuttgart, Germany
patrick.gralka@visus.uni-stuttgart.de
[4] Institute of Software Technology, University of Stuttgart, Stuttgart, Germany
dusan.okanovic@iste.uni-stuttgart.de
[5] JARA-HPC, Jülich, Germany
[6] Jülich Supercomputing Center, Forschungszentrum Jülich, Jülich, Germany
m.a.hermanns@fz-juelich.de
[7] Visual Computing Institute, RWTH Aachen University, Aachen, Germany
tom.vierjahn@acm.org
[8] Westphalian University of Applied Sciences, Bocholt, Germany

Abstract. Performance analysis is an integral part of developing and optimizing parallel applications for high performance computing (HPC) platforms. Hierarchical data from different sources is typically available to identify performance issues or anomalies. Some hierarchical data such as the calling context can be very large in terms of breadth and depth of the hierarchy. Classic tree visualizations quickly reach their limits in analyzing such hierarchies with the abundance of information to display. In this position paper, we identify the challenges commonly faced by the HPC community in visualizing hierarchical performance data, with a focus on calling context trees. Furthermore, we motivate and lay out the bases of a visualization that addresses some of these challenges.

1 Introduction

The process of optimizing performance of parallel applications is an integral part of a successful software strategy in high performance computing (HPC). However, the process of identifying performance bottlenecks and understanding behavioral phenomena in parallel applications is complex and tends to involve a problem-specific set of tools and visualizations. It is usually possible to identify some of the performance bottlenecks by solely examining metrics from a single application execution. However, properly identifying and finding complex bottlenecks depends on the ability to compare measurements from different executions,

A. Bhatele et al. (Eds.): ESPT/VPA 2017/2018, LNCS 11027, pp. 233–249, 2019.
https://doi.org/10.1007/978-3-030-17872-7_14

comparing different software versions or runtime configurations. Because the investigative process requires advanced, domain-specific knowledge, determining the right visualization to reveal relevant behavior to the experts is challenging.

Performance profile data can take various forms, as discussed in more detail in Sect. 2. Often, the context for such data follows a hierarchical structure in potentially multiple dimensions (e.g., the Cube data model [1]). The calling context is often of particular interest to the performance expert, as it describes the structure of the application, and identifying a performance phenomenon in the context of the software helps in understanding it. A calling context tree (CCT) [2] is a compact summarization of the relationships between caller-callee entities in an application. Manipulating and reasoning upon the CCT is central to numerous performance engineering activities. As such, most code execution profilers produce performance reports anchored on a CCT or similar construct [3–8].

High performance computing applications can produce a large number of CCTs in multiple dimensions: (1) parallelism, (2) time, and (3) commit history. Evolution in terms of parallelism is seen when performance measurements across processing elements (processes, threads, etc.) or across different execution scales (number of nodes, cores, etc.) are compared. In this case, the CCT may contain an additional dimension with values for each processing unit, or each processing unit is associated with its own CCT. Evolution in terms of the time dimension is often reflected by tracking time steps or iterations in the application [9]. Evolution in terms of commit history involves comparing the performance of different versions of the code.

Visualizing CCTs is crucial for understanding the performance of HPC simulation codes, but due to the large scales in each of the dimensions mentioned above as well as the potentially large size of the CCT itself, visualization of the relevant data is challenging.

This paper describes a flexible framework to visualize execution profiles of parallel programs. The key feature of our framework is to express the transition between various complementary interactive visualizations. The combination of these visualizations describes a flow that covers the CCTs, the function graph, processes/computational units, and the metric list. Transitions between views are enabled by simply selecting some relevant visual elements using the mouse.

In this paper, we outline the types of data that are stored using CCTs (Sect. 2), the related work (Sect. 3), and typical user operations on the data (Sect. 4). Subsequently, we propose a prototype for a CCT visualization framework that allows HPC experts to quickly key in on the underlying cause of performance issues at scale (Sect. 5). We conclude with some future work (Sect. 6).

2 HPC Domain Data

Several kinds of performance data are collected in HPC with different purposes. Measurements of a single execution of one application can be recorded for analyzing the performance of this single execution. The measurement of two or more executions (on different process counts, on different architectures, etc.) can be recorded for doing performance comparisons of these executions. For regression analyses, we may compare historical performance data of a single application or an entire system (all applications executed during a period of time) over time.

The HPC community is interested in several sub-components of the hardware and software stack that contribute to execution time and/or energy consumption. Execution time of an HPC application may depend on:

- Time spent in serial computation
- Data movement in the memory hierarchy
- Communication on the network
- Input/output to the filesystem
- Overlap between different application phases/components
- Sharing of the network and I/O resources by multiple jobs/applications

Since there are many potential sources of performance degradation, and it is difficult to attribute performance characteristics to the components listed above, there is not a definitive guide on performance engineering in HPC. Instead, whether comparing datasets from different executions or searching for bottlenecks in a single execution, the performance analysis process depends on advanced, domain-specific knowledge of the performance engineering experts, and is usually tool-specific, hardware-specific, and/or problem-specific.

3 State of the Art

Current production performance tools typically use straightforward means to represent CCTs. Cube and hpcviewer, the performance data browsers for Score-P [3] and HPCToolkit [10], respectively, use text-based tree views or tree tables similar to those often found in file browsers. Figure 1 shows an example of the Cube callpath display. Data spanning multiple CCTs (e.g., multiple processes in a parallel application) is shown on a unified tree using aggregate values. These tree views are easy to implement for tool developers and easy to interpret for users. VIPACT shows a hybrid tree and flat profile view with "halo nodes" showing the distribution of runtimes across processes [11].

Despite its simplicity, there are drawbacks to the traditional tree view presentation:

- All tree nodes have the same size, making it difficult to visually distinguish interesting nodes in the CCT from uninteresting ones. Coloring helps to some extent, but a large number of uninteresting nodes can clutter the display.
- Related functions or function groups (i.e., common subtrees) are visually separated over possibly large distances.
- Typical tree views show only scalar values for tree nodes, limiting the kind of information that can be displayed.
- Laborious interaction: Typically, users must expand each tree branch individually, often requiring lots of clicks to reach nodes of interest. However, both cube and hpcviewer implement a "hotpath" option which automatically expands the most expensive sub-branch.

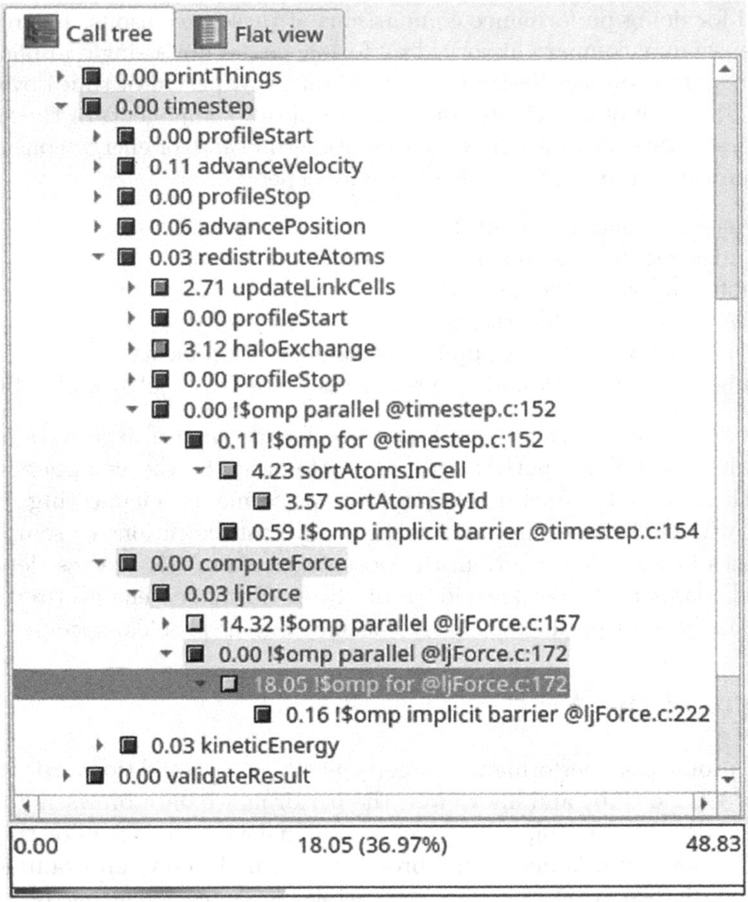

Fig. 1. Traditional callpath display in the Cube profile viewer.

An important insight here is that a tree view is not necessarily the ideal form to present CCTs. We therefore explore more compact visualizations that better highlight portions of interest.

In the context of memory performance analysis, Gralka et al. [12] presented a tool to visually explore detrimental memory access patterns. Besides a scatterplot where each low-level memory access is depicted as an individual point, they show the call tree as a flame graph [13]. Such a representation of a call tree encodes hierarchy but also duration, and lends it use in trace-based visualizations, such as HPCTraceViewer [14] and Vampir [15]. In principle, a flame graph is a variation of Kruskal's icicle plot [16]. The techniques presented by Trümper et al. [17] and De Pauw et al. [18] use tree visualizations of this type, as well. A similar visualization is indented tree, for instance used by De Pauw et al. [19,20]. The disadvantage is that these visualizations consume a significant portion of screen space. Another kind of tree visualization is radial representation, which has been used by Adamoli and Hauswirth [21], and Moret et al. [22] to depict CCTs. In a radial representation, functions with a relative small self-time can degenerate from radial boxes to small lines in the visualization, which we expect to occur quite often in the context of simulation software with an interactive design. However, we adopted the basic idea of a radial representation to augment the nodes in our graph-based alternative *Function View* with an arc of radial boxes showing the share of execution time with respect to a specific calling function.

4 Data/Visual Analytics Operations on a CCT

We deem a specific set of user operations necessary that a visual analytics tool should support in order to help users in the analysis of CCTs. An important aspect of CCTs that needs to be managed by user operations is their size and scale. **Filtering** helps to reduce the size of CCTs and helps the user to focus on the interesting parts of the tree. This requires a tool to expose selectable metrics and thresholds, or queries to have the user communicate interesting nodes for subselection to the tool.

In the same context, **grouping** is a helpful operation, as well. Navigating through a large CCT is difficult. If the user could group the nodes in the tree, for instance with respect to their name or load module (library), the tree would resemble something that the user is more familiar with, such as the general architecture of the software. Especially in the context of computational science and engineering codes, we expect to have repeating patterns, for instance from iterative solvers, in a CCT. A visual analytics tool should provide the means to group the nodes of a pattern into a single entity and to unfold them again depending on whether the user wants to gain an overview of the tree or wants to drill down into details. This operation is effective only if analyzed metrics can be aggregated into the grouped entity.

Another set of operations should help the user to cope with multiple trees, e.g., from different runs, or different inputs per run. The basis for most of these operations is a **matching** between the nodes in two or more trees. Most of this matching should be done automatically. However, in very complex trees we expect automatic matching to fail. Unfortunately in such cases, a user-driven matching on the raw data will be often too time-consuming. A user-operated **clustering** can help a user during manual matching to focus on more dissimilar parts in the trees. Adamoli and Hauswirth [21] provide a list of methods and metrics for clustering and comparison of CCTs.

In general, an important hint towards interesting behavior that a user wants to analyze are the differences in trees according to one metric or a set of metrics, or topological changes. Thus, a visual analytics tool should support the **union** or **subtraction** of two or more matched CCTs and highlighting according to detected similarities or differences.

For different optimization strategies (performance, throughput, power consumption, etc.) the user will need the capability to **overlay** different metrics on the nodes of a CCT. For example, after matching or subtracting CCTs, being able to select and view different metrics on the highlighted node(s) is crucial for understanding the performance of HPC simulations.

5 Prototype of a Flow-Based Visualization Framework

This section outlines a framework for visualizing the execution of HPC applications. The framework allows for several visualizations to be hooked together and is able to support a navigation flow between them. In Sect. 4, we described a set of user operations that a comprehensive framework should support. Note that, given the outlined framework is a prototype, not every aspect of these operations is included in the following framework. However, we encourage the reader to extend our framework to a tool ready for production use.

5.1 Flow-Based Navigation

Figure 2 gives a high level representation of the flow supported by our framework. The flow is modeled as a directed acyclic graph of four nodes. Each node represents a family of views on the data commonly considered when dealing with performance assessment and performance correction activities. In particular, we support the following views.

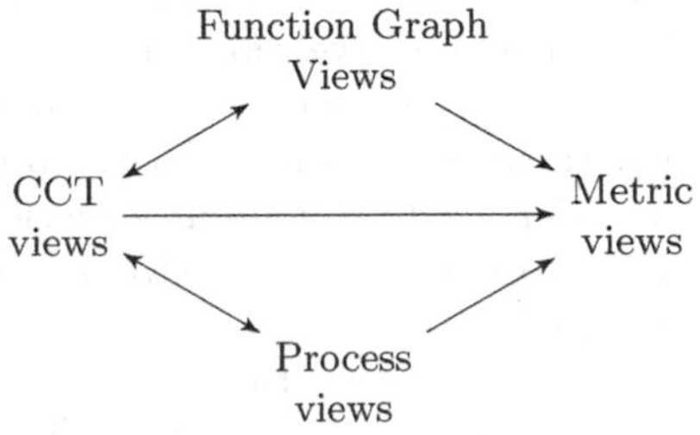

Fig. 2. Flow supported by our framework

CCT Views: A CCT is considered as a standard and intuitive representation of a program execution. This node describes visualizations of a CCT. A CCT may be large, which may turn a simple visualization ineffective. In particular, these views may filter out irrelevant parts of the CCT (*e.g.,* the use of a particular library or architectural layer), and fine-tune the visualization (*e.g.,* by using a particular or customized tree layout, user-defined color mapping to highlight some properties of each node). Therefore, the CCT view supports the *filtering* and *grouping* operations mentioned in Sect. 4. An example of a CCT view is given in Fig. 4.

Function Graph Views: CCT may be verbose, particularly in presence of loops. Considering the graph of function calls may be relevant for some activities (*e.g.,* debugging, code maintenance, code understanding). Being able to visualize functions calls complements the *CCT views.* Such views have to consider the fact that function calls may form graphs, possibly with cycles. The view should therefore accommodate such characteristics. Three examples of function graph views are given along the paper (Figs. 5, 6, and 9).

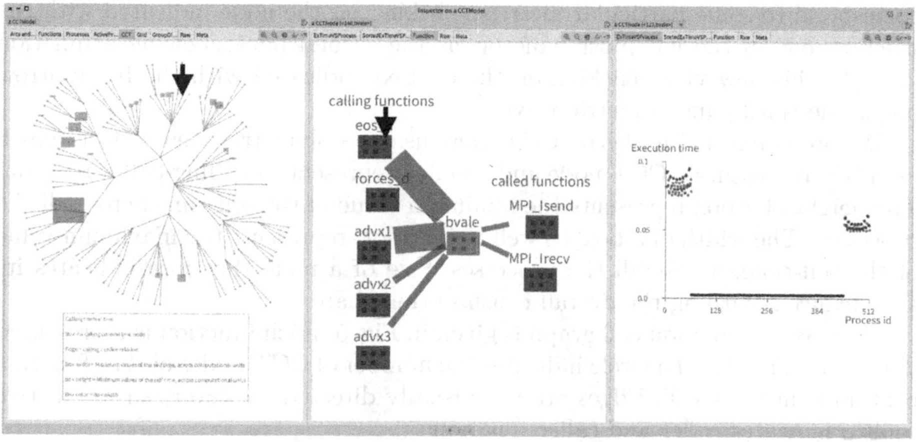

Fig. 3. Flow example for an execution of the ZeusMP/2 benchmark. Selected elements are indicated with a thick black arrow.

Process Views: HPC applications typically run over a large number of execution units, typically CPU and GPU cores. Focusing on the execution units is relevant to characterize the use of the available resources. A process view may support a particular HPC-related activity. For example, measuring the load balancing across the execution units or identifying underused units. This can be seen as a *clustering* to gain an overview as described in Sect. 4. An example of a process view is given in Fig. 7.

Metric Views: An execution is accompanied with numerous metric reports to characterize, e.g., memory consumption, CPU uses, and cache uses. Numerical reports should be adequately presented using state-of-the-art visual representations. These views relate to the *overlay* operation. However, it requires links to the other views, especially the tree and function views.

This position paper claims that *manipulating these views in an explicit fashion and expressing multiple flexible flows is key to incrementally build flexible and open analyzing HPC tools.*

5.2 A First Flow Example

We illustrate the use of our framework on the basis of a Cube measurement report of the execution of the ZeusMP/2 benchmark [23] of the SPEC MPI 2007 benchmark suite [24] on 512 processes of the IBM Blue Gene/P supercomputer JUGENE [25], formerly operated by Forschungszentrum Jülich GmbH, Germany.

Figure 3 presents a flow made of the path *CCT view* → *Function view* → *Metric view*. On the left hand side, the figure shows the calling context tree represented as a radial visualization. The shape and the color of each node correspond to some particular metrics. Clicking on the node indicated with the black arrow, in the left most pane opens the second pane showing a function view. In this new view, clicking on the context indicated with the black arrow opens the third pane, a metric view.

As presented in Fig. 4, the CCT view uses a polymetric view [26] in which each box represents a CCT node and an edge represents a calling-callee relation. The height of a box represents the minimum value of the self-time across all the processes. The width of a box, as well as its color, represents the maximum value of the self-time, across all the processes. Size of a node therefore indicates its significance regarding the overall consumption share.

The overall function call graph is given in Fig. 5. Each function is represented as a circle. The size of a circle indicates the number of CCT nodes of that function contained in the CCT. Edges are not visually directed, however, an interactive tooltip indicates caller and callee functions.

Clicking on a CCT node opens a window pane that shows a function graph. Figure 6 illustrates functions, represented as outer boxes. Each function contains the CCT nodes of the encapsulating function. The figure is obtained by clicking on a CCT of the `nudt` function. We see that `nudt` has created two CCT nodes since the box representing `nudt`, at the center, has two small inner boxes. Each of these inner boxes represents a CCT node. Callers of the `nudt` are located left of it, and functions called by `nudt` are located on the right hand side. Edges indicate the control flow between the functions. The width of the edges indicates the number of calls.

Figure 7 illustrates a process view. In this visualization, each box represents a process/computational unit. Three metrics are used to represent a process: the width indicates the maximum self-time value across all CCT nodes, the height indicates the minimum value, and the color fading represents the average. The figure clearly shows that the usage of the computation units is not homogeneous. A grid layout is used to order the boxes.

Clicking on a CCT node, either from the *CCT view* or from the second *Function view* opens a *Metric view*. It indicates the execution time of the selected entity across all the processing units. Figure 8 illustrates the execution time of a particular CCT node across all the computational processes.

The example of the flow supports cyclic function call graphs. Although convenient and intuitive, the visualization can be improved in case that the call graph has no cycles, as shown in our alternative function view, described below.

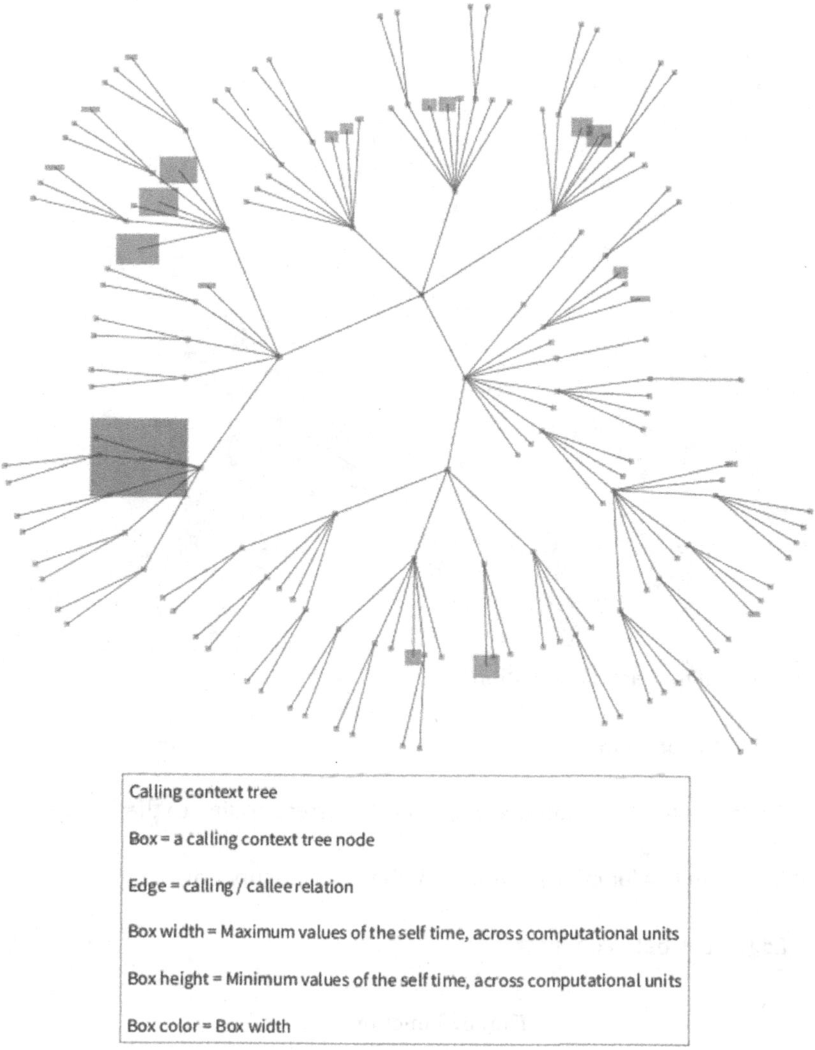

Fig. 4. Example of a CCT view

Detail about each visual element is available at all times. First a mouse tooltip indicates the relevant information, including the node name and the relevant metrics. The tooltip appears by moving the mouse above the visual element one wish to have information from. Clicking on a node triggers a new view. The new spanned view may be optionally replaced with the complete list of associated metrics (accessible from the *Raw* tab, in Fig. 3).

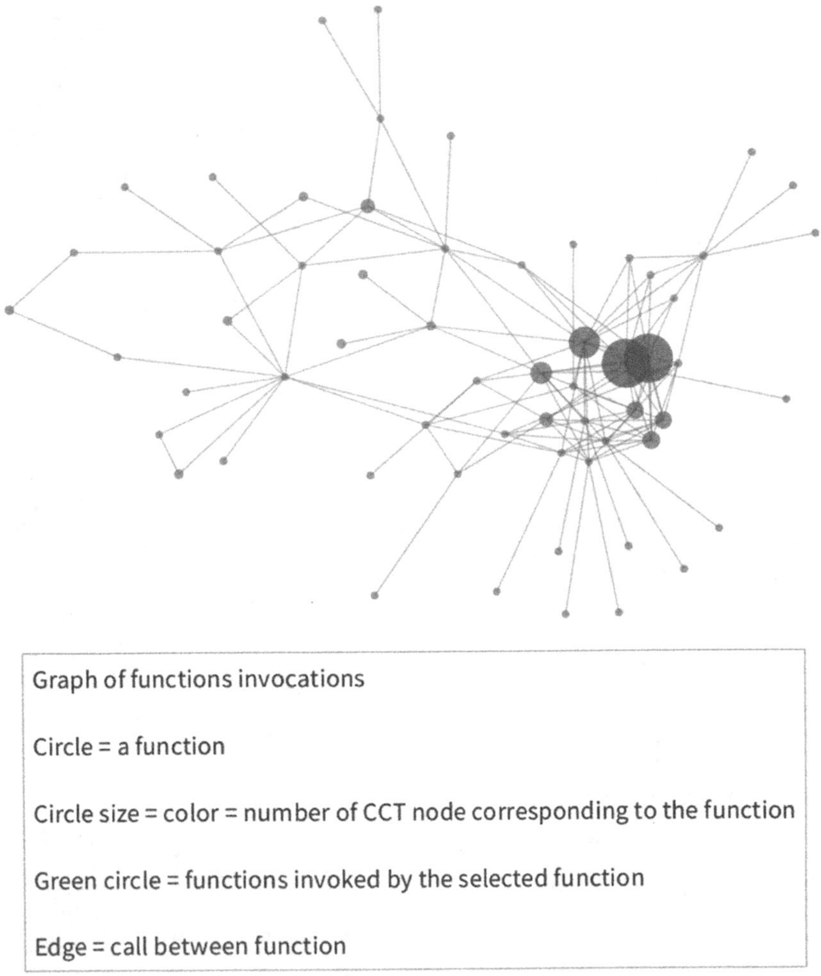

Graph of functions invocations
Circle = a function
Circle size = color = number of CCT node corresponding to the function
Green circle = functions invoked by the selected function
Edge = call between function

Fig. 5. Function view

5.3 Alternative Function View

In the case that the function call graph is simpler, we propose an alternative *Function view*, which gives more detail on the causal-effect of self-time. The visualization was generated on the basis of a Cube measurement report [27] of the execution of the Sweep3D benchmark [28] on 294,912 processes of the IBM Blue Gene/P supercomputer JUGENE [25], formerly operated by Forschungszentrum Jülich GmbH, Germany.

Figure 9 represents a function as a circle. The size of the circle represents the self/exclusive execution time. Edges represent calls between functions. In this scenario, the control flow goes from the left to the right of the figure. Functions with a significant amount of exclusive time (*i.e.*, large circle) have their names

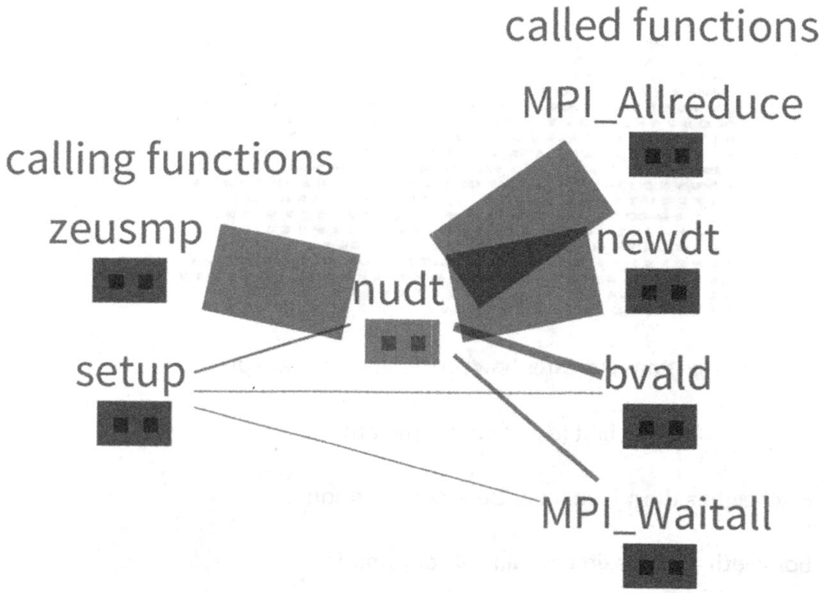

Fig. 6. Function view

on it. Less significant functions have no name in the visualization (however the name remains visible via tooltips).

Each large function has an arc around it. Each portion of this arc represents the share of that function's execution for a given calling function. The share is indicated with the size and the color of the arc. In Fig. 9, each individual call to a function is drawn separately. However, the calls can be bundled in order to reduce clutter. While, for instance, grouping only the calls that contribute an average share of execution time – i.e., those that behave similarly – the outliers will remain visible and call for attention.

This *Function view* is more detailed than the previous one (Fig. 5). However, its applicability if the data contains cycles or large number of nodes still needs to be evaluated on more data.

5.4 Data and Visualization Challenges

The typical visual analytics challenges, for instance described by Keim et al. [29, 30], apply as well to the analysis of CCTs. This section revises these challenges with respect to our framework.

Scalability. The **issue of scale** has more than one aspect. First, CCTs themselves can become very large if we analyze complex applications such as parallel simulation software (e.g., SPH [31,32]). Such large trees, with potentially hundreds of thousands of nodes, require a sensible pre-processing step prior to visualization to prevent visual overload. Second, many issues we want to address

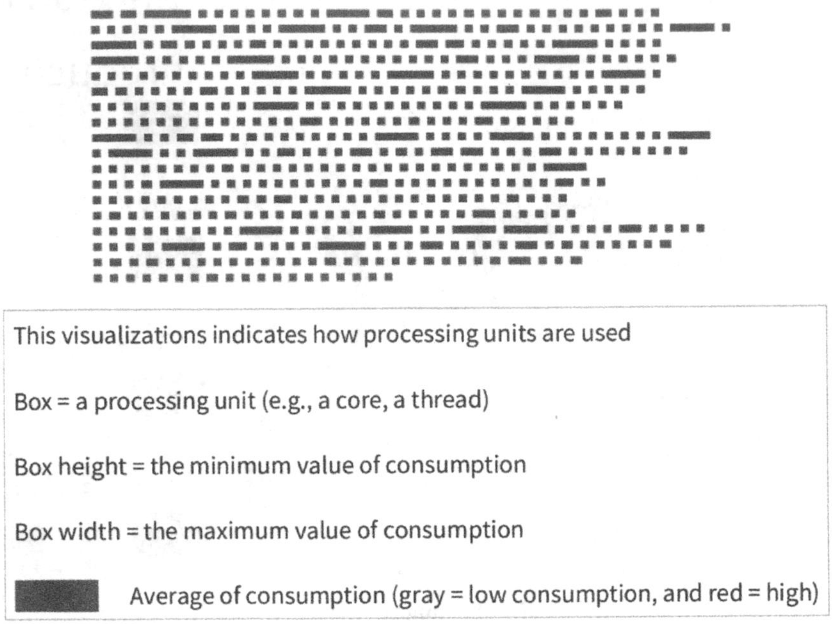

This visualizations indicates how processing units are used
Box = a processing unit (e.g., a core, a thread)
Box height = the minimum value of consumption
Box width = the maximum value of consumption
Average of consumption (gray = low consumption, and red = high)

Fig. 7. Process view

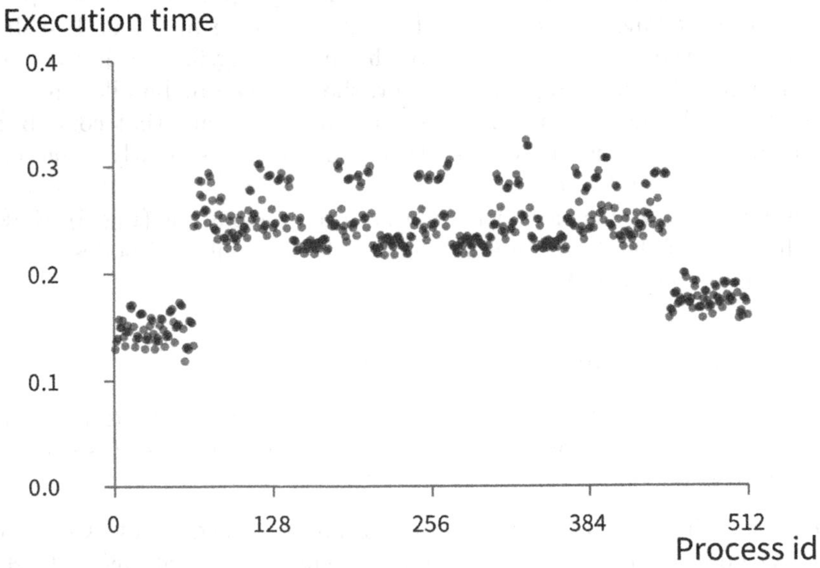

Fig. 8. Metric view

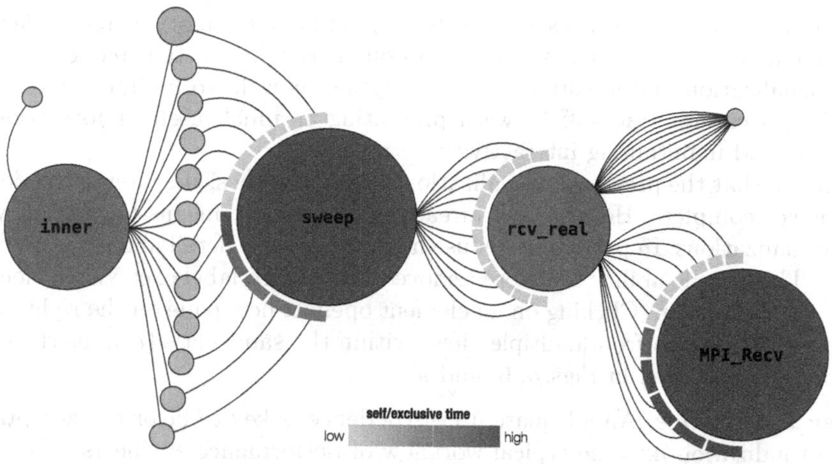

Fig. 9. Second example of the function view: calls are depicted as a directed acyclic graph with calling-direction from left to right. Currently, each call is depicted separately. However, these can be bundled according to some user-defined statistics, with only the outliers still being drawn individually.

require the comparison of CCTs across processes, timesteps, application runs, or input decks, which may involve a large number of trees. Moreover, there is no guarantee that CCTs of different processes, timesteps, or application runs are identical, even for identical inputs. Thus, the trees have to be matched, requiring heuristics or user interaction to deal with structural differences in the trees.

The first aspect remains open, as we assume the CCTs to be readily available for the described prototype for the sake of conciseness of its presentation. To address the second aspect, our framework promotes the uses of relatively simple visualizations for which practitioners can easily jump from one to another.

The flow supported by our framework is based on the "Visual Information Seeking Mantra" formalized by Shneiderman [33]. It consists of supporting a sequential flow of actions: first getting an overview and then zooming and filtering with details on demand. This mantra is a recognized way to design advanced graphical user interfaces.

Indeed, the user can start exploring the visualization from the *CCT view* and drill down into the overall execution information by moving into other views.

The visualization uses visual cues and some elementary interaction to cope with the exploitation of large visualizations. In particular, nodes are translucent to avoid occlusion in presence of overlapping, nodes can be drag-and-dropped, outgoing nodes are highlighted when locating the mouse on a particular nodes, and the view can be zoomed-in and out.

Interaction. The second challenge is to provide **suitable interaction possibilities** to the user, as user feedback is an integral part of each step in the visual analytics model. For the analysis of a CCT, a visualization has to support the user in typical analysis tasks, such as finding outliers, comparing trees, selection and comparison of sub-trees, etc. A thorough user interaction model requires the visualization and ideally the data analytics, as well, to be interactive. This involves a careful trade-off between presenting as much useful information as possible and maintaining interactivity.

Given that the presented visualizations are prototypes, the interaction design is not yet complete. However, we already provide some means to interact with the visualizations. In particular, mouse hovering reveals detail about a particular node. This simple ability therefore removes the need to label each visual element in our visualization. Clicking on an element opens a new pane on the right. Tabs are useful to switch from multiple views within the same class (*e.g.*, as the three function views given in Figs. 5, 6, and 9).

User Experience. An adequate user experience is key to favor the acceptance of a visualization into the typical workflow of performance engineers.

Currently, our prototype is not empirically validated. We did run pilots on a number of benchmarks, both available from the public domain such as Zeus, and proprietary ones. These pilots were crucial to improve the overall experience of the visualizations. As a future work, we plan to carry out empirical evaluation of the framework. In particular, controlled experiments and case studies are two experimental designs that seems adequate to evaluate the experience and performance of performance engineers.

Semantics. Finally, deriving **semantics** and augmenting a visualization with that information to support the user is a challenge, as well. We have to rely on knowledge from performance engineering to find suitable metrics to facilitate automated derivation of semantics from the performance data of simulation runs. A visualization can provide several means to display semantic information. We can utilize color, area, or size, but also additional visualizations that are interactively linked to a CCT.

Our framework is able to integrate new visualizations and customization of existing visualizations. The framework is implemented in Roassal [34], an agile framework to build visualizations.

6 Conclusion

In this paper, we provide an overview of performance data available in HPC, as well as the challenges encountered in their visualization. Particularly, we focus on visualization of CCTs, which are used in performance analysis of parallel codes. Since traditional tree representation is not suitable for large sets of data common in HPC, we propose a flow-based framework for visualizing the execution of parallel applications. The advantage of such an approach is that it connects several visualizations, and facilitates interaction by providing a navigation flow between them. At the time of writing this paper, our visualization framework is a prototype that requires an empirical evaluation. In particular, we envision the framework to enable expressing constructions to handle *scalability* and *interaction*.

Future work will focus on extending the framework with different visualization approaches and connecting them to source code, as well as allowing domain scientists to evaluate the framework. Since CCTs are used not only in HPC performance analysis, but also in software performance engineering [35], we plan to evaluate this framework in both settings. In addition, we plan to carefully evaluate the expressiveness of our approach by conducting empirical evaluations.

Acknowledgment. The ideas presented in this paper originated during the GI-Dagstuhl Seminar 18283, sponsored by the Gesellschaft für Informatik e.V. (GI), where all the authors on this paper were participants. The first author would like to thank LAM Research for its financial support.

This work was partially funded by the Deutsche Forschungsgemeinschaft (DFG) in context of SFB 716, project D.3, as well as the Priority Programme "DFG-SPP 1593: Design For Future—Managed Software Evolution" (HO 5721/1-1), and by the Excellence Initiative of the German federal and state governments. This work was performed under the auspices of the U.S. Department of Energy by Lawrence Livermore National Laboratory under Contract DE-AC52-07NA27344 (LLNL-CONF-756548).

References

1. Saviankou, P., Knobloch, M., Visser, A., Mohr, B.: Cube v4: from performance report explorer to performance analysis tool. Procedia Comput. Sci. **51**, 1343–1352 (2015)
2. Ammons, G., Ball, T., Larus, J.R.: Exploiting hardware performance counters with flow and context sensitive profiling. In: Proceedings of the ACM SIGPLAN 1997 Conference on Programming Language Design and Implementation, PLDI 1997, pp. 85–96 (1997)
3. Mey, D., et al.: Score-P: a unified performance measurement system for petascale applications. In: Bischof, C., Hegering, H.G., Nagel, W., Wittum, G. (eds.) Competence in High Performance Computing, pp. 85–97. Springer, Heidelberg (2011). https://doi.org/10.1007/978-3-642-24025-6_8
4. Schulz, M., Galarowicz, J., Hachfeld, W.: Open, speedshop: open source performance analysis for linux clusters. In: Proceedings of the 2006 ACM/IEEE Conference on Supercomputing, SC 2006. ACM, New York (2006)
5. Adhianto, L., et al.: HPCTOOLKIT: tools for performance analysis of optimized parallel programs. Concurr. Comput. Pract. Exp. **22**(6), 685–701 (2010)
6. Böhme, D., et al.: Caliper: performance introspection for HPC software stacks. In: West, J., Pancake, C.M. (eds.) Proceedings of the International Conference for High Performance Computing, Networking, Storage and Analysis, SC 2016, Salt Lake City, UT, USA, 13–18 November 2016, p. 47. ACM (2016)
7. Alcocer, J.-P.S., Bergel, A., Ducasse, S., Denker, M.: Performance evolution blueprint: understanding the impact of software evolution on performance. In: 2013 First IEEE Working Conference on Software Visualization (VISSOFT), pp. 1–9, September 2013
8. Blanco, A.F., Alcocer, J.-P.S., Bergel, A.: Effective visualization of object allocation sites. In: Proceedings of 6th IEEE Working Conference on Software Visualization, VISSOFT 2018 (2018)

9. Szebenyi, Z., Wylie, B.J.N., Wolf, F.: SCALASCA parallel performance analyses of SPEC MPI2007 applications. In: Kounev, S., Gorton, I., Sachs, K. (eds.) SIPEW 2008. LNCS, vol. 5119, pp. 99–123. Springer, Heidelberg (2008). https://doi.org/10.1007/978-3-540-69814-2_8
10. Adhianto, L., et al.: HPCTOOLKIT: tools for performance analysis of optimized parallel programs. Concurr. Comput. Pract. Exp. **22**(6), 685–701 (2010). http://hpctoolkit.org
11. Nguyen, H.T., et al.: VIPACT: a visualization interface for analyzing calling context trees. In: Proceedings of the 3rd Workshop on Visual Performance Analysis, VPA 2016, November 2016
12. Gralka, P., Schulz, C., Reina, G., Weiskopf, D., Ertl, T.: Visual exploration of memory traces and call stacks. In: 2017 IEEE Working Conference on Software Visualization (VISSOFT), pp. 54–63, September 2017
13. Gregg, B.: The flame graph. Commun. ACM **59**(6), 48–57 (2016)
14. Tallent, N.R., Mellor-Crummey, J., Franco, M., Landrum, R., Adhianto, L.: Scalable fine-grained call path tracing. In: Proceedings of the International Conference on Supercomputing, ICS 2011, pp. 63–74. ACM, New York (2011)
15. Nagel, W.E., Arnold, A., Weber, M., Hoppe, H.-C., Solchenbach, K.: VAMPIR: visualization and analysis of MPI resources. Supercomputer **12**, 69–80 (1996)
16. Kruskal, J.B., Landwehr, J.M.: Icicle Plots: better displays for hierarchical clustering. Am. Stat. **37**(2), 162–168 (1983)
17. Trümper, J., Telea, A., Döllner, J.: ViewFusion: correlating structure and activity views for execution traces. In: Proceedings Theory and Practice of Computer Graphics, pp. 45–52 (2012)
18. De Pauw, W., Jensen, E., Mitchell, N., Sevitsky, G., Vlissides, J., Yang, J.: Visualizing the execution of Java programs. In: Diehl, S. (ed.) Software Visualization. LNCS, vol. 2269, pp. 151–162. Springer, Heidelberg (2002). https://doi.org/10.1007/3-540-45875-1_12
19. De Pauw, W., Heisig, S.: Visual and algorithmic tooling for system trace analysis: a case study. ACM SIGOPS Oper. Syst. Rev. **44**(1), 97–102 (2010)
20. De Pauw, W., Heisig, S.: Zinsight: a visual and analytic environment for exploring large event traces. In: Proceedings of the 5th International Symposium on Software Visualization, SOFTVIS, pp. 143–152. ACM, New York (2010)
21. Adamoli, A., Hauswirth M.: Trevis: a context tree visualization & analysis framework and its use for classifying performance failure reports. In: Proceedings of the 5th International Symposium on Software Visualization, SOFTVIS, pp. 73–82. ACM, New York (2010)
22. Moret, P., Binder, W., Villazón, A., Ansaloni, D., Heydarnoori, A.: Visualizing and exploring profiles with calling context ring charts. Softw. Pract. Exp. **40**(9), 825–847 (2010)
23. Böhme, D., Geimer, M., Wolf, F., Arnold, L.: Scalasca analysis report for SPEC MPI.2007 benchmark 132.zeump2 on 512 processes in virtual- node mode on Blue Gene/P, April 2018. https://doi.org/10.5281/zenodo.1211448
24. Müller, M.S., et al.: SPEC MPI2007-an application benchmark suite for parallel systems using MPI. Concurr. Comput. Pract. Exp. **22**(2), 191–205 (2010)
25. Attig, N., et al.: Blue Gene/P: JUGENE. Computational Science Series, pp. 153–188. CRC Press, Taylor & Francis Group, Boca Raton (2013)
26. Lanza, M., Ducasse, S.: Polymetric views–a lightweight visual approach to reverse engineering. Trans. Softw. Eng. (TSE) **29**(9), 782–795 (2003)

27. Wylie, B.J.N., Geimer, M., Mohr, B., Böhme, D., Szebenyi, Z., Wolf, F.: Scalasca analysis report of the ASCI Sweep3D benchmark on 294,912 processes in virtual-node mode on IBM Blue Gene/P with manually annotated iterations, August 2018
28. Los Alamos National Laboratory: ASCI SWEEP3D v2.2b: 3-dimensional discrete ordinates neutron transport benchmark (1995). http://wwwc3.lanl.gov/pal/software/sweep3d/
29. Keim, D.A., Mansmann, F., Schneidewind, J., Thomas, J., Ziegler, H.: Visual analytics: scope and challenges. In: Simoff, S.J., Böhlen, M.H., Mazeika, A. (eds.) Visual Data Mining. LNCS, vol. 4404, pp. 76–90. Springer, Heidelberg (2008). https://doi.org/10.1007/978-3-540-71080-6_6
30. Keim, D., Andrienko, G., Fekete, J.-D., Görg, C., Kohlhammer, J., Melançon, G.: Visual analytics: definition, process, and challenges. In: Kerren, A., Stasko, J.T., Fekete, J.-D., North, C. (eds.) Information Visualization. LNCS, vol. 4950, pp. 154–175. Springer, Heidelberg (2008). https://doi.org/10.1007/978-3-540-70956-5_7
31. Crespo, A.J.C., Rogers, B., Dominguez, J.M., Gomez-Gesteira, M.: Simulating more than 1 billion SPH particles using GPU hardware acceleration, pp. 249–254 (2013)
32. Griffin, K., Raskin, C.: Scalable rendering of large SPH simulations using an RK-enhanced interpolation scheme on constrained datasets. In: 2016 IEEE 6th Symposium on Large Data Analysis and Visualization (LDAV), pp. 95–96. IEEE (2016)
33. Shneiderman, B.: The eyes have it: a task by data type taxonomy for information visualizations. In: IEEE Visual Languages, College Park, Maryland, USA, pp. 336–343 (1996)
34. Bergel, A.: Agile Visualization. LULU Press, Morrisville (2016)
35. Woodside, M., Franks, G., Petriu, D.C.: The future of software performance engineering. In: Future of Software Engineering, FOSE 2007, pp. 171–187 (2007)

PaScal Viewer: A Tool for the Visualization of Parallel Scalability Trends

Anderson B. N. da Silva[1(✉)], Daniel A. M. Cunha[2], Vitor R. G. Silva[2], Alex F. de A. Furtunato[3], and Samuel Xavier-de-Souza[2]

[1] Pró-Reitoria de Pesquisa, Inovação e Pós-Graduação, IFPB, Joao Pessoa, Brazil
anderson.silva@ifpb.edu.br

[2] Dept. de Eng. de Comp. e Automação, UFRN, Natal, Brazil

[3] Diretoria de Tecnologia da Informação, IFRN, Natal, Brazil

Abstract. Taking advantage of the growing number of cores in supercomputers to increase the scalability of parallel programs is an increasing challenge. Many advanced profiling tools have been developed to assist programmers in the process of analyzing data related to the execution of their program. Programmers can act upon the information generated by these data and make their programs reach higher performance levels. However, the information provided by profiling tools is generally designed to optimize the program for a specific execution environment, with a target number of cores and a target problem size. A code optimization driven towards scalability rather than specific performance requires the analysis of many distinct execution environments instead of details about a single environment. With the goal of providing more useful information for the analysis and optimization of code for parallel scalability, this work introduces the PaScal Viewer tool. It presents an novel and productive way to visualize scalability trends of parallel programs. It consists of four diagrams that offers visual support to identify parallel efficiency trends of the whole program, or parts of it, when running on scaling parallel environments with scaling problem sizes.

Keywords: Parallel programming · Efficiency · Scalability · Performance optimization · Visualization tool

1 Introduction

The number of cores in supercomputers continues to grow. Taking advantage of this to increase the performance of parallel programs is a continuous challenge. Developers must understand how their program behaves when more cores are used to process data, when more data need to be processed, or both—when data need to be processed by more cores.

This research was supported by High Performance Computing Center at UFRN (NPAD/UFRN).

A. Bhatele et al. (Eds.): ESPT/VPA 2017/2018, LNCS 11027, pp. 250–264, 2019.
https://doi.org/10.1007/978-3-030-17872-7_15

Many techniques and profiling tools have been developed to assist programmers in the process of collecting and analyzing data related to the execution of their program [10]. These tools provide a large amount of information, measurements, details, and characteristics of the program. All of this information is usually related to one single execution of the program in a particular environment. The configuration of this environment includes the number of cores, their operating frequency, and the size of the input data or the problem size. Among the various collected information, the elapsed time in each function of the code, the number of function calls, and the memory consumption of the program can be cited to name just a few [7]. It is possible to measure the parallel efficiency of the program in the analyzed environment. However, this value would probably change if the same program is executed in different environments. For this reason, from the information collected from a single run alone, it is not possible to evaluate how the efficiency will evolve when the program is executed with a different number of cores or with a different problem size. To discover the efficiency trends, developers need to perform the same analysis in many different environments. Then, they can compare the data manually and say if and when the algorithm tends to be scalable.

The information provided by these profiling tools is very useful to optimize the program execution for a single environment, with a target number of cores and a target problem size. However, when the goal is to analyze and optimize the code for parallel scalability, developers need to focus their attention on the variation of efficiency values when the program runs in many distinct execution configurations. In this case, it is more relevant to know fewer details about many executions than many more details about a single execution. In addition, current profiling tools use different techniques for collecting and analyzing data and, in some cases, they are developed for specific architectures and/or different parallelization models. These tools present the information collected in large data tables or complex graphs, and because of that, demand a "good" knowledge of their visualization interfaces [13]. Some approaches, such as [6], present the efficiency values for different environments in a single line chart. From such chart, developers could infer the program scalability trends, but this task is not always simple for a large number of environment configurations are depicted. Weak scalability trend are also difficult to infer from these line charts.

SPERF is a simple tool that can automatically instrument parallel code with the insertion of time measurement [8]. From these measurements, developers can assess the execution time of each parallel region or regions of interest. With these specific time measurements, developers can verify the efficiency of the whole program or part of it. They can check, for example, if the scalability of the program as a whole deteriorates because of a specific region. In this way, they can focus in code regions that breaks scalability, much in the same way they do for optimizing single-run performance bottlenecks using traditional tools. This work uses the output of SPERF to construct visualization diagrams that unveils scalability trends. However, since the output of SPERF is a formatted text file, it can also be generated by another tool or by a productivity script.

This paper presents a visualization tool for the scalability analysis of parallel programs. For this, the tool takes as input the execution time measurements of a program in different configuration environments as provided by SPERF, translates these values into the corresponding efficiency values, and presents, through simple diagrams, the efficiency trends of this program. The objective of the tool is to avoid a tedious manual comparison of efficiency values. The tool is independent of architecture, parallelization model or profiling tool. It displays four color diagrams related to each analyzed region. One diagram holds the efficiency values and the other three show the variation of these values: when the number of cores is fixed; when the problem size is fixed; and when the number of cores and the problem size change proportionally at given rates. This tool can assist developers during the scalability analysis of their parallel programs in a simple and productive way. It helps on the identification of hot spots that when refactored could optimize the program scalability.

The remainder of this work is organized as follows Sect. 2 describes the tool and its color diagrams. The results of a simple case study are presented in Sect. 3. Section 4 presents the related work. And finally the contribution is summarized in Sect. 5 with an outlook of future works.

2 The PaScal Viewer

This work presents a tool that introduces a novel and productive way to view the scalability trends of a parallel program, named Parallel Scalability Viewer or simply PaScal Viewer. For this, the tool translates the efficiency values collected from program executions into four color diagrams. These diagrams offer support to identify efficiency variation when the program runs on parallel environments and when it processes different amounts of data. In this sense, the tool aids developers in the identification of parallel scalability, including the analysis of whether this scalability is weak or strong, for the whole program or parts of it.

The tool is presented as a web-based application implemented in the Python programming language and the Django framework [4]. The color diagrams are drawn using Bokeh, an interactive visualization library [11].

2.1 The Color Diagrams

The proposed color diagrams simplify the understanding and the visualization of the scalability trends from a parallel program. Figure 1 presents the four diagrams generated from execution data collected from a theoretical program with the following characteristics:

- The serial execution time is given by $T_{\text{Serial}} = n^2$;
- The parallel execution time is given by $T_{\text{Parallel}} = n^2/p + log2(p)$;
- p corresponds to the number of cores and n corresponds to the problem size;

Each diagram is presented as a graphic of two axes. The horizontal axis corresponds to the number of cores and the vertical axis corresponds to the

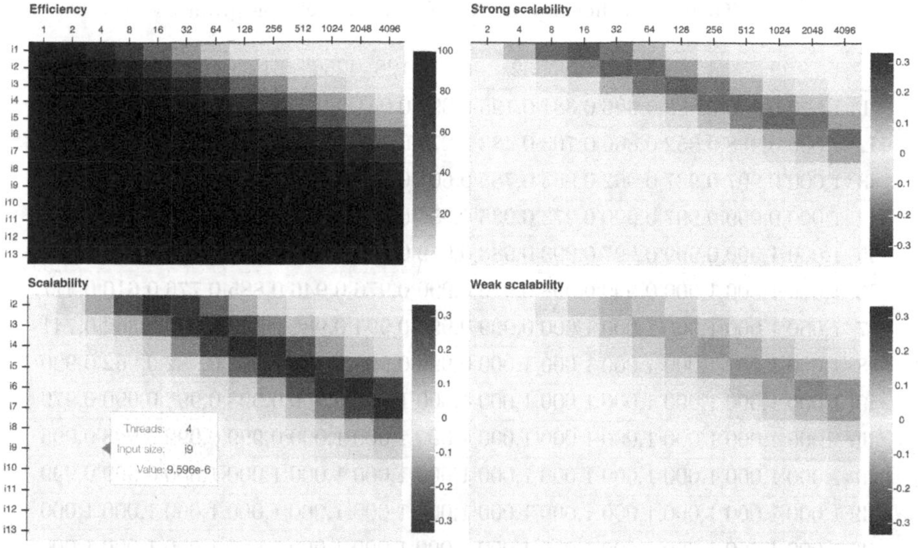

Fig. 1. Scalability diagrams of a theoretical program. The number of cores varies according to 1, 2, 4, 8, 16, 32, 64, 128, 256, 512, 1024, 2048 and 4096. The problem size, i1 to i13, varies according to 10, 20, 40, 80, 160, 320, 640, 1280, 2560, 5120, 10240, 20480 and 40960. (Color figure online)

problem size. Both are organized in same order presented in the input file. The numerical values of each diagram element can be visualized in a tooltip, as shown in Fig. 1.

The diagram located on the upper left corner of Fig. 1 presents the parallel efficiency values. Each element of the diagram, represented by a color, corresponds to a particular execution scenario, with a specific number of cores and problem size. The numerical values depicted in this first diagram are showed at Table 1 and Fig. 2. These values serve as base for constructing the other three diagrams and provide a general view of the program behavior.

The other three diagrams present the results of the difference between the efficiency values represented in the first diagram for each two bordering execution scenarios. The colors in these diagrams change according to two distinct ranges. One range for the positive values and another for the negative ones. In the case of Fig. 1, the color range for the positive values varies from white to green (from #FFFFFF to #004337, in RGB) and for the negative values varies from white to brown (from #FFFFFF to #5D3506, in RGB).

The diagram located on the bottom left corner allows the scalability analysis of the program when the number of cores is fixed and the problem size increases. From it, developers can observe the general scalability trends of a program with relation to the increase of problem size. In this diagram, each element corresponds to the difference between efficiency values of two bordering configurations that use the same number of cores but with higher problem size. The

Table 1. Efficiency values of a theoretical program.

	1	2	4	8	16	32	64	128	256	512	1024	2048	4096
i1	1,000	0,956	0,838	0,626	0,381	0,195	0,091	0,041	0,018	0,008	0,004	0,002	0,001
i2	1,000	0,988	0,952	0,866	0,703	0,483	0,278	0,141	0,066	0,031	0,014	0,006	0,003
i3	1,000	0,997	0,987	0,962	0,903	0,785	0,601	0,390	0,218	0,110	0,052	0,024	0,011
i4	1,000	0,999	0,997	0,990	0,973	0,935	0,856	0,717	0,524	0,327	0,179	0,090	0,043
i5	1,000	1,000	0,999	0,997	0,993	0,983	0,959	0,910	0,814	0,659	0,464	0,282	0,152
i6	1,000	1,000	1,000	0,999	0,998	0,996	0,990	0,976	0,946	0,885	0,776	0,610	0,417
i7	1,000	1,000	1,000	1,000	1,000	0,999	0,997	0,994	0,986	0,969	0,933	0,862	0,741
i8	1,000	1,000	1,000	1,000	1,000	1,000	0,999	0,998	0,996	0,992	0,982	0,962	0,920
i9	1,000	1,000	1,000	1,000	1,000	1,000	1,000	1,000	0,999	0,998	0,995	0,990	0,979
i10	1,000	1,000	1,000	1,000	1,000	1,000	1,000	1,000	1,000	0,999	0,999	0,998	0,995
i11	1,000	1,000	1,000	1,000	1,000	1,000	1,000	1,000	1,000	1,000	1,000	0,999	0,999
i12	1,000	1,000	1,000	1,000	1,000	1,000	1,000	1,000	1,000	1,000	1,000	1,000	1,000
i13	1,000	1,000	1,000	1,000	1,000	1,000	1,000	1,000	1,000	1,000	1,000	1,000	1,000

values of each cell is given by

$$f(x, y+1) - f(x, y), \quad (1)$$

where x represents the number of cores and y represents the problem size, both, presented in the efficiency diagram.

The diagram located on the upper right corner allows the scalability analysis of the program when the problem size is fixed and the number of cores increases. From this diagram, developers can observe the strong scalability trends of a program. The elements of this diagram show the difference between the efficiency values of two bordering configurations that use the same problem size. In this case, the values are given by

$$f(x+1, y) - f(x, y). \quad (2)$$

The diagram located on the bottom right corner allows the observation of weak scalability trends. The weak scalability trends can be identified in this diagram if the efficiency values increase or remain constant when the number of cores and the problem size used in executions scenarios increases with the same rate. In this case, the elements correspond the difference between the efficiency values of two bordering configurations in relation to the configuration that uses the higher number of cores and the higher problem size. These values are given by

$$f(x+1, y+1) - f(x, y). \quad (3)$$

These diagrams allow the visualization of the scalability trends of a program in a more dynamic and productive way because it is simpler and easier to focus the attention on a color variation than in the analysis of data presented in tables or line charts, as in Table 1 or Fig. 2. The PaScal Viewer presents the file name and the number of code lines that originated each diagrams set.

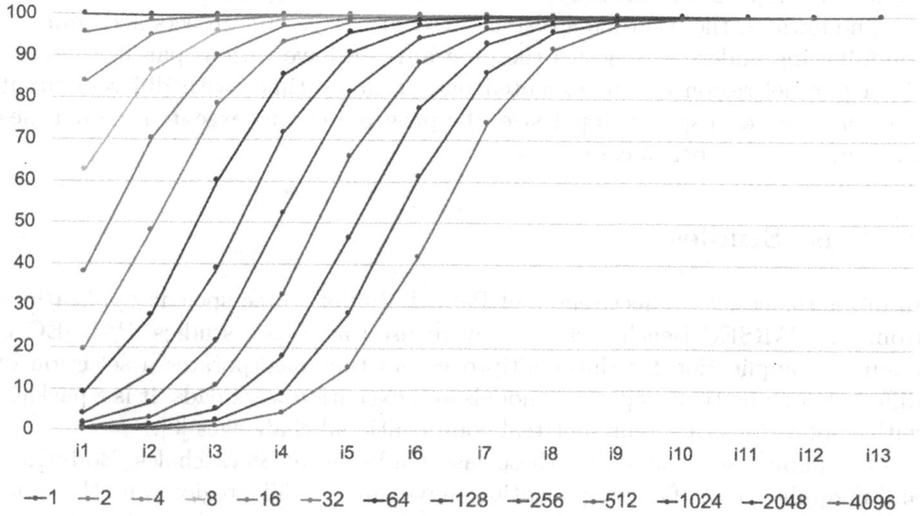

Fig. 2. Line chart with efficiency values in % of a theoretical program.

From the diagrams of Fig. 1, one can infer that: (a) to any number of cores, when the problem size increases the efficiency values increase too, therefore, the program can be considered generally scalable; (b) there is a limit to each problem size at which the increase of number of cores means efficiency improvement; increasing cores above this limit holds efficiency values constant; (c) increasing the number of cores with any constant problem size decreases the efficiency values, therefore, the program is not strongly scalable; and (d) there is no efficiency drop when the number of cores and the problem size increases at the same rate; therefore the program is weakly scalable.

2.2 Input File Format

The four diagrams of PaScal Viewer are drawn from execution time measurements of a program. The tool does not measure the execution times. It reads them from an input file, translates them into efficiency values and then draw the diagrams.

The input file can be generated directly by a profiling tool, such as SPERF. SPERF is a simple profiling tool that allows the instrumentation of C/C++ programs and that exports the analysis data to .json, .xml and .csv file formats [8]. The input file can also be generated manually, or from another comfortable tool or script. It is a simple text file that contains data from all parts of the program, as shown in Fig. 3 for the .json format. The data consists of the identification of each part analyzed, the number of cores, the problem size and the execution times of all execution scenarios. The data structure allows the inclusion of time measurements to various executions. The PaScal Viewer uses the median of these values to compute the efficiency translated into the diagrams.

The data on the .json file are structured in arrays and objects according to the following understanding: (a) the program can have various parallel regions; (b) a parallel region can be executed one or many times with different input sizes; and (c) for a specific input size, the program can be executed many times with different number of cores.

3 Case Studies

In order to show the effectiveness of PaScal Viewer, three specific applications from the PARSEC Benchmark Suite were used as a case studies. PARSEC is a suite of application for chip-multiprocessors that incorporates a selection of different combinations of parallel models and execution workloads. It is a package with applications that represent real computational challenges [3].

The applications chosen for these case studies were Blackscholes, Bodytrack and Freqmine. Two of these applications have inner parallel regions and therefore allow the analysis of the effect of their scalability on the efficiency trends of whole application. Freqmine is the one that has no inner regions. The applications were executed in a 32-core shared memory machine with 1, 2, 4, 8, 16 and 32 cores and with 10 distinct problem sizes: i1, i2, i3, i4, i5, i6, i7, i8, i9 and i10. The i2 problem size is twice as large as the i1 problem size; the i3 problem size is twice the as large as i2 problem size, and so on. The SPERF tool was used to collect the execution time measurements and to generate the .json input file for the PaScal Viewer.

3.1 The Blackscholes Application

Blascksholes is an application from the financial domain analysis that solves a partial differential equation to calculate the prices of a given number of financial options. This application has just one inner parallel region.

The diagrams of Fig. 4 refer to the whole program and the diagrams of Fig. 5 describe the behavior of the inner parallel part. From the diagrams of Fig. 4, one can infer that: (a) for any number of cores, the program presents better efficiency values for smaller problem sizes, and almost does not scale when the problem size increases; (b) the program is not strong scalable in any scenario; and (c) the program is not weakly scalable in any scenario.

```
[
    {
        "region":"<initial_line>, <final_line>",
        "filename":"<file_name>",
        "executions":[
            [
                {
                    "argument":"<id_of_problem_size>",
                    "runs":[
                        {"threads":1,"time":100},
                        {"threads":2,"time":51},
                        {...}
                    ]
                },
                {
                    "argument":"<id_of_problem_size>",
                    "runs":[
                        {"threads":1,"time":100},
                        {"threads":2,"time":51},
                        {...}
                    ]
                },
                {...}
            ]
        ]
    },
    {
        "region":"<initial_line>, <final_line>",
        "filename":"<file_name>",
        "executions":[...]
    }
]
```

Fig. 3. The structure of the PaScal Viewer input file.

The diagrams of Fig. 5 allow the following interpretation: (a) the region presents better efficiency values for higher number of cores; (b) the region is scalable because it does not present efficiency drop for increasing problem sizes; (c) the increase in the number of cores does not improve the efficiency of the region, so it is not strongly scalable; and (d) the region does not present weak scalability considering that increasing the number of cores and problem size proportionally does not improve the efficiency of the region.

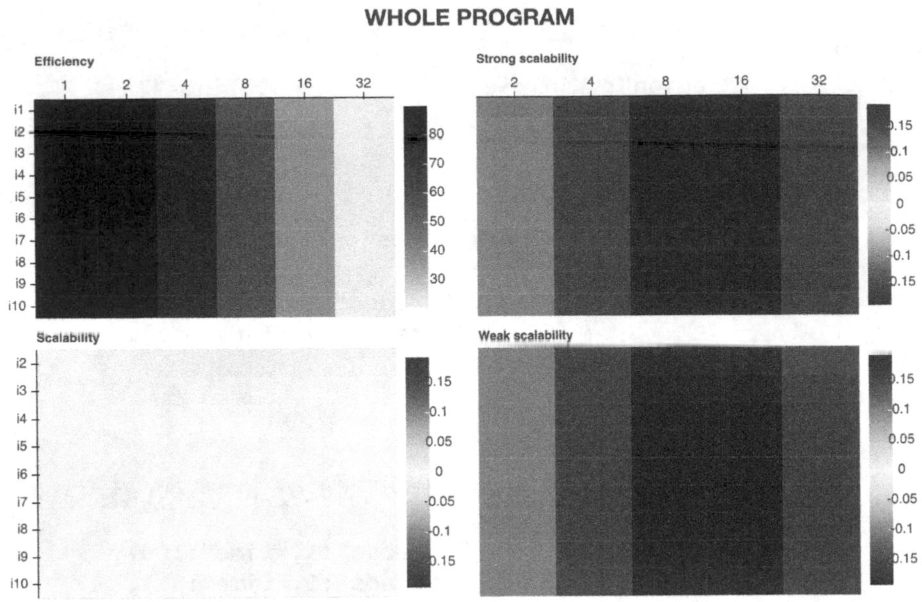

Fig. 4. Scalability diagrams for the whole Blackscholes application.

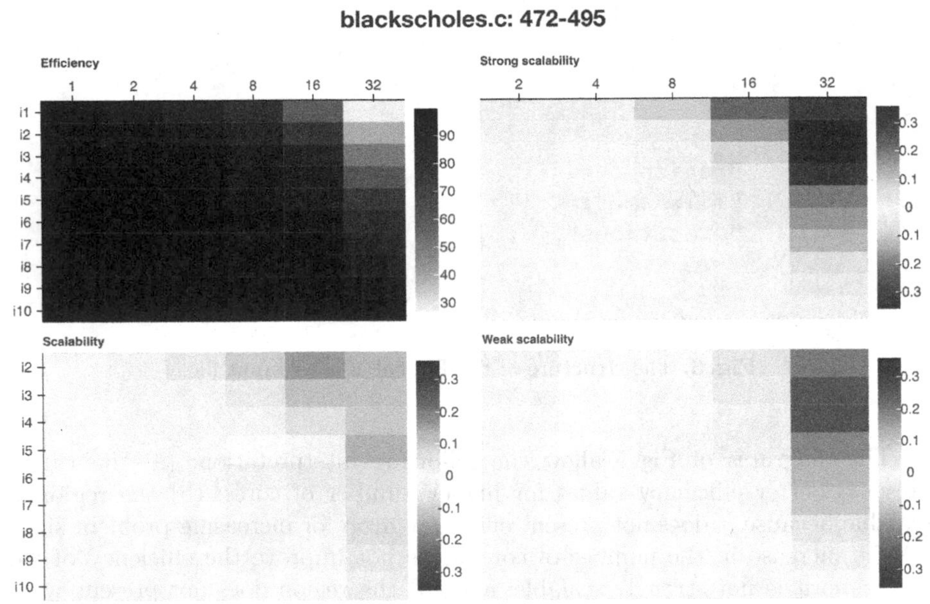

Fig. 5. Scalability diagrams for the inner parallel region of the Blackscholes application.

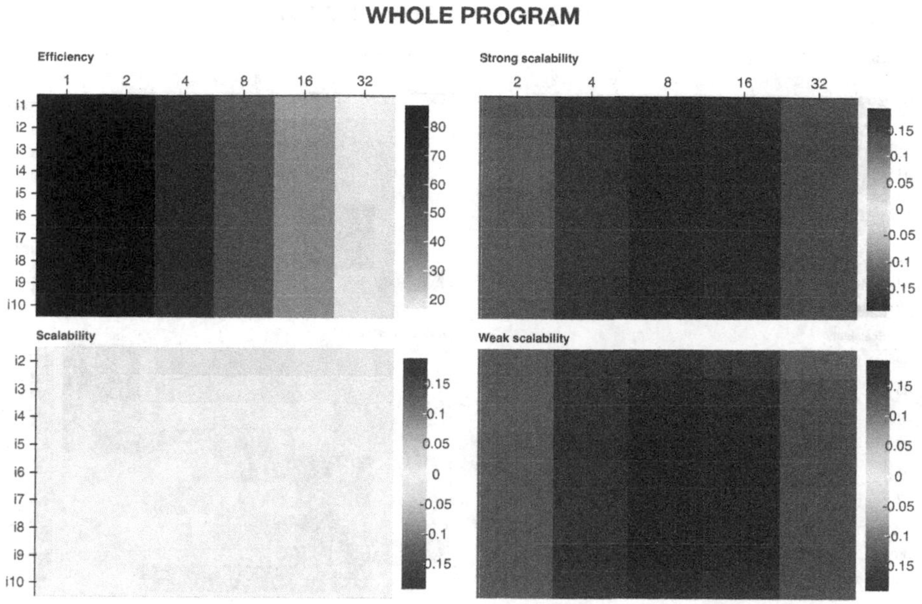

Fig. 6. Scalability diagrams for the whole Bodytrack application.

3.2 The Bodytrack Application

Bodytrack is an application of computer vision that tracks a human body from the analysis of an image sequence [3]. This application has three inner parallel regions.

The diagrams of Fig. 6 refers to the whole program. The diagrams of Figs. 7, 8 and 9 describe the behavior of three inner parallel regions of the program. From the diagrams of Fig. 6, one can realize a similar behavior to Blackscholes where: (a) the program presents better efficiency values for smaller problem sizes; (b) the program is not strong scalable; and (c) the program is not weakly scalable. Although the two programs present resembling scalability trends, one can identify that the Bodytrack scale less than Blackscholes as the problem size increases.

The diagrams of Figs. 7 and 8 demonstrate similar scalability trends for the two analyzed regions. The analysis of these diagrams allow the following interpretation: (a) for any number of cores, there is efficiency drop when the input size increases, with exception of i10 input size; (b) the regions are scalable for just the i10 input size; (c) the increases in the number of cores worsen the efficiency of the regions, so they are not strongly scalable; and (d) the regions do not present weak scalability. From the number of cores and input sizes presented in this case study, one can not infer if for input sizes greater than i10 the scalability indexes will continue to increase.

The diagrams of Fig. 9 allows the following interpretation: (a) for any number of cores, there is no clear improvement on the scalability trends; (b) the region is

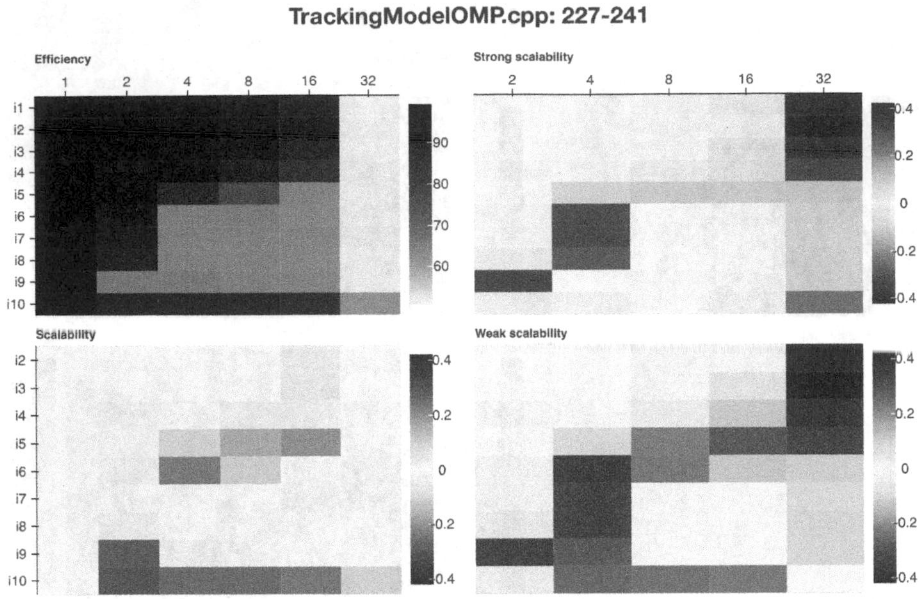

Fig. 7. Scalability diagrams for the first inner parallel region of the Bodytrack application.

not scalable because, in many cases, it presents efficiency drop when the problem sizes increases; (c) it is not strongly scalable; and (d) the region does not present weak scalability.

From the inner regions diagrams, one can infer that the efficiency drop of Bodytrack application to larger input sizes is related to the scalability of their inner parallel regions. In this case, the scalability of the whole program deteriorate influenced by its inner parts.

3.3 The Freqmine Application

Freqmine is an application that identifies patterns in a transaction database through data mining techniques. It is an array-based version of the frequent pattern-growth method for frequent itemset mining.

The diagrams of Fig. 10 refer to the analysis of whole program and allow the following interpretation: (a) the Freqmine program presents a continuously improving efficiency trend with better values for larger number of cores and input sizes; (b) it is scalable because it does not present efficiency drop for any increasing problem size; (c) the increase in the number of cores does not improve the efficiency of the program, so it is not strongly scalable, however, for smaller input sizes, as larger the number of cores the less is the loss of efficiency; and (d) it tends to present weak scalability for larger problem numbers of cores and problem sizes although weak scalability could only be seen for input size around the i8.

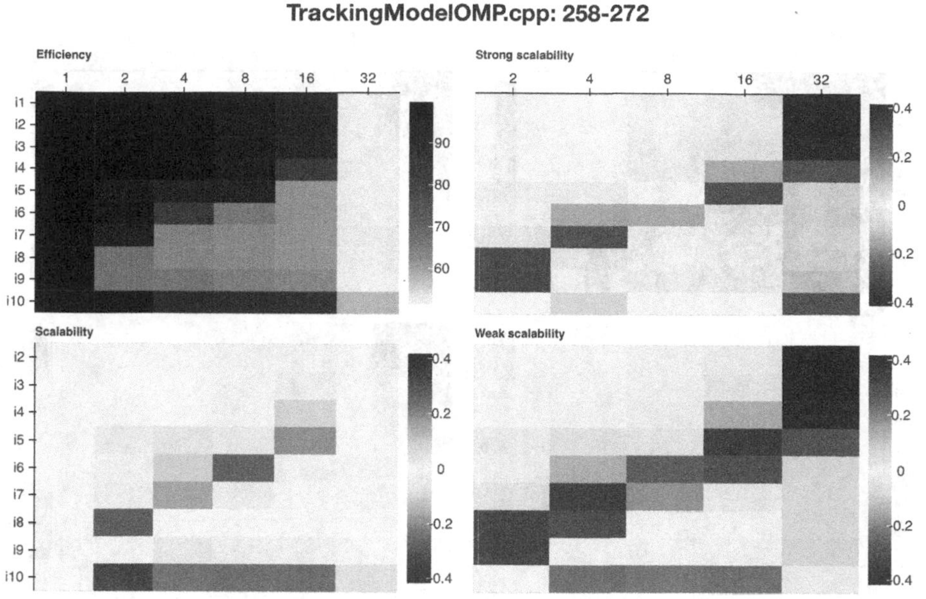

Fig. 8. Scalability diagrams for the second inner parallel region of the Bodytrack application.

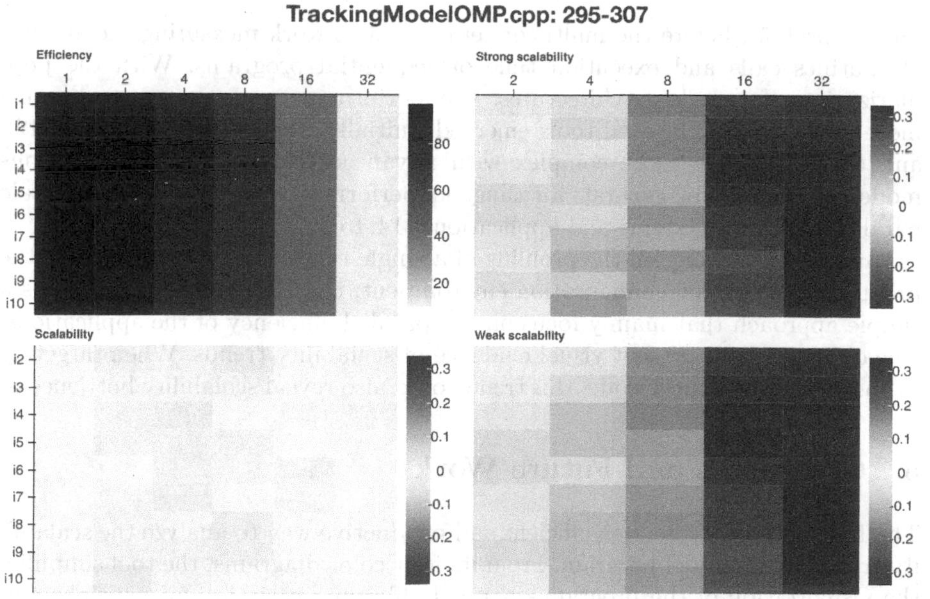

Fig. 9. Scalability diagrams for the third inner parallel region of the Bodytrack application.

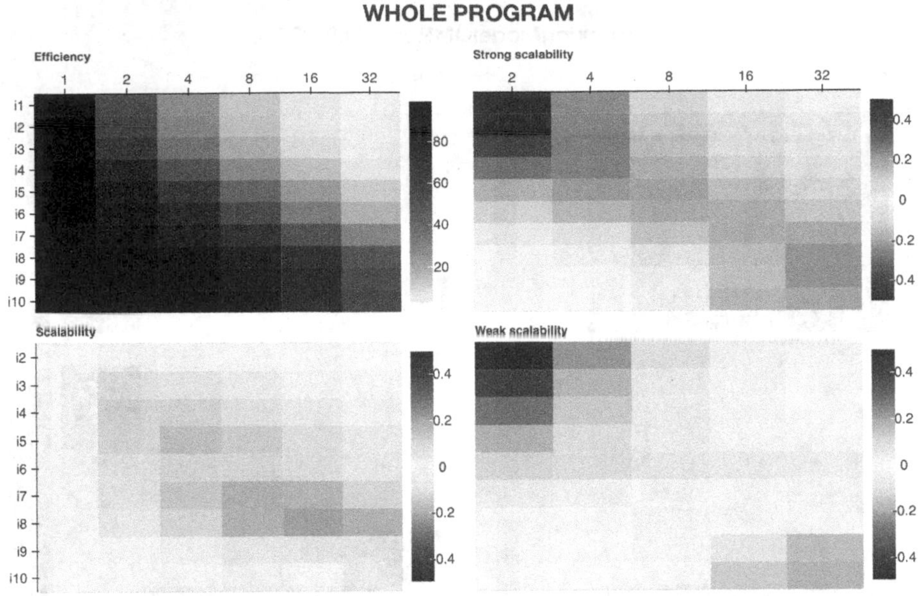

Fig. 10. Scalability diagrams for the whole Freqmine application.

4 Related Works

Since Gprof [5], before the multi-core era, profilers work measuring the amount of routines calls and execution time of sequential programs. With the popularization of parallel architectures, the performance measurements became more sophisticated. Several tools emerged, initially with basic resources [9,12], and then becoming more complex with advanced features and visualizations modes [1,2], and, in general, focusing on performance metrics for large-scale parallel computer systems and applications [14,15].

Instead of focusing on the profiling of a single run for the optimization of the program in a specific configuration environment, the PaScal Viewer proposes a simple approach that mainly focus on the parallel efficiency of the applications. The objective is to present visual evidence of scalability trends. When targeting to specific regions of the code, this trend could also reveal scalability bottlenecks.

5 Conclusion and Future Works

The PaScal Viewer offers an efficient and productive way to analyze the scalability trends of a parallel program. From its four color diagrams, the tool simplifies the visualization of the program's parallel efficiency variation for multiple runs with various distinct configuration scenarios. It allows the identification of low scalability hot spots. That way, developers can focus their attention in these hot spots to optimize the program scalability.

As future work, the proposed tool will bring an interface that presents the diagrams of inner parts of a program hierarchically. This hierarchical view can help to identify more clearly how low scalability hot spots can impact the scalability of the whole program. Additionally, support to analyzing the scalability trends of finer parallel constructs like loops are also being investigated.

References

1. Adhianto, L., et al.: HPCTOOLKIT: tools for performance analysis of optimized parallel programs. Concurr. Comput. Pract. Exp. **22**(6), 685–701 (2010). https://doi.org/10.1002/cpe
2. Bell, R., Malony, A.D., Shende, S.: *ParaProf*: a portable, extensible, and scalable tool for parallel performance profile analysis. In: Kosch, H., Böszörményi, L., Hellwagner, H. (eds.) Euro-Par 2003. LNCS, vol. 2790, pp. 17–26. Springer, Heidelberg (2003). https://doi.org/10.1007/978-3-540-45209-6_7
3. Bienia, C., Kumar, S., Singh, J.P., Li, K.: The PARSEC benchmark suite: characterization and architectural implications. In: Proceedings of the International Conference on Parallel Architectures and Compilation Techniques, pp. 72–81 (2008). https://doi.org/10.1145/1454115.1454128
4. Django-Software-Foundation: Django web framework (2005). https://www.djangoproject.com
5. Graham, S.L., Kessler, P.B., McKusick, M.K.: Gprof: a call graph execution profiler. In: Proceedings of the 1982 SIGPLAN Symposium on Compiler Construction, SIGPLAN 1982, pp. 120–126. ACM, Boston (1982). https://doi.org/10.1145/800230.806987
6. Huck, K., Malony, A.D.: PerfExplorer: a performance data mining framework for large-scale parallel computing. In: ACM/IEEE SC 2005 Conference, SC 2005 (2005). https://doi.org/10.1109/SC.2005.55
7. Khamparia, A., Banu, J.S.: Program analysis with dynamic instrumentation Pin and performance tools. In: 2013 IEEE International Conference on Emerging Trends in Computing, Communication and Nanotechnology, ICE-CCN 2013, pp. 436–440 (2013). https://doi.org/10.1109/ICE-CCN.2013.6528538
8. LAPPS-UFRN: Sperf 2.0. https://gitlab.com/lappsufrn/Sperf2.0
9. Nagel, W.E., Arnold, A., Weber, M., Hoppe, H.C., Solchenbach, K.: VAMPIR: visualization and analysis of MPI resources. Supercomputer **63**(1), 69–80 (1996)
10. Nguyen, H.T., et al.: VIPACT: a visualization interface for analyzing calling context trees. In: Proceedings of VPA 2016: 3rd Workshop on Visual Performance Analysis - Held in Conjunction with SC 2016: The International Conference for High Performance Computing, Networking, Storage and Analysis, pp. 25–28 (2017). https://doi.org/10.1109/VPA.2016.9
11. NumFOCUS: Bokeh. https://bokehplots.com
12. Pillet, V., Labarta, J., Cortes, T., Girona, S.: PARAVER: a tool to visualize and analyze parallel code. In: Proceedings of WoTUG-18: Transputer and Occam Developments, pp. 17–31 (1995)
13. Sairabanu, J., Babu, M.R., Kar, A., Basu, A.: A survey of performance analysis tools for OpenMP and MPI. Indian J. Sci. Technol. **9**(43) (2016). https://doi.org/10.17485/ijst/2016/v9i43/91712, http://www.indjst.org/index.php/indjst/article/view/91712

14. Shende, S.S., Malony, A.D.: The TAU parallel performance system. Int. J. High Perform. Comput. Appl. **20**(2), 287–311 (2006). https://doi.org/10.1177/1094342006064482
15. Wolf, F., et al.: Usage of the SCALASCA toolset for scalable performance analysis of large-scale parallel applications. In: Resch, M., Keller, R., Himmler, V., Krammer, B., Schulz, A. (eds.) Tools for High Performance Computing, vol. 228, pp. 157–167. Springer, Heidelberg (2008). https://doi.org/10.1007/978-3-540-68564-7_10

Using Deep Learning for Automated Communication Pattern Characterization: Little Steps and Big Challenges

Philip C. Roth[1(✉)], Kevin Huck[2], Ganesh Gopalakrishnan[3], and Felix Wolf[4]

[1] Oak Ridge National Laboratory, Oak Ridge, TN 37831, USA
rothpc@ornl.gov
[2] University of Oregon, Eugene, OR 97403, USA
khuck@cs.uorgeon.edu
[3] University of Utah, Salt Lake City, UT 84112, USA
ganesh@cs.utah.edu
[4] Technische Universität Darmstadt, 64289 Darmstadt, Germany
wolf@cs.tu-darmstadt.de

Abstract. Characterization of a parallel application's communication patterns can be useful for performance analysis, debugging, and system design. However, obtaining and interpreting a characterization can be difficult. AChax implements an approach that uses search and a library of known communication patterns to automatically characterize communication patterns. Our approach has some limitations that reduce its effectiveness for the patterns and pattern combinations used by some real-world applications. By viewing AChax's pattern recognition problem as an image recognition problem, it may be possible to use deep learning to address these limitations. In this position paper, we present our current ideas regarding the benefits and challenges of integrating deep learning into AChax and our conclusion that a hybrid approach combining deep learning classification, regression, and the existing AChax approach may be the best long-term solution to the problem of parameterizing recognized communication patterns.

Keywords: Deep learning · Automation · Application characterization

This manuscript has been co-authored by UT-Battelle, LLC, under contract DE-AC05-00OR22725 with the US Department of Energy (DOE). The US government retains and the publisher, by accepting the article for publication, acknowledges that the US government retains a nonexclusive, paid-up, irrevocable, worldwide license to publish or reproduce the published form of this manuscript, or allow others to do so, for US government purposes. DOE will provide public access to these results of federally sponsored research in accordance with the DOE Public Access Plan (http://energy.gov/downloads/doe-public-access-plan).

A. Bhatele et al. (Eds.): ESPT/VPA 2017/2018, LNCS 11027, pp. 265–272, 2019.
https://doi.org/10.1007/978-3-030-17872-7_16

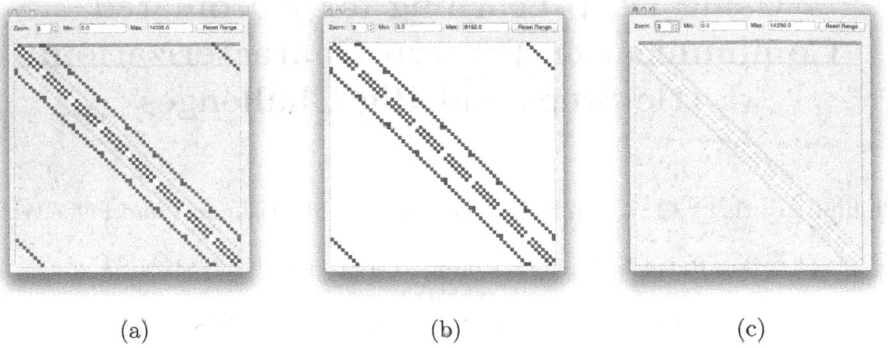

Fig. 1. Removing a recognized, parameterized communication pattern (b) from an example residual communication matrix (a), resulting in a new residual matrix (c). Screen captures originally presented in [9].

1 Introduction

Over the past few years, one of us (Roth) has been developing an approach for automatically recognizing and characterizing the communication patterns of parallel applications [7,9]. The approach uses search and a library of known communication patterns like Broadcast and 3D Nearest Neighbor. The input to the approach is a representation of a parallel application's communication behavior. Logically, this information is represented as an Augmented Communication Graph [7] (ACG), a graph that captures the volume and operation count of the collective and point-to-point communication operations performed by each process during an application run. At each step of its search, the approach examines the communication data that has yet to be explained (called the *residual*) to see if it can recognize any communication patterns from its pattern library. If it recognizes a pattern in a residual, it determines the parameters of the pattern (such as its *scale*, the amount of data that was transferred in the operation) and then refines its search by removing the contribution of the parameterized pattern to form a new residual, from which it continues its search. Figure 1 demonstrates this recognize-parameterize-remove operation. Because the approach might recognize multiple patterns within a residual, the search results form a tree where each path from the tree's root to its leaves represent a collection of parameterized patterns that have been recognized in the original communications data. The path whose leaf has the smallest residual represents the collection of patterns that best explains the original communications data. By reporting the name and parameters of each pattern along this path, the approach generates a concise description of the application's communication behavior that is easier to manage than a full communications event trace and more accurate than summary statistics.

The approach has a few known limitations. One important limitation is that it does a poor job of handling patterns where the amount of data transferred between senders and receivers may vary, such as a nearest-neighbor pattern used in a molecular dynamics simulation. Although we have explored heuristic techniques for determining a pattern's scale that avoid trapping the search in local search space minima [7], our recognition implementation still assumes that the amount of data transferred in a pattern does not depend on the particular sender and receiver and thus may fail to explain all of the application's observed communication behavior if this assumption is not true.

AChax is a Python-based tool that implements this automated communication characterization approach for applications that use a Message Passing Interface [4] (MPI) implementation for communication and synchronization. The tool's distribution includes a library that provides interposition functions for many MPI communication calls made by an application as it runs, and outputs an ACG that captures the application's MPI communication behavior. After a brief dalliance with using graphs built using the Graph-tool Python module [3] as an internal ACG representation, the tool once again represents ACGs using an adjacency matrix encoded in a NumPy [5] matrix because the tool's analysis performance is much better using matrices than when using the Graph-tool-based ACG representation.

A presentation at a recent tools workshop describing AChax [8] spurred us to form an informal working group techniques and challenges with automated pattern recognition in performance, debugging, and characterization tools. Although our discussion ranged widely, the AChax pattern recognition challenges turned out to be the dominant topic. We have long known that we can view the AChax pattern recognition problem as an image recognition problem. (Indeed, capturing the human expertise required to recognize patterns within visualizations of communications adjacency matrices is the primary motivation for the AChax work.) Because of deep learning's well-demonstrated capability for automatic image classification, including images that are "fuzzy" or otherwise obfuscated, deep learning seems tailor-made for the AChax communication pattern recognition problem and we spent a significant part of our working group discussion on exploring the potential benefits and challenges of its use in the AChax context.

In this position paper, we capture the gist of our workshop discussion, and add more detail and perspective based on subsequent consideration and hands-on experimentation using deep learning for the AChax image recognition problem. We describe how we might use our current AChax implementation to train a model using a deep neural network (DNN) and how we might use that model for communication pattern recognition. We discuss the challenges of using a model for parameterizing a recognized pattern. And we present our very early experience with training and using a model to recognize some of the patterns from AChax's current pattern library that lead us to propose that a hybrid strategy combining deep learning with our traditional recognition approach may be the best option for a future AChax implementation. It is also worth noting that at least some of us are *not* deep learning experts and are approaching this study to establish whether the proposed approach is feasible enough to warrant further investigation that includes team members with stronger deep learning expertise.

2 Integrating Deep Learning into AChax

At first blush, the integration of deep learning into our existing communication pattern characterization approach seems like an easy prospect. From a high-enough conceptual level, it seems as simple as replacing our current pattern recognition approach with one that feeds a residual matrix into a model trained to recognize the patterns from our existing library. From a practical perspective, because AChax is implemented using Python and because several of the common deep learning implementations such as TensorFlow [1], Theano [2], and PyTORCH [6] provide well-documented Python interfaces, it should be relatively easy to make use of one of these frameworks in our current AChax software. Nevertheless, considering the details reveals several significant challenges to be overcome.

2.1 Training

A model's DNN must be trained to recognize the patterns from the AChax pattern library. AChax's current implementation eases this training activity, because each pattern in AChax's pattern library is implemented as a Python class that implements both a *generator* and *recognizer* method.[1] A pattern's generator method takes a collection of parameters meaningful to the pattern (such as the dimensions of a 3D nearest neighbor pattern), and generates a matrix representing the parameterized ACG of that pattern. This "pure" matrix is used by some patterns as a mask during the pattern recognition step, and by all patterns when removing the recognized pattern from a residual.

A version of AChax that uses deep learning could use these generated matrices to produce training data. How best to label that data remains an open question. At a minimum, the label could include only the pattern's name, in which case we expect the resulting model to be useful only for identifying the type of pattern that is most strongly represented in the input residual matrix. Some other method would be needed to determine the pattern's parameters (e.g., the approach currently used within AChax). Although this approach might seem to add little value over the existing AChax approach, we believe it could be a necessary part of adding the ability to recognize patterns with varying amounts of data transferred between source and destination processes. At the other end of the spectrum, we could include the pattern's name and *all* of the parameters used to generate the training matrix in its training set label. This approach would likely result in an unfeasible number of classification categories, and we suspect that this level of specification would result in a model that is overfitted to the training data.

[1] The Garbage pattern is an exception: it only provides a generator method because this pattern's only purpose is to introduce "noise" into synthetic workloads used in unit testing.

The sweet spot is likely to be somewhere between these extremes, leading to a model that can identify not only the pattern's name but also *some* information about its parameters that would accelerate the AChax recognizer's ability to determine the complete parameterization. For instance, it may be the case that a trained model can recognize the dimensions of a 2D or 3D nearest neighbor pattern, or from which side or corner a sweep pattern originates. It may also be beneficial to use a two-phase approach whose first phase involves classification of the basic pattern, and whose second phase attempts to discriminate between the specific alternatives that might be present for that basic pattern. We discuss a few more aspects of parameterization in Sect. 2.2.

In addition to these questions of *how* to train a model to support identification of a pattern's parameters, there is also a question of *when* to do this training. Because we would be training our model with ACG matrices representing "pure" patterns, it might be an appealing idea to pre-generate an application-independent library of trained models for process counts commonly used in application runs (e.g., all powers of two between 16 and 16384). In practice, however, we expect this general-purpose library of trained models to be of limited use: by definition, it would not support applications for which non-power-of-two process counts are the best choice, and it would not support applications that subdivide their processes into smaller groups and communicate within these subgroups (e.g., using MPI sub-communicators). Instead, it seems more likely that a deep learning-based AChax would train its model on demand when invoked with a specific ACG matrix, though it may be possible to save its trained model to an *application-specific* model library.

2.2 Recognition and Parameterization

Applying the trained model to a residual matrix results in a vector of probabilities P, one per training category, such that the probability of the residual containing training specification category i is P_i. If one of these probabilities is much larger than the others, the model has given clear indication that the associated training category is highly likely to be present in the residual. But if several probabilities are nearly equal, the meaning is less clear. If those probabilities are large, we would interpret the model's output as indicating the patterns are present in the residual at nearly equivalent scales. In this case, AChax would refine its search along each of the patterns and rely on its ability to eventually distinguish between the quality of the resulting search paths once its search is done. On the other hand, if the probabilities are small, we assume that patterns from the associated training categories are not present and the search can be pruned at that point.

As noted above, there are many open questions regarding use of deep learning for parameterization of recognized patterns, and using classification can take us only so far with respect to parameterization. We expect that some parameters will require us to use a regression model instead. In particular, we expect to need regression to predict the scale of a recognized pattern. The scale indicates how much data was transferred between source and destination processes during the communication operation. It remains to be seen whether using regression to estimate the pattern's scale outweighs the accuracy of AChax's current approach of examining each of the values associated with the recognized pattern within the residual and setting the scale based on those values (e.g., their maximum or average), but the regression approach may prove to be more useful for patterns with varying amounts of data transferred between source and destination processes.

3 Early Experiments

As a first step in determining whether it is both feasible and useful to incorporate deep learning into AChax, we conducted a few simple experiments to determine whether we could train a model to recognize several of the basic patterns from the existing AChax pattern library. We conducted our experiments using TensorFlow 1.10.1, Python 3.6, and a development version of AChax from the "acg-matrix" branch of its repository. Because we were more concerned with the trained model's accuracy than its performance, we ran the experiments on a Mac OS X laptop that already had the required software stack to run TensorFlow models. For all experiments, we constructed models for a hypothetical application that was run with 256 MPI processes.

In our simplest experiment, we constructed 1000 images, each of which represented a "pure" Broadcast or Reduce pattern with randomly-selected root process, or 2D 5-point Nearest Neighbor pattern, each with randomly selected scale. We used 950 images to train our model, and 50 to test its accuracy. With this simple training/testing set, the model reached close to 100% accuracy in five training epochs, but still achieved 100% accuracy on its training images. Adding noise to the training and testing images caused a slight decrease in the model's training accuracy, but it still achieved nearly 100% accuracy with its training set.

Although the ability to recognize a single communication pattern from a (possibly noisy) image is a necessary capability for use within AChax, it is hardly sufficient. Rather, AChax needs the ability to recognize communication patterns in images with multiple patterns. To test this capability, we trained a model as described above, and used it to predict the likelihood of presence of its known patterns in a test set of 5 images, each containing all three communication patterns, with noise. Figure 2 shows an example of one of these multi-pattern images. For each of the five images, with or without noise, the trained model predicted the image contained one of the three patterns with 100% confidence. From an AChax perspective, this may be a desirable behavior because it allows the tool to easily choose which pattern remove next, we mistakenly expected the model to output priorities that reflected each pattern's degree of "presence" within the image as determined by each pattern's scale. We assume that the model chose exactly one pattern in each of our test matrices because each of our training matrices contained only one pattern, and we assume that we would have to train using matrices representing combinations of patterns to obtain the prediction behavior we originally expected.

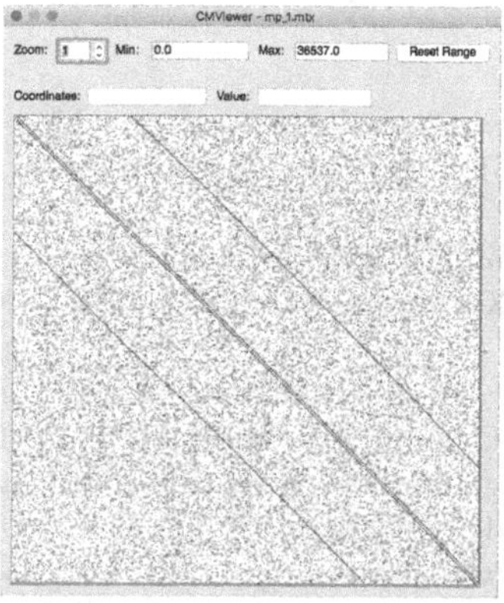

Fig. 2. Example multi-pattern image used to test our trained deep learning model.

4 Summary

Deep learning seems tailor-made for the pattern recognition problem of the AChax automated communication pattern recognition tool. It seems especially attractive for addressing the current AChax limitation of being unable to completely account for the communication from patterns where the amount of data transferred depends on the specific source and destination processes. In this position paper, we discussed our current ideas about how deep learning might be integrated into the AChax search-based communication pattern recognition approach, the challenges of doing so, and some very early experiences in using a trained model to recognize synthetic communication patterns generated by the current AChax implementation. Our experience indicates that using a trained deep learning model to recognize patterns is feasible, but may require both classification and regression, or a hybrid approach combining deep learning with our existing parameterization techniques to identify the full parameter set to associate with recognized patterns.

Acknowledgments. We thank David Poliakoff of Lawrence Livermore National Laboratory for his helpful feedback about this paper and the tools workshop presentation that motivated it.

This material is based upon work supported by the U.S. Department of Energy, Office of Science, Office of Advanced Scientific Computing Research under contract number DE-AC05-00OR22725.

This work is supported in part by the US Department of Energy Office of Science SciDAC RAPIDS project under subcontract 4000159855 to the University of Oregon from Oak Ridge National Laboratory.

References

1. Abadi, M., et al.: TensorFlow: large-scale machine learning on heterogeneous distributed systems (2015). http://download.tensorflow.org/paper/whitepaper2015.pdf
2. Al-Rfou, R., et al.: Theano: a Python framework for fast computation of mathematical expressions. arXiv e-prints abs/1605.02688, May 2016. http://arxiv.org/abs/1605.02688
3. Graph-tool: efficient network analysis (2018). https://graph-tool.skewed.de
4. Gropp, W., Lusk, E., Skjellum, A.: Using MPI: Portable Parallel Programming with the Message-passing Interface. Scientific and Engineering Computation, 2nd edn. MIT Press, Cambridge (1999)
5. NumPy (2018). http://www.numpy.org
6. Paszke, A., et al.: Automatic differentiation in PyTorch. In: NIPS 2017 Autodiff Workshop, December 2017
7. Roth, P.C.: Improved accuracy for automated communication pattern characterization using communication graphs and aggressive search space pruning. In: Bhatele, A., et al. (eds.) ESPT/VPA 2017/2018. LNCS, vol. 11027, pp. 38–55. Springer, Cham (2019)
8. Roth, P.C.: Scalable, automated characterization of parallel application communication behavior. In: 2018 Scalable Tools Workshop, July 2018
9. Roth, P.C., Meredith, J.S., Vetter, J.S.: Automated characterization of parallel application communication patterns. In: Proceedings of the 24th International Symposium on High-Performance Parallel and Distributed Computing (HPDC 2015), Portland, Oregon, USA, pp. 73–84, August 2015. https://doi.org/10.1145/2749246.2749278

Visualizing Multidimensional Health Status of Data Centers

Tommy Dang(✉)

Texas Tech University, Lubbock, TX 79409, USA
tommy.dang@ttu.edu
http://www.myweb.ttu.edu/tnhondan

Abstract. Monitoring data centers is challenging due to their size, complexity, and dynamic nature. This project proposes a visual approach for situational awareness and health monitoring of high-performance computing systems. The visualization requirements are expanded on the following dimensions: (1) High performance computing spatial layout, (2) Temporal domain (historical vs. real-time tracking), and (3) System health services such as temperature, CPU load, memory usage, fan speed, and power consumption. To show the effectiveness of our design, we demonstrate the developed prototype on a medium-scale data center of 10 racks and 467 hosts. The work was developed using feedback from both industrial and acadamic domain experts.

Keywords: Scatterplots · Visual features · High-dimensional data · Data center visualization · High-performance computing systems · Redfish RESTful API · Nagios Core · Baseboard management controller

1 Introduction

Data centers are increasingly complex and hence monitoring such systems is a daunting task for system administrators. In 2013, the Distributed Management Task Force (DMTF) released *Redfish* [17], an open industry standard specification for server configuration that aims to supersede IPMI over the network (IPMI over LAN). The web servers are expected to provide end users with simple, secure management of scalable platform hardware by enhancing security and reliability to Baseboard Management Controller (BMC). Redfish uses industry standard RESTful API architecture over Hyper Text Transfer Protocol Secure (HTTPS) using JavaScript Object Notation (JSON) format based on Open Data Protocol (OData) as depicted in Fig. 1. Redfish-enabled technologies enable IT systems to operate in harmony. Most importantly, a Redfish-enabled system delivers, and single API for everything [13]. One of the critical advantages of REST APIs is that it introduces a great deal of flexibility, allowing any software clients with RESTful capabilities to interact with *Redfish* firmware.

Building on top of Redfish RESTful interface, this paper introduces a visual analytic prototype for monitoring high-performance computing (HPC) system

A. Bhatele et al. (Eds.): ESPT/VPA 2017/2018, LNCS 11027, pp. 273–283, 2019.
https://doi.org/10.1007/978-3-030-17872-7_17

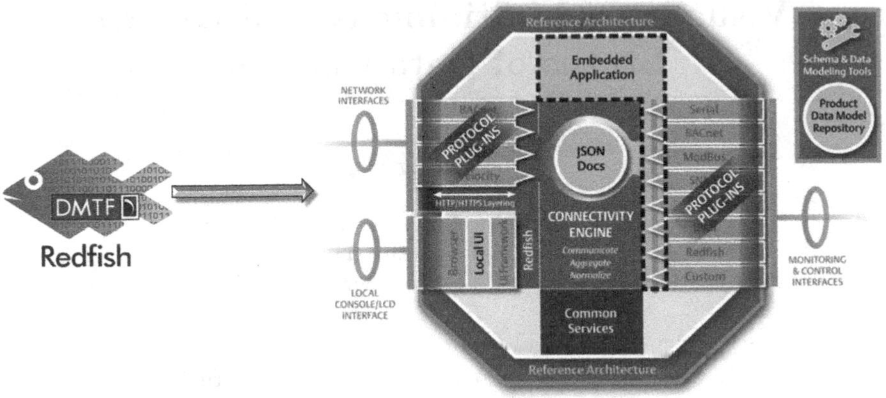

Fig. 1. Redfish reference architecture [13].

events. The goals of this prototype are: (1) to monitor the multidimensional health status of multiple hosts and racks in real-time, (2) to support system administrators in detecting unusual correlation of these services in a complex and highly dynamic system, and (3) to help in performing system troubleshooting and debugging. We demonstrate our prototype at a data center at a university.

The rest of this paper is organized as follows: We first summarize existing techniques for visualizing HPC in the next Section. Then we provide an overview of visualization tasks and describe the design and supported interactive features of our prototype in detail. In Sect. 4, we present the results of an informal study with HPC experts from a university and an industrial company. We argue that using visual features of pairwise projection we can capture abnormal correlations between various health dimensions in the data center. More importantly, these visual features can be computed automatically and notify the system administrator significant events. Finally, we conclude our paper with future plans for visual monitoring and predicting through the integration with Nagios and Redfish API.

2 Existing Approaches

Although not fully explored, there are many existing tools that support monitoring high-performance computing systems. For example, LLView [14] is a client-server based application which allows monitoring the utilization of clusters controlled by batch systems like IBM LoadLeveler, PBSpro, Torque, or IBM Blue Gene system database. However, multidimensional analysis proposed in this work is not in focus of LLview.

Ganglia [16] is an open source PHP-based web front-end interface that allows users to gather information via real-time dynamic web pages. This information, including CPU usage, memory usage, disk usage, network statistics, the number of running processes, is plotted on similar graphs. It leverages the widely used XML technologies for data representation. The advantage of real-time responsive

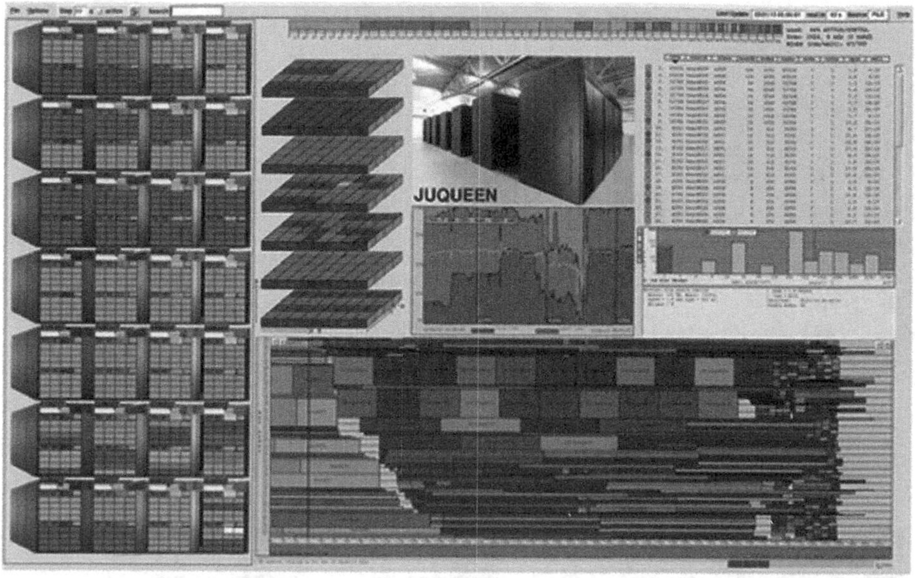

Fig. 2. Main window of LLview [14]: graphical monitoring of batch system controlled cluster.

on the web front-end, however, leads to high latency due to the size of the XML tree. Thus, Ganglia is not practical on the less powerful machines when the amount of data is large (Fig. 2).

Nagios Core [6] is another open-source monitoring system that is capable of handling a variety of servers and operating systems with the industry standard. It provides a primary web interface for the core monitoring engine as depicted in Fig. 3(b). To trace a problem, however, an administrator cannot capture a holistic monitoring view by using the Nagios web interface. Even though basic filtering operations are provided, system status overview, which is useful to correlate the isolated temporal/spatial issues, can be lost [5,11]. Figure 3(a) shows an example of the JSON query on CPU temperatures (on the left) and the corresponding results (on the right) returned from the server.

These existing tools inspect system status independently. This paper takes into account the correlations between various dimensions such as CPU temperature, memory usage, fan speed, power consumption, and I/O bandwidth. Analyzing the relationships of multidimensional data is essential to understand system behaviors as a whole [2].

3 Visualization Components

Through in-depth discussions with domain experts, we have identified the set of design goals: (1) Provides spatial and temporal overview across hosts and racks, (2) Allows system administrators to quickly narrow down to the event of interest

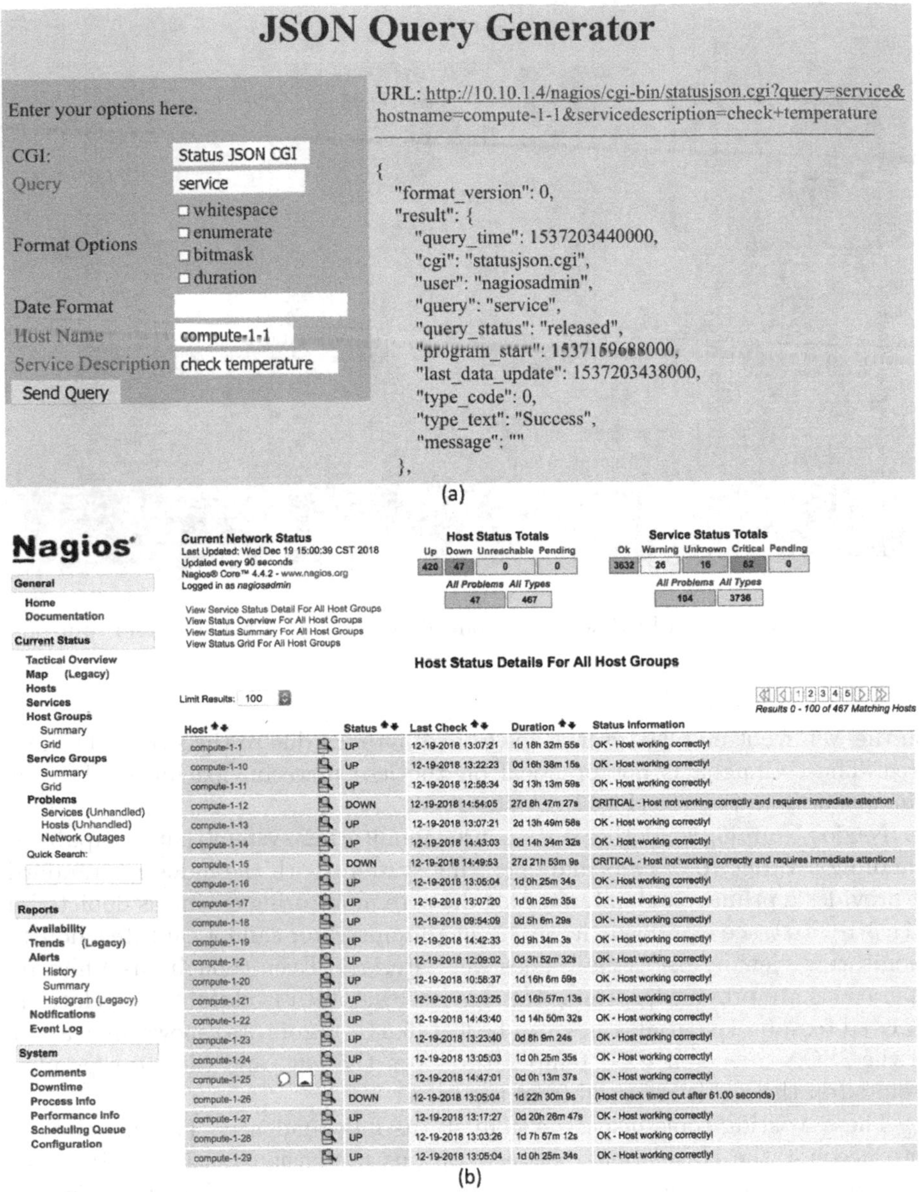

Fig. 3. Nagios Core [6] interfaces: (a) System summary in a simple listing format and (b) Json query on CPU temperatures and the corresponding results.

for system debugging, and (3) Inspects the correlation of system health services in a single view. To meet these goals, this paper proposes several visualization tasks:

- **Overview Display (T1).** Display an overview of real-time system status on the corresponding spatial layout [15].
- **Details-On-Demand (T2).** Users can inspect multidimensional historical data of a host in the system via a simple click [18].
- **Filtering (T3).** Highlight critical events on a host [3] and the associated time stamps [12].
- **Multidimensional analysis (T4).** Explore the correlations between dimensions [4,10] such as fan speeds, memory usage, and power consumption.

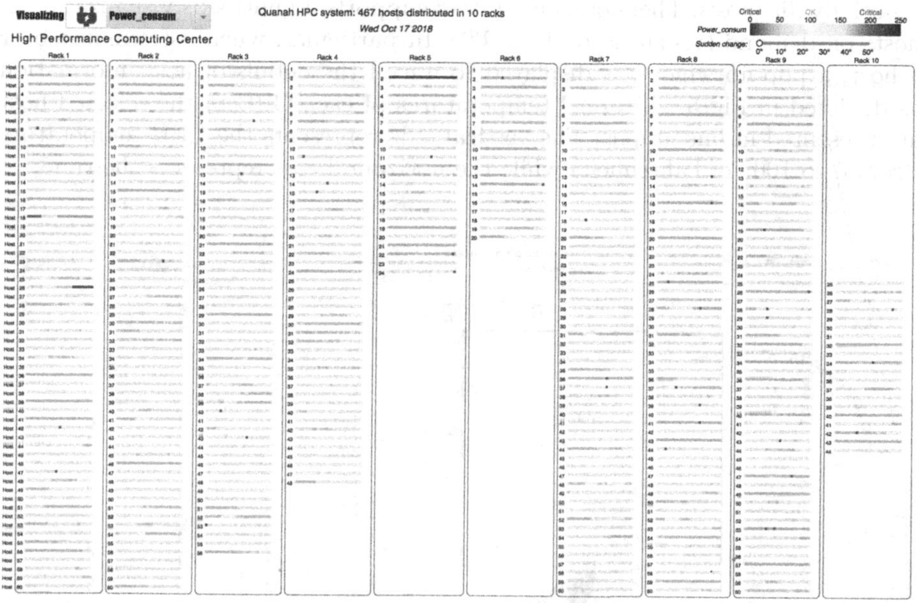

Fig. 4. Visualizing power consumption on Wednesday, October 17, 2018, of the 467-node Quanah cluster at Texas Tech University.

We leverage the Nagios Core engine for data retrieval through a RESTful API web interface. In other words, we iteratively request health status of every host int he system. For each host, we obtain a set of updated status as shown on the right panel of Fig. 3(a). In the next section, we present our approach for displaying status updates of hundreds of hosts within a single view. In the next section, we first introduce the HPC system at Texas Tech University and then visualization components and the supported interactions.

3.1 HPC System Spatial Layout

Figure 4 shows a snapshot power consumption of the 467-node Quanah cluster at Texas Tech University at noon on Sunday, May 13, 2018 (the visualization task

T1). Within a rack, hosts are listed top down. Rows are power consumption time series (the temporal distance between two consecutive cells is 3 min, the updating period set up on the cluster. Rectangles on each row are the computed power consumption, which is colored: red is high power consumption nodes while blue is low power consumption nodes.

3.2 Multidimensional Analysis of Health Status

Through our discussions with domain experts, it is essential to have a holistic view of the entire data center on multiple dimensions for system monitoring and especially diagnosis. Therefore, our system supports a multi-axis visualization of hosts on demand (visualization task **T2**). In particular, when users mouse over a host, a pop-up window is displayed to unveil the details of host information as depicted in Fig. 5. Historical temperatures of each CPU in the selected host are presented in line graphs: The vertical axis represents the CPU temperature (from 0 to 100° of Fahrenheit) while the horizontal axis represents the time.

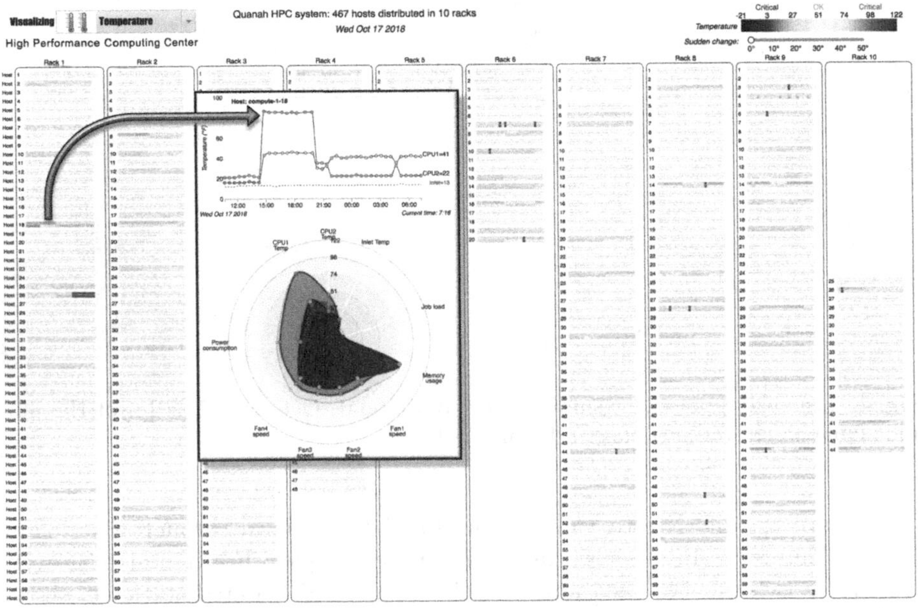

Fig. 5. Visualizing CPU temperature on Wednesday, October 17, 2018 of the 467-node Quanah cluster. Hosts experiencing a sudden temperature increase of 25° in 3 min.

The spider or cobweb chart [7] in the lower panel of the pop-up window shows health dimensions of the selected host (visualization task **T4**) which are grouped by category: CPU temperature (degrees Fahrenheit), job load (number of jobs assigned on the the given host), memory usage (from 0% to 100%), fan speeds, and power consumption (in watts). The purpose of this chart is to enable users to detect similar multidimensional patterns and how they change over time.

We decide to use the spider chart to display multidimensional health status of data center since the mental images of spider charts allow users to capture and compare historical data between different hosts quickly. Figure 6 shows four examples of spider charts from four random hosts in the Quanah cluster at Texas Tech University. In particular, each closed curve on the spider charts represents a multidimensional observation. The observed period is from 11 am to 7 pm on Wednesday, October 17, 2018.

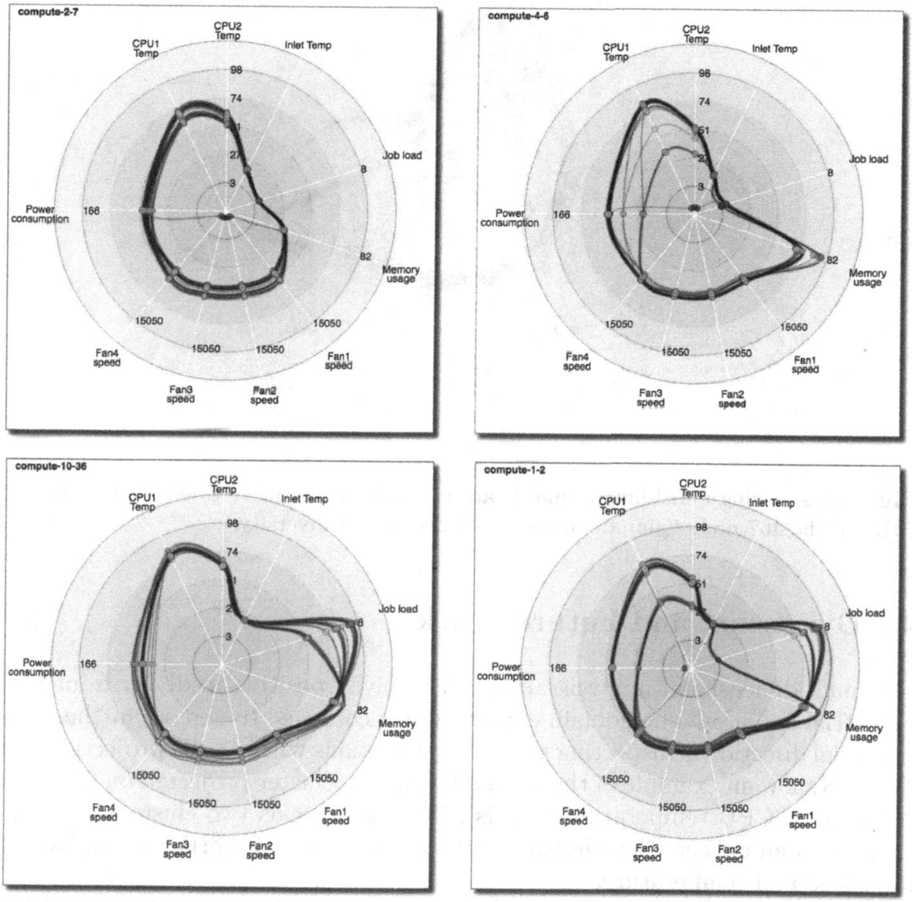

Fig. 6. Visualizing multidimensional heath status of four hosts in the data center.

Users can request to show multidimensional spider chart across hosts in the system at a time stamp. Figure 7 shows our multidimensional visualization of 467 hosts at Texas Tech University at 2 pm on Wednesday, October 17, 2018.

Brushing and linking between the summary view and HPC spatial layout can be done via *mouse over*. Our prototype also supports a range of interactive features, such as zooming and filtering (visualization task **T3**). In Fig. 5, we only display hosts which experienced a sudden CPU heat up of over 25° Fahrenheit within the two consecutive time stamps.

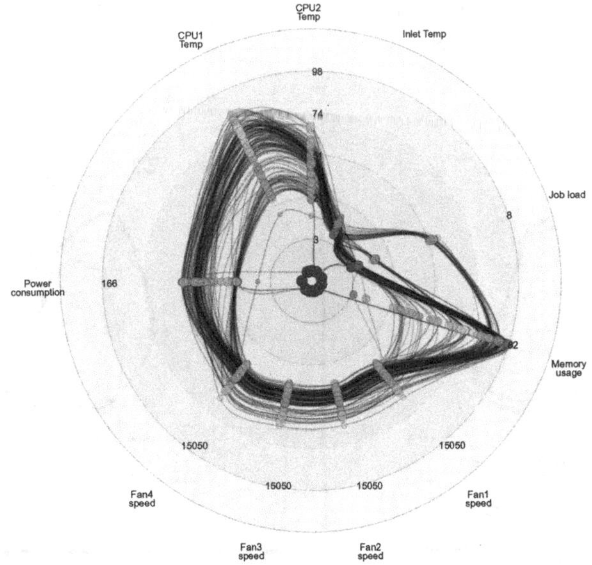

Fig. 7. Visualizing multidimensional heath status at 2 pm on Wednesday, October 17, 2018, of the 467-node Quanah cluster at Texas Tech University.

4 Discussion and Future Work

Our multidimensional analysis approach received positive feedback from both industrial and academic domain experts and encouraged to explore further. One potential direction is inspecting pairwise correlations within a 2D projection [19]. Figure 8 show an example of the 467-node Quanah cluster projected on fan speed (x axis) vs. CPU temperature (y axis). The plot reveals two clusters along the x axis and an outlier (the *compute 4–17*) at the lower left corner which has low fan speed and temperature.

Instead of having a human looking into every single scatterplot, visual features [20] can help to simplify this process by highlighting only unusual correlations. The following examples in Fig. 9 summarize possible 2D projections that can be captured using these visual features [9].

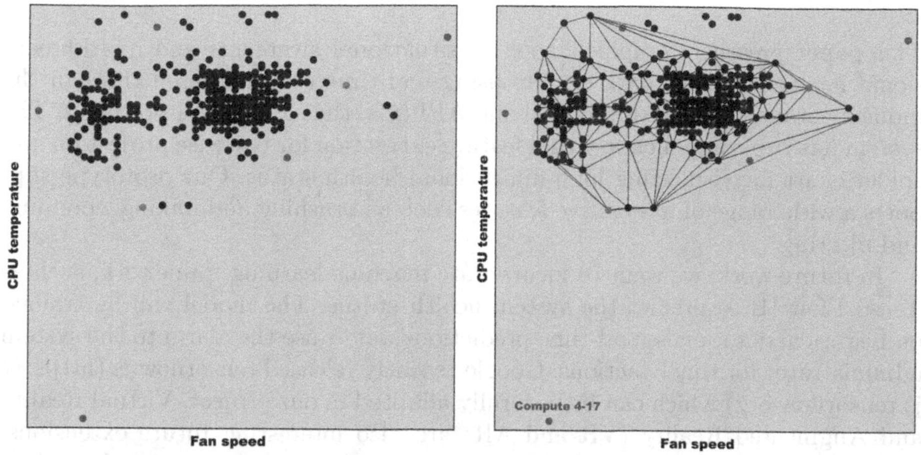

Fig. 8. Visualizing multidimensional heath status of all 467 hosts in the Quanah cluster at Texas Tech University: *Fan speed* vs. *CPU temperature*.

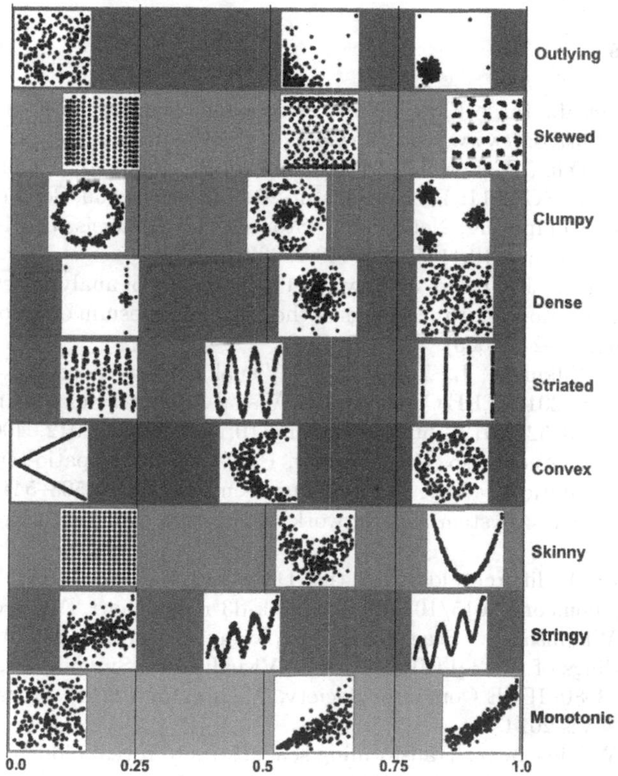

Fig. 9. Some example scatterplots and their measures [8]. In each row, the scatterplots with a low score on the associated measures are on the left while the scatterplots with a high score on the associated visual features are on the right.

5 Conclusion

This paper present a graphical tool for situational awareness and multidimensional health status of data centers using real-time data gathered through the industry-standard Redfish protocol and API (v.s. the aging IMPI protocol). The system has two components: visual feature extraction for pairwise projection and spider chart for visualizing high-dimensional health status. Our prototype supports a wide range of interactive features such as brushing and linking, zooming, and filtering.

In future work, we want to incorporate machine learning framework, such as TensorFlow [1] to predict the system health status. The model will be trained on historical data, make real-time predictions, and raise the alarm to the system administrator for timely actions. Google recently released tensorflow.js (https://js.tensorflow.org) which can be naturally adapted in our project. Virtual Reality and Augmented Reality (VR and AR) are also interesting future extensions. VR and AR interfaces enable real-time monitoring beyond traditional displays by experiencing interactive visualization techniques on mobile devices as well as within immersive environments.

References

1. Abadi, M., et al.: TensorFlow: large-scale machine learning on heterogeneous systems (2015). https://www.tensorflow.org/
2. Allcock, W., Felix, E., Lowe, M., Rheinheimer, R., Fullop, J.: Challenges of HPC monitoring. In: SC 2011: Proceedings of 2011 International Conference for High Performance Computing, Networking, Storage and Analysis, pp. 1–6, November 2011. https://doi.org/10.1145/2063348.2063378
3. Amar, R., Eagan, J., Stasko, J.: Low-level components of analytic activity in information visualization. In: Proceedings of the IEEE Symposium on Information Visualization, pp. 15–24 (2005)
4. Anand, A., Wilkinson, L., Dang, T.N.: Visual pattern discovery using random projections. In: 2012 IEEE Conference on Visual Analytics Science and Technology (VAST), pp. 43–52 (2012). https://doi.org/10.1109/VAST.2012.6400490
5. Andrienko, N., Andrienko, G., Gatalsky, P.: Exploratory spatio-temporal visualization: an analytical review. J. Vis. Lang. Comput. **14**(6), 503–541 (2003)
6. Barth, W.: Nagios: System and Network Monitoring. No Starch Press, San Francisco (2008)
7. Bremer, N.: A different look for the D3.js radar chart (2015). https://www.visualcinnamon.com/2015/10/different-look-d3-radar-chart. Accessed Oct 2018
8. Dang, T., Wilkinson, L.: Scagexplorer: exploring scatterplots by their scagnostics. In: Proceedings of the 2014 IEEE Pacific Visualization Symposium, PACIFICVIS 2014, pp. 73–80. IEEE Computer Society, Washington (2014). https://doi.org/10.1109/PacificVis.2014.42
9. Dang, T., Wilkinson, L.: Transforming scagnostics to reveal hidden features. IEEE Trans. Vis. Comput. Graph. **20**(12), 1624–1632 (2014). https://doi.org/10.1109/TVCG.2014.2346572

10. Dang, T.N., Anand, A., Wilkinson, L.: TimeSeer: scagnostics for high-dimensional time series. IEEE Trans. Vis. Comput. Graph. **19**(3), 470–483 (2013). https://doi.org/10.1109/TVCG.2012.128
11. Dang, T.N., Pendar, N., Forbes, A.G.: TimeArcs: visualizing fluctuations in dynamic networks. Comput. Graph. Forum (2016). https://doi.org/10.1111/cgf.12882
12. Dang, T.N., Wilkinson, L.: TimeExplorer: similarity search time series by their signatures. In: Bebis, G., et al. (eds.) ISVC 2013. LNCS, vol. 8033, pp. 280–289. Springer, Heidelberg (2013). https://doi.org/10.1007/978-3-642-41914-0_28
13. of the Industry, V.: How redfish specifications can improve simplicity, visibility and control of it (2016). https://datacenterfrontier.com/redfish-specifications/. Accessed Oct 2018
14. Karbach, C., Valder, J.: System monitoring: LLview. In: Computational Science and Mathematical Methods. Introduction to the programming and usage of the supercomputer resources at Jülich November 2015 (Course no. 78a/2015 in the training programme of Forschungszentrum Jülich), 26–27 Nov 2015, Jülich, Germany (2015). https://juser.fz-juelich.de/record/279901
15. Keim, D.A., Panse, C., Sips, M.: Information visualization: scope, techniques and opportunities for geovisualization. In: Dykes, J. (ed.) Exploring Geovisualization, pp. 1–17. Elsevier, Oxford (2004)
16. Massie, M.L., Chun, B.N., Culler, D.E.: The ganglia distributed monitoring system: design, implementation, and experience. Parallel Comput. **30**(7), 817–840 (2004)
17. Organization, S.D.: Distributed management task force (2013). https://www.dmtf.org/standards/redfish
18. Shneiderman, B.: The eyes have it: a task by data type taxonomy for information visualizations. In: Proceedings of the 1996 IEEE Symposium on Visual Languages, VL 1996, p. 336. IEEE Computer Society, Washington (1996). http://dl.acm.org/citation.cfm?id=832277.834354
19. Wilkinson, L., Anand, A., Grossman, R.: Graph-theoretic scagnostics. In: Proceedings of the IEEE Information Visualization 2005, pp. 157–164. IEEE Computer Society Press (2005)
20. Wilkinson, L., Anand, A.: Grossman: D3 data-driven documents. IEEE Trans. Vis. Comput. Graph. **17**(12), 2301–2309 (2011)

Author Index

Printed in the United States
By Bookmasters